Douglas Fairbanks

Douglas Fairbanks

Jeffrey Vance

with Tony Maietta

Robert Cushman

PHOTOGRAPHIC EDITOR

UNIVERSITY OF CALIFORNIA PRESS
BERKELEY   LOS ANGELES   LONDON

ACADEMY OF MOTION PICTURE
ARTS AND SCIENCES

University of California Press, one of the most distinguished university presses in the United States, enriches lives around the world by advancing scholarship in the humanities, social sciences, and natural sciences. Its activities are supported by the UC Press Foundation and by philanthropic contributions from individuals and institutions. For more information, visit www.ucpress.edu.

University of California Press
Berkeley and Los Angeles, California

University of California Press, Ltd.
London, England

Frontispiece: Breaking with his trademark youthful optimism, Fairbanks allowed his character to grow older in *The Iron Mask* (1929), his last silent film.

All photographs unless otherwise acknowledged below are from the collections of the Academy of Motion Picture Arts and Sciences, Margaret Herrick Library.

Robert S. Birchard Collection: p. 102
Kevin Brownlow Collection: pp. 36 and 272 (top)
Corbis Corporation: p. 272 (bottom)
George Eastman House Motion Picture Collection: p. 173
Vera Fairbanks Collection: p. 282
Getty Images, Inc.: pp. 90 and 305
Howard Gotlieb Archival Research Center, Boston University: pp. 8, 11, and 12
Los Angeles Public Library: p. 286
Museum of Modern Art: pp. 75 (top) and 207 (top)
Natural History Museum of Los Angeles County: pp. 77 (bottom), 215 (top), 219, and 232
Jeffrey Vance Collection: pp. 184 (left), 186, and 237
Douglas Fairbanks as The Gaucho © Douris Corporation.
Stephen Steps Out © Paramount Pictures. All rights reserved. Courtesy Paramount Pictures.
Taming of the Shrew © Mary Pickford Foundation.
A Woman of Affairs © Turner Entertainment. All rights reserved.

Library of Congress Cataloging-in-Publication Data

Vance, Jeffrey, 1970–.
    Douglas Fairbanks / Jeffrey Vance, with Tony Maietta ; Robert Cushman, photographic editor.
        p.   cm.
    Includes bibliographical references and index.
    ISBN: 978-0-520-25667-5 (cloth : alk. paper)
    1. Fairbanks, Douglas, 1883–1939.   2. Motion picture actors and actresses—United States—Biography.   I. Maietta, Tony.   II. Cushman, Robert, 1946–.
III. Title.
PN2287.F3V36   2008
791.4302'8092—dc22   2008006895

Manufactured in Canada

17   16   15   14   13   12   11   10   09   08
10   9   8   7   6   5   4   3   2   1

The paper used in this publication meets the minimum requirements of ANSI/NISO z39.48–1992 R 1997) (*Permanence of Paper*).

Contents

Prologue

They began as a small band of pioneers with a common purpose: to breathe life into moving images. They flocked to Southern California and, by their work, helped evolve a new art form, the motion picture. Among these earliest Hollywood filmmakers, Mary Pickford, Charles Chaplin, and Douglas Fairbanks built an industry without ever uttering a word to their audiences. In their eyes and through their pantomime, they conveyed the breadth and depth of human experience in a manner that caught the public's imagination and won its devotion. Quickly, the images generated by the Hollywood pioneers touched every corner of the globe. An international visual language, the silent motion picture was understood by all human souls. Wherever a projector and screen were erected, humanity was brought closer together. These pioneers contributed to creating the first universal art form unique to the twentieth century.

Pickford, Chaplin, and Fairbanks were Hollywood's first cinema superstars. They achieved truly global fame and adulation, with fans referring to them on an intimate, first-name basis as Mary, Charlie, and Doug. It is difficult to appreciate, in this age of devalued celebrity, the impact they had on world cinema and world culture. Cinema was the defining art form of the twentieth century, and they, along with their partner in the formation of the United Artists Corporation, the director

The great triumvirate of Hollywood silent cinema: Fairbanks supports Charles Chaplin and Mary Pickford (in costume for *Rebecca of Sunnybrook Farm*) in an Artcraft publicity still at the beginning of their friendship in 1917.

D. W. Griffith, were among its American progenitors. Yet while history has appropriately acknowledged Pickford, Chaplin, and Griffith, Fairbanks remains underappreciated and the least understood. Indeed, his star image is dangerously close to being forgotten at the dawn of the twenty-first century.

Douglas Fairbanks's cinema is filled with optimism, ebullience, and adventure. His screen characters' restless energy and self-confidence (whether in contemporary dress or historical costume) were inseparable from his own dynamic personality. "Fairbanks's magic was that he stirred the adventure yearnings of the young and old. He had an ability to connect with and tap into all our escapist desires," remembered William Bakewell, who acted with Fairbanks in *The Iron Mask* (1929). "He made the impossible appear attainable."[1] Fairbanks's films made him the king of Hollywood and greatly contributed to defining the spirit of his time.

No one seemed to enjoy King Doug's reign more than the sovereign himself. Fairbanks tackled every new stunt or set piece of his early contemporary comedies, which took the pulse of American society of the time, with the enthusiasm and discovery of a child at play. The course of his career changed with *The Mark of Zorro* (1920), and Fairbanks became the original screen swashbuckler. Yet this epithet, applied too often to him, stands restrictive to his genius and reductive to his artistry. Fairbanks not only acted and produced his own films; he also frequently contributed to the writing and shared in their direction. He was, in fact, one of the most creative producers Hollywood has ever known. He studied, absorbed, and mastered the techniques of traditional filmmaking quickly and turned his prodigious energies to experimentation, enlisting first-class directors, distinguished writers, and the finest designers, technicians, craftsmen, and composers, and developing top talent. (Victor Fleming and William Cameron Menzies were among the artists he nurtured.) He also produced one of the earliest Technicolor feature films. His watchword was: "If it is worth doing, it is worth doing well."[2]

Fairbanks was a founder and the first president of the Academy of Motion Picture Arts and Sciences. He was an early proponent of film preservation and deposited his own film archives with the Museum of Modern Art. He emphasized that filmmaking was a craft deserving academic analysis, and in 1929, he was instrumental in the formation of the first university curriculum devoted exclusively to film study in America, which evolved into what is known today as the University of Southern California School of Cinematic Arts. Fairbanks advanced the concept of the independent actor-producer, and in 1919, he, Pickford, Chaplin,

Douglas Fairbanks, ca. 1920. Photograph by Woodbury.

and Griffith formed their own distribution company, United Artists, which, as the name suggests, put the artists in control. It would be largely responsible for moving cinema into a new era, enabling film-makers previously tethered to the big studios to become masters of their own work.

On a social and cultural level, Fairbanks was critically important to the evolution of Hollywood. He and his second wife, Mary Pickford, virtually created the image of movie stars as "American aristocracy." Fairbanks was the first actor to live in Beverly Hills, and the Fairbanks-Pickford Beverly Hills residence, called "Pickfair," was referred to as "America's Buckingham Palace" and "The White House of the West." In the 1920s, Pickfair was unquestionably one of the most famous residences in the world and a mandatory stopping point for visiting dignitaries, statesmen, and royalty. In a world still restrictively tied to Victorian mores and values, the film personality—previously widely regarded as culturally dubious and morally reprehensible—was suddenly someone eminently respectable, to admire, emulate, and even worship. Fairbanks became the living embodiment of Theodore Roosevelt's quintessential tenets of the physically strenuous life, fueled by the underlying assumption that good men inevitably rose to the top by virtue of their energy and their determination. His celebration of these virtues captivated the world, and he capitalized on this philosophy by authoring several self-help books. He also took advantage of his celebrity for good causes; his participation (along with Pickford, Chaplin, and others) in the hugely successful Liberty Loan war bond campaigns of 1917–18 resulted in the raising of millions of dollars.

Film history has thus far been unwilling to afford Douglas Fairbanks his proper place as one the foremost artists of the cinema. He is generally not even regarded as a gifted actor; instead, he tends to be identified pejoratively as a "screen personality." Inasmuch as climbs, swings, leaps, jumps, and vaulting were invariably an integral part of his performances, some contemporary critics disparagingly dismissed him as a "jumper" (a term also frequently applied to the famous Russian ballet dancer and choreographer Vaslav Nijinsky). Fairbanks preferred sliding down banisters to using the staircase; and, as the French director and theoretician Jean Epstein wrote, "windows are [his] only doors."[3]

A close examination of Fairbanks's oeuvre amply demonstrates that he was the dominant creative force in the production of superlative films and a gifted comic actor who made the transition from satirist to swashbuckler. Comedy was an essential component of his great gift. His signature mock-heroic stance, with his fists on his hips and his head tilted back in joyous laughter, exudes humor.

Fairbanks was a superb physical specimen, possessing an inherent radiance and magnetism that commanded attention. His muscu-
lar, deeply tanned, well-defined physique and considerable skills were
placed in service to visual comedy, ingenious stunts (which he famously
performed himself), or grand pageants he created on screen. Although
his body was a superb instrument and able to eloquently express character, emotion, and attitude, Douglas Fairbanks was not just a handsome athlete. He was a great artist.

Fairbanks the private man was elusive and inconsolable. He was also
peripatetic and ambitious, moving from Denver to Britain, France, and
New York City before settling in Southern California, where he helped
create the Hollywood film industry. He lived the great American dream.
He was Gatsby before F. Scott Fitzgerald invented him. "Success" was

his favorite word, and he achieved it on a colossal scale. He leapt to the forefront of popular culture in an extraordinary trajectory from actor to superstar that seemed as effortless as one of the stunts in his costume adventures. His personality was perfectly suited to stardom and the constant attention of fame. His celebrity required distance from, not closeness to, his audience.

The Douglas Fairbanks who was popularly known and documented was invented. The true Douglas Fairbanks was the man behind "a series of masks" according to his namesake son.[4] In his autobiography, Douglas Fairbanks Jr. writes: "He designed the living of his life, almost from the start, coloring it as he went along. He did it so successfully that his best friends and biographers were seldom able to see him accurately."[5]

Actors are poseurs by nature. They frequently are former childhood experts in the universal game of "let's pretend" who overcompensate for their early childhood unhappiness with reinvented personas, which they then persuasively vend to a celebrity-hungry public. Fairbanks's overcompensatory feats of derring-do would later find an eager audience. Indeed, his screen persona of "Doug" (who was also known by such monikers as "Dr. Smile" and "Mr. Pep") was his own greatest invention—a means to escape his true self. However, the essential man can nevertheless be gleaned from the constructed false self he perfected on screen.

Biographical materials about Fairbanks are scant and frequently unreliable. Although there are many books and articles attributed to him, the truth is that he seldom remained still long enough to write anything of any length. Moreover, the reminiscences of many of those who knew and worked with him tend to be self-aggrandizing efforts to elevate their own importance or contributions. The interviews conducted by the author were mostly with elderly people, groping through the fog of early memories in an effort to recall a man dead for over fifty years. Douglas Fairbanks Jr. remembered that his father laughed off the idea of factual reporting with respect to himself early in his public life.[6] He was more than prescient. Fairbanks was neither a truthful nor a comprehensive chronicler of his own life, and he contributed most of the fantastic stories or myths that swirl about it.[7] Among the many hats he wore, he especially enjoyed the role of showman.

It is undoubtedly impossible to take the full measure of the life and character of someone as prodigious as Douglas Fairbanks. One can only speculate as to the psychological reasons for his self-invention from the clues he left behind—the greatest of which are his films. Fairbanks's swashbuckling films were his Rosebud, the sled that symbolizes the childhood of the protagonist of Orson Welles's *Citizen Kane* (1941). The costume adventure films Fairbanks made between 1920 and 1929 are some of the most important works in silent cinema. They record, not only some of the high points in Hollywood creativity, but also an important component of early twentieth-century American culture, and they deserve a detailed accounting.

A Bad Case
of St. Vitus' Dance

The child inched closer and closer to the edge of the rooftop. He was alone in the yard; his mother and brother were occupied indoors with arrangements for the celebration of his third birthday. He had become restless with the preparations for the party and had wandered out into the sunlight of the spring afternoon. He spied the trellis fastened against the side of the barn, and it called out to him. Soon he had climbed to the top of the barn. There he stood, teetering at the edge of the parapet, calmly surveying the ground below.

His reverie was suddenly broken by the sound of his brother's voice calling from inside the house: "Mama, he's on the roof!" The child did not budge. Then he heard his mother respond in frustration, "Not again!"[1]

The mother ran out to the foot of the barn, where she strained to look up through the glaring sunlight at her baby boy perched on the edge, the child's brother not far behind. To find her young son in a perilous position was not uncommon of late. What troubled her most was not the constant risk-taking in which the toddler had indulged almost since he was able to crawl, but the solemn expression on his face. What was that look? His countenance betrayed neither excitement, fright, nor defiance. She ordered him down, and they silently watched as he turned, walked to the edge of the roof, sat down, flipped over the edge to the eaves, and scuttled down the latticework without effort. It was not the first time—and certainly not the last—that an audience would be entranced by the acrobatic antics of Douglas Fairbanks.

Douglas Fairbanks, ca. 1893.

While such stories of his early childhood acrobatics are somewhat suspect, the early risk-taking is beyond dispute. One revealing account has him leaping off the roof and knocking himself unconscious. This brought about a marked change. Revived in his mother's arms, the hitherto taciturn child suddenly evolved into a smiling, laughing boy.[2] The event also resulted in a scar above his left eye, which he used to elicit further maternal attention. (It would be noticeable for the rest of his life.) Whatever the varying content or chronology, the significance of these two tales lies in his discovery that when he was in action, attention was paid.

The man who would one day be known as Douglas Fairbanks was born Douglas Elton Ulman in Denver, Colorado, on May 23, 1883. In his own recollections of his early life, style invariably triumphed over content—and for good reason. By all accounts, he had been a glum, silent child, with an absent father and a controlling mother. She was born Ella Adelaide Marsh in New York in 1847 to a prosperous Roman Catholic family. Her mother's family had originally hailed from Virginia, and in later years, Ella often romanticized her past by suggesting that she too was a Southern belle. However, she and her younger sister, Belle, were born and raised above the Mason-Dixon Line. Ella married the mysterious John Fairbanks, a wealthy planter and heir to a sugar mill, whose illustrious lineage can supposedly be traced back to one of the oldest families in Massachusetts—that of the Yorkshireman Jonathan Fayerbanke—and what is thought to be the oldest existing timber frame house in North America, the "Fairbanks House" in Dedham, Massachusetts.[3]

John Fairbanks died of tuberculosis not long after the birth of their only child, John Jr., in 1873. Swindled by her husband's business partners, Ella turned to his friend H. Charles Ulman, a New York–based attorney, for help. Despite his best efforts, however, Ulman was unable to obtain restitution for the young widow and her infant son.

While living with her sister Belle outside Atlanta, Georgia, Ella was persuaded into marriage by a certain Edward Wilcox. The union was doomed from the start, however, because Wilcox was an abusive alcoholic. A second son, Norris Wilcox, failed to make the domestic situation tolerable; and, in defiance of her faith and society in general, Ella sued Wilcox for divorce in 1877. Her attorney was again H. Charles Ulman. The friendship between attorney and client blossomed, and after successfully obtaining her divorce, she did the unthinkable and defied prevailing sentiments of the time by eloping with her attentive litigator.

H. (for Hezekiah) Charles Ulman was born to German-Jewish immigrants near Philadelphia in 1833. His father, Lazarus, was mainly involved in mercantile endeavors.[4] H. Charles attended law school and

was admitted to the state bar in 1856, practicing law in Pennsylvania until the outbreak of the Civil War in 1861. Responding immediately to the call for volunteers, he became a captain in the Pennsylvania Reserve Corps. He was wounded in 1862 and transferred from active service into the Veteran Reserve Corps until his resignation in 1864. Ella was initially pleased with her multifaceted beau: he was an attorney of prominence (first in Philadelphia and later in New York), a Civil War captain, a politician, and a publisher. He was also, she later discovered, an alcoholic and a bigamist.[5]

Ulman's choice to run off with Ella forced him to abandon law and New York society. The once widowed, once divorced, and now again pregnant Ella supported his decision to go west with her and John Jr. (her second-born son, Norris Wilcox, was left to be raised by a paternal aunt) and make a fresh start in the rough-and-tumble mining territory of Colorado. In making the move west, Ulman was also putting distance between his "new family" and the one he already had—a wife and two daughters he abandoned in New York.

The 47-year-old H. Charles and the 33-year-old Ella were married in Boulder County, Colorado, on September 7, 1881, and six months later, on March 3, 1882, she gave birth to a son, Robert Paine Ulman. The western frontier failed to be the idyll that the couple had envisioned, and after a time, Ella grew increasingly disenchanted with her surroundings and her new husband—particularly as his alcohol

Robert Ulman and Douglas Ulman, ca. 1888. Photograph by Clements.

consumption increased in direct proportion to his dwindling business ventures. There was also a disturbingly restless nature to the man; he was frequently away, ostensibly pursuing his mining interests. Restlessness was a legacy passed down to his second son, Douglas Elton, born the following year at the family home at 61 South Fourteenth Street in Denver. As their family grew, Ulman moved from one ill-advised business venture to another until, financially ruined and hopelessly addicted to alcohol, he abandoned both his business and his family and joined Benjamin Harrison's campaign for president in 1888 as a paid political speaker.

Although Douglas Fairbanks rarely spoke in later years about the enigmatic man who had abandoned him at the age of 5, Ulman was evidently a frustrated actor and relished reciting long passages from Shakespeare to his son, who credited his father with instilling in him a love of the theater. Ulman also captivated his sons with tall tales of his Civil War exploits and supposed friendship with Edwin Booth (America's foremost actor and the brother of Abraham Lincoln's assassin, John Wilkes Booth), whom he had supposedly resembled as a younger man.

Moreover, Douglas Fairbanks's love of the West began with his visits to his father's mining camps in the wild country and watching his father ride horseback. Most of his memories of his father were unpleasant ones, however, which Douglas kept to himself. When he was 12, he unexpectedly ran into his father on the streets of Denver and urged him to come back home and see his mother. Ulman, in Denver on business, consented to do so, after first stopping at the bar of the Windsor Hotel with his son in tow and downing a few shots of Scotch for fortification. The reunion was an unhappy one. Ella, now divorced from Ulman on grounds of desertion, became enraged. She promptly chased her inebriated former husband out of the house, grabbed young Douglas by the hand, and led him to the local office of the Women's Christian Temperance Union, where she made him sign the temperance pledge vowing never to consume a drop of alcohol. It was a traumatic incident in Douglas's early life. He had wanted to please his mother and prove that he was special by reintroducing his father into the family, but the attempt had backfired horribly. Incidents like the row he witnessed between his mother and father fostered a lifelong need to avoid personal confrontations.

As if making them take the temperance pledge were not enough, in 1900, Ella petitioned to have her two sons' names legally changed from Ulman to Fairbanks. (She had reverted to the surname of her beloved first husband not long after Ulman's desertion in 1888.) In doing this, and having the boys confirmed in the Roman Catholic faith, she attempted to eradicate any lingering trace of H. Charles Ulman from their lives. However, Ulman had already left an indelible imprint on his youngest son, who inherited his restlessness, rodomontade, lack of introspection, and constant need to be the center of attention. Douglas saw his father only a few more times before Ulman's death in New York on February 23, 1915, at the age of 81. Ulman occasionally appeared backstage asking his son for a handout, and it was always given. Despite this, Fairbanks held a grudge against his father for his abandonment of the family.

The loss of contact with his father was difficult enough. His embittered mother's obliteration of all traces and memories of his father made matters worse. To mitigate the loss, he erected a self-protective wall to insulate himself from his pain and learned to detach himself from the people and things around him. Douglas Elton Ulman ceased to exist at the age of twelve, and Douglas Elton Thomas (his Roman Catholic confirmation name, chosen by his mother) Fairbanks now faced a painful division within himself. His substitute for emotional connection was physical action. He discovered he was happiest when pouring his seemingly boundless energy into the welcome distraction of physical challenges; when his body was maximally engaged, his disengagement from his emotions gave way to exhilaration.

He still had his mother to contend with and to care for him. While she was loving and doting, she was also demanding and difficult to please. She was image-conscious, status-seeking, and success-driven throughout her life (traits she instilled in her youngest son). She adored Douglas, but her personality and prejudices prevented her from giving her favorite child unconditional love. Jewish blood was stigmatizing in the eyes of the socially insecure would-be Southern belle, and she was ashamed of her youngest child's dark skin, which hinted at a socially inferior father. "I was the blackest baby you ever saw," Fairbanks recalled. "I was so dark even my mother was ashamed of me. When all the neighbors came around to look at the new baby, Mother would say, 'Oh, I don't want to disturb him now—he's asleep and I'd rather not.' She just hated to show off such a dark baby."[6] What he received from Ella was narcissistic love; she needed to see and love her son as a white-skinned, non-Jewish, all-American boy. Fairbanks remarked that the fact that he was born with skin darker than his brothers' fostered shame and resentment in his mother. His mother's covering his crib with a blanket and the fuss and concern she demonstrated undoubtedly contributed to his taciturn nature. This led to more maternal anxieties over her stigmatized child, because there began to be whispers among some of the neighbors that young Douglas suffered from mental retardation.[7] This was yet another factor in his growing isolation.

Fairbanks had discovered, as early as the day that he climbed onto that rooftop, that the best way of remedying feelings of isolation was to exercise his natural physical prowess. In doing so, the child was also attempting to prove to his mother that he was special and deserving of the attention he so desperately craved. The continual jumping, leaping, and bounding about somewhat curtailed the streak of morbidity that had been in him since infancy. Though it could always resurface, it was relieved as quickly as it came by a quick jump, leap, or kick-step in the air.

This tendency to become airborne at the slightest provocation did not serve him well as a student in school. As a way to curtail his hyperactivity and make him focus on his studies, his teachers would often assign him long soliloquies from Shakespeare or other passages to memorize and recite. Given his already all-consuming need for attention, this proved particularly potent, and before long his theatrical aspirations began to blossom. All of this was alarming to his mother, who sent both Robert and Douglas to Jarvis Hall Military Academy for two years, hoping this might instill some much-needed discipline in them. When the family's financial situation became precarious, Ella, who had been supporting her family in a life filled with shabby-genteel pretenses by taking in lodgers, as well as accepting assistance from her sister Belle and John Jr., ordered them home to 1629 Franklin Street. The brothers enrolled in East Denver High School on September 7, 1898, from which, just before his sixteenth birthday, Douglas was expelled. According to family lore, this was because he had adorned the school's statuary with green bows and silly hats as a St. Patrick's Day prank.[8]

None of this mattered to Douglas. Concurrent with high school, he had been attending a drama school run by two former New York actresses, the retired Margaret Fealy and her daughter, Maude (later a star in cinema prior to World War I). He was also an aspiring playwright. A surviving theater program from the Tabor Grand School of Acting's performance at Denver's Elitch Theatre from August 1898 records that Fairbanks wrote and acted in a sketch entitled "Mr. and Mrs. Moffet."[9] Burns Mantle, a Denver neighbor who later became an esteemed critic and annalist, remembered that the teenage Fairbanks "would recite you as fine and florid an Antony's speech to the Romans as you ever heard. With gestures too."[10] The very same month as his expulsion from high school, he encountered Frederick Warde, a well-known British actor-manager, who was in Denver for a week's run at the Broadway Theatre. Fairbanks attended an assembly the actor gave for the students at the high school and was enthralled. According to Warde:

While in Denver, Colorado, I made an address on the study of Shakespeare to the faculty and students of the High School. On the following day a very youthful student of the school called on me and expressed a desire to go upon the stage. Such applications were not uncommon, but this applicant, little more than a boy, had an assurance and persistence in spite of my discouragement, that attracted me. He replied frankly to all my questions, realized the gravity of the step he desired to take; told me the conditions of his life and referred me to his mother for confirmation.

The lady called on me the next day, endorsed all that her son had told me, approved of the boy's ambitions and the result was I engaged him for my company for the following season, to lead the supernumeraries and to play such small parts as his capacity and appearance would permit.

The youth was of rather less than average height but of athletic build, with frank attractive features and his name was Douglas Fairbanks.[11]

Fairbanks apparently made his professional stage debut as Florio, a lackey, in *The Duke's Jester,* an adaptation of Alexandre Dumas *père*'s novel *La Dame de Monsoreau* by Espy Williams, on September 10, 1900, in Richmond, Virginia.[12] Warde was charmed by the 17-year-old Fairbanks's boundless enthusiasm and infectious personality, but less than impressed by him as an actor. He summed up Fairbanks's performance with his troupe as "a catch-as-catch-can bout with the immortal bard."[13] Fairbanks himself liked to recall a particularly caustic review from a Duluth newspaper: "Mr. Warde's supporting company was bad, but worst of all was Douglas Fairbanks as Laertes [in *Hamlet*]."[14] Fairbanks toured with Warde's company for two years as the troupe journeyed throughout the United States, playing mainly in smaller cities and never in Fairbanks's dream destination, New York City. When Warde finally dismissed him, he kindly recommended that the young man gain more life experience in order to bring greater conviction to the roles he portrayed.

Fairbanks followed Warde's advice by traveling to Britain, where he enjoyed a peripatetic existence in England for a few months, also venturing into France. Upon his return, he first found employment in the Wall Street brokerage house of De Coppet & Doremus, later on as a clerk in a hardware store, and finally in the law offices of E. M. Hollander and Sons. Fairbanks later created the myth of his attending Harvard University during this period, disregarding the fact that he had dropped out of high school after his freshman year.[15] In 1901, Fairbanks and his mother were permanently living in New York City, Ella having sold her Denver home to join her youngest son as he attempted to find work on the New York stage. Fairbanks believed nearly two years of life experience sufficient to attain his goal: becoming a star on Broadway.

At the time of his arrival in New York City, Broadway was on the cusp of one of its golden periods, with approximately fifty theaters in operation. The "Great White Way," as it was to be dubbed the following year, stretched from Thirteenth Street north to the newly christened Times Square, and the burnishing lights that fashioned that nickname spelled out the names of a luminous generation of stars: John Drew, Anna Held, Lillian Russell, Maude Adams, Sarah Bernhardt, Minnie Maddern Fiske, and John, Ethel, and Lionel Barrymore. It was primarily an era of the star vehicle, and everyone went to the theater or vaudeville for entertainment. Fairbanks's potent mixture of ambition and energy, combined with a healthy dose of luck, enabled him to make a Broadway debut without undue hardship in the short-lived *Her Lord and Master* in February 1902. In September of that year, he appeared in *A Rose o' Plymouth-Town*, whose leading lady, Minnie Dupree, called his acting "a bad case of St. Vitus' Dance."[16] Dupree's remark is one of many contemporary accounts suggesting Fairbanks's overwhelming energy. His first starring role came with *A Case of Frenzied Finance* in April 1905. The actress Grace George saw him in the role of Fred Everett in the musical

comedy *Fantana* and, impressed with his youthful zeal, brought him to the attention of her husband, William A. Brady, one of New York's leading producer-impresarios. Though Grace George conceded that he was not very handsome, she enthused that he had "a world of personality." Brady remembered: "After one look at him I hired him in support of my wife in a play called *Clothes*. An odd young man, running over with energy to such an extent that it fatigued me to look at him sitting down—and he seldom sat."[17]

In one of the set pieces for *Clothes*, which opened in September 1906, Fairbanks had to climb a long flight of steps to a high platform. During a break in rehearsals, the fidgety Fairbanks entertained himself by walking up and down the stairs on his hands. Brady was delighted with his acrobatics and worked the bit into the play. Soon after, Brady signed Fairbanks to a five-year contract.[18] In December 1906, he had his first unqualified hit in a leading role in *The Man of the Hour*. As the play's second lead, Fairbanks had his first real taste of success, something with which he had been obsessed. He frequently doodled the word "success" over and over again on scraps of paper. He was not concerned with the specific nature of the success; he thought about it only in the most general terms. And with this play, he achieved it.[19]

During the Boston run of *The Man of the Hour*, the 25-year-old Douglas Fairbanks first set eyes on the beautiful, blonde 19-year-old Beth Sully, who had seen him in the production and been instantly smitten. At her instigation, a meeting between the two was arranged. A romance quickly developed. Sully was starstruck, and Fairbanks, for his part, was flattered by the attention. She was attractive on many levels, not least because of her wealthy family and their social connections.

One person not enthralled was Beth's father, the former "Cotton King" Daniel J. Sully. A onetime financial powerhouse, he had recently fallen on difficult times, but he still maintained his social position and was not about to let his beloved daughter become involved with an actor. Beth was determined to marry Fairbanks, however, and to appease her, he gave his blessing to the union, provided Fairbanks abandon his theatrical career and work for the Buchan Soap Company, Sully's comeback enterprise. After careful deliberation, Fairbanks accepted. Douglas Fairbanks and Beth Sully were married at the Sully mansion, called Kenneth Ridge, at Watch Hill, Rhode Island, on July 11, 1907. After returning from his honeymoon, which the couple spent in Europe (a gift of the Sully family), Fairbanks jumped into his new position as soap salesman with his usual enthusiasm. Though not a great success in securing new business deals for the struggling company, he did manage to secure a contract for Buchan's soap from Frank Case, owner of the (pre–Round Table) Algonquin Hotel, where he and Beth took up residence after their marriage. For those clients with whom he was unable to secure contracts, he at least left a lasting impression by following through on his pledge to take a bite out of a bar of "Buchan's Twenty Three Brand" soap to prove its purity.[20] The excitement of all this soon began to pale in comparison with the memories of his former stage glory; and before long, with a call to William A. Brady, he was back on Broadway.

Once Fairbanks recommitted himself to the theatrical life, he was rarely again at liberty. His stage career in the ephemeral fare popu-

As Bud Haines, with the actor-manager-playwright Thomas A. Wise, in the Broadway production of *A Gentleman from Mississippi* (1908) by Wise and Harrison Rhodes. Photograph by White.

As Steve Oldham, with Millicent Evans, in the Broadway production of *The Cub* (1910) by Thompson Buchanan. Photograph by White.

lar at the time was successful. His extraordinary physical gifts, which had previously been displayed only in bits and pieces, began revealing themselves in full; and the acrobatics delighted audiences. Brady recalled Fairbanks's return in a play called *The Cub* in November 1910:

In one scene he had to run upstairs in a two-level set and save somebody's life—probably the heroine's.

"Run?" he said, when he first saw the set, "what's the matter with jumping?"

I eyed the twelve-foot gap between stage floor and upper floor and expressed some doubts.

"Why, that's simple," he said, took a little run, caught the edge of the flooring by the stair-opening and pulled up as easy as an alley-cat taking a fence. That made a tremendous hit with the audience.[21]

Soon after his return to the stage, he left Brady's management and signed on with his friends George M. Cohan and Sam Harris, who saw great possibilities in the comic actor. After starring in the Chicago touring production of *Officer 666* for Cohan and Harris in 1912, he followed Wallace Eddinger in the New York production. Cohan wrote *Broadway*

Jones especially as a vehicle for Fairbanks, but he found the part of Jackson Jones so irresistible, he cast himself in it instead. Undeterred, Fairbanks went on to flourish in Broadway comedies and comic melodramas such as *Hawthorne of the U.S.A.* (1912), *The New Henrietta* (1913), and *He Comes Up Smiling* (1914). Of this period, Fairbanks reflected:

Long before *The Lamb* [Fairbanks's first starring film] I had done similar stunts on the stage; in fact, it was this sort of thing that commended me to my first New York manager, William A. Brady, who always liked bustle, speed and energy in the plays that he directed. In a later play in which I appeared, *Hawthorne of the U.S.A.*, I made my first appearance by vaulting a wall, and at the end of the third act I sprang from a balcony to the throat of the villain.[22]

Also contributing to the growing success of Fairbanks's career at this stage was his wife, Beth. No one was happier than she when Douglas decided to return to the stage after his brief hiatus in her father's company. Fairbanks often relied on Beth's judgment in considering properties and parts that were offered to him, and she proved to be an astute judge. On December 9, 1909, the couple became the proud parents of Douglas Elton Fairbanks Jr. With his work ever more in demand, Beth raising their son, and the entire family enjoying blissful New England summers at the Sully home in Watch Hill, Fairbanks appeared to have settled down into what most men would consider an idyllic family life.

As Anthony Hamilton Hawthorne in the Broadway production of James Bernard Fagan's *Hawthorne of the U.S.A.* (1912). Photograph by White.

As Bertie "The Lamb" Van Alstyne in the Broadway production of *The New Henrietta* by Winchell Smith and Victor Mapes (1913). Photograph by White.

As Jerry Martin in the Broadway production of *He Comes Up Smiling* by Byron Ongley and Emil Nyitray (1914). Photograph by White.

Fairbanks and the infant Douglas Fairbanks Jr. on vacation in Bourne End, England, 1910.

Douglas Fairbanks, his mother, and his wife Beth (seated with Douglas Fairbanks Jr.) in a family portrait, New York City, 1915. Photograph by Byron.

Except that Fairbanks was unlike most men. Although everything appeared tranquil, his ever-present restlessness resurfaced to undermine the stability of home life. He was by now a highly sought-after comedy star. However, he could go only so far, even on Broadway, and he began to wonder if there was not more out there—new, uncharted territories just waiting to be conquered.

One day in 1914, as he and Beth were strolling through Central Park with Junior, they were stopped by a motion picture cameraman who asked Fairbanks to do a bit of mugging for the camera. Fairbanks responded by jumping over a park bench.[23] Several weeks later, the film was viewed by Harry E. Aitken of the newly formed Triangle Film Corporation, who was struck by the celluloid image of the charismatic Broadway actor; he jumped not just over a park bench but out of the screen. Aitken approached him with an offer to appear in motion pictures.

At the dawn of the feature-film era, cinema was looked down upon by most "legitimate" theater people. Though it was not uncommon for a stage actor to work in the movies during the Broadway summer hiatus—when the stifling city heat forced most theaters to close down for the summer—this was viewed as nothing more than a mild diversion and a quick way to earn some additional income until "real" work began again in the autumn. Many lesser lights of the New York theater, and some major ones as well, including John Barrymore and the Divine

As Jerome Belden in his last Broadway play, *The Show Shop* by James Forbes (1914), a comedy concerning the foibles of theater people and show business. Photograph by White.

Sarah herself, had played in front of the movie cameras in the summertime. It was a lark; but it was certainly not something for which any respectable thespian would consider abandoning the theater.

It was with this attitude that Fairbanks greeted Aitken's offer. He was a major star on Broadway; to give it all up and accept an offer to appear full-time in the movies seemed like lunacy. However, Aitken was offering much more than he could ever hope to make in the theater, even as a major Broadway star. He consulted with his friend Frank Case, owner of the Algonquin:

Fairbanks told me he had an offer of $2,000 a week to go to Hollywood but did not know whether to accept or not. Two thousand dollars was very much more than he could possibly hope for in the theater; moreover, the employment and salary were to be continuous, fifty-two weeks in the year, not for an indefinite season as in the theater. When I pointed out to him that $104,000 was a handsome amount of money, he said, "I know, but the movies!"[24]

In the end, however, it was more than the promise of wealth that lured Fairbanks out on that rooftop again. He had achieved all he could in New York; he had to go out further—to lands unknown. His restless psyche would not have it any other way. The theater's three walls and proscenium arch proved too restricting for his restless energy. Allan Dwan, who directed ten Fairbanks films, summed it up best when he said: "Pictures were made for him. The theater was too little."[25]

The Machine
for Escape

Hollywood was in the midst of a revolution in July 1915 when Douglas Fairbanks arrived at the Fine Arts Studio, located at 4500 Sunset Boulevard. D. W. Griffith's feature-length epic *The Birth of a Nation* had been released in February, only a few months earlier, forever altering the American film industry and the way audiences experienced motion pictures. It had been produced under the aegis of Harry E. Aitken, and its phenomenal success enabled Aitken to align himself with three of the industry's leading filmmakers—Griffith, Thomas H. Ince, and Mack Sennett—to form the Triangle Film Corporation. The Fine Arts Film Company was the Griffith studio; the other two angles of the triangle were Keystone (Sennett) and Kay-Bee (Ince). Aitken's ambition was to challenge Adolph Zukor's Famous Players Company and its slogan "Famous players in famous plays" by recruiting some of the biggest theatrical stars of the day, including De-Wolf Hopper, Sir Herbert Beerbohm Tree, Billie Burke, and Douglas Fairbanks.

Fairbanks arrived in Hollywood with every reason to believe he would succeed there. The contract he had signed on June 26, 1915, paid him $2,000 per week (with a $500 increase every six months) and stipulated that all his films were to be personally supervised by Griffith. In addition, his first starring vehicle, *The Lamb* (1915), was suggested by one of his stage successes: the rich idler Bertie, "the lamb" in *The New*

Despite obstacles such as the minister (Fred Warren) being imprisoned for vagrancy and his would-be bride being sequestered in a hotel room by her father, Jimmie Conroy is undeterred from eloping in *The Matrimaniac* (1916).

Harry E. Aitken flanked by stars of the Triangle–Fine Arts Film Company, February 1916. Back row (from left to right): Dorothy Gish, Seena Owen, Norma Talmadge; center row: Robert Harron, Harry E. Aitken, Sir Herbert Beerbohm Tree, Owen Moore (Mary Pickford's first husband), Wilfred Lucas; front row: Douglas Fairbanks, Bessie Love, Constance Talmadge, Constance Collier, Lillian Gish, Fay Tincher, DeWolf Hopper.

Henrietta,[1] who was renamed Gerald and inserted into a new scenario written by Griffith, using the pseudonym Granville Warwick. Griffith did indeed supervise the film, but he did not direct it—or any other film starring Fairbanks.[2] A Griffith disciple, William Christy Cabanne, was assigned to direct *The Lamb,* and he made little effort to temper Fairbanks's theatrical performance style to conform to the more subtle technique required for motion pictures. Cabanne's negligence may have been deliberate. There was a growing resentment in the established film community of the astronomical salaries and preferential treatment given Broadway interlopers. An apocryphal story attributed to Griffith's cinematographer G. W. "Billy" Bitzer had Fairbanks purposely masked in makeup that gave him a ghostly appearance in early scenes in order to sabotage his debut.[3] When Fairbanks discovered the malicious prank, his good humor disarmed his co-workers; he loved

Gerald is abducted by rampaging Yaquis in a scene from *The Lamb* (1915), Fairbanks's first starring vehicle for Triangle–Fine Arts. Charles Stevens, reportedly the grandson of the Apache leader Geronimo, is at left. Stevens appeared in small roles in many of Fairbanks's films and served as the Fairbanks company mascot.

practical jokes, and his own future film sets would be notorious for them. However, in the future, Fairbanks would be the primary perpetrator. In this respect and many others, he established himself almost immediately as the de facto boss of his own films.[4]

Fairbanks worked diligently and quickly learned film technique without displays of star attitude. However, his overpowering personality was an irritant to some, including Griffith, who dismissed his new male star with the comment, "He's got a head like a cantaloupe and can't act."[5] Fairbanks later remembered: "D.W. didn't like my athletic tendencies. Or my spontaneous habit of jumping a fence or scaling a church at unexpected moments which were not in the script. Griffith told me to go to Keystone comedies."[6] At the time, Griffith was having to supervise a large program of Triangle films in return for Aitken's financing of the film project that would become his epic *Intolerance* (1916), and he wanted to relieve himself of the burden of supervising the Fairbanks comedies. The status-conscious Fairbanks found Griffith's suggestion galling.

Despite the obstacles that beset his first weeks at Fine Arts, Fairbanks found the process of film production exhilarating, with challenging stunts to master and new situations to help stage and photograph. The thin story line of *The Lamb* afforded Fairbanks, in the role of the idler Gerald, the opportunity to be abducted by crooks, abandoned in the desert, captured by Native Americans, and entangled in a fight between Yaqui braves and Mexican soldiers. By the film's conclusion, the lamb has turned into a lion and rescues both himself and the damsel in distress (Seena Owen) in the sort of rough-and-tumble Wild West adventures that Fairbanks had fantasized about in his childhood. He loved every minute of it.

When production of *The Lamb* was completed, Fairbanks returned to New York City, where he happily reunited with his family at the Algonquin Hotel. He believed his first starring vehicle to be only a modest effort, but events proved him wrong. *The Lamb* was selected as the submission from the Fine Arts division for the inaugural Triangle film program, held at the Knickerbocker Theatre in New York City on September 23, 1915. In an early attempt to put movie admission on a par with that of live theater, tickets were priced at a steep $3. Dignitaries like the newspaper magnate William Randolph Hearst, the pianist Ignacy Jan Paderewski, the artists Howard Chandler Christy and James Montgomery Flagg, and the writers Irvin S. Cobb and Rupert Hughes were in attendance to legitimize the event. The evening, comprising one Fine Arts film, one Kay-Bee film, and one Keystone comedy in a triple bill, proved a triumph for Triangle and a major boost for Fairbanks. Indeed, in contrast to the other expensive stage stars hired by Triangle, only Fairbanks made a really successful transition to film. The *New York Times* reported:

For Mr. Fairbanks last evening was in the nature of a triumph. For some years a favorite comedian of the legitimate stage, he then made his first appearance in motion pictures. For some mysterious reason he succeeds where others fail. His engaging personality easily and undeniably "registers"—as the film folk say. He is amusing, graphic, individual, effortless. He even has a humorous walk of his own, and no one in last evening's audience at The Knick will be overcome with surprise if he attains a motion picture popularity such as the distinguished Mr. Chaplin has experienced. It is not surprising that, after seeing this film in the

Florian Amidon is puzzled by his unfamiliar surroundings in the dual personality drama *Double Trouble* (1915). Fairbanks plays both the effeminate, mincing Florian Amidon and his aggressively masculine alter ego Eugene Brassfield. The unidentified actor playing the homosexual bellman is even more feminine than Fairbanks's Florian.

studios, the directors hurried out and legally bound Mr. Fairbanks hand and foot for the next three years.[7]

The Lamb was a smash hit, and with its success, Fairbanks threw in his lot with the movies. The formula for his Triangle–Fine Arts features quickly emerged, in which Fairbanks plays an ineffectual, callow youth confronted by a series of challenges through which he undergoes a marked transformation, to emerge triumphant in the concluding reels. The obstacles Fairbanks faces in the films are of a very physical nature and showcase his energy and athleticism. All but one of the Fairbanks Triangle–Fine Arts films were five-reel features (i.e., approximately seventy-five minutes' running time) and each cost approximately $40,000 to produce.[8]

His third film, *His Picture in the Papers,* was a significant achievement in the development of Fairbanks's comedies. Produced at the Reliance studio in Yonkers on the East Coast, away from Griffith's disdainful eye, it solidly established Fairbanks as the American ideal of pep, vim, and vigor. Furthermore, the film brought him together with two collaborators who were to play a profound role in the evolution of his screen persona: the writer Anita Loos and her future husband, the director John Emerson. Griffith's head writer, Frank Woods, felt that these three

Pete Prindle delights in seeing himself in *His Picture in the Papers* (1916).

misfits on the Fine Arts lot were well suited to each other, and the results bore out his assumption. Indeed, Emerson and Fairbanks were predisposed to work well together. They had known each other during Fairbanks's years on Broadway and both were members of the Lambs, a theatrical club in New York City. The youthful Loos, whose age and diminutive stature belied her satiric and expansive views on life, amused and intrigued Fairbanks from the start. *His Picture in the Papers* was the first in a string of nine successful screen collaborations: Loos's scenarios and intertitles provided a sharp edge and commentary to the action on screen and a theme on which they focused their wit. (The theme of *His Picture in the Papers* was, according to Emerson and Loos, "the great American love of publicity.")[9]

Emerson, who co-wrote and directed the film, kept the action moving at a breakneck pace. In this comedy, on which the trio lavished three months of production, Fairbanks plays Pete Prindle, the health food–loathing son of a health food magnate—the sort of fellow who follows a healthy vegetarian dinner with the family with a clandestine dessert of a juicy steak. When he falls in love with a simpatico "vegetarian" (she prefers red meat to radishes as well), Christine Cadwalader (Loretta Blake), he is told that he can obtain her hand in marriage only if he claims half of his father's health food business. His father advises him that to secure his inheritance he must successfully publicize "Prindle's 27 Vegetarian Varieties" and get "his picture in the papers." Thus begins a series of comic misadventures that delighted Fairbanks's audience, who thrilled at the sight of this seemingly ordinary young man executing extraordinary feats to accomplish his goals. In the Fairbanks world, everything was his private gymnasium. For Fairbanks, a room was "a machine for escape," Alistair Cooke writes.[10] Audiences were fascinated by his screen persona—his broad, strong hands, dancer's small feet, and compact, gymnast-like physique. Yet it was his smile, his most distinctive physical attribute, that most set him apart. The Fairbanks grin flashed like the lights on a cinema marquee.

Much credit has been given to Loos and Emerson for the evolution of Fairbanks's screen character. A good deal of this was somewhat exaggerated by Loos herself in her autobiographical books and in interviews. Fairbanks had long been his own creation, and as his film career gained momentum, he assumed even more control. Anita Loos accurately recorded their collaboration in a 1939 interview with Louella Parsons:

Neither John [Emerson] nor I should get entire credit for those early pictures of Doug's, for he sat in on the writing, and contributed as much as we did.

I don't suppose that Doug ever made any picture that he didn't do at least 50 percent of the writing. He knew his own technique, and he had a rare faculty for understanding what people liked. He was full of ideas and gave us many of the best gags that were used. No writer could object to having help from a brain as fertile, as stimulating and as original in its story conceptions as Doug's.[11]

Emerson's and Loos's most valuable input was assisting Fairbanks in translating his character from stage to motion pictures. What was required of his collaborators, Alistair Cooke observes, "was no rare skill, but a willingness to let Fairbanks' own restlessness set the pace of the shooting and his gymnastics be the true improvisations on a simple scenario."[12] The films were promoted as a showcase for his personality and promised plenty of action. *His Picture in the Papers* opened at the Knickerbocker Theatre on February 10, 1916, and proved a great critical and commercial success, with *Variety* proclaiming, "Douglas Fairbanks again forcibly brings to mind that he is destined to be one of the greatest favorites with the film-seeing public."[13] Years later, *His Picture in the Papers* remained one of Fairbanks's favorites among his early films.

On his fourth film for Triangle, *The Habit of Happiness* (1916), Fairbanks began his long and important collaboration with the director Allan Dwan, which resulted in some of the finest films of both their careers. Dwan began directing in 1911 and quickly earned a reputation for his technical innovations (his background was as an electrical engineer). Prior to working with Fairbanks, Dwan had directed such silent stars as Mary Pickford (*A Girl of Yesterday* [1915]) and Lillian Gish (*An*

Sunny Wiggins teaches the power of laughter in *The Habit of Happiness* (1916), the first of the Fairbanks comedies that instilled the virtues of cheer and optimism. The flophouse was a studio set erected in New Jersey, but the flophouse residents populating it were actual vagrants recruited from local shelters. Fairbanks's initial attempts to make them laugh failed miserably. It was only when Allan Dwan, the film's director, encouraged Fairbanks to tell increasingly ribald stories and jokes that he managed some success.

▶ Fairbanks with cast and crew (including leading lady Bessie Love and director Allan Dwan) during production of *The Good Bad Man* (1916) at the Triangle–Fine Arts studio in Hollywood.

▶ The affluent Reggie Van Deuzen dons working-class attire and courts the dance hall girl Agnes (Bessie Love) in *Reggie Mixes In* (1916). Love wrote in her autobiography: "Nothing was ever accidentally good about Fairbanks' work. Everything was carefully planned."

Innocent Magdalene [1916]). The two men developed an instant rapport; their congenial demeanor stemmed from a similar sense of humor, an athletic nature, and a restless spirit. Dwan remembered, "I'd move *with* Doug—work with him and surround him with athletes. He worked with speed and, basically, with grace. Stunts *per se* were of no interest to him or to me. The one thing that could possibly interest either one of us was a swift, graceful move—the thing a kid visualizes in his hero."[14]

In addition to *The Habit of Happiness*, Dwan directed Fairbanks in *The Good Bad Man*, *The Half Breed*, and *Manhattan Madness*—all in 1916—for Triangle–Fine Arts. Their collaboration would extend to ten films in all. "He was very creative and on-the-ball all the time," Dwan remembered. "He wasn't doing you a favor in coming to work. It was a real privilege to work with him."[15]

In *Flirting with Fate* (1916), a dark comedy about a starving artist determined to end his life, August Holliday "can draw everything except a salary." Harold Lloyd and Buster Keaton would make similar films.

Fairbanks, nearly nude, as Lo Dorman, the title character of *The Half Breed* (1916), just before he dives from the rock and swims in the river, a scene devised by director Allan Dwan to appease Beth Fairbanks's objections to her husband's appearing as a "dirty, filthy character." Dwan remembered: "That made her happy. We had proved that he took a bath."

Steve O'Dare is a westerner in New York who loses a bet but wins a wife (Jewel Carmen) in *Manhattan Madness* (1916), an unusual, fast-paced mix of comedy, western, and thriller that was well received by critics and audiences alike, showing Fairbanks that he could get away from standardized formulas.

In the midst of these successful, formulaic early comedies, Fairbanks indulged in a couple of curiosities. *The Half Breed* (1916) is a straight dramatic film (adapted by Loos from "In the Carquinez Woods" by Bret Harte) in which Fairbanks plays the title role of the son of an Amerindian woman betrayed by a white settler—an early sympathetic depiction of a Native American in motion pictures. The other, *The Mystery of the Leaping Fish* (1916), undoubtedly the most bizarre film Fairbanks made, is a burlesque on Sherlock Holmes. Subsequent generations elevated it to cult status for its comic treatment of drug abuse. Tod Browning, a director who later achieved lasting fame for his forays into the macabre in collaborations with Lon Chaney and who also directed *Dracula* (1931) and *Freaks* (1932), is credited with the scenario in which Fairbanks plays the cocaine-addicted detective Coke Ennyday. The stage actor William Gillette had recently adapted his hugely popular stage success into a film (*Sherlock Holmes*, 1916); and taking a page from that famous

Coke Ennyday protects Inane, the "Little Fish-Blower of Short Beach" (Bessie Love), from the McCarty brothers in a gag still from *The Mystery of the Leaping Fish* (1916). The inflatable rubber fish—a flotation toy for bathers created expressly for this film—was shrewdly patented by J. P. McCarty and his brother, who acted in the production as well as serving as its visual effects specialists.

detective's exploits, Browning fashioned a character so dependent upon cocaine (the "seven percent solution" used by Sherlock Holmes) that he requires constant injections to maintain consciousness. The entire scenario is a hallucinogenic odyssey into the absurd, with Fairbanks, attired in a checkerboard suit (with matching automobile) attempting to thwart drug smugglers from carrying their contraband powder into port concealed inside inflatable rubber fish. However interesting the premise, the film's irony is never addressed: "Ennyday (an addict) prevents illegal importation of the very thing which he is addicted to," the film historian Arthur Lennig observes. "If this inconsistency is supposed to be ironic or humorous, the effect does not succeed."[16]

This muddled two-reel (25-minute) comedy was filmed twice. It was first directed by William Christy Cabanne and then again, after Cabanne was fired, by John Emerson, who remade the entire film with the assistance of Browning.[17] Fairbanks disliked *The Mystery of the Leaping Fish* so intensely that he wanted it withdrawn from distribution.

The film's most interesting aspect is unquestionably its unbridled attitude toward drug abuse and addiction. Cocaine was a controlled substance in the United States after the passage of the Harrison Act of 1914, and heroin was not made illegal until the Dangerous Drugs Act of 1920. Drug abuse was still widely considered a social indiscretion in 1916; reformers targeted alcohol as the greatest cause of America's ills. Charles Chaplin trod similar ground the following year in his early masterpiece *Easy Street* (1917), in which Charlie accidentally sits on an

Cassius Lee foils a plot to smuggle arms to Mexico during the Mexican Revolution and rescues the distressed damsel in *American Aristocracy* (1916).

addict's needle, the effects of which give him superhuman powers to defeat the villains.

It was during this period that Fairbanks and Chaplin first met, at a dinner arranged by the actress Constance Collier at Fairbanks's home. The two most popular male stars in pictures had an instant rapport. "That night was the beginning of a lifelong friendship," Chaplin remembered in his autobiography.[18] Undoubtedly a major factor in the intense bond between the two men was their shared experience: both were on the cusp of amazing worldwide celebrity of a previously unknown scope. Though the ensuing years brought inevitable tensions and separations, the two men cherished their unique bond. Chaplin reflected in 1966 that Fairbanks was "the most charming man I ever met. He was a marvelous man, a great man. . . . He was everything [. . .] and he was interested in everybody. He was very frank—we didn't always see eye to eye—but he was my very dear friend."[19]

Fairbanks's last films for Triangle were *American Aristocracy* (filmed in and around Watch Hill, Rhode Island, and featuring the screen debut of the 6-year-old Douglas Fairbanks Jr.), *The Matrimaniac*, and *The Americano* (all three 1916). In twelve feature films and one two-reel short made over eighteen months, Fairbanks served his screen apprenticeship and established himself as one of the highest-paid film stars in the industry, earning a reported $15,000 per week, a tremendous leap from his $2,000 per week initial salary. Only Pickford and Chaplin were paid as much for their film work.[20]

American engineer Blaze Derringer single-handedly foils a revolution in the mythical South American republic of Paragonia in *The Americano* (1916).

However, Fairbanks quickly became dissatisfied with the arrangement. "Actually, I'm working for nothing," he said. "My pictures have been netting the studio more than a million a year each and when you multiply that by a dozen pictures, you can see I really am, comparatively, working for nothing."[21] Fairbanks resolved to leave Triangle and become his own employer; with that objective in mind, he traveled to New York in December 1916 to consult with his attorney as to how he might be able to terminate his contract with Triangle. The loophole they found was the clause to the effect that D. W. Griffith was to supervise Fairbanks's films, which had been all but ignored by Triangle after *The Lamb*.[22] Now, it served as Fairbanks's portal to freedom.

In February 1917, Fairbanks announced the formation of the Douglas Fairbanks Pictures Corporation, which would distribute its own productions through Artcraft Pictures Corporation. Furthermore, Fairbanks intended to take Anita Loos, John Emerson, and other key personnel, such as the cinematographer Victor Fleming and the character actor and company mascot Charles Stevens, with him. Triangle countered with an injunction against Fairbanks, and a settlement was quickly reached, in which, in exchange for being released from his contract, Fairbanks agreed to pay Triangle an unspecified sum of money. The injunction against him was lifted, and he became his own producer. In his new role, Fairbanks would push his own physical capabilities in tandem with the capabilities of the growing art form of the motion picture.

Doug

Hero and Popular Philosopher

There is one thing in this good old world that is positively sure—happiness is for *all* who *strive* to *be* happy—and those who laugh *are* happy.

Douglas Fairbanks, *Laugh and Live*

Fairbanks had much to be happy about in the winter of 1917.[1] He had caught a comet by its tail, and the sky was truly the limit; he was setting out on his own at a time when success in Hollywood had yet to be defined. For a man addicted to the rush of adrenaline, it was the ride of a lifetime. Tempering his effervescent enthusiasms was shrewd business counsel from an astute and powerful new friend, Mary Pickford. Thanks to her advice and behind-the-scenes guidance, Fairbanks negotiated a contract with the Artcraft Pictures Corporation, a division of Famous Players–Lasky Corporation, to distribute the films of his newly organized production company, Douglas Fairbanks Pictures Corporation. Demonstrating an incisive business acumen that would become legendary, Pickford had, through Adolph Zukor, instigated the formation of the company the previous year to distribute her films.

With the most famous woman in the world also on the Artcraft roster, Fairbanks considered himself in excellent company. Artcraft afforded independence, a level of autonomy, and top dollar, because it did not block-book its productions but rather sold them individually to exhibitors. As his own producer, Fairbanks assumed greater creative control over every aspect of his films. Exploiting his artistic

"Doug," the popular philosopher, in a 1917 Artcraft publicity portrait. Booth Tarkington famously wrote that same year: "Fairbanks is a faun who has been to Sunday-school. He has a pagan body which yields instantly to any heathen or gypsy impulse—such as an impulse to balance a chair on its nose while hanging from the club chandelier by one of its knees—but he has a mind reliably furnished with a full set of morals and proprieties: he would be a sympathetic companion for anybody's aunt. I don't know his age; I think he hasn't any. Certainly he will never be older—unless quicksilver can get old." Photograph by Apeda.

freedom to invent and play a screen version of himself, "Doug" epitomized Fairbanks's boundless optimism and indefatigable energy in a series of good-natured satires of contemporary fads and foibles. "Doug" always championed the twin virtues of health and optimism. On screen and off, Fairbanks became an exemplar of the American zeitgeist during this early period of his career and helped to define American masculine ideas in the twentieth century. Alistair Cooke later christened this aspect of Fairbanks's screen persona "The Popular Philosopher."[2]

Fairbanks's ascendance at Artcraft was fortuitous, because the burgeoning motion picture industry had left the nickelodeon age by 1913 to become the most popular form of commercial entertainment the world had ever known. In the larger cities, vast picture palaces were built seating thousands and equipped with symphony orchestras. Every evening in midtown Manhattan, the streets around Times Square were closed to traffic in order to accommodate thousands of moviegoing pedestrians. The impact of some performers on these mass audiences was profound. Fairbanks quickly became more than a movie actor; he was a symbol—a beacon of assurance to an anxious nation tentatively taking the first steps toward entering the world war. "At a difficult time in American history, when the United States was keeping a precarious neutrality in the European war, Douglas Fairbanks appeared to know all the answers and knew them without pretending to be anything more than 'an all-around chap, just a regular American,'" Alistair Cooke explains.[3]

Fairbanks expounded on his own personal philosophy in a series of self-help books, beginning with *Laugh and Live* (1917), a boyishly naïve text shrewdly mass-marketed to America's idealistic youth. It was followed by *Making Life Worth While* (1918) and smaller, pamphlet-sized books: *Initiation and Self-Reliance* (1918), *Taking Stock of Ourselves* (1918), *Whistle and Hoe—Sing as We Go* (1918), *Assuming Responsibilities* (1918), *Profiting by Experience* (1918), and *Wedlock in Time* (1918), all published by the Britton Publishing Company. Fairbanks's modest contribution to self-help literature contained the oversimplified idea that everyone had control over various aspects of their lives. Fairbanks pitched his precepts: the power of positive thinking, the virtues of good health, and the power of good-natured laughter. He epitomized the traditional American idea of the invention and reinvention of one's self.

Fairbanks espoused the principles, but Kenneth Davenport ghostwrote the books. Fairbanks had become indebted to Davenport during their early days on Broadway, when the two struggling actors shared not only a dressing room but also a warm woolen overcoat, which Fairbanks wore one particularly cold New York day. Davenport became tubercular shortly thereafter, and Fairbanks never forgave himself. He employed

Fairbanks does a handstand for the amusement of some Boy Scouts, ca. 1924. Boys and young men were his most loyal audience, and he marketed his films to them in various ways, including a series of articles in the Boy Scout publication *Boys' Life* between 1923 and 1933. His final book, *Youth Points the Way* (1924), was initially serialized in *Boys' Life* before being published as a single volume.

Davenport as a factotum, working as secretary, confidant, screenwriter, and ghostwriter. In addition to the self-help books, Davenport also wrote Fairbanks's monthly page in the popular motion picture magazine *Photoplay* for six months (November 1917–April 1918). It was another cog in the wheel of Fairbanks's effective marketing machine. Fairbanks loved publicity and was learning how to promote his star image through ghosted writings, in addition to what his public relations team generated on his behalf. He also interviewed well and could effortlessly generate copy on a wide variety of subjects.[4] An examination of film industry trade publications, movie magazines, and the rotogravure and entertainment pages of newspapers of the time indicates that Fairbanks's breezy and charming popular image masked an astute showman who was in the vanguard of twentieth-century self-promotion.

Fairbanks in front and back views of his famed physique, ca. 1919.

Davenport was one of several key personnel working for Fairbanks during this period. Fairbanks's coterie were selected for their compatibility as much as for their talent. In addition to Davenport, there were the publicist Bennie Zeidman, the writer Tom Geraghty, the ex-wrestler Bull Montana, and the former pugilist Spike Robinson. Most important of all, Fairbanks's brothers John and Robert served as senior advisors, mediators, and, when necessary, moderators of their younger brother's overly ambitious flights of fancy. Fairbanks invented and portrayed his dreams of success. John and Robert helped him implement them.

Together the three Fairbanks musketeers constructed a contemporary star image for "Doug" that was so powerful that it helped extinguish the last lingering effects of the pious, stuffy, and hypocritical Victorian era to usher in a new age, confirmed by the so-called emancipated youth of the World War I period. The seeds that were sown in the Triangle–Fine Arts films germinated as the later Fairbanks comedies came to reflect the hopes, dreams, and concerns of Woodrow Wilson's America. Fairbanks shot to the top of movie fan magazine polls as the second most popular male movie star in America; only Chaplin was more popular. Chaplin's screen character costume was imitated ad nau-

Fairbanks uses a camera lens (for the Bell & Howell 2709 motion picture camera at center) as an ear horn while the cinematographer Victor Fleming and leading lady Arline Pretty look on in amusement during production of *In Again–Out Again* (1917), Fairbanks's first film produced by his own company, and his first Artcraft release.

seam in Charlie Chaplin look-alike contests. Douglas Fairbanks's off-screen dress, dark tan, and mannerisms were imitated as well, as was his choice of words ("Doug" popularized the expression "gee whiz").[5] He was, as Alistair Cooke sums him up, "a young vigorous man as uncompromising as his splendid physique, unfazed by tricky problems of taste and class behavior, gallant to women, with an affection for the American scene tempered by a wink."[6]

The quintessentially American nature of his screen persona nevertheless resonated throughout the world. The European response to his films was later expressed by the French critic Alfred Gheri: "Douglas Fairbanks is a tonic. He laughs and you feel relieved."[7] The war in Europe had been raging since 1914, and the escapism that American comedies provided was gratefully received. When America entered the war in April 1917, "My father tried to 'join up,'" Douglas Fairbanks Jr. remembered. "But the White House intervened. They wouldn't allow him to enlist."[8] They understood the propaganda power of the cinema and realized that the 34-year-old Fairbanks had more clout in front of a camera than he was ever likely to have on the front lines.

He demonstrated that clout with his first Artcraft film, *In Again— Out Again* (1917), a minor comedy that packed a major punch, both for Artcraft-Fairbanks interests and for the war effort. Fairbanks plays Teddy Rutherford—another of his prototypical ineffectual young men

Fairbanks campaigns for the third Liberty Loan drive at the Sub-Treasury Building, New York City, April 8, 1918. Some twenty to thirty thousand people gathered at the junction of Broad and Wall streets to see Fairbanks. Only a small portion of the crowd could hear him speak (he had only a simple megaphone for his public address). However, as in his films, he used his body as the best way to express himself; quickly dispensing with the megaphone, he launched into pantomime to convey his message. It was Fairbanks's first real exposure to mass adulation. Photograph by Paul Thompson.

Fairbanks represents democracy and Bull Montana represents Prussianism in *Sic 'Em, Sam* (1918), a promotional short subject for the fourth Liberty Loan bond drive directed by Albert Parker and distributed by the Federal Reserve.

transformed by circumstances and revealed to have great hidden resources. This time, he makes light fun of the pacifist movement (the opening scene is a spoof on the New Jersey "Black Tom" sabotage explosion). In doing so, he helped stoke the combative fires of a nation anxious about entering the war and sending its young men "over there."

Equally important was his participation in the third and fourth Liberty Loan bond drives of 1918. Fairbanks appeared in Washington, D.C., with Mary Pickford, Charles Chaplin, and Marie Dressler on April 6, 1918, to launch the third Liberty Loan campaign selling war bonds. On the first stop of the tour, the group met with President Wilson at the White House. Fairbanks next went to New York City, where on April 8 he spoke—with Chaplin—at the junction of Broad and Wall Streets to an estimated twenty to thirty thousand people.[9] To achieve maximum impact, the stars split up for the remainder of the tour, Fairbanks heading to the midwestern states, while Pickford journeyed to the Northeast and Chaplin to the South. This third Liberty Loan campaign succeeded beyond anyone's wildest expectations; the cumulative intake of the tour tallied approximately $3 million. In addition, the stars made short films to promote the purchasing of war bonds. Among Fairbanks's contributions were *Swat the Kaiser* (1918) and *Sic 'Em, Sam* (1918), distributed free to American cinemas.

Meanwhile, audiences were also clamoring for "Doug," the screen character they had come to love. *Wild and Woolly* (1917), Fairbanks's second independent production, was a brilliant return to form; it is the finest of the surviving Fairbanks-Emerson-Loos collaborations and perhaps the best of the thirteen films he made for Artcraft. It was also one of Fairbanks's personal favorites. "I really am living this picture," he said during production.[10] From his first appearance, in which his character is enthusiastically enjoying a campfire repast (the camera slowly pulls back to reveal the visual comedy of the situation: it is a playtime façade set up in his very Park Avenue bedroom), to the final frantic roundup in Arizona, Fairbanks has such a rollicking rowdy good time that it is difficult not to get caught up in the sheer delight of his performance.

Based on an original story by Horace B. Carpenter, the film's humorous theme, as Emerson and Loos wrote, was that "sometimes the practical joker finds his own joke turned against himself with dire results . . . we also satirized the more or less common idea of the easterner regarding the west."[11] Jeff Hillington (Fairbanks), son of an eastern railroad tycoon and a lover of dime novel stories of America's great romantic frontier, is offered the chance to escape his stultifying city life to go west and investigate the possibility of adding a spur to his

Jeff Hillington is fired with a nostalgia for the life and virtues of the Old West in *Wild and Woolly* (1917).

father's new mainline railroad in the town of Bitter Creek, Arizona. Jeff imagines Bitter Creek to be a lawless "wild and woolly" outpost of the untamed frontier, just like those depicted in his pulp novels. The residents resolve to give him what he expects, and retrofit modern Bitter Creek into a lawless boom town to impress him. He arrives guns cocked and ready for action; action he gets, as residents stage every western cliché imaginable, including a shoot-out (with blanks) in which Jeff defends the honor of a pretty young woman, Nell Larrabee (Eileen Percy). As the highlight of his visit, the townspeople have planned a fake train robbery that Jeff will naturally thwart and thus be proclaimed a hero. Two scheming varmints, Steve Shelby (Sam de Grasse, also spelled De Grasse) and Pedro (Charles Stevens), seize the opportunity to perform some real thievery of their own and set about hatching a scheme to carry out their intended stickup. In the meantime, Jeff has become enamored with Nell and means to romance her at a big dance planned for the night of the "robbery." Shelby and Pedro rob the train and abduct Nell with the intention of taking her away with them to Mexico. To keep the townspeople at bay while they make their escape, Shelby intoxicates a group of local Native Americans and entices them to hold the townspeople at gunpoint. The intended hoax is quickly explained to Jeff, who then becomes a real buckskin buckaroo by rounding up the band of inebriated Indians, liberating Nell, gunning down Shelby and Pedro, and emerging as the true hero of the day.

Fairbanks had a deep interest in western history, literature, and art. In addition to being fascinated with the physically strenuous life of Theodore Roosevelt, he adored the adventure fiction of Richard Har-

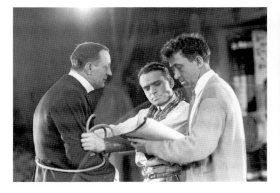

Fairbanks confers with the director, John Emerson, on the proper way to lasso Joseph Singleton (at left) during production of *Wild and Woolly*.

Fairbanks and Anita Loos discuss a script outside Fairbanks's dressing room at the Lasky Studio in Hollywood during production of *Wild and Woolly*.

Fairbanks playfully wields his lariat on location during production of *Wild and Woolly* for the amusement of the director, John Emerson (holding the megaphone at center), the cinematographer, Victor Fleming (behind the Bell & Howell 2709 camera), and the leading lady, Eileen Percy (on horse in background).

ding Davis and was an enthusiastic collector of paintings by Frederic Remington and Charles M. Russell. He believed in Manifest Destiny. The American frontier, South America, Africa, and the outposts of the British Empire piqued his curiosity and sense of adventure. Glen Mac-Williams, his second cameraman for many films, remembered:

When he was making westerns, he was in his glory. He was like a little boy playing cowboy. A lot of people don't believe this, but the whole time I was with him, he never had a stunt man. He kept real cowboys around him all the time. And he never sat still. He was

Billy Gaynor encourages his childhood sweetheart Ethel Forsythe (Eileen Percy) to embrace nature and get back to basics in the comedy *Down to Earth* (1917), which satirized hypochondria.

Fairbanks as "Fancy Jim" Sherwood on location for *The Man from Painted Post* (1917), a story of cattle rustling filmed at the Riverside Ranch near Laramie, Wyoming.

always rehearsing, building up stunts, practicing, working. He'd figure out a stunt and we'd build the whole picture around it.[12]

The film moves at a vigorous pace, with an enthusiasm and energy that rivaled D. W. Griffith's. In fact, the film historian William K. Everson notes, "Fairbanks, always much influenced by Griffith, sometimes outdid Griffith (and even the later Eisenstein) in the number and brevity of his shots. . . . *Wild and Woolly* moved at a fantastic pace, many shots running no more than five frames."[13] The film was an enormous success as a comedy-western and time has proven it to be one of the most enduring and endearing of the Fairbanks comedies.

By the time of *Reaching for the Moon* (1917), Fairbanks' fifth Artcraft release, the Fairbanks team was firing on all cylinders. The film, a Ruritanian romance, with Fairbanks dreaming himself to be royal, was the last Fairbanks-Emerson-Loos collaboration. Its premise foreshadows the costume adventures to come and is a fitting finale to their celebrated partnership. Once Emerson departed, Fairbanks engaged Allan Dwan,

Alexis Caesar Napoleon Brown dreams himself a prince in *Reaching for the Moon* (1917), which teased the concept of "new thought" (mental manipulation of physical events) and Ruritanian romances, both fashionable at the time with American audiences. In the upper photo, Alexis duels with Black Boris (Frank Campeau) to claim his crown as the sovereign of Vulgaria. Charles Stevens is at left. Eugene Ormonde is in the top hat.

In the lower photo, the officer at far right is played by Erich von Stroheim, who also served as technical director on this comedy as well as several other Fairbanks films made for Triangle–Fine Arts and Artcraft.

his colleague from Fine Arts, as his principal director, with Arthur Rosson (a disciple of Dwan's), Joseph Henabery, and Albert Parker alternating to relieve Dwan when his duties became too overwhelming. The first Fairbanks-Dwan collaboration for Artcraft, *A Modern Musketeer* (1917), proved to be significant as the link between his contemporary comedies and the later costume films.

A flamboyant action comedy based on E. P. Lyle Jr.'s story "D'Artagnan of Kansas" (1912), *A Modern Musketeer* winningly combines elements of comedy and melodrama. Moreover, as the title suggests, it was the harbinger of the great things to come, for in it Fairbanks dons the cloak and sword of the legendary fourth musketeer for the first time. Fairbanks was testing the waters of public acceptance of himself in a costume film. Appearing as d'Artagnan in early sequences, Fairbanks is wonderfully acrobatic as the Gascon swordsman, particularly in his first sequence, in which his chivalrous nature is showcased as he slays a tavern full of adversaries to obtain the lost handkerchief of a damsel in questionable distress. However, most of *A Modern Musketeer* is dedicated to exploring the exploits of Ned Thacker (Fairbanks), who emulates d'Artagnan as a result of his mother's prenatal influence. (His romantic mother read the Dumas novel incessantly during her pregnancy with Ned, resulting in his being instilled with the spirit of the Gascon hero.) The Kansas community can barely contain the frustrated young man, who literally climbs the steeple of a nearby church to vent

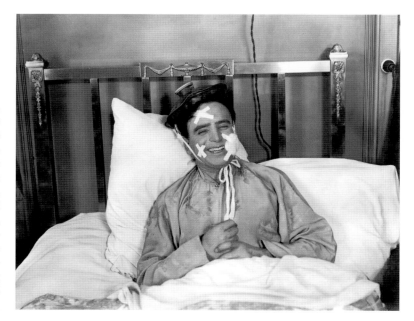

In *Reaching for the Moon*, Alexis's recovery from an attack by Black Boris's American agents is cheerful. Alexis is described in an opening title as "a young man of boundless enthusiasm, whose physical self is chained to a desk in a button factory, but whose spirit, led by vaulting ambition, walks with the kings of the earth—and sometimes stubs its toe." His spirit is not the only thing prone to occasional injury.

his pent-up energy. His father takes a page from Dumas's novel and provides Ned with the twentieth-century equivalent of d'Artagnan's plug horse: a Model T Ford. As the irrepressible young man makes his way across the dusty prairie, he happens upon a trio whose transcontinental auto tour has been disrupted by a washed-out bridge. He is immediately enamored with the youngest member, pretty Elsie Dodge (Marjorie Daw), who is accompanied by her 45-year-old suitor, Forrest Vandeeter (Eugene Ormonde), and her mother (Kathleen Kirkham). Ned comes to their rescue by ingeniously adapting his Model T to maneuver on the nearby railroad tracks, and effortlessly conveys them to a hotel near the Grand Canyon.

The chivalrous spirit of d'Artagnan is quickly called into service at the hotel as Ned discovers that the respected Vandeeter is in actuality a bigamist and embezzler. Further, he finds that a Navajo chief, Chin-dedah (Frank Campeau), intends to abduct Elsie and make her his latest "bride." The exciting climax of the film finds Ned literally scaling down the walls of the Grand Canyon on a rope to vanquish the evil Navajo, rescue Elsie, and elicit a full confession from the villainous Vandeeter. The tableau of the Grand Canyon serves as a stunning backdrop for Ned and Elsie to embrace at the happy conclusion.

The breathtaking scenery of the Grand Canyon, superbly photographed by the cinematographers Hugh McClung, Harris Thorpe, and Glen MacWilliams, under Dwan's direction, helped to make *A Modern*

Fairbanks as d'Artagnan in *A Modern Musketeer* (1917), which prefigured Fairbanks's epic period costume productions.

Fairbanks surveys the Grand Canyon on location for *A Modern Musketeer*. "I was disappointed in the Grand Canyon," Fairbanks wrote. "I couldn't jump it."

Musketeer an outstanding artistic achievement. Cast and crew went on location in the autumn of 1917 to the Grand Canyon and the Canyon de Chelly in Arizona, where they camped in tents during the entire three-week location shoot.[14] Fairbanks was in his element on location with the stunning landscapes, the distinctive rock imagery, and the community of Navajo people. "I was disappointed in the Grand Canyon," he joked. "I couldn't jump it."[15] This may have been bravado on Fairbanks's part, because for many years it was whispered that he had an aversion to great heights.[16] What was becoming commonly known, however, was Fairbanks's aversion to love scenes. " 'Doug' could breathe freely on the tops of church steeples, hanging from a mountain crag, or diving through a window pane; the only things that choke him are the scent and epigram of the boudoir," Alistair Cooke notes.[17] Alice Belton Evans, interviewing Fairbanks in 1927, asked, "Could you tell me what are some of the most difficult things you have ever had to do in your pictures?" Fairbanks answered with alacrity: "The love scenes. I dread them."[18]

The world premiere of *A Modern Musketeer* was held at the newly constructed Rivoli Theatre in New York City on December 28, 1917. The film was a great commercial success. *Variety* declared that *A Modern Musketeer* "ranks with the best" of the Fairbanks Artcraft series of films.[19] A great sadness for film history is that six Fairbanks comedies made for Artcraft are unavailable for reappraisal. Over 80 percent of all

Fairbanks in *Headin' South* (1918), a story of the Mexican border during "the recent troubles in that locality." This gag still was shot on location in Arizona.

Fairbanks confers with the director, Allan Dwan, during production of *Mr. Fix-It* (1918).

George Travelwell investigates the woman behind the veil (Pauline Curley) in *Bound in Morocco* (1918).

Fairbanks is a cub newspaper reporter who bites into a hairbrush sandwich in *Say! Young Fellow* (1918).

Jerry Martin is shut behind his cashier's grill, not unlike the bank vice president's pet canary, which Jerry tends to as one of his responsibilities. The bird soon escapes from its cage, launching Jerry on adventures that lead him on a journey of self-discovery in *He Comes Up Smiling* (1918), which gave Fairbanks the opportunity to reprise the role he had originated on Broadway.

Lieutenant Denton with Canby (Theodore Roberts) and his daughter Bonita (Marjorie Daw) in a scene from *Arizona* (1918), set during the Spanish-American War and adapted from Augustus Thomas's play of the same name.

Fairbanks in costume aboard his trailer on location for *The Knickerbocker Buckaroo* (1919), his last film for Artcraft. The trailer was designed by his brother Robert to provide some of the comforts of home while on location. Robert Fairbanks's "camping car," which had a library, a shower with hot and cold water, and provisions for two weeks, anticipated the trailers that are de rigueur for film stars today whether on location or parked on a studio lot.

silent films have perished, and six Fairbanks Artcrafts are among the lost ones: *Headin' South, Say! Young Fellow, Bound in Morocco, He Comes Up Smiling* (which survives incomplete), and *Arizona*, all released in 1918, and *The Knickerbocker Buckaroo* from the following year.[20]

What is not lost, however, is the important role Douglas Fairbanks played in providing joy to the world during this often grim period. More men had been killed in Europe between 1914 and 1918 than in any other war in history. Across the Atlantic, foreign-born anarchists, pacifists, and communists were detained and deported from America in 1919. At the end of World War I, the so-called Spanish influenza pandemic engulfed Europe and America, with more victims than soldiers killed in the Great War. Woodrow Wilson's dream of American membership in a League of Nations failed, and famine became a nightmare throughout central Europe. Prohibition became the law of the land in America, creating a society of bootleggers and powerful gangsters. Throughout this upheaval, the movies were a refuge for those seeking temporary solace and diversion. Fairbanks was the laughing, reassuring guard of its gate; on his watch, life was an adventure to be relished and enjoyed, and there was no problem—however impractical or intimidating—that could not be solved with a wink, a laugh, a backflip, and cheerful goodwill to all humankind.

Pickfair

If you will read the story of Peter Pan and Wendy, you will know
a great deal more about Mary and Doug than you do now.

Charles Chaplin

Douglas Fairbanks's public image in 1918 was one of great assurance and confidence, yet in his private world, he was experiencing great insecurity and turmoil.[1] His marriage to Beth Fairbanks, once the anchor that had kept him secure, had deteriorated to the point where he could feel only its numbing restraint. A new and exciting world was his for the taking. His wife and child were mere vestiges of the distant past and impediments to his exciting professional future. Furthermore, he had fallen in love with Mary Pickford, "America's Sweetheart," and wanted desperately to make her his wife.[2]

With the lingering effects of Victorian mores still permeating the American consciousness, a clandestine romance between these two very married paragons of cinema was a precarious situation from a public relations standpoint. Pickford's career was particularly predicated on her successfully projecting an image of youthful, sometimes childlike innocence and virtue. She was born Gladys Louise Smith in Toronto, Canada, on April 8, 1892. Her father's early death when she was only five years old forced her to work to help support her family, because her mother Charlotte's income as a seamstress barely kept the family of four from starvation. When a theatrical company was looking for young children to appear in one of its productions, Charlotte consented to allow Gladys and her younger sister Lottie to appear onstage.

The most famous couple in the world: a portrait of Fairbanks and Pickford, ca. 1922.
Photograph by Nickolas Muray.

Soon, the eight-year-old Gladys was appearing regularly on the Toronto stage and touring with second-rate stock companies throughout Canada and the United States in undistinguished productions of melodramas and potboilers typical of the period. Still only a teenager in 1907, Gladys had gleaned enough experience and awareness of her situation to call upon the leading theatrical impresario of the day, David Belasco, and request a part in his upcoming production *The Warrens of Virginia.* "I have been an actress," she said to Belasco. "I want to be a good actress now."[3]

Impressed with her verve, Belasco hired her, after an audition, and promptly advised a name change from the plebeian Gladys Smith to the more patrician Mary Pickford (Pickford being a maternal family name). As Fairbanks had also discovered, steady work in the New York theater meant steady work only during the more temperate months of the year, and Pickford found herself unemployed during the humid New York summers. Her mother suggested some temporary work in motion pictures, the thought of which appalled the young actress's theatrical sensibility. However, as was the case throughout her life, when Charlotte pushed, Mary acquiesced, and in April 1909, she found herself at the American Biograph studios in New York working under the direction of D. W. Griffith. The young actress immediately fell in love with making films, and they reciprocated, bestowing on Pickford unprecedented fame and adulation, and setting the parameters for movie stardom. She intuitively understood that the motion picture experience was an intensely intimate one between performer and audience and that this required a subtlety in acting that was the antithesis of the stylistic film performing of the time. Through her large and vulnerably expressive eyes, she forged a powerful connection with her audiences. Her cascading golden curls and tiny five-foot frame belied a spirited and spunky demeanor that immediately endeared her to them. "Our Mary," as she came to be called by her adoring public, was soon the most powerful personality in motion pictures, starring in fifty-two feature films between 1913 and 1933. Her years of dealing with theatrical bosses had sharpened her business acumen. Blessed with savvy, "Little Mary" had learned to beat them at their own game.

Fairbanks and Pickford first met at a party at Philipse Manor, the home of the musical comedy star Elsie Janis, in Yonkers, New York, in November 1915. Pickford had seen Fairbanks in *A Gentleman of Leisure* on Broadway and in his first film, *The Lamb,* and she disapproved of his exuberance. But when they met that day, and subsequently, her feelings began to change. Pickford remembered in her autobiography:

How can I possibly convey the impact of this man's personality, the terrific vitality, the completely childlike enthusiasm? One would have had to know Douglas personally to realize the overwhelming dynamism of the man. People of attainment fascinated him, and he them. He sought them out, not because he was a snob, but because of his lively interest in how they had made their names; how they accepted their success; how it had influenced them. I don't think either of us realized . . . that we were falling in love. When the realization came, it was too late to save the loneliness and heartache and escape the cruel spotlight of publicity. We fought it, we ran away from it, not once, but times innumerable. Mother knew, and so did Douglas' mother, and she was always tender and loving to me.[4]

It was ultimately through Fairbanks's mother, Ella, that the two lovers were brought together. In December 1916, Ella Fairbanks took ill, and her health began to deteriorate rapidly. Beth Fairbanks dutifully traveled to New York City to nurse her ailing mother-in-law, but two days before Christmas, Ella succumbed to pneumonia. Fairbanks journeyed from Los Angeles and sat impassively, apparently unaffected, at his mother's funeral. He even attended a Broadway show that evening, insisting that this was what Ella would have wanted. Though he maintained this stoic mask in public, his true state of mind was revealed to Mary Pickford after he received her note of condolence. He telephoned her, begging her to see him, and they met for a late-night drive through Central Park. As they rambled aimlessly through the Ramble, she reached out to him. They stopped the car, and he began sobbing. This uncharacteristic vulnerability touched Pickford profoundly, particularly when she noticed that the clock on the dashboard had stopped at the precise moment of his breakdown. The two took it as a sign of Ella's heavenly blessing on their union (Ella had been very superstitious about clocks), and from then on they used the phrase "By the clock" as a term of ultimate endearment between them.

Though of opposite temperaments, in the manner of shared experience, the two were cut from the same cloth. Fairbanks and Pickford were both children of absent, alcoholic fathers and willful, headstrong mothers. They had both begun their careers on the stage, and later both began their motion picture careers under the auspices of D. W. Griffith. In addition, their screen personas were both dependent on the illusion of youth and vitality. The coupling of "America's Sweetheart" with "Everybody's Hero" would have been ideal had it not been for their respective unhappy marriages, hers to the film actor Owen Moore. Still, soon after this intense emotional rendezvous, Pickford, claiming emotional exhaustion, left New York—and Owen Moore—to take up permanent residence in California.

Their clandestine courtship took nearly five years, Fairbanks in passionate pursuit, Pickford in righteous retreat. Anita Loos remembered that Fairbanks was as determined and as energetically clever in his quest for Pickford as any of the characters he portrayed on screen. He took to sleeping on an outdoor porch out of Beth Fairbanks's earshot, which allowed him, under the cloak of darkness, to slide down a nearby pillar, jump into his car, and speed off for a late-night tryst with Pickford. (The difficulty lay in his return—having to retrace his steps by pushing the car silently back up the steep driveway and shinnying up the pillar undetected.)[5] These artful subterfuges continued until the Liberty Loan bond tours of World War I gave the two furtive lovers a legitimate reason to spend time together. Though the public may have been duped by their patriotic enlistment in the bond tours, Beth Fairbanks was not, and in April 1918—during the third Liberty Loan bond tour—she announced that she and Fairbanks were separating. The final interlocutory decree of divorce was granted on November 30, 1919, with Beth acquiring full custody of their son. The settlement comprised $400,000 in securities, with an additional $100,000 set up in trust for Douglas Fairbanks Jr.

Though Beth Fairbanks was resolute in the direction of her future, the "unknown woman" named in the Fairbanks divorce as co-respondent was not. Pickford was at the breaking point, vacillating between hope and despair. After continual coaxing and cajoling, Fairbanks had reached his breaking point as well. He wanted "all of Mary," his son recounted. "And he longed to be able to display their union to the world like a double trophy."[6] Finally, he played his trump card: either she obtain a divorce and marry him, or she would never see him again.

Their wedding on March 28, 1920, at the home of the Reverend J. Whitcomb Brougher, pastor of the Temple Baptist Church, was a simple, quiet affair. Both bride and groom were in the midst of production on their respective film projects, and they did not wish to call immediate attention to their nuptials, so their honeymoon was briefly postponed. Instead, the newlyweds spent their first months together as man and wife at Fairbanks's new home, perched high atop a hillside in a largely undeveloped area west of Hollywood called Beverly Hills.

Although the newlyweds nervously bided their time to gauge the public reaction to their union, their hesitation proved needless. The negative public reaction to the marriage was negligible; it was as if they had always been Mr. and Mrs. Fairbanks. "Douglas Fairbanks and Mary Pickford came to mean more than a couple of married film stars," Alistair Cooke surmises. "They were a living proof of America's chronic belief in happy endings."[7] Secure in their acceptance by their public, they set out on their official honeymoon in the grandest style possible, embarking on the first of what would become almost annual European tours. "Doug goes to Europe each year to book his royal visitors for the coming year," Hollywood wags liked to comment.[8] Arriving in London, the couple met with a near-hysterical reception, and the crowds were overwhelming to the point of terrifying Pickford. They received a similar welcome in Holland, Switzerland, and Italy, but were met with apathy when they arrived in Germany. American films had not been distributed in Germany since the United States entered the war in April 1917 and, reeling from the ravages of war, Germans had no enthusiasm for Douglas Fairbanks and Mary Pickford. Finding mass adulation more appealing than mass indifference, the two traveled to France, where they proceeded to consort with dignitaries befitting their new stature. In fact, no personages—royal or otherwise—had ever experienced such a reception as Fairbanks and his bride. The power of motion pictures had created a new world—a new empire, which was in need of sovereigns to guide it. With this thought in mind, they set sail for home, prepared for their coronation.

While on board the SS *Olympic* bound for New York City, Fairbanks made the acquaintance of a young music hall acrobat traveling to America for the first time, 16-year-old Archie Leach. The acrobat would, in time, come to know something about fame and its incalculable toll, and over forty years later, Cary Grant remembered:

Among the fellow passengers were newlyweds Douglas Fairbanks Sr. and Mary Pickford, the world's most popular honeymooners and the first film stars I ever met. They were gracious and patient in face of constant harassment, by people with cameras and autograph books, whenever they appeared on deck; and once even I found myself being photographed with Mr. Fairbanks during a game of shuffleboard. As I stood beside him, I tried with shy, inadequate words to tell him of my adulation. He was a splendidly trained athlete and acrobat, affable and warmed by success and well-being . . . and it suddenly dawns on me that I've doggedly striven to keep tanned ever since, only because of a desire to emulate his healthful appearance.[9]

Returning to their home at 1143 Summit Drive, which Fairbanks gave as a wedding present to his bride, the two American monarchs set about making it their palace. The press dubbed it "Pickfair." Situated atop eighteen acres, it combined the charm of an English cottage with the majesty of a manor. Lord Mountbatten, who spent part of his own 1922 honeymoon there, remembered, "Pickfair was certainly the best taste house—not the biggest but the best taste house—in Hollywood. It was run very much on English country house lines and in fact they really kept court there. It was like Buckingham Palace in London."[10]

Far more imposing in legend than in actual square footage, Pickfair was designed to be comfortable and welcoming in its amalgam of Colonial and Georgian styles. However, it was replete with what would become the mandatory movie star home trappings: a lush sloping lawn, an oyster-shaped swimming pool (with its own small strip of beach), stables, kennels, and tennis court. From the grounds of their well-appointed but modest principality, King Doug and Queen Mary held court. The dining-room table was set for fifteen people each evening (just in case). In deference to Prohibition and, moreover, to the teetotaler Fairbanks, no alcohol was served. The house was kept cool—some said chilly—because Fairbanks thought it was invigorating and Pickford had an aversion to steam heat. When summoned for an audience at Pickfair, one could expect to find oneself in the company, not only of film stars, but also of dukes and earls, government dignitaries, politicians of various stamps (Fairbanks was essentially apolitical and had no strong allegiance to any particular political party), and sometimes even a king or a sultan. There were none of the ribald, risqué adventures that

sometimes occurred at Pickfair's California rival to the north, William Randolph Hearst's "ranch" at San Simeon. At Pickfair, dinner was at eight, and the host and hostess were in bed by 10:30 P.M. If one wanted a nightcap, one only had to ring, and a member of the staff of fifteen would provide a warm cup of milk.

As for the hosts, despite this glittering array of visitors, they only truly reveled in the reflective glow of one another. They often referred to each other by their pet names: Hipper, for her, and Duber, for him. Fairbanks's need to be close to her bordered on the obsessive; at dinner, whether it be at Pickfair or elsewhere, he insisted he always be seated next to her. In addition, he requested that she let him know her planned destination whenever she left the house, and he forbade her to dance with any other man.

Pickford was dazzled by the energy with which Fairbanks tackled life, often sitting silently by his side at the dinner table as he expounded, in his peculiarly percussive speech pattern, on whatever subject had caught his momentary interest. For his part, Fairbanks was never happier; he was as much in love with another person as his personality allowed him to be. Just as Beth Sully had been to him earlier, Mary was an anchor of stability—keeping him safely grounded during particularly precarious flights of fancy; she was Wendy to his Peter Pan. But more than that, Pickford represented true success for him. Though he had been a hugely popular star before their nuptials, his marriage to Pickford catapulted him to heights he never would have attained without her. Having her as his wife satiated the aching hunger within him to believe that he was worthy. If the biggest star in the world could love him, then, he reasoned, he must indeed be more than worthy. She was the ultimate trophy wife. On some level, he knew this, and he made up for it by cherishing her in the most loving and generous way possible.

As the influence of the most famous couple in the world grew, so did the community around them. In 1919, when Fairbanks acquired the property, construction in the city of Beverly Hills totaled $300,000. The following year, the figure reached almost $2 million.[11] As the "first" citizens of Beverly Hills, Pickford and Fairbanks took their civic responsibilities seriously, participating in all the large community events

Doug and Mary at Pickfair, 1920. "Mary and Doug were treated like royalty and in fact behaved in the same sort of dignified way that royalty did," Lord Mountbatten remembered. "They also filled the role of running the very loose sort of society there would have been in Hollywood in those days. They were a great unifying force."

Doug and Mary enjoy the canoe run at Pickfair, 1920.

Fairbanks and Pickford celebrate their "wooden" (fifth) wedding anniversary with the planting of a Douglas fir on the grounds of Pickfair, March 1925.

of the period. Fairbanks, in particular, relished his role in making the sleepy little town a sort of exclusive and restricted principality. In a larger sense, their role as Hollywood's ambassadors to the world meant even more. Allene Talmey wrote in 1927:

Doug and Mary are, of course, the King and Queen of Hollywood, providing the necessary air of dignity, sobriety, and aristocracy. Gravely they attend movie openings, cornerstone layings, gravely sit at the head of the table at the long dinners in honor of the cinema great, Douglas making graceful speeches, Mary conducting herself with the self-abnegation of Queen Mary of Britain. Cornerstone layings, dinners, openings are duties; they understand thoroughly their obligation to be present, in the best interests of the motion picture industry.[12]

Of course, the interests of the motion picture industry were their own interests. Their work was their lifeblood. All of the trappings of Pickfair—the travels, the hosting, the dinner parties, the ceremonies— were predicated on this work; it was a love and value system that they shared, and that was everything to them. Later, when Hollywood began to change, this fundamental error of not developing a life of their own beyond the effects of the studio would not bode well for them. But as long as movies were silent, all was well with Doug and Mary. "This is a happy house," Pickford said of her sacred surroundings in 1923. "This is a house that has never heard a cross word."[13]

United Artists

I
n 1919, four of Hollywood's greatest motion picture artists, Douglas Fairbanks, Mary Pickford, Charles Chaplin, and D. W. Griffith, embarked upon a revolutionary arrangement in which they became their own distributors. The impetus was their discovery that an impending merger between Paramount Pictures/Famous Players–Lasky (the world's largest film producer and distributor) and the First National Exhibitors' Circuit (originally created to combat Famous Players–Lasky by financing and distributing productions) was imminent. The merger was conceived as a means to rein in the astronomical salaries commanded by the major movie stars.

Fairbanks and his associates responded by forming their own distribution company for their independently produced films and thereby became the true masters of their destiny. To leave no room for speculation as to what the intent of this alliance was, Fairbanks suggested naming the company "United Artists." The United Artists Corporation, which was announced on January 15, 1919, and officially incorporated on April 17, 1919, created much surprise and skepticism. "The lunatics have taken charge of the asylum," lamented the disgruntled president of Metro Pictures, Richard A. Rowland.[1] However, for the "Big Four" of United Artists, it was a formal declaration of independence and, with it, they further developed the notion of independent film production.

Fairbanks signs the articles of incorporation of the United Artists Corporation, flanked by Chaplin, Pickford, and Griffith, February 5, 1919.

The "Big Four" of United Artists, February 5, 1919.

Fairbanks and Pickford (in costume for *Through the Back Door*) place their feet in the position of the Chaplin walk, while the originator does the opposite, 1921.

The details of the incorporation were devised and drawn up by Woodrow Wilson's son-in-law Williams Gibbs McAdoo, a former secretary of the Treasury, who was subsequently retained as general counsel. Oscar Price, who had been press representative for the U.S. Treasury Department during the Liberty Loan campaigns, was elected as the first president of United Artists. McAdoo, Price, and the four owners had first met during their productive association with the third Liberty Loan bond campaign.

At the outset, United Artists was faced with problems. McAdoo and Price had no previous experience in the film industry and were in conflict with the general manager, Hiram Abrams, who had left Famous Players–Lasky to join the new organization. The key challenge was a lack of product; Pickford, Chaplin, and Griffith were under obligation to old contracts to provide films for other distributors and could not immediately begin producing for their fledgling corporation. All of the films made by United Artists were sold for distribution on their individual merits; there was no block-booking with their product. In addition to the lack of product, the small-scale UA was organized at a time when smaller corporations were being consolidated by the conglomerates. However, the struggling United Artists soon became synonymous with motion pictures of the highest quality. The organization was never a company for profit; it was designed to service producers at actual cost of distribution, allowing them to enjoy as production profit what otherwise would have been a distributor's profit. To finance the company's operations, each of the founder-partners purchased $100,000 of preferred stock, and each agreed to deliver a specified number of films to the company.

Initially, United Artists sold its films on the basis of a flat fee paid by the exhibitor, but in 1920, this policy was changed to selling on a percentage basis. The "Big Four" received the huge percentage of an 80/20 percent split of the domestic gross and a 70/30 percent split of the foreign gross profit.

The tenures of McAdoo and Price were short-lived, but the producer Joseph M. Schenck was allowed to buy into the company and became an owner-partner in 1924. He was elected chairman of UA's board of directors, and under his astute leadership, the four founders became less involved in the daily operations of the United Artists Corporation. Not only was there a paucity of theater access for UA product, however, but the corporation was in deficit owing to the mounting overhead of distributor exchanges for too few releases. Schenck was therefore given the authority to reorganize the company so as to increase the number of productions. Schenck brought to United Artists the films of Samuel Goldwyn and Gloria Swanson, as well as his own output, starring Norma Talmadge, Constance Talmadge, Buster Keaton, and Rudolph Valentino. He also formed the United Artists Theatre Circuit in order to secure suitable outlets for the company's films.

Samuel Goldwyn became the second new member-owner of United Artists in 1927. By the end of the decade, D. W. Griffith was no longer producing independently (he sold back his UA shares in 1933), and Douglas Fairbanks was producing only to honor his commitments as a partner. It was Fairbanks who kept the owners together: Chaplin and Pickford—two monumental egos—were unable to interact successfully without him. Once he lost interest in production, therefore, the organization began to fray. However, in the first years of United Artists, Fairbanks, Pickford, and Chaplin were closely connected. They scrutinized films—their own as well as others—and developed shared characteristics visible in the three actor-producers' own productions.

Inasmuch as Fairbanks was the only one of the quadrumvirate free to make films for the corporation upon its formation, he supplied United Artists with its first release, *His Majesty the American* (1919). The company's inaugural film is marked by a special introduction, preceding the film's main title, in which a special title, in simple white lettering on a black background, expresses the sentiments of the newly formed United Artists: "It is our hope and desire to attain a standard of entertainment that will merit your approval and continued support."

To break the serious tone of the proceedings, an enthusiastic Fairbanks literally rips through the title itself, does a front somersault, and excitedly proclaims to the camera via an intertitle: "Listen, folks—they made me start the ball rolling. So here's the first picture. Gee whiz!—I hope you'll like it."

Fairbanks indeed starts "the ball rolling." He plays the wealthy William Brooks, described as a "Fire-eating, Speed-loving, Space-annihilating, Excitement-hunting Thrill-Hound," who preoccupies himself by bounding about New York City, aiding the fire department (rescuing a family of three and their cat from the third floor of a raging inferno inside a tenement building) and the police force (single-handedly capturing a crafty crook) in order to escape the unhappiness of not knowing his own family. As a title explains, "He comes of a good family—but knows nothing about them. He has pots of money—and doesn't know whence it comes."

When New York City's fire and police activity no longer move at a pace that quenches his need for constant stimulation, the adventurous Brooks heads for Murdero, Mexico, in search of excitement. While in Mexico, bestowing punishment on Pancho Villa for his depredations, Brooks receives an urgent telegram summoning him to Alaine, a fictional Mitteleuropean kingdom, with the promise that his parentage will be revealed. Brooks arrives in the picturesque surroundings, tucked away in a corner of the Alps, only to discover that "agitating demagogues

Fairbanks (pointing at right) directs his crew while in the studio tank during production of *His Majesty the American* (1919). The director, Joseph Henabery, is second from left, and the cinematographer, Victor Fleming, is behind Fairbanks at right. The camera operator, Glen MacWilliams, is third from left.

William Brooks battles his way into the minister of war's office in *His Majesty the American*.

have changed a peace-loving people into a rioting succession of mobs." The traitorous Grand Duke Sarzeau (Frank Campeau), Alaine's minister of war, is orchestrating a political revolution with his equally corrupt associates. It is up to the energized American to restore order and save the day, discovering in the process that he is in fact the heir apparent, grandson of King Phillipe IV (Sam Sothern). More important,

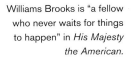

Williams Brooks is "a fellow who never waits for things to happen" in *His Majesty the American.*

the natural aristocrat is reunited with his mother, Princess Marguerite (Lillian Langdon), and finds true love with Felice, comtesse of Montenac (Marjorie Daw).

Fairbanks's American aristocrat harkens back both to Henry James and to the Horatio Alger success stories. Of course, such heroes are also typical of the romantic literature that ideally suited Fairbanks's talent both on and off-camera. His predilection for stories concerning lineage also suggests Fairbanks's preoccupation with recasting himself with his celebrity. Whether in contemporary comedies like *American Aristocracy, His Majesty the American,* and *The Mollycoddle* (1920), or such costume films as *Douglas Fairbanks in Robin Hood* (1922), *Don Q Son of Zorro* (1925), and *The Black Pirate* (1926), Fairbanks attempted to reconcile the contradictions between the self-made man and the aristocrat within himself.

Joseph Henabery, a protégé of Griffith's who had previously directed Fairbanks in the Artcraft productions *The Man from Painted Post* and *Say! Young Fellow,* as well as in the war bond short *Swat the Kaiser,* was engaged to direct the film and write the scenario with Fairbanks. Instead of the typical Fairbanks formula of good-naturedly teasing some fad or foible, the scenario of *His Majesty the American* ambitiously attempted to reflect Woodrow Wilson's vision of America's peace aims (including the League of Nations), the Fourteen Points, in a Ruritanian romance. Fairbanks, having gained White House contacts through his involvement in the Liberty Loan campaigns and his association with McAdoo,

Fairbanks (in costume) and Chaplin share a laugh during production of *His Majesty the American.*

Fairbanks exercises at the studio, ca. 1919.

had promised officials of Wilson's administration that his film would incorporate favorable material on each of the Fourteen Points, and the scenario was submitted to government officials for their approval prior to production.[2] The American government believed in film as a persuasive media by the end of the war, in stark contrast with the U.S. Supreme Court decision, *Mutual Film Corporation v. Industrial Commission of Ohio* (1915), in which the Court ruled that free speech protection did not extend to motion pictures.

His Majesty the American was the first of the Fairbanks films to be made at the Douglas Fairbanks Studios on the W. H. Clune studio lot in Hollywood (Raleigh Studios in the twenty-first century). The art director, Max Parker, conceived some ambitious settings, including a New York City tenement, a two-floor crook hideout, a royal palace, a train station, and a grand ballroom, among the many sets depicting locations in New York, Mexico, and the imaginary kingdom of Alaine. Large crowds were employed to fill the grand settings. Victor Fleming, who had regularly worked with Fairbanks as a cinematographer since Triangle–Fine Arts, was engaged in that capacity.

His Majesty the American was Fairbanks's most expensive film up to that time, costing nearly $175,000. With the success of United Artists riding on its initial efforts, he invested his own money in the picture. All proceeded smoothly until two-thirds of the way through production, when the U.S. Senate refused to approve America joining the League of Nations. Fairbanks and Henabery were faced with a serious problem, because the film was based on Wilson's Fourteen Points, which were no longer relevant. "I could conceive of no way to salvage the picture without doing damage by the removal of material relating to the propaganda, but the job had to be done. Luckily, some excess material, for which there was no room in the first cut, was available," Henabery remembered.[3] The film had suffered as a result, with a convoluted plot and unsatisfactory pacing of the edited material, he felt. Nevertheless, the scenario reflected in part the fantasy element that would increasingly define Fairbanks's cinema.

Dissatisfied with the finished film, Henabery was also upset by Fairbanks's divorce from Beth. A man of high moral principles with a Roman Catholic background, he never again worked with Fairbanks; but he maintained a high regard for Fairbanks himself to the very end of his life. "During my career, I worked with many fine people, but Doug topped them all," he later wrote.[4]

The film was released on September 1, 1919, with its New York City premiere at the newly constructed Capitol Theatre, touted as the world's largest cinema, with 5,300 seats, on October 24, 1919. The en-

The Douglas Fairbanks Studios, located at the W. H. Clune studio lot in Hollywood, ca. 1919.

thusiastic reception of both the film and the new theater gave United Artists a highly publicized debut. *Variety* described the film as being "a sort of Fairbanksian *The Prisoner of Zenda*,"[5] while *Photoplay* called it "a good-humored diversion in which no one, including the star, seems to take things or himself too seriously."[6]

The best of all the contemporary Fairbanks comedies, *When the Clouds Roll By* (1919), lampoons America's then-current obsession with all things psychoanalytic—from psychiatric experimentation to dream interpretation to Couéism, the autosuggestion as advocated by Émile Coué. At the end of World War I, psychoanalytic study—specifically, the general public's conception of the works of Sigmund Freud and Alfred Adler—became a popular topic in the more sophisticated urban areas of the United States. Always one to be current on the latest obsessions or fads, Fairbanks saw in this mind-study mania a rich cinematic opportunity for his second United Artists release. He devised a story in which Daniel Boone Brown (Fairbanks), an "average young man," falls victim to the experimentations of a sinister quack, Dr. Ulrich Metz (Herbert Grimwood), and Tom Geraghty wrote the scenario based on this.[7] Using the power of suggestion, Metz attempts to control the normally happy-go-lucky young man and ultimately drive him to self-destruction. Brown is first seen being fed a harrowing midnight meal of onions, lobster, Welsh rarebit, and mince pie by his manservant, Hobson (Albert MacQuarrie), who secretly works for Dr. Metz. The point

Dr. Ulrich Metz (Herbert Grimwood) plants the seeds of suggestion into a dubious Daniel Boone Brown in *When the Clouds Roll By* (1919), a comedy satirizing both superstition and fake psychology.

Fairbanks underwater in the climax of *When the Clouds Roll By*. The underwater scene was photographed through the glass wall of a water tank.

of this sadistic smorgasbord is to induce nocturnal hallucinations in the young man. After a phantasmagoria of indigestion-induced adventures, Boone awakens to discover he is two hours late for work.

His boss, who is also his uncle (Ralph Lewis), will no longer tolerate the young man's irresponsible behavior and suspends him for one week without pay. Dejected, Brown wanders aimlessly through a local park, where he happens upon a young woman, Lucette Bancroft

(Kathleen Clifford), who, he discovers, shares his superstitious beliefs and enjoys using Ouija boards. At the same time, the girl's disreputable fiancé, Mark Drake (Frank Campeau), arrives and conspires with Brown's uncle to swindle the girl's father out of acres of oil-rich land in Oklahoma. The sinister Dr. Metz, realizing that none of the involved parties has knowledge of the others, sabotages the surprise wedding of Brown and Lucette, and all appears to be lost.

On the verge of suicide, Brown discovers the machinations of Dr. Metz, however, when it is revealed that the latter is actually an escaped patient from the local insane asylum. Reason is restored to his mind (illustrated as a morality tableau depicting Brown's mental state), and he swings aboard a moving ferry, races atop a speeding train, and braves a deluge and a flood to save his beloved from the clutches of the dastardly Drake. The two are eventually reunited, and providence provides a parson to marry the couple (marooned on a rooftop) as the flood waters carry them happily away.

Executed at a breathless pace, *When the Clouds Roll By* is a masterful showpiece for the whirling cyclone of energy that was Douglas Fairbanks. The film's pièce de résistance, the elaborate dream sequence, is a virtual encapsulation of every gymnastic feat in the Fairbanks repertoire (as well as a few that neither he nor anyone else had attempted before on film). The segment begins inside Brown's stomach, as the effects of the midnight meal begin to manifest themselves. While the culinary culprits battle it out within his stomach walls, Brown bounds from his bed to assault a menacing apparition looming above him. The intimidating visage soon dissolves into a series of ghostly hands grabbing at him from all directions. In an effort to escape, he dives through his bedroom wall and lands in the midst of a large congregation of women, who confront him as he struggles to keep his pajama bottoms from falling about his ankles. Seeking again to escape, he leaps through another wall and into a swimming pool; once out, he is confronted by the contents of his midnight meal—in semi-human form. They pursue him at super speed as he, in slow motion, vaults over a series of fences (once with a front somersault and tuck) and leaps onto a waiting horse. He leaps from the horse into a room of a nearby house, where, still pursued by his malicious meal, he literally climbs up the wall and across the ceiling to escape. Eventually, he climbs onto the roof of the house, makes another spectacular leap into a chimney, and tumbles down the shaft and into a large metal cylinder at the bottom. At this point, he awakens from his dream, literally on the wrong side of the bed. He calls for his manservant to bring him his book of dream interpretation, but is informed that he is two hours late for work.

This was an enormous amount of action for such a brief sequence. The most visually stunning of these events—the sequence in which Fairbanks climbs up the wall and across the ceiling—was so memorable that Fred Astaire and the director Stanley Donen reused the idea over thirty years later for the celebrated "dancing on the ceiling" sequence in *Royal Wedding* (1951). In both instances, the effect was achieved in the same manner. In July 1920, *Literary Digest* revealed the techniques utilized to achieve the Fairbanks sequence:

They built at his studio a set showing a room open at one side and revolving on an axis like a squirrel cage. As Doug walked over to the side wall and placed his foot on it for the first step, the camera, also set with special equipment so that it would revolve, likewise turned, and so on as he walked up one side, over the ceiling, and down the other side.

To the turned camera he appeared always to be walking along the floor, head up, but in the picture registered on the film, always vertical, the star had his head out horizontally or downward, as the case happened to be. The pursuers rushing into the room were introduced by double exposure.[8]

Fairbanks also utilized other, less complicated, technical tricks in the production, such as slow-motion photography (requiring overcranking of the camera to alter the speed of the filming), fast-motion photography (achieved in the opposite manner), double exposure, and the use of miniature sets. Pushing the technical envelope became a Fairbanks trademark in later years, and this is the first significant instance of it in one of his productions.

All this innovative trickery could have lost its impact had it not been contained in a smooth and coherent production. *When the Clouds Roll By* had the working title *Cheer Up* and boasted a new leading lady, Kathleen Clifford. The sure and steady hand of Victor Fleming, Fairbanks's former cinematographer, in his first directing assignment, contributed greatly to the film's success. This talent for imposing order on chaos became Fleming's trademark and made him a top director in Hollywood's "Golden Age," when he reined in unwieldy productions such as *Gone with the Wind* (1939) and *The Wizard of Oz* (1939). His association with Fairbanks continued the following year with *The Mollycoddle* (1920), and he would later co-direct the comic travelogue *Around the World with Douglas Fairbanks* (1931).

When the Clouds Roll By premiered at the Rivoli Theatre in New York City on December 28, 1919, and was described by *Variety* as the best of the recent Fairbanks releases, and by *Photoplay* as a finer film than *His Majesty the American*.[9] The film's critical reputation increased after it was added to the Museum of Modern Art's Circulating Film Library in 1938 (it was the only "contemporary" comedy included in MoMA's initial release of Fairbanks films). "Technically, it is one of the most inventive of all the Fairbanks films," Alistair Cooke wrote in 1941. "The slow-motion chase is about the best gymnastic section of all the early comedies."[10] Viewed in the context of Fairbanks's body of work, Cooke's assessment of the film remains valid, and beyond the homage in *Royal Wedding*, one sees echoes in other films. The flood sequence conclusion, with a minister washed downstream to marry the young lovers on the rooftop of a floating house and provide a happy ending, anticipates the last moments of Buster Keaton's *Steamboat Bill, Jr.* (1928).

"Mollycoddle" was a term popularized by Theodore Roosevelt, one of Fairbanks's heroes, to denote an overly indulged and spoiled young man. In *The Mollycoddle* (1920), his third United Artists release, Fairbanks latched onto the catchword to evoke his trademark "lamb into a lion" character transformation, used from his very first film. Fairbanks plays the Arizona-born Richard Marshall V, the "mollycoddle" of the film's title, a hopeless Anglophile sporting such affectations as a monocle, cigarette holder, and walking stick, degraded by the "super-civilization" of Monte Carlo and in stark contrast to a long line of patriotic, adventurous, and chivalrous forefathers. A trio of mischievous American college students shanghai Marshall onto the yacht of Henry Van Holkar (Wallace Beery), a diamond smuggler, who mistakes him for a secret service agent. The center of the smuggler's operations is a Hopi reservation in Arizona, where Marshall eventually arrives after being thrown overboard. Galvanized into action as a result of his love for the real secret service agent on the trail of Van Holkar, Virginia Hale (Ruth Renick), and regenerated by the land of his birth, Marshall sheds his marshmallow mannerisms and confronts Van Holkar in a climactic sequence involving a fistfight between the two men beginning atop a tree, descending a mountainside, and continuing through an adobe hut, off a cliff, into a raging river, and over a waterfall. The film concludes with justice meted out to the villain and Marshall and Virginia happily paired.

The scenario of *The Mollycoddle* was suggested by a serial in the *Saturday Evening Post* by Harold McGrath and adapted for the screen by Tom Geraghty. Fairbanks reportedly spent ten weeks in the preparation of the story and other preproduction concerns.[11] He chose the character actor Wallace Beery, in his first film for Fairbanks, as the villain, and Ruth Renick, a newcomer to films, as his new leading lady. Victor

The feckless playboy Richard Marshal V in *The Mollycoddle* (1920).

Fleming was again the director, with J. Theodore Reed as his assistant and Harris Thorpe as cinematographer. The art director, Edward M. Langley, designed a faithful reproduction of Monte Carlo, with its famous casino, at a reported cost of $22,000. In the one scene, there are 300 people (including the principals).[12]

Despite this ornate setting, along with other costly expenditures, the production cost was approximately $130,000, nearly $45,000 less than the cost of *His Majesty the American*. An elaborate touring car, described as a "desert yacht," features in the film, and there is an impressively staged landslide sequence that "outdoes anything of the kind in the memory of the writer," the *New York Times'* film critic declared.[13] Perhaps most significant, there is also an animated sequence that, while somewhat primitive, effectively illustrates the diamond-smuggling subplot. *Photoplay* acknowledged that with the inclusion of this sequence, the film "boasts a bit of originality in introducing a Bray [Studios] cartoon effect in the elucidation of the plot."[14] The outlay of money served to bring a measure of prestige to the film, and the *New York Times* review observed that, aside from seeing Fairbanks himself, "People who go to see a Fairbanks picture are assured in advance of several novel and spectacular examples of cinematography."[15]

Fairbanks camped outdoors for two weeks with cast and crew at Polacca, Arizona, approximately ninety miles from the nearest railroad station at Holbrook, Arizona, where much of the location work was

Fairbanks joins in the ceremonial dance of the Hopi people in *The Mollycoddle*.

filmed. The main interest for Fairbanks in this specific northeastern Arizona locale, near the Painted Desert, was the Hopi from the reservation at Polacca, some of whom were persuaded to participate. Fairbanks adored the Hopi (he had briefly used a Hopi dance in *A Modern Musketeer*) and filmed several of their ceremonial dances, although little of the footage was used in the finished film.[16] However, in one sequence, a Hopi dance is showcased, with Fairbanks comically participating with one very heavy Hopi belle. As part of their compensation, Fairbanks promised the Hopi people an opportunity to see themselves on screen. A screen, a projector, electrical equipment, and a projectionist were sent from Los Angeles several weeks after Fairbanks returned from the location; for many of the tribe, it was their first exposure to motion pictures. Newsreels, scenes from Fairbanks's films, and the footage taken of the Hopi were projected. In the short interval since the filming, some of those shown had died, and a few among the Hopi became alarmed, taking the projected images of the deceased for ghosts.[17]

The climactic fight sequence, which the star jokingly referred to as "the two-mile battle" because of the amount of territory covered, was one of the most arduous of his career. Fairbanks had earlier sprained his wrists and broken the index finger of his right hand on location in Arizona while executing a stunt involving a horse.[18] The Hollywood stuntman Richard Talmadge (known at the time as Silvio Metzetti) was therefore hired to do the daring stunt that begins the sequence, in which Fairbanks leaps from the top of a cliff onto a tree some fifteen feet away to fight the villain, played by Wallace Beery. Talmadge later recalled that his work on *The Mollycoddle* "was common knowledge at the time. I was hired to do a special stunt because Doug had gotten hurt and couldn't do it." Talmadge wore Fairbanks's clothes and performed the stunt with Talmadge's brother standing in for Wallace Beery.[19]

The Mollycoddle premiered at the Mark Strand Theatre in New York City on June 13, 1920, where it was well received by critics and the public. *Variety* called it "One peach of a feature."[20] Reviewing it for *Photoplay*, Burns Mantle wrote that it was "good screen entertainment" and that "if the Fairbanks pictures are to retain their popularity they must come to stand for something more than a series of stunts. His jumping days are not over, by several years, and he may find a few new leaps in Europe, but he has pretty well covered those in his own, his native land. Therefore I think he was a wise Douglas to do *The Mollycoddle*. It indicates his determination to stand on his own as an actor as well as a handsome athlete."[21]

However, the old values would soon fade away as the emancipated youth of the "Lost Generation" ushered out the values for which "Doug" was a great champion. His optimistic go-getter character would be appropriated by Harold Lloyd, who began to make feature-length films just as Fairbanks abandoned contemporary comedies. Indeed, *The Mollycoddle* might easily have been a Lloyd vehicle, and some of the gags from the Fairbanks film (Doug being followed by the village cats after escaping a fish house) are very similar to gags in Lloyd's first feature-length masterpiece, *Grandma's Boy* (1922).

Although Fairbanks made his first costume adventure, *The Mark of Zorro*, before *The Nut*, he was unsure whether he would be accepted in a costume film. Once again assuming the role of the cosmopolitan cavalier was not an assignment Fairbanks relished. A producer with his eye on the bottom line, Fairbanks made *The Nut* (1921) thinking that it would be fully accepted by exhibitors as well as the public as a proven commodity. The success of *The Mark of Zorro* and the relative failure of *The Nut* determined Fairbanks's career path for the next decade.

Admittedly a minor work, *The Nut* is frequently dismissed in critical assessments of Fairbanks's career. This is unfortunate, for it contains some fascinating sequences and reveals much about the actor-producer's state of mind at the time it was made. The issue that dogs *The Nut* is the very issue that was dogging Douglas Fairbanks himself; the man and the film suffer from an identity crisis. Fairbanks had become disengaged from his screen character; his supple sermons belonged in the past, along with his idealistic heroes Theodore Roosevelt and Billy Sunday. Fairbanks wrote in the year *The Nut* was released of the shift in his work: "Anyone who has seen *The Mollycoddle* or *The Nut* must have noticed that something strange has happened. In *The Mollycoddle* the

Charlie Jackson with sparklers and incense in hand, about to literally set the party on fire, with Marguerite de la Motte in *The Nut* (1921).

smiles are only occasional and sustained for but a brief period of time, and in *The Nut* they have disappeared almost altogether, like the last few flickers of a lamp that is going out."[22]

Reflecting Fairbanks's half-hearted commitment to the project, *The Nut* comes to life only in fits and starts. It begins with Charlie Jackson (Fairbanks) deep in slumber. He is awakened by his nearby parrot (which exclaims, "Ten o'clock" in an animated caption); Jackson is slowly removed from his bed (revealed to be on wheels) and slid into his sunken bathtub filled with warm water. This sequence depicts Jackson's Rube Goldberg–like time-saving devices, the implication being that he is an eccentric, or rather a "nut," as well as a mere puppet in a machine of his own creation. Upon the completion of his automated bath (three whirling sponges do the washing, a towel on a spindle dries him off), standing on a conveyor belt, Jackson selects his clothes for the day—an ingenious contraption of bed, bath, and beyond. The brilliance of the sequence suggests Fairbanks's flair for the type of mechanical gags Buster Keaton showcased in such two-reel comedies of the period as *The Scarecrow* (1920) and *The Electric House* (1922), and it is a precursor to the feeding-machine sequence of Chaplin's *Modern Times* (1936).

After this inspired opening, the major story line of the film is introduced: Jackson makes ill-fated attempts to assist his neighbor and sweetheart, Estrell Wynn (Marguerite de la Motte), who, an intertitle explains, "believes that homes radiate a constructive influence and that

Charlie Jackson is a free—and sometimes surreal—spirit in the modern world of *The Nut*.

a group of slum children brought into a refined home for an hour each day will become good citizens—just like that." Jackson entertains prospective benefactors at a party for Estrell, but when he introduces some of his inventions, they backfire horribly, causing a rift between the two and opening the way for a rival, the villainous Philip Feeney (William Lowery). The film careens from one implausible situation to the next, from attempts at social commentary (Estrell's absurd theory), drawing-room comedy (a clever sequence in which Jackson "impersonates" a series of famous figures), slapstick (Jackson appropriating three dummies from a wax museum), and melodrama (Jackson's race to the rescue to save his sweetheart from the clutches of the lascivious Feeney). The climax of the film is an elaborate escape in which Jackson and Estrell climb up and down the heating pipes within Feeney's gambling house. The conventional "The End" title is altered by the inclusion of a squirrel finishing its meal, with the title "The End of *The Nut*" superimposed over the image for one last laugh.

The picture is like a chaotic funhouse, filled with magical masquerades, illusions, and gimmicks of great momentary amusement. However, the material is in dire need of a cohesive plot—or at least a clear perspective—to make it truly enjoyable. The story of *The Nut* was devised by Fairbanks's crony Kenneth Davenport and adapted by William Parker and Lotta Woods. Like *When the Clouds Roll By*, the tale begins in Greenwich Village, and the entire production was filmed at the Douglas Fairbanks Studios in Hollywood as envisioned by the art director, Edward M. Langley. The production had no fewer than three cameramen (a first for a Fairbanks film): Harris Thorpe was the cinematographer and operator of the first camera; William McGann operated the second; and Charles Warrington (Fairbanks's still photographer) operated a third. In addition to the foreign and domestic negatives, Fairbanks reportedly manufactured a third negative for his personal library.[23] *The Nut*, briskly shot in eight weeks and four days, was made at an approximate production cost of $131,048.20.[24]

The film's novice director, J. Theodore "Ted" Reed, had met Fairbanks in Detroit during the third Liberty Loan bond drive. Impressed with his buoyant personality, Fairbanks arranged for Reed to join the Fairbanks organization, where he worked as part of the scenario staff and later coordinated publicity work for the Fairbanks productions. After he had worked as assistant director on *When the Clouds Roll By*, *The Mollycoddle*, and *The Mark of Zorro*, Fairbanks gave Reed the chance to direct *The Nut*.

Fairbanks was, as *Variety* noted in its review, "less of the acrobat and more of the comedian" in *The Nut*.[25] Indeed, there are few of the typical

Fairbanks with director J. Theodore "Ted" Reed during production of *The Nut*. Reed acted as Fairbanks's production manager from 1923 until the advent of talking films, when he was made director of the sound department at the United Artists Studios, a position he held from 1929 to 1931. He served as president of the Academy of Motion Picture Arts and Sciences in 1933–34.

Fairbanks stunts, partly because of an accident during production. The final scene of the film required Fairbanks to jump through a window in an effort to apprehend the villain, Feeney. In making the leap, Fairbanks caught his toe on the window sill and fell hard onto the pavement, breaking his left hand and wrenching his back.[26]

The shortest and most modest of all his silent feature films produced for United Artists, *The Nut* concludes with the wedding of Charlie and Estrell, but the pressbook indicates there was a scene following the wedding, in which "Charlie is taken to the Vanderbrook home where he discovers that the supposed senior Vanderbrook he attempted to meet was in reality the steward." This scene is missing from the film as preserved by the Museum of Modern Art. It may have been eliminated just prior to the film's release.[27]

Also missing from the finished film, despite the claims of many film historians, is Charles Chaplin. It is clearly a Chaplin imitator, not Chaplin himself, who appears briefly in the party sequence wearing the Tramp costume. In the film, Charlie Jackson entertains his guests with a series of "impersonations" by darting behind a large screen and re-emerging each time dressed as a different famous figure. The joke is that Fairbanks is obviously not any of the figures he "appears" to be; Napoleon Bonaparte, Ulysses S. Grant, Abraham Lincoln, and Tom Thumb are impersonated by other actors. The masquerade ends when the façade collapses, revealing the actual impersonators hiding behind the screen (along with a Chaplin imitator).

The confusion may partly be the result of the fact that Chaplin did act in the production (sans Tramp costume). Ted Reed recalled in 1956 that he needed someone to pass Fairbanks going down a street to enliven the scene. Chaplin happened to be observing the filming and volunteered. "How about your contract?" Reed asked, referring to Chaplin's obligations to First National. "I'll keep my back to the camera," Chaplin replied. In the first take, Chaplin stopped Fairbanks and asked him for a light—an embellishment that the short scene was not able to withstand. In the second take, Chaplin deliberately tripped on the curb for comic effect.[28] Unfortunately, this sequence—which may or may not have ended on the cutting room floor—does not appear in the MoMA print or the surviving outtakes held by the George Eastman House. Chaplin was not the only famous face who volunteered to appear in the film. Mary Pickford discreetly appears as a party guest; in addition, her niece Gwynne plays a child inside the wax museum.[29]

The Nut premiered at the Mark Strand Theatre in New York City on March 6, 1921. Burns Mantle, writing in *Photoplay*, summed up the critical consensus when he wrote, "*The Nut* is not as good as some of the other Fairbanks pictures, but, being fair, you will have to admit it is at least seven times better than most of the pictures you pay the same price to see."[30] Released between *The Mark of Zorro* and *The Three Musketeers*, *The Nut* has inevitably been overshadowed by the costume films that surround it.

Making His Mark

The Mark of Zorro (1920)

T*he Mark of Zorro* is a landmark, not only in the career of Douglas Fairbanks, but also in the development of the action adventure film. With this, his thirtieth motion picture, Fairbanks was transitioning from comedies to the costume films for which he is best remembered. Instead of reflecting the times, *The Mark of Zorro* offers an infusion of the romantic past with a contemporary flair. The film proved to be an ideal test of the public's acceptance of Fairbanks in costume stories and a new persona. Up until then, most costume films had been turgid affairs; Fairbanks contributed his winning charm, humor, and athleticism executed in a modern manner. His approach—particularly his ingratiating humor—gave his films great appeal to audiences of the 1920s and helped usher in a renaissance of costume adventures. Beyond reenergizing his career and redefining a genre, Fairbanks's *The Mark of Zorro* helped popularize one of the enduring creations of twentieth-century American fiction, a character who was the prototype for comic book heroes such as Batman.

The idea of making bigger and more spectacular films had been in the back of Fairbanks's mind for several years. In fact, friends and advisors kept prodding him in that direction and had suggested folk heroes and fairytales as subjects. However, Fairbanks was enjoying great success with his contemporary comedies and had no strong desire to alter a successful formula. However, by 1920, events indicated that a change in course was required.

The fearless Zorro uses a gun to keep men filling a tavern at bay in *The Mark of Zorro*.

The devastating effects of World War I were measured, not only in a generation lost, but also in an innocence lost among its survivors. As a result, the desire to escape from the disillusionment and cynicism of the times prevailed, and Fairbanks's choice to experiment with a costume adventure proved to be a shrewd decision. The values his contemporary comedies had celebrated were vanishing. Furthermore, the problems of the period included the high cost of living, Prohibition, and the League of Nations controversy. Adding to the social ills, exhibitors were beginning to grumble about the response the Fairbanks films were receiving from audiences. Dennis F. "Cap" O'Brien of United Artists wrote the Douglas Fairbanks Pictures Corporation: "Exhibitors have been complaining because you have failed to develop sufficient love interest in your pictures. . . . Women do not care to see your pictures because . . . of a lack of love interest in them . . . , and of course, men do not go to the matinees so the afternoon business is not as big as it should be." O'Brien recommended getting away from "the type of picture you have been making . . . do something with real dramatic values in it which you can do better than any male star in the business."[1]

Although there are conflicting versions as to who placed Johnston McCulley's five-part story "The Curse of Capistrano" in Fairbanks's hands, the best evidence suggests that Ruth Allen, a former actress, play agent, and family friend, recommended the story, an action adventure based on a true-life character in early California history.[2] Fairbanks was at first uninterested; it was Pickford who read it while they were en route to Europe on their honeymoon. Based on her enthusiasm for the story, he read it himself and quickly cabled instructions home to acquire the rights and begin preparations for its preproduction.

Instead of involving Fairbanks with current fads and foibles, *The Mark of Zorro* provided his audiences with the antidote of escape. He was, he later confessed, "a little timid" about such a transition.[3] However, the desire to play in a costume film (particularly *The Three Musketeers*) was great. Moreover, the success of Ernst Lubitsch's *Madame DuBarry* (1919) and *Anna Boleyn* (1920) proved that costume spectacles were once again fashionable with the public. Looking upon his costume film as an experiment, he proceeded with caution. Filming was easy, because many of the film's Spanish California locations were virtually outside the windows of the studio. Furthermore, the source material bore important similarities to his most popular contemporary comedies: action mixed with comedy, and the dual nature of the protagonist.

Having made the commitment, Fairbanks began assembling his team. Fred Niblo was engaged to direct his first of two films for Fair-

Don Diego Vega extends his snuff to diffuse the bluster of Sergeant Gonzales (Noah Beery) in *The Mark of Zorro*. Fairbanks and Beery had first worked together in the Broadway production of *As Ye Sow* in 1905.

banks. Niblo largely established his reputation with Fairbanks and went on to direct such important silent films as *Blood and Sand* (1922) with Rudolph Valentino, *Ben-Hur: A Tale of the Christ* (1925), and two Greta Garbo vehicles, *The Temptress* (1926) and *The Mysterious Lady* (1928). Ted Reed was hired as Niblo's assistant director. William McGann and Harris Thorpe, who had filmed Fairbanks's previous two United Artists releases, were again engaged as the cinematographers. Edward M. Langley provided the art direction and Eugene Mullin worked with Fairbanks in adapting Johnston's story into a film scenario. Marguerite de la Motte (who had previously appeared in the supporting role of Lena in *Arizona*) was engaged as leading lady, in which role she was required to generate more romantic chemistry with the star than was the case in any prior Fairbanks pairing. The capable character actors Robert McKim, Noah Beery, Charles Hill Mailes, Claire McDowell, Snitz Edwards, and Sydney De Grey rounded out the principal cast.

Zorro laughs at Sergeant Gonzales's swordsmanship.

One of the best stuntmen in Hollywood, Richard Talmadge, who had performed the special stunt in *The Mollycoddle,* was again on the payroll to assist Fairbanks in the choreography of stunts. In rehearsals, Talmadge mainly served as a model; Fairbanks, along with his trainer, Lewis Hippe, watched him go through the action in order to eliminate flaws and minimize hazards. Once a stunt routine was effectively refined to Fairbanks's satisfaction, the star himself executed the feat for the cameras. In addition to contributing his own physical prowess, Talmadge was influential in developing the graceful, gymnastic-style athleticism Fairbanks achieved in his costume films. Invaluable expertise was also provided by a Belgian fencing master, Henry J. Uyttenhove, the fencing coach at the Los Angeles Athletic Club, who choreographed all of the film's dueling sequences.

As the film begins, oppression is rife in early nineteenth-century Spanish California. The evil Governor Alvarado (George Periolat) and the lecherous Captain Ramon (Robert McKim) abuse their power and hold the missions around Reina de Los Angeles under a ruthless militia. A masked avenger, Zorro (Spanish for "fox"), appears as a champion of the oppressed, punishing officials and protecting the helpless. The mysterious swordsman carves his initial, with the tip of his rapier, into the flesh of his victims: the mark of Zorro. Natives and caballeros alike are enthralled and terrified by the exploits of the deft dueling outlaw, except for an effete young nobleman, Don Diego Vega (Fairbanks), recently returned from Spain. The young man's father (Sydney De Grey) wishes him betrothed to Lolita (Marguerite de la Motte), the daughter of Don Carlos Pulido (Charles Hill Mailes), a nobleman made poor by the governor. Don Diego, however, is not interested in courting the beautiful Lolita, preferring to spend his time idly performing party tricks with his ever-present handkerchief. His behavior is a stratagem; the foppish Don Diego is Zorro in disguise. As Zorro, he conquers the blustering Sergeant Gonzales (Noah Beery), confronts the licentious Captain Ramon, and courts the lovely Lolita. His double identity is unknown to all but his faithful mute servant Bernardo (Tote Du Crow). Captain Ramon imprisons the Pulido family and subsequently abducts Lolita. Zorro galvanizes the local caballeros into action to rid California of its corrupt officials, rescues Lolita, and reveals his true identity. After vanquishing Captain Ramon and forcing the governor to abdicate, he hurls his sword into the ceiling rafters, where its point penetrates a beam, declaring, "Till I need you again!" Amidst the plaudits, Don Diego leaps to Lolita's side and clasps her in his arms.

Production of *The Mark of Zorro* was accomplished in eighteen weeks at the Douglas Fairbanks Studios and on location in Roscoe (present-day Sun Valley), California, where the major exterior sets were built, including a faithful reconstruction of the Old Plaza Church of the City of Los Angeles as it appeared in 1830.[4] The film was a close adaptation of McCulley's story, although Fairbanks added key elements. He provided *The Mark of Zorro* with not only its definitive title but also two of its most identifiable characteristics. First, in "The Curse of the Capistrano," there is no mention of Zorro's famous "mark"—the "Z" carved into his victims. The "mark" was an innovation of the film, used as a visual trademark. Second, Don Diego Vega's foppish and foolish nature, as suggested by the parlor tricks he performs with his handkerchief, was also a Fairbanks embellishment. Fairbanks himself enjoyed devising such sleight-of-hand tricks off-screen. Johnston McCulley incorporated these elements into his next Zorro story, published in 1922, which was unquestionably influenced by the Fairbanks film.[5]

The Mark of Zorro is well cast, and the performances are restrained for the time (save for that of the comic villain Beery), yet at the same

time expressive. Apart from a few good dueling sequences, one of which finds Zorro cheerfully dueling with his opponent while sitting cross-legged, Indian-style, on a table, and the superb chase near the end of the film, Niblo's direction is mostly uninspired by later silent film standards; many sequences are blocked as if taking place on a proscenium-arch stage. However, the direction of *The Mark of Zorro* was as good as the best commercial work of 1920. It is Fairbanks who transforms and dominates the film, and his dramatic and suspenseful entrance is notable. The film begins inside a tavern one rainy evening. The local caballeros are conferring intently about the masked Zorro, who has carved his trademark "Z" on the face of one of Sergeant Gonzales's soldiers. The braggart Gonzales boasts he will be the one to capture the slashing outlaw. Suddenly there is a rap on the door, and all inside freeze with anticipation. The door slowly opens, and a figure, obscured by the night and a large umbrella, steps inside. As the onlookers hold their breath, the umbrella is eventually raised and the figure is revealed to be not the dreaded Zorro but the dandy Don Diego.

The wonderful chase toward the end of the film gave Fairbanks a showcase for various acrobatic feats as he eludes the governor's cortege. The sequence as a whole is one of Fairbanks's most celebrated trajectories and without question one of the best swashbuckling sequences in cinema. This chase is considerably elaborated from that in the original story. Fairbanks mixes the action with moments of deft comedy, such as Zorro momentarily stopping for refreshment. Perched on a windowsill, he dispenses advice to the woman whose hospitality he is enjoying; "I give you a safe rule, good landlady. Never do anything on an empty stomach—but eat!"

The premiere of *The Mark of Zorro* was held at the Capitol Theatre in New York City, where it broke all records; in one week, the film garnered a box office total of $48,103.43.[6] It opened at the Mission Theatre in Los Angeles to good reviews and excellent box office receipts. The film also performed particularly well in foreign markets, where the earlier Fairbanks contemporary comedies were not as easily understood or appreciated. *The Mark of Zorro* was produced at a cost of approximately $169,187.05 and in its initial release grossed over three times that amount domestically; it was Fairbanks's most profitable film up to that time.[7] Indeed, it was a tremendous hit with audiences

The foppish and effeminate Don Diego Vega does not impress Lolita (Marguerite de la Motte) with the tricks he performs with his handkerchief in *The Mark of Zorro*.

The dashing and virile Zorro, however, successfully romances Lolita.

throughout the world. While it became part of Fairbanks lore that the critical response to *The Mark of Zorro* was overwhelmingly positive, contemporary reviews show some dissension. Some critics were mystified by Fairbanks's desertion of his comedic contemporary character for a romantic adventure hero.

The *New York Times* wrote "there are moments in the motion picture which must delight anyone, no matter how preposterous they are." The reviewer found the non-Fairbanks scenes to be slow and thought that the film, on the whole, was "somewhat tamer" than the usual Fairbanks product.[8] *Variety* was enthusiastic: "Here is romance and into the bargain a commercial film . . . Douglas Fairbanks is once more the Doug that crowds love."[9] The Pulitzer Prize–winning writer Carl Sandburg pronounced in his review: "Doug's latest picture will be considered by thousands to be his best. It is well within the conservative bounds of a critic to pronounce *The Mark of Zorro* one of his best . . . Fairbanks does some splendid bits of acting."[10] The *Dramatic Mirror* disliked the film, declaring, "Zorro is not up to expectations, and bears one of the most sickening scenes ever depicted upon the public screen, namely the beating of a priest upon the bare back by way of showing man's fiendishness and utter disregard for religion."[11]

The Mark of Zorro achieved one of its goals in contenting those members of the public who wanted more romance from Fairbanks. No less an authority on 1920s sex than the famous romantic novelist Elinor Glyn wrote in 1921: "*The Mark of Zorro* (Douglas Fairbanks) is the most all-round delightful play I have ever seen," citing the film's romance and depiction of "love in an adventurous spirit" as its outstanding traits.[12] Frederick James Smith in *Motion Picture Classic* summed up the prevailing sentiment about Fairbanks for audiences of the time: "Doug is the personification of youth and high adventure; he is the spirit of all the things you and I, out in the darkened spaces this side of the screen, have ever dreamed of being. He is Everyman as he would like to be, if he could break the shackles of the commonplace and the everyday."[13]

The reputation of *The Mark of Zorro* has grown steadily since its initial release as the far-reaching effects of Fairbanks's contribution to the source material and to the swashbuckler genre have become more apparent. Characteristics that are famously part of the Zorro legacy, such as the duality of the everyman/superman hero and the "calling card" of

Zorro effortlessly outwits a member of the governor's cortege in *The Mark of Zorro*'s wonderful chase sequence, which showcases Fairbanks in many acrobatic feats.

Zorro defends Lolita from the lascivious Captain Ramon (Robert McKim).

A portrait of Fairbanks as Zorro in his first classic costume adventure, *The Mark of Zorro*.

the letter "Z," are directly traced back to Fairbanks. The film has been imitated and remade, the best remake being *The Mark of Zorro* (1940) starring Tyrone Power. However, no one ever equaled the ebullience and distinction that Fairbanks gave to his original production.

With this film, Fairbanks defined and popularized the swashbuckler genre. All the practitioners after him—Errol Flynn, Tyrone Power, Gene Kelly, Burt Lancaster, and Johnny Depp among them—draw upon the Fairbanks heritage and his contribution to the mosaic of the swashbuckling hero. Moreover, had it not been for Fairbanks's *The Mark of Zorro*, popular culture might not have a comic book hero named Batman. Bob Kane, who created Batman, stated in several interviews that one of his primary inspirations for the Caped Crusader was the athleticism of Fairbanks and, in particular, his characterization of Zorro,

The supposedly effete Don Diego Vega in *The Mark of Zorro.*

making Fairbanks a direct antecedent.[14] Furthermore, the dual nature of the protagonist, the secret identity, a hallmark of superhero iconography, was popularized by Fairbanks.

Fairbanks's exploration of the different natures of masculinity is a source of continuing comment.[15] Although his contemporary comedies frequently portrayed him as various lambs, playboys, millionaires, milquetoasts, and mollycoddles transformed into go-getters, *The Mark of Zorro*'s juxtaposition of the effete Don Diego and the vigorous Señor Zorro is the most distinctive delineation. McCulley's character fascinates, because both identities are masks. Don Diego Vega is neither fop nor fox. The paradox intrigued both Fairbanks and viewers alike.

The Mark of Zorro remains one of the most important and satisfying of the Fairbanks films. The period setting, cape, and mask accentuated the sheer beauty and escapist escapades absent in his contemporary comedies. Fairbanks's nicotine-fueled Zorro showcases the star at his most ballistic and his most balletic up to that time. The overwhelmingly positive public reaction to *The Mark of Zorro,* and the relative failure of his last contemporary comedy, *The Nut,* was all the proof he needed that his career instincts were correct. It would spur him on to greater challenges. As Gavin Lambert postulated in *Sequence* in 1949: "He will be remembered as the only figure of his time to attempt a revival of the heroic spirit in popular terms. What was overlooked, perhaps, in the excitement of the moment, was that Fairbanks had to create an old-fashioned world to contain his antics."[16]

The Great Leap

The Three Musketeers (1921)

The popular success of *The Mark of Zorro* signified a shift, not only in the films of Douglas Fairbanks, but also in Fairbanks himself. As the architect of his own films, he had long wished to assert himself by building productions on a grand scale and, in his own way, equaling the finest films of Griffith, Chaplin, and Pickford. With the enthusiasm of this renewed purpose, he set to work realizing his long-held ambition of bringing his hero of heroes, d'Artagnan of Alexandre Dumas's *The Three Musketeers,* to the screen. More than any other character he portrayed, Fairbanks identified with the brave and inexhaustible d'Artagnan, and he embarked upon the production with a brio unseen in any of his previous films. *The Three Musketeers* was the first of the grand Fairbanks costume films, filled with exemplary production values and ornamentation. Indeed, one ornament extended beyond the film; Fairbanks wore d'Artagnan's moustache—cultivated for *The Three Musketeers*—to the end of his life. With *The Three Musketeers,* he at last found his métier and crystallized his celebrity and his cinema.

Fairbanks often remarked that Chaplin and Pickford possessed "genius," while he had only "a small talent."[1] He was being somewhat disingenuous; he made such remarks to draw attention to himself in order to get the validation he craved. Yet the statement does reveal some essential truths about the man and his perceived position among the united artists. Fairbanks understood that he was not a conventional

D'Artagnan has commandeered a feast of the Cardinal's Guards and in addition takes some of their hats as a souvenir in *The Three Musketeers.*

Fairbanks, sporting the moustache he kept for the rest of his life, during a production meeting for *The Three Musketeers*. Photograph by Kadel & Herbert.

The three Fairbanks musketeers: John, Douglas, and Robert Fairbanks, 1921.

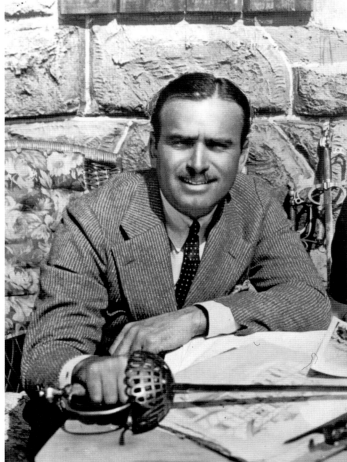

actor; he saw himself as a unique cinema personality, athlete, and dancer with a flawless sense of screen rhythm, grace, and movement. Cognizant of his own limitations, he began to employ individuals who had claims to artistry. *The Mark of Zorro* opened the door to opportunity, and Fairbanks leaped at the chance. By 1921, Fairbanks had been making movies for six years, and his restlessness could no longer be contained. Film critic and historian Richard Schickel observed:

It seems that he wanted to exert himself as what would later be termed, somewhat derogatorily, a "creative producer" in order to compensate for the narrowness of his range. . . . He appears to have loved the process of mounting his increasingly elaborate films, absorbing himself in the million-and-one details of the work. It was man's work—business—in the age when business was said to be the business of America, and it appears to have greatly pleased him to set hundreds of craftsmen to work on projects that would, ultimately, employ similar numbers of players.[2]

To mount the first of these lavish productions, Fairbanks looked no further than his United Artists partner D. W. Griffith for a model. Griffith was renowned for establishing the period and characters of his films through delicately interwoven subplots that converged in a spectacular climax. Fairbanks wanted to emulate him by creating a similarly majestic structure for the Dumas classic. The first film version of the novel, *I tre moschettieri* (1909), was produced in Italy and received international distribution. There were several other versions in the silent era, most notably Thomas H. Ince's American production, *D'Artagnan* (1916) (rereleased in 1921 under the title *The Three Musketeers* in order to capitalize on the success of Fairbanks's film), and Henri Diamant-Berger's French version, *Les trois mousquetaires* (1921). However, Fairbanks had an emotional connection to the character that these filmmakers had not. D'Artagnan was his touchstone; he looked to the exuberant Gascon youth as his ideal screen self.

The character Fairbanks so closely identified with his creative fantasies was based on Charles de Batz-Castlemore. Born in Gascony in 1623, he traveled to Paris as a youth, adopted the name of Sieur d'Artagnan, and served in the king's elite Mousquetaires de la Garde (Musketeers of the Guard) until his death at the siege of Maastricht in 1673. Memorialized by the French novelist Gatien de Courtilz de Sandras in *Mémoires de M. d'Artagnan* (1700), he found immortality with the French novelist and dramatist Alexandre Dumas *père*, who wove d'Artagnan into his historical romances *Les trois mousquetaires* (*The Three Musketeers*)

Athos (Léon Bary), Aramis (Eugene Pallette), d'Artagnan, and Porthos (George Siegmann) raise their swords, point to point, symbolizing "One for All— All for One," in *The Three Musketeers*.

(1844), *Vingt ans après* (*Twenty Years After*) (1845), and *Le Vicomte de Bragelonne, ou Dix ans plus tard* (*The Vicomte de Bragelonne, or Ten Years Later*) (1847–50).

D'Artagnan was a role Fairbanks was born to play. Audiences had already had a tantalizing glimpse of his d'Artagnan in *A Modern Musketeer;* now, like the character he was about to immortalize, he was poised to take the leap wholly and without compromise. To ensure that this leap would be a successful one, he set about employing gifted collaborators who aspired to artistry. He once again turned to Fred Niblo, who had directed *The Mark of Zorro,* to helm the production. Perhaps his most significant choice for *The Three Musketeers* was to enlist the services of his old friend Edward Knoblock, the American-born British playwright, scenarist, and novelist best known for his play *Kismet* (1911),

D'Artagnan proves himself to be "the best swordsman in France" as Aramis, Athos, and Porthos look on.

who happened to be an authority on French history and the culture of the reign of Louis XIV. (In addition to preparing the screen adaptation from Dumas's novel with Fairbanks, Knoblock supervised the scenery and costumes.) The screenplay ultimately used was greatly simplified and confined itself to the episode involving the queen's diamond brooch. Another significant alteration was d'Artagnan's love interest, Constance Bonacieux, who becomes the niece, rather than the wife, of M. Bonacieux in order to avoid problems with film censors. Furthermore, Constance is spared the death she suffers in the novel in order to provide the film its requisite happy ending. In the film, she is reunited with d'Artagnan by Cardinal Richelieu, who serves as the deus ex machina and facilitates d'Artagnan's reunion not only with Constance but with his beloved three musketeers.

Lotta Woods was the scenario editor, sifting through the nearly 1,500 volumes Knoblock and Fairbanks reportedly collected for the production. Arthur Edeson was employed as cinematographer. Previously, he had been chief cinematographer for the actress Clara Kimball Young. Fairbanks had been impressed by Edeson's work on Young's film *For the Soul of Rafael* (1920) and signed him to a contract. Edeson was the cinematographer for three of Fairbanks's biggest films (*The Three Musketeers*, *Douglas Fairbanks in Robin Hood*, and *The Thief of Bagdad*), and his credits include such classic or important early films as *Stella Dallas* (1925), *The Lost World* (1925), *The Big Trail* (1930), *Frankenstein* (1931), *The Invisible Man* (1933), *Mutiny on the Bounty* (1935), *The Maltese Falcon*

Arthur Edeson, the cinematographer, pulls Fairbanks and the director, Fred Niblo, in a prop pull cart in a gag still taken during production of *The Three Musketeers*.

D'Artagnan courts Constance Bonacieux (Marguerite de la Motte) while keeping the royal court waiting.

(1941), and *Casablanca* (1942). Reflecting upon his association with Fairbanks, Edeson later remarked, "To anyone who worked with him, moviemaking today seems prosaic and cramped by comparison."[3]

Fairbanks gathered a fine cast; the assemblage appears more impressive in retrospect, because several of the actors went on to achieve greater fame, their career opportunities greatly expanded by their association with Fairbanks. The principals included Marguerite de la Motte as Constance Bonacieux, Léon Bary as Athos, George Siegmann as Porthos, Eugene Pallette as Aramis, Mary MacLaren as Anne of Austria, Barbara La Marr as Milady de Winter, Nigel de Brulier as Cardinal Richelieu, and Adolphe Menjou as Louis XIII.

And then, of course, there was Fairbanks himself, who with conviction and absolute sincerity believed himself to be the ideal d'Artagnan. Fairbanks had remembered the character of d'Artagnan from an idealized perspective of youth. When he was confronted with the reality of the Dumas character, however, he was a bit taken aback. Fairbanks recalled:

You know if you get right down to cases, that fellow [d'Artagnan] was a brute and a bully. He went around picking quarrels with everybody and killing folks who hadn't done anything to get killed for. . . . It was hard to make a picture out of him. It sounded all right in the book, but when you showed it in the picture you had to show men being run thru with swords and dying . . . that could have been a horrible thing. We steered away from the idea that he was killing people and that the people were dying by always giving his fights a comic finish.[4]

The bullyboy d'Artagnan was thus softened to make the character more palatable to audiences—and more palatable to the actor. More to the point, d'Artagnan was made to fit the personality and idealized characteristics of Douglas Fairbanks rather than the other way around. Instead of delving into the more unpleasant aspects of d'Artagnan, the fourth musketeer, Fairbanks eliminated these qualities and replaced them with the familiar "Doug" characteristics that audiences had come to expect. In this respect, d'Artagnan emerges as a sort of "French Cowboy," as one reviewer described him, rather than the unrepentant Gascon upstart of Dumas's novel.[5] No doubt this assessment pleased Fairbanks at the time, given his penchant for all things western. However, it was such compromises that made Fairbanks dissatisfied with the film just a few years later, which partly provided the impetus to revisit the character in *The Iron Mask*.[6]

Whereas *The Mark of Zorro* had been produced with caution and conservative production values, *The Three Musketeers* had lavish sets, a large cast, and magnificent costumes. Edward M. Langley, the art director, went to great pains to make certain the settings, from d'Artagnan's rustic Gascony home to Louis XIII's ornate rooms, were reproduced as faithfully as possible, using etchings from historic books brought from all parts of the world to ensure authenticity.[7] The Scottish sculptor William Hopkins was engaged to do the modeling for *The Three Musketeers* under the direction of Langley. An imitation bronze statue of Britain's King Charles I standing five and half feet tall in the chambers of the Duke of Buckingham, a small detail justified as integral to the success of the film, was a source of pride among the artists of the production. Hopkins explained his methodology thus: "Much has been written about the attention paid to details in motion pictures but to my mind no reason has ever been given for it. Most properties play an inconspicuous part anyway and details may be slighted. However, in *The Three Musketeers* the properties stand forth so boldly that they must be absolutely historically correct, or their imperfections would be immediately apparent."[8]

The plot of the film presents high adventure against a fairly accurate historical background. In 1625, the royal court of France is the center of an elaborate game between the jealous and malleable King Louis XIII and the devious and iron-willed Cardinal Richelieu. D'Artagnan, a young Gascon, arrives in Paris determined to fulfill his ambition of joining the musketeers, the king's elite regiment of guards. He presents himself to de Tréville, captain of the musketeers, and is told he must first serve an apprenticeship elsewhere. He immediately involves himself in duels with the three best French swordsmen of the day: Athos, Porthos, and Aramis. Skillfully defending himself in battle, he earns the friendship of the three musketeers and is immediately welcomed into their company. With equal speed, d'Artagnan wins the heart of the queen's pretty young seamstress, Constance. Cardinal Richelieu conspires to maneuver Anne of Austria, the queen, into a scandal with her paramour, the Duke of Buckingham, when he requests a token of remembrance since she will no longer permit him to see her. She gives him a diamond brooch that had been a gift from her husband, and he returns with it to England. Richelieu, seizing a golden opportunity to undermine the queen's authority, suggests to the suspicious king that the queen wear the treasured jewel to an upcoming court ball. The queen enlists the king's three musketeers—plus one—to embark on the treacherous journey across France to England to retrieve the trea-

D'Artagnan struggles to retrieve the queen's diamond brooch from the cardinal's spy, Milady de Winter (Barbara La Marr).

sured brooch from Buckingham and save her honor. Richelieu, aware of her plan, assigns his guards, along with his spy, Milady de Winter, to thwart the musketeers in their mission. One by one, the musketeers are bested and, in the end, it is d'Artagnan alone who remains to secure the precious jewel and return it to his queen. D'Artagnan's accomplishment of what was thought to be an impossible mission earns him the gratitude of the queen, the love of Constance, the lifelong animosity of the cardinal, and a commission into the ranks of the king's musketeers. At the film's conclusion, d'Artagnan is presented to Louis XIII before the whole court, his three loyal friends accompanying him. The motto of the *bonshommes* remained always, "One for All—All for One."

When the seventeen-week production began in the spring of 1921, most—if not all—of Fairbanks's team knew what lay in store. *The Three Musketeers* utilized not one but two motion picture studios in Hollywood. The Douglas Fairbanks Studios was utilized for the small sets, while the adjacent Robert Brunton Studios (Paramount Pictures in the twenty-first century) was used for the elaborate interior scenes. All tallied, there were 116 actors, not counting extras, on the lots at any given time. Fairbanks was the dominant force, and although he treated his director well, he was the final arbiter. He needed someone to play off of, a sounding board, and, if need be, a scapegoat. As Douglas Fairbanks Jr. explained, his father's directors were basically "Super-assistants. They were day-to-day, hour-to-hour coordinators and executives on the

D'Artagnan, wounded and nearly fainting, successfully completes his mission of returning the diamond brooch to Anne of Austria.

▶ Fairbanks rehearses the one-handed handspring.

▶ D'Artagnan vanquishes one of the Cardinal's Guards with a dagger in a stunning single-handed handspring in the most famous acrobatic feat in *The Three Musketeers*.

set . . . while he encouraged their honest expression of views and welcomed their reactions, he always reserved the right to overrule them."[9]

One of the outstanding achievements of the production is the construction of the action scenes, a collaborative effort between Fairbanks, Niblo, and the fight choreographer, H. J. Uyttenhove. Indeed, there are more brilliantly staged action shots and stunts in the famous fight sequence with the Cardinal's Guards, lasting only a few minutes on the screen, than in some entire action films of the period. The best of all the stunts was unquestionably Fairbanks's left-handed handspring balanced on a short dagger, generally considered the single most difficult stunt of his career.

Fairbanks and members of the cast spent three months taking fencing lessons from Uyttenhove. Even performers such as Adolphe

Menjou, whose role as Louis XIII required no duel scenes, took advantage of the lessons. In his boundless enthusiasm, Fairbanks reportedly broke twelve rapiers in the filming of the final script's sixteen dueling sequences.[10] Menjou later recalled that Uyttenhove instructed Fairbanks one way, but when the cameras rolled and Niblo yelled action,

Doug went completely unorthodox. He was all over the set, jumping over chairs and on top of tables, slashing away with his rapier as though it were a broadsword. The fencing instructor, who was an expert swordsman, tore his hair. Never in his life had he seen such an exhibition. He screamed and protested, but Doug did it his way. When the picture was released, fencing experts all over the world groaned at Doug's antics, but there were millions of movie-goers who thought he was the world's greatest swordsman.[11]

Adolphe Menjou also remembered:

Doug worked just as hard as he played, and he expected his company to do the same. I remember how surprised I was one day when he said to me, "You're going to be a success in this business because you take it seriously. I notice you're always on the set fifteen minutes early."

In spite of all the horseplay and the practical jokes and the social activity on the Fairbanks lot, Doug invariably got the very best performances out of his actors. I think that was because they were relaxed and having a good time. And the spirit of fun that prevailed at the studio always seemed to show up in Doug's pictures. There was a tongue-in-cheek, devil-may-care sort of quality in all his films that nobody else has ever been able to duplicate.[12]

Fairbanks celebrated his thirty-eighth birthday during the production of *The Three Musketeers* and received many presents from family, friends, and admirers throughout the world. Pickford presented him with a couple of small boats and a slide for the Pickfair swimming pool, as well as a Bedouin tent and daybed for his den. Also presented to him was a large parchment plaque with a photograph of Fairbanks as d'Artagnan, created with a tribute written by Knoblock and containing the signature of every member of the cast and crew. John Fairbanks, who continually fretted over his brother's mounting production expenses, gave his younger brother a rubber purse.[13]

D'Artagnan eludes the Cardinal's Guards by sliding down the balustrade to make his get-away. "I did not consciously . . . perform a single stunt that d'Artagnan himself might not have done," Fairbanks wrote in 1922. "The standing slide down the balustrade, after the audience with Richelieu, has been objected to by some critics because it is not in Dumas' story, but Dumas' hero might well have done it, and to my way of thinking it was not out of character. Exhibitors tell me that this proved one of the most popular bits in the picture."

It was certainly a time of some introspection. Fairbanks was transitioning to a new phase of his life and career. One of the ghosts from his past, the veteran British actor-manager Frederick Warde, who had published his autobiography the previous year, visited the studio and reminisced with Fairbanks. "For a man who couldn't act, you seem to be doing all right in the picture business," Warde reportedly told him.[14]

The general belief that Fairbanks was more a personality than an actor in the conventional sense was borne out at the time of the film's release. *Picture-Play* noted in its review of the film that when Fairbanks "broke loose with his incredible adventures there was a wink beneath his plumes and curls which said plainer than words: 'Under all this fuss

Fairbanks (in costume) with Pickford in the studio Japanese dining room during production of *The Three Musketeers*. While Fairbanks was in production with the Dumas classic, Pickford was immersed in her screen version of Frances Hodgson Burnett's novel *Little Lord Fauntleroy*.

and feathers, it's me!' "[15] Douglas Fairbanks Jr. wryly noted: "Whether it was d'Artagnan with Douglas Fairbanks or Douglas Fairbanks pretending to be d'Artagnan I don't know. It was an interchangeable identification."[16] As a screen personality, few have equaled Fairbanks, and no one but Chaplin has surpassed him. He may not be the definitive screen d'Artagnan, but the bravura he brought to his swashbuckling characters has left indelible traces in all who assay similar roles. The key difference between Fairbanks and all who have followed is that he *was* that larger-than-life personality he portrayed in his films, while the others are simply acting like him. Curiously, Fairbanks's d'Artagnan in *The Three Musketeers*—the role the consensus was that he was born to play—has not aged as well as his more nuanced interpretations of Zorro, Ahmed the thief, the Black Pirate, the Gaucho, or even the mature d'Artagnan of *The Iron Mask*. Saddled with a bad wig and an unfamiliar moustache (at times Fairbanks appears not to be sure what—if anything—he is to do with the hair above his lip, and at times he twirls it like the villain in a hoary melodrama), Fairbanks gives a performance laden with the dramatic poses and systematized set of gestures associated with the system of expression developed by the French aesthetician of movement François Delsarte, although the "I smell a rat" gesture he performs at various moments when he senses something is amiss has the desired comic effect.

Fairbanks recalled the difficulty he experienced with his big emotional scene as d'Artagnan. Fairbanks as d'Artagnan approaches the

A portrait of Fairbanks
as d'Artagnan.

commandant with his letters of introduction but is rejected as a musketeer because he does not belong. Fairbanks was famous for becoming
quickly inhibited in the playing of big emotional scenes. On the day the
scene was to be filmed, Fairbanks recalled, "Fred Niblo, my director,
said in a voice of agony and woe, 'Now Doug, remember this is the big
scene: this is the picture.'" Fairbanks wilted under the pressure. "How
could I cry after that?" Fairbanks remembered. "Dumas and the spirit
of d'Artagnan sneaked away and left me flat and we had to resort to the
good old glycerine squirter."[17]

In the postproduction phase, Louis F. Gottschalk, who had composed
and compiled the score to D. W. Griffith's *Broken Blossoms* (1919) to great
acclaim, prepared a score for *The Three Musketeers*. Gottschalk conferred
at length with Fairbanks, Niblo, and Knoblock before commencing

the assignment. The result was a score far short of the level of *Broken Blossoms*. However, although Gottschalk's score is particularly weak in the action sequences, and utterly unable to capture the comic aspects of the action, it is notable for placing Fairbanks in the vanguard with respect to film music. Few producers placed any importance on whether a properly prepared music score enhanced their films; the majority were content with subjecting their productions to the banal improvised scores films more often than not received. Although compiled scores and thematic music cue sheets were prepared for the earliest Fairbanks films, Fairbanks's increased involvement with the music and exhibition of his productions began with *The Three Musketeers*.

The world premiere of *The Three Musketeers* took place on August 28, 1921, at the Lyric Theatre, a Broadway theater with just two screenings daily as opposed to a conventional cinema with multiple screenings per day, to add prestige to Fairbanks's production. The engagement was further enhanced by a full orchestra in the pit playing Gottschalk's score, a spoken prologue written in verse by Edward Knoblock (which Fairbanks later adapted as his prologue speech to *The Iron Mask*) and performed by the actor Stephen Wright costumed as d'Artagnan. The premiere boasted a personal appearance by Fairbanks himself with Pickford, Chaplin, and Jack Dempsey as his guests. The premiere was a sensational event. *Variety* reported:

For an hour before the unwinding of the first reel a crowd lined the sidewalks on both sides and literally jammed 42nd Street to Broadway. The magnet was the personal appearance of Fairbanks and of Mary Pickford, and, quite unexpected, Charlie Chaplin and Jack Dempsey. There were demonstrations outside and they continued inside the theatre and throughout the showing of the film, the four celebrities occupying a stage box . . . $2 tickets for the initial showing sold as high as $5.[18]

Despite the appearance of Pickford, Chaplin, and Dempsey, the *New York Times* noted, "It was distinctly a Fairbanks evening, and he was forced three times to respond to the plaudits of the crowd—before and after the film and during the intermission."[19] The *New York Herald* expounded:

It is a kind of combination of Dumas, Douglas, and delirium. One moment it boils with action and the next it snaps and sparkles with humor like d'Artagnan's own rapier. The spectators alternately whistled with glee at Fairbanks's prowess and the next shrieked with laughter at his comedy—even the serious-faced

The composer Louis F. Gottschalk, Fairbanks (in costume and holding an unlit pipe), and Pickford examine a reel of 35 mm film at the Robert Brunton Studios during production of *The Three Musketeers.* Gottschalk wisely kept his cigarette unlit in his right hand while holding the highly flammable nitrate film stock.

Charlie Chaplin laughed in the Pickford-Fairbanks box. It increased in speed and fury as it progressed, until but one word fits it—rip-roaring. Fairbanks ripped and the audience roared.[20]

Photoplay declared: "A great picture . . . romance, adventure, humor—great direction, great scenario, great acting—it is one of the finest photoplays ever produced, a real classic. . . . Fairbanks has never done better work; his performance is an everlasting credit to him and to the screen."[21]

Robert E. Sherwood, an admirer of and later collaborator with Fairbanks, was a film critic before he became a Pulitzer Prize winner. (He was an original member of the Algonquin Round Table, screenwriter, playwright, editor, and speechwriter to President Franklin D. Roosevelt.) Sherwood began his review for *Life:*

When Alexandre Dumas sat down at his desk, smoothed his hair back, chewed the end of his quill pen, and said to himself, "Well I guess I might as well write a book called *The Three Musketeers*," he doubtless had but one object in view: to provide a suitable story for Douglas Fairbanks to act in the movies.... Never has a famous character from a famous novel found finer treatment in a movie.... Not only is the physical grace and superb poise there—but also the intense fire, the animation of spirit that was so vital a part of Dumas' magnificent hero.[22]

The Three Musketeers was released in the same year as such screen masterworks as Rex Ingram's *The Four Horsemen of the Apocalypse*, starring Rudolph Valentino, Pickford's *Little Lord Fauntleroy*, Chaplin's *The Kid*, D. W. Griffith's *Orphans of the Storm*, starring Lillian and Dorothy Gish, and Henry King's *Tol'able David*, starring Richard Barthelmess, and accorded equal prestige and popularity. *The Three Musketeers*, which had a production cost of $748,768.76, grossed over $1.4 million domestically and performed well in foreign markets, with the exception of France and French-speaking countries.[23]

The importance of Fairbanks's *The Three Musketeers* lies in the fact that it was his career leap to the kind of action film popular today. Indeed, the poet Vachel Lindsay, who acclaimed the cinema as an art as early as 1915, wrote in 1921: "The action picture will be inevitable.... Charlie Chaplin and Douglas Fairbanks have given complete department store examples of the method." Specifically mentioned was *The Three Musketeers* as Fairbanks's "one great piece of acting," which Lindsay praised as "marvelous acting in the school of the younger [Tomasso] Salvini."[24]

Fairbanks called the film "my most ambitious venture to date."[25] In the final analysis, the reverberations of *The Three Musketeers* upon the life and career of Douglas Fairbanks can scarcely be overestimated. Despite its importance to Fairbanks's career and the plaudits it enjoyed, the film has not, however, held up as well as *The Mark of Zorro* and most of the other Fairbanks costume films. In an attempt to be true to aspects of the novel and the court intrigue, it sacrifices enchanting and exhilarating action for ponderous scenes and performances enacted in the traditional grand manner of silent film costume drama. The film's most exciting sequence—the duel involving the Cardinal's Guards—occurs much too early, and the film never again achieves such momentum; rather, it simply becomes submerged in plot. The art direction, although sumptuous, fails to convince as seventeenth-century France. The ambition of *The Three Musketeers* is its undoing, but its ambition was

A portrait of Fairbanks with the debonair moustache of the swashbuckling d'Artagnan. The moustache, like the dark tan he flaunted, quickly became a nationwide fad.

what made the remaining Fairbanks costume films possible. Fairbanks was aware of the film's shortcomings, and rectified his missteps when he revisited the subject for his silent screen valedictory, *The Iron Mask*. Artistic qualms aside, the critical and commercial success of *The Three Musketeers* gave Fairbanks the artistic capital to proceed wholeheartedly down the road of the costume adventure. For the remainder of his great career, he emphasized his roles as producer and, in one form or other, the d'Artagnan screen persona he devised for this film.

Scaling the Heights

Douglas Fairbanks in Robin Hood (1922)

Douglas Fairbanks in Robin Hood is arguably the most important legacy of the rich life and career of Douglas Fairbanks. The towering sets are long gone, and the characters have been reimagined and reinterpreted, but the foundation the film was built upon—and the culture it created—exists to this day. At a time when the future of the Hollywood film industry was precarious owing to a succession of scandals, Fairbanks mounted an ambitious production of virtually unprecedented spectacle and pageantry, not only producing his greatest popular sucess but creating an early prototype of the movie "blockbuster." Fairbanks is at his dashing and romantic best in the film, which is filled with marvelous stunts that audiences enjoyed watching more than once to try to determine how they were accomplished.

The success of *The Three Musketeers* gave Fairbanks the impetus to embark upon a grand-scale costume film. There was also a desire on his part to create something of lasting value for the cinema. If *The Three Musketeers* was the film from which Fairbanks benefited the most personally and professionally, *Douglas Fairbanks in Robin Hood* was Fairbanks returning the favor to the art of filmmaking. The creation of *Douglas Fairbanks in Robin Hood* consumed nearly a year of his life, and the experience established the matrix for all of his subsequent silent film productions. Indeed, it was the first of his productions to be fully realized in every aspect.

Robin Hood, apple in hand, makes his entrance through a window of Nottingham Castle in *Douglas Fairbanks in Robin Hood.*

Edward Knoblock had initially proposed that Fairbanks produce an adaptation of Sir Walter Scott's *Ivanhoe*. From this grew the idea of a film drawing upon the Robin Hood legends, and both ideas were subsequently submitted to United Artists headquarters in New York City for the sales department to make its recommendations. They reported that Robin Hood was the more saleable. Although Fairbanks was pleased with this report, he had no clear idea of where to go in developing the scenario. He had been fascinated by Robin Hood since boyhood, but he was unsure whether the story would make an ideal vehicle for him.[1] Owen Wister's *The Virginian*, Booth Tarkington's *Monsieur Beaucaire*, and a sequel to *The Mark of Zorro* were other projects he was seriously developing. However, his brother Robert was keen to have him pursue the idea of the English outlaw who robbed the rich to give to the poor, and to further that end, he brought some bows and arrows and a target to the studio. "And the first thing you know Doug got crazy about shooting these arrows," Allan Dwan remembered. "We got an expert to come up and teach him everything correctly, and it fascinated him so much that it sowed the seeds of *Robin Hood*."[2]

Consequently, Fairbanks instructed members of his staff to begin researching one of the supposed periods of Robin Hood (sometimes associated with the reign of Richard the Lion-Hearted) and departed with Pickford on a trip to Europe. He also amassed many more ideas during his trip abroad. His latent Anglophilia surfaced in Britain, where he and Pickford met the Prince of Wales and Lord Mountbatten, with whom they would later become good friends. As a result, his enthusiasm for the Robin Hood film increased a hundredfold.

Fairbanks returned before Christmas and assembled his creative team for the first day of preproduction on New Year's Day, 1922. Robert Florey, the future film director, who was then employed by Fairbanks in the capacity of foreign publicity head, was among the assembled group and recorded Fairbanks as declaring: "I've just decided that I'm going to make the story of Robin Hood. We'll build the sets right here in Hollywood. I'm going to call it *The Spirit of Chivalry*."

"I will never forget the forcefulness with which Douglas made this pronouncement. He pounded his fist on a small table. Nobody said a word." Fairbanks, according to Florey, continued:

Mary and I are going to have to buy a new studio, where we can all work together. I'm thinking of the old Jesse Hampton Studio on Santa Monica. There's nothing but fields around there, and we can put up some really big sets—Nottingham in the twelfth century, Richard the Lion Heart's castle, a town in Palestine,

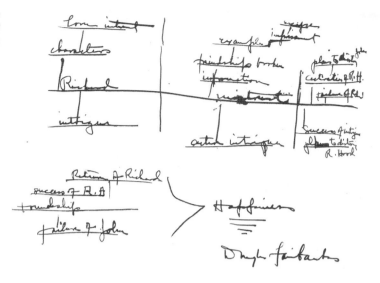

Sherwood Forest, and the outlaw's lair. There's a big field to the south where we can set up the Crusader's camp in France. We'll have several thousand costumes designed from contemporary documents, we'll order shields, lances, and swords by the thousand, we'll stage a tournament, we'll—

"And how much is all that going to cost?" asked John Fairbanks, Douglas's brother, who was company treasurer. "That's not the point," replied Douglas. "These things have to be done properly, or not at all."

"By midday on January 1, 1922," Florey continued, "everyone was convinced that Douglas was absolutely right. *Robin Hood* must be made."[3]

The pronouncement made an impression not only on Fairbanks's associates but also on the entire Hollywood community. Hollywood was in a slump; box office receipts had dropped, and production had waned owing to a succession of scandals, the Roscoe "Fatty" Arbuckle manslaughter case and the mysterious murder of the director William Desmond Taylor being the most prominent. In an effort to prevent national censorship (cinema was not then entitled to First Amendment protection) and to preserve the film industry by curbing practices objectionable to the public and instigating reforms on and off screen, the movie studios formed the Motion Picture Producers and Distributors of America (known today as the Motion Picture Association of America), headed by former U.S. postmaster general Will H. Hays. Unemployment in Hollywood was high in January 1922. The preparations on the Fairbanks production commenced a return to more prosperous

Lotta Woods, Kenneth Davenport, Fairbanks, and Edward Knoblock work on the scenario on the grounds of Pickfair.

times, with plenty of employment for work crews and extras starting at $7.50 a day.[4] Indeed, the film unquestionably reinvigorated the entire industry. The first person Fairbanks engaged was Allan Dwan to direct. Dwan told *Motion Picture* in 1923: "Douglas Fairbanks is, in my opinion, a great factor for progress in the motion picture profession. He has vision. Several prominent producers increased their production appropriations when they learned of the manner in which *Robin Hood* was being produced. At a time when retrenchment was the signal word everywhere, he had the convictions and the courage to press forward."[5]

So dire was the state of the industry at the time that no bank was willing to finance the film; Fairbanks surmounted the obstacle by financing it entirely himself. His critics thought that Fairbanks was being foolish and that the project might bankrupt him. Fairbanks remained sanguine and undeterred. Indeed, as Alistair Cooke wrote, the whole production was "an act of bravado worthy of 'Doug.'"[6]

Fairbanks and Pickford purchased the former Jesse D. Hampton Studios at Santa Monica Boulevard and Formosa Avenue in West Hollywood for a reported $150,000 and renamed it the Pickford-Fairbanks Studios.[7] Fairbanks was very excited about the new facilities and his new project from the start. A series of extensive conferences about the story and characters commenced with his staff. The one thing delaying the start of the picture was his indecision as to how to go about it and on what scale. Beginning with this film, a former Pennsylvania physician, Dr. Arthur Woods—husband of Lotta Woods and brother of the screenwriter Frank Woods—became Fairbanks's research director. Woods led a team researching the old ballads, legends, and stories of Robin Hood. Sixty people were employed to conduct research in libraries in New York City, Los Angeles, and London. Books, engravings, photographs, and other documentation were meticulously collected and sifted, and a "Robin Hood Library" was established. The compilation of facts dealing with the history of the time was to provide atmosphere rather than to create a factual account of the period. Indeed, the atmosphere Fairbanks was striving for was less an evocation of the Middle Ages than chivalry as suggested in nineteenth-century romantic literature. As the film historian Rudy Behlmer has noted, "the accent is on sweep, romance, chivalrous deeds, and acrobatics."[8] The primary influences on the scenario were *Ivanhoe*, Alfred Noyes's poem "Sherwood" and play *Robin Hood*, the Elizabethan dramatist Anthony Munday's two plays about the Earl of Huntingdon, and Howard Pyle's *The Merry Adventures of Robin Hood*, as well as other Pyle illustrations and the illustrations of N. C. Wyeth. After the film was released, Fairbanks bemoaned the fact that he had received letters from intelligent people criticizing his film for deviating so far from the book. "If these critics know what book they are talking about," Fairbanks stated, "they have a distinct advantage over me."[9]

Eventually, as with all his subsequent costume films, the general idea of the plot was first laid out on an enormous wall chart. From this, another chart was produced, breaking down the overall plot line into sequences, and from there on, another, even more detailed chart of scenes, until eventually the scenario took shape in Fairbanks's unique form; it was ultimately credited to "Elton Thomas," his two middle names. Ted Reed, production manager for most of Fairbanks's costume films, described the process in 1925:

There is no scenario. All the camera shots are made according to [a] blueprint, which we term the "Shooting Schedule."

As a matter of fact the big work on a Fairbanks picture is done strictly from blueprints two yards in area. These blueprints are

Fairbanks and Pickford, in February 1922, pose at the entrance of the newly acquired Pickford-Fairbanks Studios at 7200 Santa Monica Boulevard in West Hollywood, where the pair made many of their finest films.

Fairbanks stands behind a large bulletin board (in a cleverly staged joke to appear as if he has grown a pair of very long legs) and confers with the director, Allan Dwan (at right), and research and scenario staff, including Dr. Arthur Woods and Lotta Woods (at left), during preproduction of *Douglas Fairbanks in Robin Hood*. The prints at the top of the board illustrate costumes of the period. The shipping tags at the center of the board represent a research concept that has yet to be decided. Beneath the bulletin board is Zorro, Pickford's white-haired terrier.

posted where Fairbanks and the director can readily see them. The "Set Plot" and the "Shooting Schedule" are the bibles . . .

The "Set Plot" has very little on it. It is only a tabulation of sets, by name, horizontally and of principal players vertically. Crossmarks carried out opposite each player's name under the sets show in which sets the players will appear during the production. The only other division is of the list of sets into exterior and interior. . . .

The "Shooting Schedule" is prepared almost simultaneously with the "Set Plot." It tells the story of the picture in about 2,000 words and is devoted only to essential action. The usual continuity, or script, with its . . . full description of several hundred scenes and imaginary camera positions are not there. Fairbanks also is stimulated in the way of ideas by using his story in outline while producing it, as he feels then he has more license to add inspired touches as he goes along.[10]

Fairbanks did not invent breakdown boards, breakdown sheets, storyboards, and shooting schedules, but his use of them was uniquely his own. The *Douglas Fairbanks in Robin Hood* (hereafter *Robin Hood*) schedule was the beginning of the Fairbanks system. Ted Reed remembered that with *Robin Hood*, "The system carried out the story on shipping tags pinned to a board." Just a few years later, it evolved "into the even more tabloid blueprint form."[11] The efficiencies were of great help; the preproduction phase of *Robin Hood* lasted only three months.

Fairbanks authorized the construction of an enormous Norman-English castle as the centerpiece of his film. The size of the structure exceeded that of the Babylonian set created for *Intolerance*, until then the largest motion picture set ever built. During construction, Fairbanks traveled to New York with Pickford to settle a lawsuit. Upon his return to California on March 9, Florey recalled:

He demonstrated some new tricks for the photographers, and shook hands with everyone. From their faces, he realized there was a surprise in store for him.

"Let's go and see what you've been doing at the studio," he said. I climbed into Douglas's car, so that I could see his look of astonishment when he saw the splendid set. The chauffeur drove across Pasadena in a whirlwind of photographers and newsreel men, who were mounted on vehicles, trying to get to the studio before us. At the corner of Santa Monica and La Brea, about two hundred yards from the studio, Douglas caught sight of the castle

The castle set of *Douglas Fairbanks in Robin Hood*, designed by Wilfred Buckland, was the largest set yet built for a Hollywood production. The size was further enhanced with a glass shot to create the appearance of even higher towers in the background.

for the first time. He opened his eyes very wide and exclaimed, "My gosh! It's astounding . . . it's fantastic!"[12]

The towering castle set stood ninety feet high. When Fairbanks inspected the sets with his associates, what he saw did not seem conducive to intimacy or personality. Indeed, Fairbanks was appalled when he first saw the sheer size of his castle set; he initially believed he would be overwhelmed. "I can't compete with that," he told Dwan. "My work is intimate. People know me as an intimate actor. I can't work in a great vast thing like that. What could I do in there?"[13] According to Dwan, Fairbanks threatened to abandon the production, but the director induced him to return to the studio one morning:

I took him onto the set. About forty feet up, there was a balcony. I'd hung a big drape from the ceiling, sweeping down across that balcony to the ground.

"Now," I said, "you get into a sword fight with the knights, and they chase you up the stairs, battling all the way. You fight like mad, and you succeed in getting away, but as you run out onto the balcony, some more knights rush out of the door at the end and you're caught between them. You haven't a chance. So you jump on the balustrade, and you're fighting them—"

And then I stopped talking. He said, "Yeah, *then* what do I do?" I showed him. I climbed onto the balustrade and jumped into this drape. I had a slide, a kid's slide, hidden inside it and I slid right down that curtain to the ground, with a gesture like he used to make, and I ran out through the arch to freedom.

He bought it like that. "I'll do it!" he shouted. He immediately sent out for some people, ran up to the balcony, explained it to them, jumped in the drape and slid down. He did it a thousand times—like a kid.[14]

The castle set was the creation of the supervising art director, Wilfred Buckland, who first worked for Fairbanks at Artcraft. Buckland came to film after working as David Belasco's set designer on Broadway and later worked on pictures with Cecil B. DeMille and Mary Pickford. Irvin J. Martin and Edward M. Langley provided invaluable support as associate art directors. Mitchell Leisen, an expert on sartorial research, who, like Buckland, had been associated with Cecil B. DeMille, was the costume designer. (Leisen later became a top Hollywood director.) Arthur Edeson was again cinematographer, with Charles Richardson operating the second camera. The services of Henry J. Uyttenhove were

Fairbanks rehearses a stunt at the studio. "My father's stunts were as carefully planned and rehearsed as any Fred Astaire or Gene Kelly routine," Douglas Fairbanks Jr. remembered. "There would be months of meticulous preparation in and out of the set."

obtained once again to choreograph all the scenes involving swordplay. Fairbanks's leading lady was recommended to him by Elinor Glyn; Enid Bennett was cast as Lady Marian. The cast also included Wallace Beery as King Richard the Lion-Hearted, Sam de Grasse as Prince John, and Paul Dickey as Sir Guy of Gisbourne. Under Dwan were a technical staff, a costume staff, and a historical research staff. Fairbanks enjoyed the services of two highly capable engineers—Dwan and his brother Robert—to solve the many technical issues in the preproduction phase.

Dwan later explained the Fairbanks methodology for the production: "we knew that atmosphere was something beyond authenticity and the absence of anachronisms. It was the atmosphere we strived for far above everything else."[15] The art direction of the exceedingly handsome production was founded on principles of the British theatrical designer Gordon Craig, the German impresario Max Reinhardt, and the American theatrical designer Robert Edmond Jones.[16] In addition to the Norman-English castle, with its enormous drawbridge, portcullis, towers, and battlements, Buckland and his associates designed the castle interior, a banquet room, and a convent. The interiors were so vast they could only be lit with sunlight and reflectors, and Dwan and Edeson were inspired to devise many ways to use the enormous sets. Edeson's compositions and arrangement of lighting effects (most of the castle interior scenes were night scenes filmed during the day) were justly celebrated for making brilliant use of Buckland's sets. The trade journal *American Cinematographer* praised his work and held the film up as an example to critics who might claim that motion picture cinematography lacked artistic composition.[17] Edeson achieved his effects with an emphasis on the use of a low foreground in contrast to the natural height of the castle and towers. The main set was without precedent: 550 feet long and 180 feet high. To match the length, the walls were 85 feet high.[18] The theory was that they required a low horizon to show a tremendous sweep of wall and a broad panorama. Dwan and Edeson also emphasized full-length figures, with close-ups only sparingly utilized. For three weeks, Edeson spent hours on the set planning his camera setups from blue prints and charts in consultation with Dwan. Edeson recalled: "Mr. Fairbanks had the courage of a trail blazer, else he never would have attempted a production on such a scale. . . . [The creative team] were seeking to make a picture which would stand the test of years. It was our purpose to set a standard which would be a real standard and endure the wear of time."[19] When Fairbanks wanted the castle exteriors to appear even larger, Edeson ingeniously supervised glass shots to create the illusion of greater size.[20]

Mitchell Leisen's exacting standards provided costumes correct in every respect. Leisen also designed the enormous drape that Robin Hood slides down to make his escape. According to Dwan, the drape was seventy feet long and made of burlap painted to look like an elaborate tapestry. Leisen had to carefully arrange the drape to conceal the children's playground slide in back of it that allowed Fairbanks to manage the famous feat.[21] Leisen remembered that Fairbanks worked as hard as he played, and that the actor-producer was "fascinated by the period and was very knowledgeable about everything in it. Once he got wound up in a project, he couldn't stop."[22]

The film begins with an intertitle containing lines from Charles Kingsley's "Old and New," a favorite poem of Fairbanks's since boyhood: "So fleet the works of men, back to their earth again; / Ancient and holy things fade like a dream."[23] The title is followed by a short sequence in which ancient castle ruins are magically reconstituted to their former glory. An introductory title explains, "History—in its ideal state—is a compound of legend and chronicle and from out of both we offer you an impression of the Middle Ages—." The main action opens with an enormous drawbridge being slowly lowered and the procession of squires, knights, and the king's jester preceding the

Wallace Beery (in costume as King Richard the Lion-Hearted); Robert Florey, the future film director, employed by Fairbanks in the capacity of foreign publicity head; the cinematographer, Arthur Edeson; Fairbanks; and the director, Allan Dwan, during production of the tournament scene in *Douglas Fairbanks in Robin Hood*. Fairbanks is leaning against the pedestal of "Big Bertha," a megaphone four feet in diameter and ten feet long, designed by Dwan for the mammoth production to make the director heard by the 1,200 extras hired for such large scenes. In the background, at left, are wind machines (mounted on the back of trucks) used to animate pennants and guidons.

king himself, Richard the Lion-Hearted. The pageantry and spectacle intensifies with a grand tournament in which Richard's favorite, the brave Earl of Huntingdon, is pitted against the devious Sir Guy of Gisbourne, confidant to the King's brother, Prince John. Handily defeating his opponent, Huntingdon is celebrated as the victor and proclaimed second-in-command on the Third Crusade. However bold and loyal Huntingdon is on the tournament field, he is reticent and shy of the many fair maidens who flock to him, but his chivalrous nature draws him to a lovely young woman in distress, Lady Marian Fitzwalter, who is being pursued by Sir Guy. Huntingdon manages to thwart Gisbourne's lascivious advances and wins the gratitude and heart of

Lady Marian. The two pledge lifelong devotion before Huntingdon embarks with Richard to Palestine to defend the Holy Sepulchre. Unbeknownst to the king and his loyal followers, Prince John, with the complicity of Gisbourne, is planning to seize the throne in Richard's absence. He does so and begins a reign of oppressive tyranny, plunging the country into economic despair and spreading fear throughout the land. Marian succeeds in getting word to Huntingdon of the current state of affairs through his squire, who has been left behind to protect her. Torn between love and honor, Huntingdon vows to return to England but fears that advising the king of the current situation will cause him to abandon his Holy Crusade. The evil machinations of Sir Guy bring Huntingdon into disfavor with King Richard, and he is imprisoned. Huntingdon manages to escape with the help of his squire and returns to England, where he finds the situation graver than he had imagined, and he is informed of the apparent death of Marian. He vows vengeance upon John and retreats deep into Sherwood Forest, where the displaced persons of the countryside have congregated. The Earl of Huntingdon disappears, and in his place appears Robin Hood, a devil-may-care avenger of the poor who commands an outlaw band of "Merry Men." Robin Hood slowly begins to undermine the power of Prince John's evil rule. The outlaw and his men return the valuables taken by Prince John's soldiers from a convent. An old nun, recognizing Robin Hood as Huntingdon, reunites him with Marian, who has gone into hiding at the convent. A spy informs John of the convent reunion, and Marian is subsequently abducted from the nunnery and held as John's prisoner. Meanwhile, Robin Hood captures the town of Nottingham and, in an effort to rescue Marian, infiltrates the royal castle. He is captured and condemned to a crossbow execution. However, Robin Hood's Merry Men (joined by the returned Richard the Lion-Hearted in disguise) enter the castle, and Richard's shield deflects the arrows. The film concludes with Richard restored to the throne and the marriage of Huntingdon and Lady Marian celebrated.

During the fifteen weeks of production of *Douglas Fairbanks in Robin Hood*, which began on April 3, 1922, it became Hollywood's foremost tourist attraction.[24] Visitors arrived at the studio by the hundreds to watch the filmmaking, providing Fairbanks with a new audience each day to stimulate him.[25] Illustrious visitors included the athlete Jim Thorpe and the literary giants Sir Arthur Conan Doyle and W. Somerset Maugham. Although there was some location shooting in Thousand Oaks, California (this area of the Thousand Oaks community is called Lake Sherwood as a result of the Fairbanks connection), most of the

Huntingdon, astride his white charger, waits for the start of the tournament.

Robin Hood, the devil-may-care avenger of the poor, with his outlaw band of "Merry Men."

Robin Hood defends Lady
Marian Fitzwalter (Enid
Bennett) from Prince John
(Sam de Grasse).

filming was confined to the new studio facilities, where Pickford had a five-room bungalow and offices on an acre of lawn in one part of the lot, while Fairbanks was equally comfortable in the quarters and offices he maintained on the property; his facilities included a Turkish bath and swimming pool. Surviving outtakes reveal the Fairbanks production to have been a particularly happy unit.[26] Not everyone shared the merriment, however; the huge cost of the proceedings ultimately became too much for Fairbanks's elder brother John, who suffered a stroke. John Fairbanks never resumed his duties, and Fairbanks and his brother Robert jointly assumed responsibility for the financial and administrative duties that John had capably performed.

"Nothing was too good for the production," Enid Bennett remembered. "I had a most wonderful time playing Maid Marian. Of course the part was not too demanding, I just walked through it in a queenly manner. But everything was so lavish. Douglas Fairbanks was wonderful, inspiring." She also recalled that, like Huntingdon in the picture, Fairbanks in real life "was very timid about love scenes."[27] Fairbanks used this limitation to his advantage in the film. Huntingdon is inexperienced and awkward with women, fleeing from the women who flock to him after his victory in the tournament, begging him to wear their favors. He resorts to jumping into the moat to escape them, and when he comes up for air, he happens to see a woman washing her clothes and submerges once again before she can lay eyes on him.

Robin Hood, strapped to a post, as Prince John's crossbowmen are poised to shoot him in the dramatic climax of *Douglas Fairbanks in Robin Hood.*

Fairbanks's characterization of Robin Hood contrasts vividly with the serious, armor-laden Huntingdon. From the start, Fairbanks made it clear that he did not "want to look like a heavy-footed Englishman tramping around in the woods."[28] His Robin Hood is lithe and as light as the feather in his cap, exuding innocence and insolence and wearing a grin from ear to ear. Whether cavorting through Sherwood Forest or leaping from battlement to tower high above the castle, Fairbanks's Robin Hood exhibits a ballet dancer's grace. Fairbanks described his own conception of the Robin Hood character as being "typified by the breeze. . . . All motion and wholesomeness."[29] Fairbanks also clearly draws upon Peter Pan as inspiration. One of his great moments as Robin Hood is his marvelous slide down the huge drapery in the vast

Robin Hood eludes his pursuers within the enormous Nottingham Castle.

▶ Fairbanks performs a spectacular leap (the effect was achieved with the aid of a hidden trampoline) in *Douglas Fairbanks in Robin Hood*. "There was no living man as graceful as he was," Allan Dwan remembered.

castle hall, a signature stunt everyone in the film's original audience remembered.[30] Fairbanks built upon this in conceiving the most celebrated sequence of his career, sliding down the sails in *The Black Pirate*. Although the role is British, Fairbanks's Robin Hood is irrepressibly the American Doug, and his Merry Men often prance ridiculously in their efforts to emulate their inimitable leader's bounding enthusiasm. Will Rogers was to parody their movements in the two-reel comedy *Big Moments from Little Pictures* (1923).

Comedy was an important part of the spirit of the picture. Perhaps the best example of this is near the end of the film. King Richard impatiently calls out to Huntingdon to join the revelry; the Merry Men, sitting in a line on the very balcony from which Huntingdon and Lady Marian have fled to their nuptial chamber, all topple backward from

their perch over the ledge and out of view at the sheer force of Richard's bellow. The irreverence with which Fairbanks and his team imbue this scene is typical of the film. As Kevin Brownlow has noted, "A hilariously irresponsible element of comedy pervades the entire picture."[31]

A well-known tale from the production concerns Robert Fairbanks's wariness of his brother's determination to charge up the chain of the rising drawbridge to infiltrate Nottingham Castle. The stunt was exceptionally dangerous, and an accident would precipitate a delay, at tremendous financial loss. (Fairbanks reportedly carried nearly a half million dollars of life insurance with Lloyd's of London in addition to his usual coverage.)[32] A stuntman was suggested, and Fairbanks finally acquiesced. During rehearsals, it was clear to all that the stuntman was unable to provide the requisite combination of athleticism and grace, and orders were given to find a replacement the next day. An acrobat was found and rehearsed in the stunt, and instructions were given for costume and makeup. When the cameras rolled, the company was delighted that the acrobat looked even more like Fairbanks than he had in rehearsals and was imbuing the sequence with characteristic

Chaplin visits Fairbanks at the studio during production.

▶ Wallace Beery, Enid Bennett, and Fairbanks listen to a primitive radio during a break in filming.

gestures that had been considered inimitable. Only when the acrobat reached the top of the drawbridge did Dwan and Robert Fairbanks realize that Fairbanks himself had doubled as his own double.[33]

The drawbridge set also provided a legendary missed opportunity. On a visit to the Pickford-Fairbanks Studios, Chaplin was greatly impressed by the magnificent drawbridge and asked if he could use it for a scene in one of his comedies. "What use can you make of it?" inquired Fairbanks. Chaplin explained: "I will shoot a close-up of myself, all prepared for bed, coming to the front entrance. I will put out the cat, wind up the old alarm clock, and put out my empty milk bottle for the milkman and then raise the drawbridge for the night."[34] Unfortunately, this never made its way into a Chaplin film.

Once production was completed on July 28, 1922, Dwan recalled, four negatives were created, each of which was approximately 12,000 feet long. To film the 48,000 feet, 192,000 feet were shot, or less than 50,000 feet for each 12,000 used—a low shooting ratio for such a large and experimental production.[35] In an effort to dissuade concurrent

imitations (as had occurred with *The Three Musketeers*) of the public-domain property Robin Hood, the star titled and copyrighted his film as *Douglas Fairbanks in Robin Hood*. The advance publicity for the film was without precedent; it was the most anticipated Hollywood film up to that time. Victor L. Schertzinger, who had compiled a score to Thomas H. Ince's important production *Civilization* (1916), was hired by Fairbanks to compose original music and compile existing music to score *Robin Hood* for eighteen players. The assignment was completed in haste, and, despite the guidance of the showman Sid Grauman and assistance from A. H. Cokayne, John Cranshaw, and four copyists, the score suffers from a repetition of musical ideas, particularly the tournament music and marches. Nevertheless, the atmospheric score serves the action well and contains several memorable melodies. The song "O Promise Me," appropriated from Reginald De Koven's light opera *Robin Hood*, serves as the love theme for the reunion of Huntingdon and Lady Marian at the convent, as well as for the concluding scene in their wedding chamber. One minor Schertzinger theme, further developed and given lyrics by Sid Grauman, was touted as the film's "theme song" and sold as sheet music under the title "Just an Old Love Song." In fact, only the verse of "Just an Old Love Song" is used in the score; the chorus was added with the lyrics at the time of publication.[36]

Fairbanks's publicist Pete Smith (who later gained fame for the *Pete Smith Specialties* short subjects made for M-G-M from 1931 to 1954) was assigned the responsibility of handling the "road show" presentations of this production, which included New York City, Boston, Philadelphia, Chicago, and Los Angeles. (The European market was handled differently; in Britain, the premiere was held at the London Pavilion under the direction of the great theatrical manager Charles B. Cochran). As a road show presentation, *Robin Hood* was a sensation. At the Capitol Theatre in New York City, the film played to 100,000 people in the first week. As part of his press junket, Fairbanks posed for photographs on the roof of the Ritz-Carlton Hotel with bow and arrow in hand. Not content merely to pull on the bowstring for the press, as Allan Dwan recalled, "some deviltry within him made him let go of the arrow and away it flew" across Madison Avenue, ultimately penetrating the backside of a furrier, Abraham Seligman, who had made the unfortunate choice of keeping his window open while Fairbanks was in the city hyping his new film.[37] Superficially wounded, Seligman was visited by a contrite Fairbanks in the hospital the next day, and the wayward arrow cost Fairbanks a reported $5,000 to settle amicably.

The film had a production cost of $930,042.78—more than the cost of D. W. Griffith's *Intolerance* and nearly as much as Erich von Stroheim's *Foolish Wives* (1922).[38] It went on to earn over $1.5 million domestically, however, through its United Artists distribution.[39] The actual profit is impossible to determine, because Fairbanks "road-showed" the film in major U.S. cities as well as in Britain and France before allowing it a United Artists release, which complicates the measurement of the grosses.[40] Road-showing was a method developed by Griffith; the producer would rent a theater and run a film as a regular theatrical attraction with only two performances a day, charging prices comparable to those for live theater. This gave the production a tremendous opportunity to build publicity, as well as various opportunities for creative accounting. In addition to the "Just an Old Love Song" sheet music, a special souvenir booklet was created of the Elton Thomas scenario and sold at theaters during the period of exhibition, providing Fairbanks with additional revenue. In view of the cost of production, Fairbanks understood that the margin of profit for his film would never be great. However, the margin of loss in the event of failure might have proved

Fairbanks demonstrates with a bow and arrow on the roof of the Ritz-Carlton Hotel in New York City for the benefit of the newspaper reporters while promoting *Douglas Fairbanks in Robin Hood* in October 1922.

disastrous to his future career as a producer. The film's success was a great achievement against considerable odds.

The most spectacular road show presentation of the film was under the direction of Sid Grauman, whose Egyptian Theatre in Hollywood opened with *Robin Hood* on October 18, 1922, with elaborate dedication ceremonies and a prologue entitled "Nottingham Castle Pageant" staged by Victor L. Schertzinger. Many of cinema's luminaries were in attendance, greeted as they arrived at Grauman's superbly designed picture palace by bright lights, a red carpet, and a swarm of adoring fans and zealous photographers; it was one of the first "Hollywood premieres," as they are still called to this day. In an era when films typically played for a week and exceptional films for a month, *Robin Hood* ran nearly six months at the Egyptian, effectively eliminating any first-run distribution possibilities in the Los Angeles area. Hollywood streetcar conductors stopped announcing their Hollywood Boulevard stop with the usual cross street of "McCadden Place" and began shouting, "All out for *Robin Hood.*"[41]

Robin Hood, touted as "the greatest film show on earth,"[42] enjoyed laudatory reviews, many of which contained more than a few superlatives. Leading the way was Robert E. Sherwood, writing in the *New York Herald,* who proclaimed:

Here is a motion picture which is so far ahead of any spectacle that has ever gone before that it is impossible to appraise it in the same terms that have been applied to previous efforts. It represents the high-water mark of film production—the farthest step that the silent drama has ever taken along the highroad [sic] to art. . . . But back of all this vast display is an intelligence which is indeed rare. *Robin Hood* did not grow from the bank roll; it grew from the mind. And this is the chief reason for its superiority.[43]

The *New York Times* reviewer enthused:

To Zorro and D'Artagnan, Douglas Fairbanks has added Robin Hood, and Robin Hood is the greatest of the three. . . . Fairbanks has gone beyond anything he has ever done before. He has made a picture which, for magnificence of setting, richness of pageantry, beauty and eloquence of photography and impressiveness of action has probably never been equaled before, surely not surpassed.[44]

Carl Sandburg, writing for the *Chicago Daily News,* declared it "a screen classic" and "Douglas Fairbanks' masterpiece." Fairbanks had made a personal appearance at the Chicago opening, and Sandburg noted: "The outpouring of people who couldn't get into the theater but waited around for a look at him was probably the largest crowd of its kind that the local theater district has seen. It was a testimony to a unique personal popularity."[45] Reviewing the Hollywood premiere at the Egyptian in the *Los Angeles Times,* Edwin Schallert thought the film "A revelation in artistry, its advent was a symbol of a new triumph. . . . The tyranny of cinema prose was shaken and the democracy of cinema poetry was, mayhap, proclaimed. Certainly, this is the great picture of the year. Undoubtedly, too, it is the most artistic picture in the history of ocular narrative."[46]

Fairbanks poses inside the newly built Grauman's Egyptian Theatre in Hollywood.

The film went on to receive the *Photoplay* Gold Medal of Honor, a notable distinction in 1923, before the formation of the Academy of Motion Picture Arts and Sciences and its annual awards of merit. *Photoplay* pronounced: "In spite of the fact that a dozen or more men and women played important parts in the production of this picture, the credit for the conception and the execution of the idea goes to Mr. Fairbanks."[47]

This is the film in which Fairbanks attained great art. René Clair, later a celebrated French filmmaker, wrote in 1923 that the film "disarms criticism" and that audiences should

judge *Robin Hood* as you would judge a ballet or a fairy-pantomime. Look at it for just a moment with simple eyes. Pay attention only to the perfection of the motions, of the motion: the cinema was created to record it. *Robin Hood* is an army of banners on the march, steel-clad horses galloping, free men dancing in a forest, sprints through a castle built for giants, leaps that traverse space, streams, forests, countrysides.[48]

Not everyone was disarmed. For Vachel Lindsay, the film was "a heavy exhibit of armor that does not move." He deemed it "a failure" precisely because of the pageantry and spectacle of the first half.[49] Similar criticism has been frequently leveled at the film in the decades since then, despite the fact that *Robin Hood* is a meticulously constructed work, and the first half contains much action, essential character motivation, and the atmosphere of medieval England. Every scene contributes to the themes of the film (loyalty, love, fidelity of friendship, heroism) and the overall "impression" of the period. Fairbanks anticipated the criticism; the spectacle of the first half came as a surprise to audiences who had come to expect stunts, rather than spectacle, as soon as Fairbanks appeared on screen. "I believe that without a thorough presentation of the hero in the character of the Earl of Huntingdon, his exploits as Robin Hood would have been much less effective," Fairbanks maintained.[50]

Lindsay's opinion notwithstanding, the enormous sets and pageantry did not weigh down the film. Alistair Cooke, who preferred Fairbanks unfettered by large-scale backgrounds, assessed the film favorably, observing: "This all-American construction job did not, however, involve strangulation of the Fairbanks character by drapes and décor. The décor was still a background and did not impede the flying figure of the hero."[51] Richard Schickel sums up the film best, writing that *Robin Hood* finds Fairbanks in transition and calling it

a Janus-like film—looking backward to the Dashing Doug of the early films, forward to the Douglas Fairbanks to come, when the spectacular showman's side of his nature would be in the ascendant. In no other film would the conflict between these two aspects of his personality be so obvious, and so obviously unresolved. The public, however, did not notice or did not care. *Robin Hood* represented the height of their love affair with him.[52]

The position that *Robin Hood* held in the silent era as a milestone in the development of film art has been diminished somewhat by the enormous popularity of *The Adventures of Robin Hood* (1938), starring Errol Flynn. Flynn's boyhood hero was Fairbanks, and one sees an influence on his acting style: the broad smiles, hands on hips, athleticism, and humor.[53]

Douglas Fairbanks in Robin Hood was first made available for nontheatrical distribution by the Circulating Film Library of the Museum of Modern Art in 1938.[54] However, the only way to assess it properly is on a large screen with live orchestral accompaniment. Indeed, it may not be possible to evaluate today the film seen by audiences in 1922. As early as June 1923, it was reported that new scenes, not part of the original version, had been added under Fairbanks's supervision to strengthen the film.[55]

Robin Hood asserted Fairbanks's claim to leadership in Hollywood, and his influence can be seen in the spectacles released the following year: Cecil B. DeMille's *The Ten Commandments, The Hunchback of Notre Dame* starring Lon Chaney, and James Cruze's western epic *The Covered Wagon,* as well as a storm of other costume films. Fairbanks ushered in a new era of motion pictures, emphasizing an elaborate scale of production—along with a high level of artistry—that was an important achievement in the development of cinema. The trick, which much of his competition failed to capture, was the wit and vitality he brought to his costume adventures; by comparison, many of the large-scale films of the 1920s seem merely bloated. The magic and spectacle of the movies is clearly evident in Fairbanks's superb rendering of the Robin Hood legend. *Douglas Fairbanks in Robin Hood* captured Fairbanks at his peak.

Apogee

The Thief of Bagdad (1924)

A n epic romantic fantasy-adventure inspired by several of the *Arabian Nights* tales, *The Thief of Bagdad* is the greatest artistic triumph of Fairbanks's career. The superb visual design, spectacle, imaginative splendor, and visual effects, along with his bravura performance (leading a cast of literally thousands), all contribute to making this his masterpiece. The magic of his dynamism—his physical presence, his movements, and his humor—and the magic of the silent cinema are at their zenith in *The Thief of Bagdad*. Fairbanks's thief is completely different from the roles his audience had come to expect from him; he is less the all-American Doug here than a ballet dancer in the style of Nijinsky. His humor is still very much in evidence, as well as his trademark grin, yet close-ups are used infrequently and indeed are somewhat wasted on him. The full effect captures both the grin and the bare chest he displays throughout much of the film. The prodigal production cost $1,135,654.65.[1] The film took over sixty-five weeks to make, and the sets covered six and a half acres. The film was not only his most ambitious but also one of the largest and most expensive made up to that time. *The Thief of Bagdad* overshadows *Robin Hood* in its size and scope, and Fairbanks was at his personal and professional apogee in it.

Fairbanks in the titular role in *The Thief of Bagdad*. Photograph by Charles Warrington.

Fairbanks shows off his stunning 40-year-old physique in an early costume test for *The Thief of Bagdad.*

Fairbanks originally intended to follow *Robin Hood* with a sequel to *The Mark of Zorro* involving pirates, and he had discussions with Ernst Lubitsch about directing such a production. However, he was adamant that his pirate film be photographed in color and was dissatisfied with the limitations and difficulties of color cinematography at that time. Concurrently, he was given a beautiful edition of *The Arabian Nights* (then in vogue as a result of a new translation), and he started to read it before he went to sleep one evening. Fairbanks, who seldom read anything of length, pored over the volume all night, and the next day, he abandoned the pirate film in favor of an *Arabian Nights*–themed fantasy.[2] By the end of November 1922, Fairbanks had commenced the early preproduction phase. (Preproduction did not officially begin until May 7, 1923.) He would ultimately spend eight months in research and planning.

Fairbanks, director Raoul Walsh, and production consultant Edward Knoblock at the Pickford-Fairbanks Studios inspect the costumes of the various supporting and day players. Every cast member and costume was tested before the cameras. "When finally the extra people were selected from many hundred—three thousand in fact—they were put into their costumes and photographed, in groups of fifteen, before they were definitely engaged," Knoblock remembered.

Fairbanks's selection of his creative team for *The Thief of Bagdad* was inspired. His most important choice was Raoul Walsh as director. Prior to *The Thief of Bagdad*, Walsh was well known as an actor for his portrayal of John Wilkes Booth in D. W. Griffith's *The Birth of a Nation* and as a director of many films, including *Regeneration* (1915), an impressive drama of gangster life in the Bowery, based on fact. The success of *The Thief of Bagdad* launched Walsh's career as a major Hollywood director, maker of such classics as *What Price Glory?* (1926), *High Sierra* (1941), and *White Heat* (1949). The type of fantasy-spectacle Fairbanks envisioned was not Walsh's element, as he later conceded. Fairbanks typically encouraged his chosen directors to give more than even they thought themselves capable of contributing.[3] He was confident of Walsh's capabilities in the coordination of the production and enjoyed his sense of humor; Walsh was an inveterate practical joker, and Fairbanks loved practical jokes. Walsh's style and temperament were well suited to bring out the best in Fairbanks's self-parody and narcissism. As for Walsh, he held Fairbanks in the highest regard, later remembering him as "a fine man" and "a perfectionist."[4] However, Fairbanks was the real force both in front of and behind the camera, and he frequently took charge of the difficult scenes. He was a cinema auteur over thirty years before the concept was developed; he put his own identifiable stamp on his films. Indeed, Walsh was hardly mentioned in the reviews of *The Thief of Bagdad*.

After a long search, Fairbanks eventually hired William Cameron Menzies as art director, with Irvin J. Martin as consulting art director. An impressive team of associate artists were also put on the Fairbanks

Fairbanks, in costume, supervises the filming of a scene in
The Thief of Bagdad.

Ahmed offers the princess
(Julanne Johnston) the rose
he has plucked from
her garden.

payroll: Anton Grot, Paul Youngblood, H. R. Hopps, Harold W. Grieve, Park French, William Utwich, and Edward M. Langley. Circulating prints of *The Thief of Bagdad* omit all production credits, but the key members of the crew were Mitchell Leisen, who had designed the costumes for *Robin Hood*, once again the costume designer, with Paul Burns as master of wardrobe and properties. Arthur Edeson, in the last of the three films he was to photograph for Fairbanks, was again cinematographer, with Richard Holahan, P. H. Whitman, and Kenneth MacLean

Ahmed threatens a Mongol slave girl (Anna May Wong) with his dagger, while the princess sleeps in her bedchamber.

serving as camera operators. James O'Donohoe was engaged as assistant director. Ted Reed returned to serve capably as production manager. Robert Fairbanks's engineering expertise was once again heavily tapped in his capacity as technical director. Norris Wilcox, Fairbanks's half brother, was given the position of company manager.

The film's cast included the comedian Snitz Edwards as the thief's "evil associate," Charles Belcher as the holy man, Brandon Hurst as the caliph, Sojin Kamiyama (billed simply as Sojin) as the malevolent Mongol prince, and Noble Johnson as the Indian prince. Inexplicably, a woman, Mathilde Comont, supplied with a moustache, was given the role of the corpulent Persian prince, which she played convincingly, rounding out the excellent ensemble.

Fairbanks had seen the sultry Evelyn Brent in *The Spanish Jade* (1922) and placed her under contract as his leading lady. Still photographs survive of the two costumed for the film. However, in June 1923, Brent abruptly left the film and was replaced by Julanne Johnston, a former vaudeville dancer. Although a limited actress, Johnston possessed the requisite grace, beauty, and dignity. It was rumored at the time that Fairbanks's interest in Brent had been more than professional, and that Pickford insisted upon her immediate dismissal, although there is little evidence to support this claim.[5] Unquestionably, the most dynamic female casting was the hiring of Anna May Wong as the princess's Mongol slave. Fairbanks had seen her in the early two-color Technicolor production *Toll of the Sea* (1922) and believed she would be ideal for the part. Her role in *The Thief of Bagdad* catapulted her to international fame.

Dr. Arthur Woods once again led the scenario research, with his wife, Lotta Woods, as scenario editor. Edward Knoblock, who had previously adapted *The Three Musketeers* for Fairbanks, provided invaluable assistance in the preparation of the story and was heavily involved in every aspect of preproduction. Knoblock, whose play *Kismet* was a major inspiration, was ultimately credited as the film's consultant.

Fairbanks described the character he wanted to portray thus: "Our hero must be every young man of this age who believes that happiness is a quantity that can be stolen, who is selfish, at odds with the world and rebellious toward conventions on which comfortable human relations are based."[6] The scenario staff found the film's theme in a quatrain from Sir Richard Francis Burton's unexpurgated English translation of *The Arabian Nights:* "Seek not thy happiness to steal / 'Tis work alone will bring thee weal / Who seeketh bliss without toil or strife / The impossible seeketh and wasteth life."[7]

Fairbanks simplified this to the dictum "Happiness Must Be Earned," on which his staff built the scenario of a lowly thief who triumphs over adversity to win the hand of the princess. The episodic structure is more apparent here than in any of his other costume films. The thief confronts a series of tests, "The Valley of Fire," "The Valley of the Monsters," "The Cavern of the Enchanted Trees," "The Old Man of the Midnight Sea," and "The Abode of the Winged Horse" among them. Fairbanks's characterization exudes insouciance, and he holds the film together beautifully with his grace and humor, particularly in the burlesque, Griffith-like last-minute race-to-the-rescue climax.[8]

Eschewing enormous manuscripts, Fairbanks once again employed a series of charts, including a set plot and shooting schedule, mounted on walls of various studio offices. He was thereby able to visualize the whole production. Douglas Fairbanks Jr. remembered:

My father went about the plotting of *The Thief of Bagdad* like the parsing of a sentence. "Happiness Must Be Earned" was the theme of the film, and this was written on an enormous chart. Under the word "Happiness" would be the state of mind of the hero and heroine. "Must Be" were the factors set against them in opposition. And "Earned" would be broken down to what the action was that earned the "Happiness." All of these ideas emanating from "Happiness Must Be Earned" were brought together at the bottom of the chart.[9]

The scenario and scope of the production exceeded those of *Robin Hood,* and at its final length of fifteen reels (approximately 152 minutes at the suggested projection speed of 85 feet per minute), *The Thief of Bagdad* was the longest film Fairbanks ever made.

The production was an enormous undertaking and required all the prodigious energy and enthusiasm that Fairbanks singularly possessed. His daily routine, which he firmly established with this production, was to awake between five and six o'clock in the morning and take a pre-breakfast jog on his own around the grounds of Pickfair for about an hour. After a light breakfast of fruit (occasionally augmented with toast, coffee, or a hard-boiled egg), he dressed and drove to the studio, arriving between eight and nine o'clock. The first order of business was to visit the various departments. The *New York Times,* doubtless aided and abetted by Fairbanks's press agent, captured his daily routine during this period:

As Doug approaches each department head he makes that executive smile and feel "at home," because he believes that when a man's heart is happy his arm works willingly. At first he is all business, though without severity. He finds out how the department is progressing. Getting a satisfactory answer, he smiles, leans against a wall or a desk and says: "Did you ever hear this one?"

The executive grins as though his favorite brother were standing beside him, says "No" and looks up expectantly. Doug tells

Fairbanks, a "hands-on" producer, applies the finishing touches to a bit player's costume.

Fairbanks, as producer, stands at the center of the camera platform and supervises the filming. At left, holding the megaphone, is the director, Raoul Walsh.

him a story. His yarns are always short and to the point. He chops them down as he does the subtitles in his pictures. At the end there is generally a surprise "punch" and a good laugh. Where he gets his stories from, nobody knows. Some there are who say he "dreams 'em." But he always has a fresh stock on hand.

Overflowing with the joy of living, Fairbanks resumes his rounds. If a fence happens to be in his way, he jumps it. It is a passion with him to meet and overcome obstacles. He believes in putting obstacles in his way, mental and physical, to develop his powers of resistance and aggressiveness. Therefore he would rather leap over a hedge or a fence than pass under a triumphal arch. He gets more thrills out of it.[10]

Fairbanks began filming as soon as he made the daily rounds, stopping for a light lunch at 12 noon before resuming work in the afternoon. Between four and five o'clock, he stopped work altogether for a game of his own creation, a combination of tennis and badminton known as "Doug," which enjoyed a brief popularity in the 1920s. "We play with a specially made racket," Fairbanks wrote in 1924, "and the shuttlecock or puck used makes a very fast game; for, unlike the tennis ball, it may not touch the ground."[11] Following this rigorous workout, Fairbanks repaired to the large Turkish bath complex for a steam bath, sauna, ice-cold plunge, and a session with his masseur. Friends were encouraged to visit, with Chaplin among the regulars enjoying the facilities and conversation. "If Chaplin or Barrymore was present, it [the conversation] would be hilariously bawdy. Dad, who rarely told dirty jokes himself—and strictly forbade them in front of the ladies—was nevertheless a wonderful, coughing, weeping, guffawing audience for other people's raunchy stories," his son remembered.[12] Fairbanks returned to Pickfair for dinner, usually held at eight o'clock. His daily routine during production was to be in bed by ten P.M., in order to sleep for eight hours.

The athletic and other training equipment at the studio was kept in a gymnasium facility on the lot with the Latin phrase "Basilica Linea Abdominalis" ("Waist Line Temple") posted above the entrance. For *The Thief of Bagdad*, Fairbanks vigorously trained for weeks on trampolines to perfect the famous sequence in which the thief outwits his pursuers by leaping from one life-sized earthenware jar to another with the bounce of a rubber ball. He began with little jumps from one trampoline to another. As in a high jump, hurdle sticks were raised for him to leap over, and the height was increased as he continued to perfect the stunt. Ultimately, Fairbanks was able to jump barriers higher than

Fairbanks plays "Doug" at the studio during production of *The Thief of Bagdad*. He filed a patent on the game in 1923 (registered January 1, 1924), and "Doug" subsequently enjoyed a brief vogue.

▶ Ahmed effortlessly jumps from jar to jar in *The Thief of Bagdad*. The stunt required weeks of training and the use of trampolines hidden within the various jars.

the jars themselves, so that when the sequence was filmed, he was able to make the jumps (with trampolines inside the jars) without any appearance of effort. Fairbanks stood nearly five feet eight inches tall and weighed 150 pounds in his fortieth year. His physique would have been the envy of a professional athlete half his age. "All muscle and not an ounce of fat," Raoul Walsh remembered.[13] According to Douglas Fairbanks Jr., however, outward appearances were somewhat misleading. Fairbanks's personal physician was beginning to note that his circulation was "not all that it should be and that he was extending himself beyond the wise limits for his age. He scorned the advice and kept on

pressing himself physically to the limit."[14] Unquestionably, his heavy smoking contributed to the onset of his circulatory problems.

Fairbanks's fitness regime was simply constant motion. "Doug" may have been the only structured exercise, but the entire day was one continuous workout. The stuntman, fight choreographer, and actor David Sharpe, who began his career as an extra working for Fairbanks, recalled in 1952:

Fairbanks had a frightening energy. It was a constant hassle around him from morning to night. . . . All of his acrobatics were genuine. . . . The entire studio was rigged up like a gymnasium. There were trampolines, swings, horizontal bars, ropes, hand rings, punching bags, even a dirt track for sprints out at the back. It was like a present-day Army obstacle course. He'd come racing out of his administration building office and never stop running and jumping until he hit the dirt track clear out in back a half mile away. He'd swing onto a gate, vault over it, leap from there to a portico, bounding like a kangaroo. And he loved to entice others to join him. . . . He always had a swarm of fighters, wrestlers, knife throwers and stunt men around him. . . . There was never anyone like Fairbanks. He was the indispensable man.[15]

The ethereal, spectacular setting for *The Thief of Bagdad* was determined by Fairbanks in the early planning stages. He wanted the design of the film to first and foremost convey the extravagance of imagination manifest in the *Arabian Nights* tales. Sergei Diaghilev's Ballets Russes had a great impact in America, as in Europe, defining modern dance in the early twentieth century. Fairbanks was inspired not only by Nijinsky but by *Scheherazade,* Diaghilev's great success, choreographed by Michel Fokine, danced by Nijinsky to the music of Rimsky-Korsakov, and with costumes and décor by Léon Bakst. Fairbanks originally hired the illustrator Maxfield Parrish to design the film, but his conception was deemed impractical, and Fairbanks tried more than one replacement before engaging William Cameron Menzies, the brilliant young (he was not yet thirty) production designer whose career as arguably Hollywood's foremost art director was launched with this film. *Things to Come* (1936), *Gone with the Wind* (1939), and *Michael Todd's Around the World in 80 Days* (1956) were among Menzies's subsequent triumphs. Based on Bakst's ideas, Fairbanks, Walsh, Edeson, and Menzies and his consulting artists developed the integrated, coherent, curvilinear Art Nouveau design on which the film pivots. Applied to the Art Nouveau décor, Menzies's pen-and-ink effects, which registered like drawings on screen,[16] were revolutionary in cinema. Prior to *The Thief of Bagdad,* set designs and décor in major films like Griffith's *Intolerance* were a tasteful mixture at best and in most cases a jumble. Menzies's sets for *The Thief of Bagdad* created an ethereal world of its own, with cast and setting melded in rhythm and motion. "It is as if a set of mobile black-and-white, pen-and-ink drawings has come to life, creating an animated *mise-en-scene,*" John C. Tibbetts and James M. Welsh note in their study of Fairbanks. "Some fifty years later it seems that one of the essential formulas for popular success that the Disney Studio was later to exploit is here given its most effective early rendering."[17] Experiments with models convinced Fairbanks that the surfaces for the various sets should be simple yet immense. The city of Bagdad was conceived with various sparkling domes, minarets, and pagodas, an enormous palace, streets with archways, swirling stairwells, and cantilevered balconies that all appeared weightless and imaginary. Despite the massive scale, the various settings could be dominated by Fairbanks's thief. Indeed, the sets were a limitless playground of improvisation and provided numerous opportunities for Fairbanks's flights and leaps. Yet when Menzies's sets were built and tests were made, the sets—intended to look fantastical—became too literal and substantial. The solution became a staple film—and later television—method of creating large sets without the impression of weight. Fairbanks explained:

A production design illustration depicting Ahmed descending into the Midnight Sea in search of the star-shaped key.

A special problem that faced us for *The Thief of Bagdad* was my desire that a dream city should not look too well anchored on its foundations. It is easy enough to make a thing fantastic and un-real, but I wanted it to seem light in addition. By using a somewhat weird design, by painting trees and branches black even where we had real ones, by the use of light backgrounds instead of the cus-tomary dark tones which are thought to bring out the figures more clearly, by confining our colors to gray, silver, black and white for everything except the actual costumes, we obtained an unusual effect; but sets built on the ground will look as if they were.

To get away from this solidity, we painted our buildings darker at the top than at bottom. This seemed to make them less solid and heavy at the bottom. We also built upon a highly polished black floor that had reflections. The vertical line of a house meets the horizontal line of the ground and ends there. Our polished floor reflects the building lines and lifts our city. And this black floor caused considerable extra work. There was endless brush-ing and polishing week after week.[18]

The enormous palace of Bagdad set, populated with hundreds of extras. Fairbanks ordered the construction of the large "Bagdad" sign above the set, visible to virtually all in still rural 1920s Hollywood, to dissuade producers from stealing shots of his set. Douglas Fairbanks Jr. recalled that portions of the set were "a source of wonder and curiosity for hordes of sightseers" for many years after.

In the film's souvenir book, Fairbanks elucidated this point in an article entitled "Translating Fantasy into Pictures":

To further the illusion, the environment of the characters was designed out of proportion to human fact. Flowers, vases, stairs, windows and decorative effects were given a bizarre quality suggestive of the unreal.

Even the tinting and toning of the film is subtly co-related with the action; a roseate glow for the romantic moments; a garish green where the terrifying monsters appear; a soft Uranium sepia where the beautiful golden haze glows about the dream city of Bagdad.[19]

The Bagdad set occupied six and a half acres; the bazaar alone covered over two acres, with a concrete floor four inches thick, which had to be re-enameled several times a week. The spectacular sets were the

A portrait of Fairbanks
as Ahmed the thief. The
tattoo design on Fairbanks's
right biceps became his
personal emblem.

upward and outward extensions of the *Robin Hood* sets—the same foundations, but with a different facing that ingeniously transformed Nottingham Castle into the palace of Bagdad. The production design for *The Thief of Bagdad* is a remarkable monument of 1920s Art Nouveau design, as well as a creation that integrated the actors into the fairy tale settings. The accomplishment is a landmark in early cinema art direction.

"The art director, the set dresser, the costume designer—we all worked together as closely as possible," Mitchell Leisen remembered; "we had 3,000 extras . . . [on some days] for *The Thief*, and I had to design different costumes for all of them. . . . the costumes were much more complicated than *Robin Hood* had been."[20] After several false starts, Leisen created the simple yet daring costume in which Fairbanks danced through much of the film. Fairbanks's thief appears in his early scenes bronzed and bare-chested, wearing large golden hoop earrings,

Fairbanks rehearses with the magic rope during production. Note the crew members just visible at extreme left.

a pencil-slim moustache, and a head scarf (which also served to conceal and anchor the actor's wig), his right biceps adorned with a silver crescent-and-star design. Fairbanks's sheer pantaloons were suggested by the trousers worn in the Diaghilev-Bakst ballet *Scheherazade*. These diaphanous drawers, particularly in the sequence depicting him the morning after the thief's flogging, are revealing enough to still evoke comment from audiences in the twenty-first century. His movements are beautiful, fluid, and graceful, the exaggerated movements of a dancer, perfectly suited to the stylized fantasy and enormous scale of the production. In *The Thief of Bagdad*, Fairbanks consciously emphasized his athleticism; his graceful, dance-like poses enable him to successfully integrate himself into the film's ornate, oversized design.

The film's set pieces include the magic rope that hangs from nowhere, various monsters, the magic carpet, a winged horse, a cloak of invisibility, and an army raised out of thin air from seeds thrown on the ground. Fairbanks assembled a visual effects team of artisans and technicians that included Edeson, Coy Watson, and Hampton Del Ruth, director of mechanical effects. Most of the men hired were specialists in comic films, where trick photography was frequently employed.[21]

Fairbanks was impressed by the German spectacles he had seen on his trip abroad, such as Ernst Lubitsch's *Carmen* (*Gypsy Blood*, 1918), *Madame Dubarry* (*Passion*, 1919), and *Sumurun* (*One Arabian Night*, 1920), as well as by Dimitri Buchowetzki's *Danton* (*All for a Woman*, 1921) and Viacheslav Tourjansky's *Les contes de mille et une nuits* (*The Tales of a Thousand and One Nights*, 1921). He was particularly influenced by Fritz Lang's *Der Müde Tod* (*Destiny*, 1921), which he had seen in Berlin in 1921, and from which he borrowed many visual effects for *The Thief of Bagdad;* he especially liked the sequence with an ancient Chinese wizard and the magic carpet scenes in *Destiny*, which prefigure those in *The Thief of Bagdad*. Fairbanks even went so far as to purchase the American distribution rights to *Destiny*. Lang complained that Fairbanks acquired the American rights to his film primarily to study and improve upon the Lang film's visual effects with impunity.[22] In Fairbanks's defense, most of the film industry was being influenced by the German films of the time; Fairbanks's challenge to himself was to surpass the German productions as well as top himself. "Although my father was artistically impressed by the better German films, he did not like them as commercial enterprises and usually opposed suggestions that United Artists distribute them," Douglas Fairbanks Jr. observed.[23] Fairbanks primarily embraced the concepts of stylized performance and stylized sets from the German films.

He managed to surpass the German films of the period technically in all but one respect. Fairbanks was outshone by one aspect of another Lang film, *Siegfrieds Tod* (*Siegfried*, 1924), the first of a two-part version of the Nibelungen legend, which was distributed in the United States in 1925. The rubbery dragon Fairbanks slays in the Valley of the Monsters sequence pales in comparison with the sixty-foot mechanical dragon in Lang's film, which spews both fire and blood. Lang's dragon took months of careful work to achieve and was operated by a crew of technicians.[24] However, Fairbanks's mechanical team did create some memorable monsters, including a giant bat and a prodigious sea spider.

Some of the film's visuals were achieved simply: the magic rope was suspended by a piano wire; the winged horse was a horse outfitted with wings on wires running on a treadmill in front of a black backdrop; the army raised out of thin air from seeds thrown on the ground was realized with exploding flares. The most difficult visual effect to design as well as perform was the magic carpet, which had to swoop over the city of Bagdad. Robert Fairbanks decided that it was best to use a crane, the highest camera-stand ever built up to that time. Constructed of steel by Llewellyn Iron Works and operated with a derrick and hoist, the crane was ninety feet high, with platforms for the camera operators.

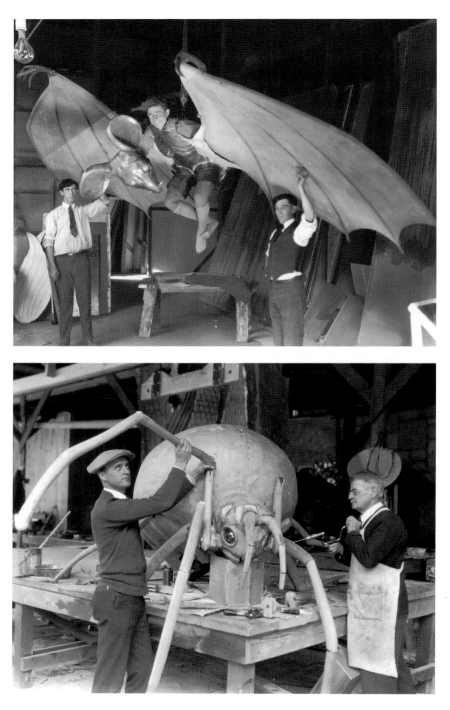

A behind-the-scenes photo reveals Paul Malvern portraying the gigantic bat that attacks Ahmed in the Valley of the Monsters sequence.

Two property technicians work on the assembly of the giant sea spider, one of the sinister creatures Ahmed encounters in the Valley of the Monsters.

Coy Watson Jr., whose father had the enormous responsibility of being in charge of all the wire work, remembered that the carpet itself was "a three-quarter-inch flat piece of steel, five feet by eight feet in size and covered with a Persian carpet with an eight-inch fringe hanging down around the edges."[25] It was suspended by six "invisible" piano wires and moved at twenty-five miles an hour; undercranking the cameras made it appear to move much faster. *Science and Invention* magazine published a two-page article on "The Mechanical Marvels of *The Thief of Bagdad*" in its May 1924 issue, revealing the innovative techniques employed: black backdrops, double exposure, glass shots, and models.[26]

The production design and visual effects were meticulously planned and tested; every player had a camera and costume test. This encompassed not only the sixteen principals, but several minor roles and hundreds of extras. In all, 20,000 feet of costume, makeup, and visual effects tests were filmed.

The Thief of Bagdad, subtitled "An Arabian Nights Fantasy," begins with the theme of the film, "Happiness Must Be Earned," spelled out in the sky by stars in a brief prologue sequence in which an entranced boy listens as a holy man tells the story of the film. This transitions into the story of Ahmed, a crafty and cynical thief, who bounds about the city of Bagdad a thousand years ago deftly picking purses, vaulting balconies, and effortlessly jumping in and out of a succession of huge jars. Ahmed's philosophy is expressed in the intertitle, "What I want—I take. My reward is <u>here</u>. Paradise is a fool's dream and Allah is a myth." Ahmed infiltrates the palace and attempts to pose as a prince—one of four suitors for the hand of the princess (Julanne Johnston). He wins her favor and is ennobled by his love for her. He is exposed as a thief by the caliph (Brandon Hurst) and flogged. The princess saves his life and professes her love. She sends her remaining suitors away for a journey of seven moons, consenting to wed the one who returns with the greatest treasure. Aided by the princess's Mongol slave (Anna May Wong), one of her suitors, the Mongol prince Cham Shang the Great (Sojin), plots to assemble a secret army within Bagdad's walls and capture the city. Ahmed enters a mosque and seeks the advice of a holy man (Charles Belcher, the holy man of the film's prologue and epilogue), who tells him: "Allah hath made thy soul yearn for happiness, but thou must earn it." He is advised to seek the magic Chest of Nazir and sets out on his journey, during which he confronts temptation and is attacked by sundry monsters. He emerges victorious and returns to Bagdad. Meanwhile, the suitors have obtained their treasures: the Persian prince (Mathilde Comont), a magic carpet; the Indian prince (Noble Johnson), a magic crystal; the Mongol prince, a magic apple.

The Mongol prince raises his secret army and captures the city in a surprise attack. Ahmed returns to Bagdad and with his magic Chest of Nazir conjures up a massive army to retake the city and restore the caliph to power. Ahmed and the princess are reunited and sail away together on the magic carpet to the Land of Love. The film concludes with an epilogue, a continuation of the prologue, in which twinkling stars once again spell out its theme: "Happiness Must be Earned."

Production of *The Thief of Bagdad* began on July 5, 1923, with nonstop work excepting Sundays and Christmas Day. The production phase lasted a little over twenty-eight weeks. Fairbanks was proud of his large,

◁ This behind-the-scenes still reveals that the magic carpet was suspended from the platform of an enormous crane by six steel wires. Fairbanks was assured that each wire was guaranteed to hold 300 pounds. As he was first hoisted aloft, he remarked, "I'd like more than a guarantee in a place like this!"

Effective flying scenes were crucial to the successful execution of the magic carpet sequences. Fairbanks hired Coy Watson, who had achieved amazing mechanical effects with piano wire for comedy producer Mack Sennett. The photo at top right reveals the six steel piano wires Watson attached to the carpet to suspend it in the air. In the bottom photo the wires are undetectable, thus achieving the illusion of the carpet in flight. The neutral backdrop afforded the cinematographer the opportunity to double-expose the negative with clouds painted on a rolling canvas; an off-camera fan providing a breeze completes the in-flight effect.

Fairbanks with the Jazz Age icon Babe Ruth, wearing his New York Yankees uniform and ready to play, along with another baseball great, Walter Johnson (third from left). The publisher G. Logan Payne is on the far left. Chuck Lewis, Fairbanks's trainer, stands behind Fairbanks (sixth from left).

cosmopolitan cast and crew and was amused to recall afterward that the flashes of temper that sometimes marked the production process had resulted not so much from the work as from "complications of international temperament."[27] Raoul Walsh's interaction with the hordes of extras was sometimes fraught with difficulties. According to Walsh, extras were recruited by the casting director and three assistants going to south-central Los Angeles in four big buses with placards on them that read: "Free Ride! See Douglas Fairbanks in person making *The Thief of Bagdad*!" The response was such that hundreds had to be turned away. The film benefited from the busloads of colorful characters, but there were also difficulties handling them, and Walsh had to stop more than one fight with his own fists. "This maneuver achieved a double result," he recalled. "It catered to Doug's love of an audience while he worked, and it got us more extras than we needed."[28] The extras were not the only onlookers. Each day brought visitors. "The daily audience appeared to put more snap into Doug's performance and he kept his brother Robert, the production manager, busy herding newcomers onto the set to gasp and applaud," Walsh remembered.[29] Of the many distinguished visitors to the set of *The Thief of Bagdad*, none was more inspiring to the actor-producer than Anna Pavlova. Appalled at the revelation that none of the great Russian ballerina's work had been properly documented for posterity, he immediately arranged an impromptu filming of her most famous dances, including "The Dying Swan," at the studio. As with the ceremonial Hopi dances he had filmed during production of *The Mollycoddle*, Fairbanks lavished time on Pavlova to preserve an art of which he saw himself as an enthusiastic patron. *The Thief of Bagdad* wrapped on January 26, 1924, with Fairbanks relieved that the arduous production was finally at an end.

The sample print of the film having been approved by Fairbanks on January 31, 1924, the postproduction phase, which began February 1, 1924, went by swiftly, owing to the meticulous preparations. William Nolan, the editor, had systematically cut the 480,000 feet of film (exposed on multiple cameras) that had been shot. Fairbanks hired the poet George Sterling to write the intertitles and give them a lyrical quality.[30] Fairbanks oversaw all aspects of postproduction and had a hand in everything—even the film posters, which were works of art, particularly a special one-sheet poster designed by Anton Grot. Fairbanks had been impressed by Grot's painting *The Shepherd's Dream* and wanted a similar poetic quality for one of the posters. Grot's image of Fairbanks astride a winged horse soaring through the clouds is certainly one of the finest film posters ever rendered.

Early on, Fairbanks had decided that *The Thief of Bagdad* must have an exceptional musical score. Rather than following the usual practice of compiling one from existing music, he hired the American composer Mortimer Wilson to create an original score. Wilson was known for the versatility of his chamber music, symphonies, and other classical works. His only previous music for cinema was "1849," an original overture for *The Covered Wagon*, which brought Wilson to the attention of Fairbanks. Wilson viewed each scene shortly after it was taken and put his impressions to music.[31] Fairbanks himself was not a musician but had very definite views about music for film. "Make your score as artistic as you can and don't feel that you have to jump like a banderlog from one mood to another at the expense of the development of your musical ideas," he advised Wilson.[32] Original film scores like Wilson's were exceedingly rare; Victor Herbert's score for *The Fall of a Nation* (1916) and Sigmund Romberg's score for Stroheim's *Foolish Wives* (1922) are among the few original scores from the silent era. (Joseph Carl Breil's score for *The Birth of a Nation* used mostly existing music.) Wilson's Opus 74 was celebrated at the time of *The Thief of Bagdad*'s New

York City world premiere. The score "made musical history," Theodore Stearns asserted in the *New York Morning Telegraph*:

What has handicapped the few real composers of original scores to accompany a big movie, up to date, has been that producers and directors eternally insist upon the music changing instantly with the changes in the picture. . . . It would mean, in the case of *The Thief of Bagdad*, changing the musical idea at the rate of once a minute for two hours and a half. This attempt is made, however, in most moving-pictures, and the result—nine times out of ten— is a hodgepodge of something commenced, nothing ever satisfactorily finished. . . . [Wilson develops his ideas] consistently without having to worry about the flashes to and fro on the film, and still his music reflects the action and backgrounds.[33]

Wilson's score continues to have a reputation among musicologists. Martin Marks, writing in *The Oxford History of World Cinema*, describes it as "richly worked out in terms of both thematic structure and orchestration, its lavish design is fitting for so opulent a film and presages the achievements of Erich Korngold and the great composers of Hollywood scores in the sound period."[34] The musicologist and conductor Gillian Anderson proclaims it "a landmark in the history of motion picture music."[35] However, Wilson's music—including his intricate *The Thief of Bagdad* score—is seldom performed.

The world premiere of *The Thief of Bagdad* was held at the Liberty Theatre in New York City on March 18, 1924. A crowd of five thousand gathered outside the theater for a glimpse of Fairbanks and Pickford. F. Ray Comstock and Morris Gest managed the elaborate road show engagement. Gest, a master showman in the spirit of his father-in-law, David Belasco, was hired by Fairbanks at great expense to oversee all the American road show presentations of the film, which boasted "full scenic and stage effects, a band of Arabian musicians, with the instruments of their native country, as well as a Mohammedan Prayer Man."[36] Fairbanks was active in all aspects of the exhibition and exploitation of his films, even down to such details as the number of billboards to reserve.[37]

"It is an entrancing picture, wholesome and beautiful, deliberate but compelling, a feat of motion picture art which has never been equaled and one which itself will enthrall persons time and again," Mordaunt Hall wrote in the *New York Times*.[38] Hall made mention of Gest's elaborate presentation and the fact that the theater was given "a thoroughly Oriental atmosphere, with drums, ululating vocal offerings, odiferous

incense, perfume from Bagdad, magic carpets, and ushers in Arabian attire, who during the intermission made a brave effort to bear cups of Turkish coffee to the women in the audience."[39]

The *New York Herald Tribune* declared it "the greatest thing that ever has been put on the screen!"[40] *Photoplay* also gave the film a rapturous review:

Here is magic. Here is beauty. Here is the answer to the cynics who give the motion picture no place in the family of arts. Here is all the color and fantasy of the greatest work of imaginative literature, *Arabian Nights,* done so beautifully, so perfectly, that it is an everlasting credit to its producer and an everlasting joy to those who see it. Into the words of this great classic, Douglas Fairbanks has blown the breath of life. . . . It is a work of rare genius, and the entire industry, as well as the public, owes him a debt of gratitude.[41]

Robert E. Sherwood wrote in *Life* magazine that *The Thief of Bagdad* was "the top" of movie art: "There may well be higher peaks than that achieved by *The Thief of Bagdad*—but if there are, they have not as yet been charted on any of the existing contour maps. . . . Fairbanks has gone far beyond the mere bounds of possibility: he has performed the superhuman feat of making his magic seem probable."[42]

Carl Sandburg wrote in the *Chicago Daily News:* "Probably no one photoplay since the motion picture business and art got going has been greeted so enthusiastically in the circles known as highbrow and lowbrow. . . . Douglas Fairbanks is the producer of it, also the leading player, and it represents the quintessence and distillation of what he has learned about movies since he started in, among the first of the film workers." Like many others, Sandburg saw the film more than once; the following year, he called it a "masterpiece" and "a rare, brilliant picture that sort of wakes us up and at the same time makes us a little sleepy—a glad and mysterious picture, this one, *The Thief of Bagdad*."[43]

In a 1926 article titled "The Great Douglas Fairbanks," the poet and film aesthetician Vachel Lindsay recommended seeing *The Thief of Bagdad* ten times, as he had; he called it "architecture-in-motion" and "sculpture-in-motion," two of Lindsay's own film aesthetic values, which were on ample display in the film. "I say that in *The Thief of Bagdad* and *The Black Pirate*, Douglas is fighting like a gentleman and a scholar for Griffith's place," Lindsay proclaimed. "The history of the movies is now David Wark Griffith, Douglas Fairbanks, and whoever rises hereafter to dispute their title."[44]

Although the reviews were ecstatic, the film was not the success in general release that Fairbanks had anticipated. Audiences preferred him in simpler stories with less fantasy. The film historian Benjamin Hampton wrote in 1931:

But beautiful as it was, *The Thief of Bagdad* suffered from the same weakness as Griffith's *Intolerance:* it was too much entertainment for an audience to assimilate. Too many superb settings, too many great mobs, too many chapters shifting rapidly from one to another. The ordinary brain could not absorb in one evening all the glories that Fairbanks offered, and the average patron left the theater rather bewildered by the amazing spectacle.

Films like *The Thief of Bagdad*, *Ben-Hur: A Tale of the Christ*, and *The King of Kings* were nevertheless "noteworthy achievements of the American civilization that inspired them," Hampton declared.[45]

In his 1962 book *The Movies in the Age of Innocence*, Edward Wagenknecht assesses *The Thief of Bagdad*'s lackluster box office and critical revisionism thus:

The great Fairbanks films came in a bad period. The old, specious wartime idealism had sagged, imagination had sagged with it, and producers were showing a sad tendency to confine themselves not only to the contemporary but even to the duller aspects of the contemporary. Fairbanks was not alone in resisting this tendency. . . . But the influence of his example was great, and none of the others came within hailing distance of his work.[46]

The surrealists, of course, adored Art Nouveau. Jean Goudal praised *The Thief of Bagdad* "for that faerie [*féerie*] Marvelous . . . the essential elements of which [are] the *geometry of line* and the *illogicality of detail*," citing two images in particular: "the gate of the town that opens and closes through the connecting and disconnecting of identically formed panels, and Douglas Fairbanks soaring above the unreal clouds on his scleroid horse."[47]

Maurice Bardèche and Robert Brasillach in *The History of Motion Pictures* were the first to put forward the idea that Fairbanks in *The Thief of Bagdad* "almost succeeded in burying himself under the sets and the props."[48] Alistair Cooke's influential monograph, published two years later, developed this critical line against the film, preferring the earlier, less-pretentious Fairbanks films. *The Thief of Bagdad*'s sheer size "suffocated the old beloved sprite in a mess of décor," Cooke opined; its hero, he wrote, was "a boy grotesquely buried in a library of costume."[49] Cooke explained that for those who knew the "slap-happy, All-American" Doug, *The Thief of Bagdad* "didn't click. A world public that knew and loved the pattern of Fairbanks' heroics was impatient of overlong romantic and processional pauses in between the gymnastics."[50] Other critics have followed Cooke's lead. "The armies of period historians, costume designers, special effects men and art directors . . . do not support their leader so much as swamp him," Alexander Walker writes. "Where once he danced on air, Doug now stands on ceremony."[51]

Conversely, David Robinson and Richard Schickel see the film as Fairbanks's masterpiece. Robinson wrote in 1973:

In fact Fairbanks is never, I feel, dwarfed or dominated by the monumental settings he devised. He was simply working on a larger stage, in a larger gymnasium. . . . In fact, *The Thief of Bagdad* now seems one of Fairbanks' best, most accomplished, and certainly durable pictures. With absolute deliberation he places himself in gigantic settings—the Cave of Fire, for instance, or the battle with the dragon—in which his minuscule figure remains always the focus of activity. No distance can reduce the indomitable vitality of the unmistakable figure.[52]

"*The Thief of Bagdad* is unquestionably Fairbanks's masterpiece," Schickel opined in an interview.[53]

Part of the difficulty in properly appreciating *The Thief of Bagdad* involves the varying quality of the presentations of the film. The film's copyright was not renewed, and *The Thief of Bagdad* has thus fallen into the public domain. As a result, the prints circulating are not always of the best quality. Furthermore, many do not adhere to the original tints and are simply black-and-white. James Card, the first curator of the motion picture collection at George Eastman House, laments:

There are so few of the basic classics around that even have a vague resemblance to the original. Fairbanks's *Thief of Bagdad* is an example; in a poor print, this film is nothing. But seeing one of those original release prints, with the blending of the tinting and the dawn effects, where the color comes slowly into the clouds and slowly fades out again—it's just an extraordinary experience. No black and white duplicate, however beautifully graded, can equal it. Anything less than that is just not that film—it's some other film. You can't take a painting of Titian's, for example, as a cheap color reproduction in a book, and have the slightest conception of what the painting is like in reality.[54]

Also, the film often contends with less-than-ideal musical accompaniment. To accompany *The Thief of Bagdad* with a lone piano or even a theater organ is comparable to mounting a ballet with simply a keyboard for musical support. Fortunately, *The Thief of Bagdad* has been revived occasionally under ideal conditions. Memorable screenings were held at the Dominion Theatre in London in December 1984 and at Radio City Music Hall in New York City in March 1987 with a musical score by Carl Davis based on the compositions of Rimsky-Korsakov and performed by seventy-three musicians. (*The Thief of Bagdad* with Davis's score was also broadcast on British and American television.)

The Thief of Bagdad has influenced nearly every subsequent *Arabian Nights*–inspired film, including the early feature-length animated film by Lotte Reiniger, *Die Abenteuer des Prinzen Achmed* (*The Adventures of Prince Achmed*, 1926); Alexander Korda's production of *The Thief of Bagdad* (1940), with Menzies as associate producer and involved with the design; *Sinbad the Sailor* (1947), starring Douglas Fairbanks Jr.; several Ray Harryhausen films; and Pier Paolo Pasolini's *Il fiore delle Mille e una notte* (*Arabian Nights*, 1974). Korda's superb *The Thief of Bagdad* is a classic of its kind, but one of the film's directors, Michael Powell, conceded that Fairbanks's film was inimitable, declaring: "From Fairbanks, I learnt to be satisfied with nothing but the best."[55]

The Thief of Bagdad did not equal the gross of Robin Hood, and for his next film project Fairbanks took on the less ambitious Don Q Son of Zorro. However, The Thief of Bagdad was Fairbanks's favorite of all his films and continues to hold that place among his admirers.[56] The film remains a testament to the best of Hollywood creativity and imagination, and Fairbanks's leadership role with respect to the film's innovations and artistry cannot be overestimated.

The Son Also Rises

Don Q Son of Zorro (1925) and Douglas Fairbanks Jr.

D*on Q Son of Zorro*, Fairbanks's sequel to his first great swash-buckling success, *The Mark of Zorro*, not only recaptures much of the latter's charm and vitality but is an entertaining and vital work in its own right. Despite the inevitable echoes of the earlier film, there are also several marked differences. Instead of assuming a dual identity as he had in *The Mark of Zorro*, Fairbanks plays dual roles here: Don Diego Vega, thirty years later, and his 20-year-old son, Cesar.[1] This film is not as fast-paced as *The Mark of Zorro*, nor is the star himself; Fairbanks's athleticism is now firmly subordinated to the graceful movements of a dancer. Indeed, Fairbanks described the film as "a romantic melodrama," rather than his typical swashbuckling adventure.[2] What *Don Q Son of Zorro* may lack in action and spontaneity is compensated for with a greater sense of cinematic sophistication, the grandeur of the art direction, and a superb cast. With his extraordinary lithe figure, the 42-year-old Fairbanks convincingly plays Cesar, Zorro's high-spirited son, who is depicted in the film as being slightly more than half the actor-producer's age. However, off-screen, Fairbanks's illusory image of perpetual youth was waning with the emergence of Douglas Fairbanks Jr. as a rising star in Hollywood. This development was a source of considerable vexation to Fairbanks and strained relations between father and son.

After the relative financial disappointment of *The Thief of Bagdad*, Fairbanks wanted to produce a sure-fire hit and determined the timing was right to revisit Zorro. He had previously secured the rights to

Cesar lights his cigarette with the end of his whip in *Don Q Son of Zorro*.

Fairbanks as Don Cesar de Vega in *Don Q Son of Zorro*.

Fairbanks as the elder Don Diego de Vega in *Don Q Son of Zorro*.

Johnston McCulley's sequel, "The Further Adventures of Zorro," which
appeared in 1922 in *Argosy All-Story Weekly*, intending to use this as the
basis for his eventual *Mark of Zorro* sequel. He instead hired Jack Cunningham, who had prepared the scenario for the western epic *The Covered Wagon,* to adapt Kate and Hesketh Prichard's novel *Don Q's Love
Story* as the basis for the screenplay. (Fairbanks revisited and revised
"The Further Adventures of Zorro" for *The Black Pirate* the following
year.) His stalwart husband and wife scenario staff, Lotta Woods and
Dr. Arthur Woods, again worked as scenario editor and research director, respectively. *Don Q Son of Zorro,* set in Spain, involves Cesar being
falsely accused of murdering an Austrian archduke (foreshadowing the
impetus for World War I) and his father's traveling in haste from California to aid his son and clear the family name. The theme of the film,
"Truth crushed to earth shall rise again if you have the yeast to make it
rise,"[3] was a twist on a famous quotation from the poet William Cullen
Bryant; Fairbanks supplied the conditional clause himself.

The British character actor Donald Crisp, who had established himself as the villainous Battling Burrows in D. W. Griffith's *Broken Blossoms* and would later go on to play fatherly roles in *How Green Was My*

Leaving a lovers' tryst, Cesar
is summoned to the palace
by order of the queen.

Valley (1941) and *Lassie Come Home* (1943), was engaged as the film's
nominal director. In addition to *Don Q Son of Zorro*, Crisp's best-known
directing credit is Buster Keaton's *The Navigator* (1924). Additionally,
Crisp was asked by Fairbanks to play the role of Don Sebastian. Fairbanks joked that if he was to play two parts, so would Crisp. Furthermore, Fairbanks believed that the actor-director might guide the cast
to better effect when closely operating with them in the action.[4]

The leading lady for Fairbanks's new film was the 18-year-old Mary
Astor, who had appeared with John Barrymore in *Beau Brummel* (1924)
and went on to appear again with Barrymore in *Don Juan* (1926), as well
as in other classic films, such as *The Prisoner of Zenda* (1937) and *The
Maltese Falcon*. The Swedish actor Warner Oland (best known for his
portrayal of Charlie Chan in a series of films in the 1930s) was given the
sympathetic role of the Archduke Paul. The Danish actor Jean Hersholt,
who had memorably played the despicable Marcus in Erich von Stroheim's *Greed* (1924), was engaged to play the unscrupulous schemer

Don Fabrique Borusta. Albert MacQuarrie, who had memorably played the manservant Hobson in *When the Clouds Roll By,* among his many small roles in Fairbanks films, was casting director of the production and cast himself as Colonel Matsado. Fairbanks's sister-in-law, Lottie Pickford Forrest, was engaged as the servant girl Lola; she had appeared in a similar part as a maid in *Dorothy Vernon of Haddon Hall* (1924), the most Fairbanksian of the Mary Pickford films, and no doubt she was hired as a gesture to please his wife.

Arthur Edeson's contract with Fairbanks had expired with *The Thief of Bagdad,* and he opted for a position with First National. Henry Sharp, for more than six years chief cinematographer for Thomas H. Ince Studios, was engaged as cinematographer for *Don Q Son of Zorro* and later made three more films with Fairbanks. In a 1963 interview, Sharp described his association with Fairbanks as "the great thing in my career." Sharp recalled, "Fairbanks ran a picture I had just done for Ince called *Enticement* [1925] in order to see Mary Astor, as he was thinking of using her as the female lead role in *Don Q.* She was hired, and after I met with Robert Fairbanks, Doug's brother and general manager at the studio, Ted Reed, his production manager, and Doug, they hired me as well."[5]

In addition to using camera illusions to effectively achieve his dual role, Fairbanks enlisted the prominent makeup artists Perc and Ern Westmore to handle all aspects of the production's makeup and hairdressing demands. (For a week Fairbanks shaved off his famous moustache in order to play Don Diego Vega.) The costume designer Paul Burns devised four costumes for the trim Fairbanks; as Cesar, Fairbanks is memorably attired in tight-fitting, bell-bottomed trousers, bolero jacket, and wide, flat-brimmed hat.

Fairbanks garnered ideas for the sets depicting Madrid for *Don Q Son of Zorro* as a result of his close involvement with Pickford's production of *Rosita* (1923), directed by Ernst Lubitsch, which was set in Seville. Edward M. Langley was supervising art director of *Don Q Son of Zorro*, with Francesc Cugat, Anton Grot, and Harold W. Miles as art dirctors, and Harry Oliver as consulting artist. All of the designers Fairbanks employed had their own important specialties. For example, Cugat, reportedly from Barcelona, was invaluable in ensuring the authenticity of the sets, while Oliver confined himself to the dressing of finished sets. Thirty-five sets were created for the film in all, many of which appear on an operatic scale, including memorable rooms in the royal palace, a students' club, narrow, winding streets typical of Spain, and a peculiar inn, as well as a faithful re-creation of Don Diego Vega's California home as it appeared in *The Mark of Zorro*. Perhaps the most challenging sets were those for the ruins of the Vega ancestral castle, which involved full-scale construction (one reaching the height of 125 feet), as well as models and glass shots.

Fairbanks had been impressed by the manner in which the Belgian fencing master Fred Cavens handled the fight choreography in the French comedian Max Linder's burlesque of the Fairbanks version of *The Three Musketeers*, entitled *The Three Must-Get-Theres* (1922). When Pickford enlisted Cavens's expertise for *Dorothy Vernon of Haddon Hall*, Fairbanks met the Belgian and secured his services to choreograph all the swordplay for *Don Q Son of Zorro*. However, although there is much swordplay in the film, it is Fairbanks's mastery of the Australian stock whip that dominates all of his fight sequences.

The Australian stock whip, a long, sinuous lash fastened to a short handle, was the novelty of the film and made the production particularly interesting for Fairbanks. He trained with Reginald "Snowy" Baker, arguably Australia's greatest all-around athlete, for six weeks to master the weapon. Douglas Fairbanks Jr. remembered, "It didn't take long before Dad was able to whirl the long blacksnake, make it crack like a pistol shot, and then snap a cigarette out of a brave and steady mouth fifteen or more feet away."[6]

Fairbanks family lore suggests Fairbanks's fascination with whips originated with "Hardrock," an old prospector dexterous with a mule whip whom Fairbanks fondly remembered from his youth in Colorado.[7] In Fairbanks's hand, the whip becomes an appendage to his character

Fairbanks practices the Australian stock whip during production.

of Cesar, and with it he is able to break a bottle in half, slice in two an invitation to the archduke's ball (and later the contract for a forced marriage), extinguish a lighted candle, disarm a swordsman, capture a runaway bull charging through a populated city square, swing, mount, and vault various walls, light a cigarette, coil the ruthless Colonel Matsado into submission, remove a cigarette from Don Fabrique's mouth, and lash Don Sebastian to defeat.

The ability of Fairbanks the actor to master such weapons in itself is admirable. However, it was also to the credit of Fairbanks the producer-showman that he was able to find unusual items that were, to quote the film historian Paul Rotha, "essentially filmic." Rotha explained: "At first glance, these gestures may be explained by the Fairbanks enthusiasm, but they are to be attributed to more important reasons than the sheer love of doing things right. He saw in those accomplishments some basis for filmic actions other than mere acrobatics. He realised that the actions were superbly graceful in their natural perfection, as indeed are any gestures born out of utility."[8]

The action of the film unfolds with Don Cesar de Vega (Fairbanks) of California honoring family tradition by journeying to Madrid for a period of travel and study. His skill with his distinctive whip brings him to the attention of the queen (Stella De Lanti) and her visiting cousin, Archduke Paul of Austria (Warner Oland). But the whip also brings him into conflict with the vicious Don Sebastian (Donald Crisp) of the Queen's Guard. Cesar falls in love with Dolores de Muro (Mary Astor), whose father is lord chamberlain of the royal household and a trusted

Cesar crosses swords with Don Sebastian (Donald Crisp) in *Don Q Son of Zorro* as members of the students' club watch from above.

Don Fabrique (Jean Hersholt) gets his nose tweaked by Cesar as Archduke Paul (Warner Oland) looks on with approval.

advisor to the queen. At the archduke's ball, while Cesar pledges his love to Dolores, Don Sebastian assassinates the archduke and frames Cesar for the murder. A witness, Don Fabrique Borusta (Jean Hersholt), holds the important playing card upon which the archduke has written the name of his assassin before his death. The crafty Don Fabrique retains the card as blackmail against Don Sebastian in order to advance his own interests. Cesar feigns his own death and retreats to the ruins of the Vega ancestral castle, where he plots to prove his innocence and redeem the family name. His father, famously known as Zorro, receives news of his son's plight at his home in California and recalls his own battles and the sword with which he righted wrongs in the past. In a flashback, a brief sequence from *The Mark of Zorro* is shown with Zorro hurling his sword into a wall and declaring, "Till I need you again!" The elder Zorro removes his sword from high above, where it has been lodged for many years, and journeys to Spain to aid his son. Meanwhile, Cesar, posing as "Don Q" (hence the film's title) bests the ruthless one-eyed commander Colonel Matsado (Albert MacQuarrie) and disguises himself as the latter in order to get vital information to prove his innocence. In a climactic standoff, Zorro stands side by side with his beleaguered son to valiantly defend the family honor, and the Vega name is ultimately cleared. The film concludes with Cesar paying homage to his father's famous "Have you seen this one?" legerdemain; he reveals Dolores concealed behind a cape and embraces her at the fadeout.

Mary Astor had had a lively affair with her leading man John Barrymore and evidently expected similar attention from Fairbanks during the production of the film. Instead, as she later recalled, Fairbanks "was nice to me, in the way a sophisticated man about town would be nice to a small and reasonably well-behaved child."[9] Despite their relationship off-screen, the two share a charming romantic sequence in the film, in which Cesar serenades Dolores with a guitar and later leaps to her window, where he recites from the balcony scene from *Romeo and Juliet* ("With love's light wings did I o'er-perch these walls"). He also gently reads her palm. As with many of Fairbanks's leading ladies, Astor remembered that he "seemed to be awkward, and almost embarrassed in his love scenes, but he flung himself into his athletic scenes with a wholehearted gusto. He was a perfectionist in them."[10]

Not every athletic scene was perfect. Fairbanks may still have been able to look the part of a 20-year-old, but not every stunt was achieved with the illusion of effortlessness. Alistair Cooke notes that when Fairbanks uses the whip to swing from a wall, there is a "steadying stumble" when he lands. It is, Cooke concedes, "slight but so untypical" of Fairbanks—the first time anything less than perfection was allowed into a finished Fairbanks film.[11] Fairbanks was literally and figuratively slipping. He could no longer manage the fine, careless rapture of the earlier films, so as a result, the stunts were created to highlight the elegance of the movement as opposed to the sheer physical feat.

The production proceeded with the same snap Fairbanks gave to the stock whip. The elaborate charts Fairbanks innovated for his films had been further developed to satisfy his desire for greater efficiencies. Just

Cesar falls in love with Dolores de Muro (Mary Astor).

as Chaplin, Buster Keaton, and Harold Lloyd did not use scripts in the accepted sense, Fairbanks eschewed conventional scripts; he favored charts instead. Indeed, Fairbanks refined the scenarios of his films as he went along, using collaborators and friends as sounding boards for his ideas. Ted Reed explained in 1925:

The blueprint of the shooting schedule is also a tabulation. It is built up in column after column under two headings only, "Set" and "Action." Take the schedule for *Don Q Son of Zorro*. The set may be "Interior Ruined Castle" or it may be "Archduke's Servant Corridor." What to do in "Interior Ruined Castle" or in "Archduke's Servant Corridor" is as easy as finding a telephone number. Under "Action," right opposite the name of the set, one may read: "Lola tells Cesar about Robledo and leaves with rose for Dolores." Then the director proceeds to "shoot" [the scene]. . . . He takes it from several angles, the next evening looks at the result on the screen, and if Fairbanks "O.K.'s" them, the stroke of a red pencil strikes out this scene from the "Shooting Schedule." When the blueprint is all red marks the camera work is finished.[12]

Though cracking the whip was a defining attribute of the character he was portraying, when others, most specifically his director, made attempts to apply that idea in the figurative sense with Fairbanks, they did not get the desired effect. "Tell him to do something and he'd take the whole afternoon off and play Doug," Donald Crisp recalled.[13] Crisp would then have to explain to Robert Fairbanks, as general manager, why the production had fallen a day behind schedule. There were, however, few such days as this, and production ended in April 1925, with a total production cost of $496,958.82.[14]

The world premiere of *Don Q Son of Zorro* was held June 15, 1925, inaugurating an eight-week engagement at the Globe Theatre in New York City before a run at the Strand Theatre. Fairbanks was not present for the premiere. Mark Larkin, publicity director for the Fairbanks organization, and Harry D. Buckley, Fairbanks's special business representative, handled the premiere showing, which included a memorable prologue of Fred Lindsay with the stock whip (which he would later repeat for the initial Los Angeles engagement) and a serviceable musical score by Mortimer Wilson. Radio, billboards, a YMCA circular tie-in, and a Grosset & Dunlap book tie-in were part of the marketing strategy. The campaign also had to counter the idea that *Don Q Son of Zorro* had anything to do with *Don Quixote*. "*Don Q Son of Zorro* is not at all related, as many have thought, to the Cervantes masterpiece *Don Quixote*," the film's pressbook is at pains to convey.[15]

Critical reaction was strong. Mordaunt Hall wrote in the *New York Times*:

Don Q Son of Zorro is just as full of new ideas as the average Fairbanks effort.... It is a swift picture with plenty of pleasing surprises and action. Mr. Fairbanks appears to have trained down to a very slender figure for the part. He springs into the saddle with amazing ease, and never makes a false move. It is an ideal part for Mr. Fairbanks, who as usual has put in no end of work in mastering the great whip as well as in showing that he is just as agile as he was years ago when he first startled audiences by his remarkable leaps.... This is a photoplay which creates no end of mirth and sustains the interest all through.[16]

Variety proclaimed: "Douglas Fairbanks is back again, and back with a picture that is Doug at his best.... it is a picture that has been designed for the Fairbanks fans.... it is Fairbanks as the public wants Fairbanks." *Variety* thought the direction "splendid and there isn't a lagging minute in the picture." The *Variety* reviewer closed his review with a comment suggesting the meticulous preparation of the film prints, as well as further indicating Fairbanks's interest in color cinematography: "The photography is excellent and there is some footage that appears to be hand colored in a manner that is most effective."[17]

Cesar wards off the Queen's Guard as he defends himself and the family name.

The film opened at Grauman's Million Dollar Theatre in Los Angeles on January 28, 1926. Fairbanks was present, took to the stage, and introduced his special guests, Mary Pickford and Charles Chaplin, both of whom spoke briefly. Donald Crisp, Warner Oland, and Jean Hersholt were also in attendance. Edwin Schallert of the *Los Angeles Times* praised the film as "one of Douglas Fairbanks's cleverest and most spirited of film divertissements. . . . he has returned to the light sort of adventure story which, in many respects, resembles his earlier productions, and yet also incorporates a picturesque and romantic flavor that is characteristic of his more recent films," while also noting that when the action "lags," the plot is mechanical.[18]

"If the little boys in the front row promise not to scream, Douglas Fairbanks will blindfold his eyes and, with one flick of the whip, put out a candle," the *Photoplay* review began. "The story is lively but clumsy; it is full of over-seeing and over-hearing and dark doings. But as it is laid

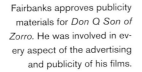
Fairbanks approves publicity materials for *Don Q Son of Zorro*. He was involved in every aspect of the advertising and publicity of his films.

in the beautiful and mythical Spain of romance, it has the advantage of taking place in a rich and gorgeous background. And Mr. Fairbanks, in Spanish clothes doing a Spanish dance, is a sight to behold. In fact, in all his pantomime, he's really more of a dancer than an actor."[19]

Motion Picture Classic noted the narcissism of Fairbanks in the two roles. "Thus as the white-haired Zorro, he applauds himself as the brisk and militant Don Q. A situation after an actor's own heart, indeed." The reviewer thought that the film was too long at ten reels and "lacks much of the spontaneity of *The Mark of Zorro*," but felt compelled "to go on record as endorsing *Don Q* as quite cheery entertainment, very well done."[20]

Iris Barry, future curator of the Department of Film at the Museum of Modern Art, wrote in the London *Spectator*:

This rapid, almost Mozartian picture is very closely akin, in another medium, to those newer ballets, like *Les Matelots*, which the Diaghilev company have invented. The patterns which the slender black figure of Fairbanks makes in the unbounded scene of the cinema are as rhythmical as the equally, practically, almost everyday movements of the Diaghilev dancers . . . he is no longer the purely-athletic film star he once was, any more than ballet-dancers are pure athletes. His movements are almost poetically graceful, and what is more they are infused with a light spirit of comedy. He is not the close friend of Chaplin for nothing.[21]

Beginning with *The Thief of Bagdad*, the ambiance of Fairbanks's celluloid world was evolving. Clearly evident in *Don Q Son of Zorro* is the shift away from the athleticism of the earlier stunts in favor of movement that accentuated Fairbanks's grace. Some critics have found the change unsettling. "It is even painful to see the unconscious athlete taking second place to a self-conscious narcissist, for this diminishes him spiritually," Alexander Walker observes. "It is the difference between an acrobat and a muscle-builder."[22]

Despite some excellent sequences, Fairbanks's use of the Australian stock whip, impressive production values, and a talented cast, *Don Q Son of Zorro* remains one of his lesser costume films. The fact that the film is a sequel is not the problem (Fairbanks frequently recycled his basic ideas). Rather, *Don Q Son of Zorro*, unlike *Robin Hood* and *The Thief of Bagdad*, suffers from simplistic characters and one-dimensional plot points, although these are somewhat disguised by the expert cast and elaborate scenery. Jean Hersholt's Don Fabrique Borusta and Donald Crisp's Don Sebastian are given far too much screen time for characters that never develop past their introductions into the story (both are corrupt from beginning to end). Fairbanks himself is much more convincing as the son than as the father, a character closer to his actual age. Although a father himself, with a son nearly the age of his fictional counterpart, Fairbanks was never comfortable playing the paternal role.

As a representation of the dynamics of a father-son relationship, *Don Q Son of Zorro* is an exemplar; Cesar reveres his father, and his father, the great Zorro, beams with pride at his son's accomplishments. It is an idyllic relationship, and not representational of the real-life dynamic between the Senior and Junior Fairbanks. While Douglas Fairbanks Jr. idolized his father, the latter had a difficult time conceding any amount of his glory to anyone, most particularly someone whose very name was a threat to his singular identity (and a reminder of his own advancing maturity).

Even in the early days of his son's life, Fairbanks admitted to being at a loss for any kind of paternal feelings. Indeed, he confessed that he had "no more paternal feeling than a lion has for his cubs."[23] Unquestionably much of this indifference is rooted in his own fatherless upbringing and lack of example. However, he managed to inflict upon his own son the very wound his mother had inflicted upon him. Embarrassed by his son's chubby appearance, he at first distanced himself from the boy and neglected him. As a result, his mother, Beth, rather than his father, was the omnipresent force during the early life of Douglas Fairbanks Jr. Beth Fairbanks was dominating and possessive but also loving and generous. She made certain that her son received the validation he needed but insisted that her former husband never be viewed in a negative light. "Her determination in my youth that I should love and respect my father and avoid bitterness on her behalf and instead understand and appreciate his situation was a wonderful way you minimize the psychological problems someone so young as I might face with his family breaking up," Douglas Fairbanks Jr. observed.[24] Throughout his life, he refused to concede that there had been any deliberate unkindness on his father's part. While he whitewashed some facts in his role as custodian of his father's legacy, it cannot be forgotten that the latter was the hero of adolescent boys throughout America, a club from which his son was certainly not excluded. "I was too shy, too plump and awkward, and he was such an evanescent sprite. . . . My hero worship of him made me even shyer."[25]

Perhaps "my pudgy mama's boy image influenced him to keep a benign distance from me," Douglas Fairbanks Jr. surmised. "Although I failed to win any real affection from him, it never occurred to me to feel sorry for myself. I minded, of course, but in silence."[26] If it was just a matter of physical appearance, then once his physically awkward period was past, all should have been well. This was not, of course, the case. As the son grew up, and it became increasingly apparent that he was going to equal, indeed surpass, his father's physical beauty, the relationship became even more strained. As Brian Connell writes in his authorized biography of Douglas Fairbanks Jr.: "For the first dozen years of his life young Douglas was subjected to his father's indifference; for most of the second decade to almost pathological opposition to his development as a screen personality; and in his third decade fought an uphill battle to win the confidence and friendship of a parent whose social and professional reputation decreased as his own grew."[27]

If his pre-adolescent son was an embarrassment to his father's fitness fanaticism, his post-adolescent son, long and lean, with blue eyes, blond hair, and an impossibly beautiful countenance, was an even worse nightmare for the elder Fairbanks: a newer and *improved* Douglas Fairbanks. Not that the son's entrance into the motion picture industry was the natural progression that one might believe. As Douglas Fairbanks Jr. remembered: "A friend of the family's, who was a stage actor and producer, said to mother, 'I think I can get Douglas a job at Paramount, in the movies.' My father heard about it and thought I was to make films for the fun of it. As far as I was concerned, it was going to be fun as I knew it was going to be better than going to school. It was quite awhile before my father knew the real reason."[28]

The real reason was that after Beth Fairbanks's disastrous marriage to the stockbroker James Evans Jr., who speculated with her divorce settlement, the family found itself in dire financial straits. When an offer came from Jesse L. Lasky, Beth readily agreed, and Douglas Fairbanks Jr. was delighted at the idea. Furthermore, a movie offer assured more contact with his father.

The reason for Lasky was simple: "My motives?" he remembered. "Douglas Fairbanks was the greatest name in [the] picture business. This was a commercial proposition to capitalize on his name."[29] It was also an opportunity to irritate Douglas Fairbanks Sr.[30] Simultaneous films in release might prove devastating at the box office for the latter; Douglas Fairbanks Jr. as a movie star suggested that his father was a much older man than his image suggested and also served as a reminder of his first marriage and divorce. Fairbanks said of his son: "He's too young and doesn't really know what he's doing. I wanted him to have the best education possible, but I don't think that's possible now. You can't work in pictures and attend a university at the same time."[31]

Shortly before his launch into films, the son met his father in Paris. "We were always embarrassed, self-conscious, and undemonstrative in each other's company," Douglas Fairbanks Jr. recalled of their early relationship.[32] However, on this occasion, they succeeded in having their one and only heated argument, in which his father "became very angry with me. He believed I was too young and should be in school and that I was being used for my name alone. We argued back and forth. I was stubborn—perhaps even rude—but held my own. I left knowing he disapproved of me and that he really didn't want to have anything further to do with me."[33]

Douglas Fairbanks Jr.'s first starring vehicle, *Stephen Steps Out* (1923), was not a success, and after a few more minor efforts, he was released from his contract. He then began visiting the Pickford-Fairbanks Studios in an effort to repair his relationship with his mercurial father. Exercising with the latter was the best means to that end. When he was exercising, Douglas Fairbanks Sr. was at his best. However, his son's increasing athletic proficiency as a result of these workouts, coupled with his youthful energy, began to threaten his father's long-held illusion of ageless virility. It became apparent that it would be difficult, if not impossible, for the elder Fairbanks to continue to cast himself as a 20-year-old when there was a younger, better-looking version available.

At sixteen, Douglas Fairbanks Jr. looked twenty-one. The director Henry King hired him for an important role in Samuel Goldwyn's production of *Stella Dallas* (1925), in which his character wears a moustache similar to his father's. King recalled receiving a telephone call from Douglas Fairbanks Sr., who was unhappy to hear that his son was to appear in a film with a moustache. "But, Henry, I'm still in pictures—don't make him look too old!"[34] To Donald Crisp, who directed Douglas Fairbanks Jr. in *Man Bait* (1926), Douglas Fairbanks Sr. snarled, "There's only *one* Fairbanks."[35] A tension grew between the two men, perhaps a contributing factor in Crisp not being assigned to direct *The Black Pirate* (although he is prominently featured in the film's cast). Despite the friction between father and son, Douglas Fairbanks Sr. was occasionally persuaded by his brother Robert or by Pickford to invite his son to Pickfair to swim in the pool. Less frequent were dinner invitations. Douglas Fairbanks Jr. later reflected:

It was unfortunate that my father was hesitant at demonstrating any paternal feeling to me in those first years in Hollywood. . . . He forgot my fourteenth birthday, and Christmas and forgot me again on both occasions the following year. . . . I was hurt. Embarrassed really. I wouldn't admit it either. If someone asked what he'd given me, I'd point to something wonderful and say, "that." Of course, he made up for it in my mind when he gave me my first car for my sixteenth birthday. I believed then and believe now they were simply oversights on his part because my father could never be consciously unkind to anyone.[36]

One of the turning points in the life of Douglas Fairbanks Jr. and the relationship between father and son arrived with his stage debut at the Belasco Theatre in Los Angeles in the John Van Druten play *Young Woodley*. The opening night, held October 17, 1927, was a glittering event with Douglas Fairbanks Sr., Pickford, Chaplin, and Gloria Swanson among the Hollywood elite in attendance. Douglas Fairbanks Jr. garnered the praise of skeptical critics, and after six weeks in Los Angeles, the play went on to a six-week engagement in San Francisco. The young Fairbanks received further encouragement from his father in the form of a first edition of Henry Irving's lectures, *The Drama,* dedicated: "To Junior 'Let your own discretion be your tutor.' Dad 1927—The occasion being your first appearance on the dramatic stage."[37]

Seated among the many luminaries on the opening night of *Young Woodley* was a 22-year-old Metro-Goldwyn-Mayer starlet, Joan Crawford. She had yet to play the role that made her a star—that of Diana

Douglas Fairbanks Jr. in a scene from his first starring vehicle, *Stephen Steps Out* (1923).

Medford, the "Jazz Baby" in *Our Dancing Daughters* (1928)—but Crawford already had a reputation in Hollywood as an ambitious, hard-
working young actress who had risen from bit player to leading lady
in only two years. By her own admission, Crawford fell hard for the
play's handsome leading man and, as was her custom when she saw
something she wanted, she went after him. The two soon became
inseparable, and their ardent courtship also attracted much attention from the press. Although in the past he had largely ignored or remained silent about his son's exploits, romantic or otherwise, Douglas
Fairbanks Sr. had serious misgivings about the relationship. He re-
frained from direct confrontations, but he let it be known through others that he was not happy with what he considered an overexploited
affair, even after the couple made their union official on June 3, 1929,
in the chapel of St. Malachy's in New York City. The press the newlyweds generated must have hit a nerve; fan magazines referred to them
as Hollywood's other—younger—first couple. "Filmland's Royal Family,
Second Edition," *Photoplay* called them.[38] It was, as Crawford recalled,

a full year after their marriage before they were finally admitted into Douglas Fairbanks Sr.'s good graces at Pickfair and regular Sunday afternoon visits. Crawford called her father-in-law "Uncle Douglas" and remembered him warmly in her autobiography:

His sense of humor was that of a Walt Disney character, his poise absolute. The night of the first great ball to which we'd been invited, my debut as it were, I was descending the long staircase on Uncle Douglas' arm when the lady in back stepped on the train of my dress. I heard the rip, I felt it straight up my back. My grand manner faltered and began to rip too. Uncle Douglas never missed a step. He leaned back, swung my torn train over his arm and kept right on, suavely guiding me down and through the long line of guests. This man became my close friend and I loved him.[39]

Relations between father and son grew warmer as well. Though Douglas Fairbanks Jr. was carving out a respectable film career for himself, appearing in films such as Clarence Brown's *A Woman of Affairs* (1928), starring Greta Garbo, and opposite his wife in *Our Modern Maidens* (1929), it was apparent that, despite his prodigious gifts, he was no Douglas Fairbanks Sr. Although he surpassed his father in both looks and range of acting ability, he was never to equal his father in reputation or popularity. In the realm of the performing arts, he would always be "Junior." But this presented another problem. Douglas Fairbanks Jr. remembered:

Now that I was nearly twenty and married, it embarrassed him to call me Junior. So he used initials instead and I became, "Jayar." Correspondingly, he didn't want to be called Dad or Father and I certainly couldn't call him Senior. I was uncomfortable with Doug, a name he never really liked anyway. "What would you like to be called if you weren't called Doug?" I asked.

"Oh, I don't know . . . Peter, I guess."

So from then on I called him Pete.[40]

Regrettably, Douglas Fairbanks Sr. never overcame the difficulty of facing what Douglas Fairbanks Jr. represented rather than who he actually was as his son. Reflecting on relations between father and son, Mary Pickford was charitable to the elder Fairbanks:

Senior was so much of a little boy himself, I don't think he felt like a father. He was a very shy person, he didn't like to show af-

Newlyweds Douglas Fairbanks Jr. and Joan Crawford at the beach, 1929. Photograph by Clarence Sinclair Bull.

Douglas Fairbanks Jr. as the dissolute Jeffry Merrick and Greta Garbo as the fatalistic Diana Merrick in *A Woman of Affairs* (1928), an adaptation of Michael Arlen's popular novel *The Green Hat*. The M-G-M production, directed by Clarence Brown, was the younger Fairbanks's best work in the silent cinema.

fection or emotion. . . . There was this sense of misunderstanding between them, augmented undoubtedly by the greed of certain people that forced his son into a position that he didn't think was right. He felt at the time that the boy was being exploited, to his injury and hurt and the detriment of his father. When that was over, I know positively he was very proud of him.[41]

Throughout his long life, Douglas Fairbanks Jr. hero-worshiped his father, forgave him, and protected him in order to shield himself from the pain of their true relationship.

Derring-Do

The Black Pirate (1926)

T he Black Pirate was the most carefully prepared and controlled work of Fairbanks's entire career. It is the epitome of the motion picture art and science possible in the Hollywood of the 1920s. Whereas previous productions such as *Robin Hood* and *The Thief of Bagdad* utilized size and scope to push the limits of cinema production, *The Black Pirate* used the nascent technology of two-color Technicolor, once again demonstrating Fairbanks's leadership position within the film industry. He alone at the time possessed the artistry, vision, courage, and financial resources to shepherd to completion the most important feature-length silent film designed entirely for color cinematography. These assets gave the Fairbanks swashbuckler an added dimension and proved to be a vital step in the development of this burgeoning technology. In addition, Technicolor's inherent limitations and cost at the time had the effect of unfettering the Fairbanks production from pageantry and visual effects, thus producing what is in essence a straightforward action adventure film. The result was a refreshing return to form and a dazzling new showcase for the actor-producer's favorite production value: himself. Fairbanks is resplendent as the bold buccaneer and buoyed by a production brimming with rip-roaring adventure and spiced with exceptional stunts and swordplay, including the celebrated "sliding down the sails" sequence, arguably the most famous set piece of the entire Fairbanks treasure chest.

Fairbanks had first contemplated a film involving pirates in 1922 for his sequel to *The Mark of Zorro*. Encouragement to undertake a pirate

A portrait of Fairbanks on top of a massive treasure chest for *The Black Pirate*.

film came from an unlikely source: the child star Jackie Coogan, who had read *Howard Pyle's Book of Pirates* and ignited Fairbanks's enthusiasm for a pirate film after the two spoke at the *Photoplay* Awards in November 1922.[1] Fairbanks was captivated by Pyle's illustrations of buccaneering on the high seas; it brought to mind the swashbuckling stories of his youth. As a child, he had been interested in pirate lore and played pirate, most often relishing the role of Captain Kidd. However, in the back of his mind, he felt that to do a pirate story justice necessitated actual color cinematography rather than the standard practice of applying tints and tones to black-and-white film.[2]

Fairbanks was a shrewd showman who carefully followed the novelties and new motion picture technologies that might enhance his own screen spectaculars. Although he had, by this point in his career, become a cinema icon, he was always in search of a gimmick or unique selling point for his films. He had been impressed by the two-color Technicolor production *Toll of the Sea*, a feature-length film produced as sort of a demonstration by the Technicolor Corporation. However, there were inherent problems with the new technology. In 1922, Technicolor had no adequate means of supplying dailies or exhibition prints in a timely manner, owing to insufficient laboratory capacity in Hollywood. Undoubtedly, this would create a huge delay in production and exhibition, as well as place a tremendous strain on the film's budget. In addition, a plethora of pirate films were either in release or in production. After careful consideration, it was determined to concentrate on *The Thief of Bagdad*.

Fairbanks and his team revisited the Technicolor situation in May 1925. By that time, Technicolor had expanded its operations and had contracted with Famous Players–Lasky Corporation to make *Wanderer of the Wasteland* (1924) in the two-color Technicolor process. Fairbanks, however, had reservations about what he saw on the screen. He wrote at the time:

This ingredient [color] has been tried and rejected countless times. It has always met overwhelming objections. Not only has the process of color motion picture photography never been perfected, but there has been a grave doubt whether, even if properly developed, it could be applied, without detracting more than it added to motion picture technic. The argument has been that it would tire and distract the eye, take attention from acting, and facial expression, blur and confuse the action. In short it has been felt that it would militate against the simplicity and directness which motion pictures derive from the unobtrusive black and white. These conventional doubts have been entertained, I think, because no one has taken the trouble to dissipate them. . . . Personally I could not imagine piracy without color.[3]

According to Herbert T. Kalmus, the president and general manager of the Technicolor Corporation, Fairbanks and his attorneys pointed out that their production of *The Black Pirate* had an estimated cost of $1 million, and requested that Technicolor provide contractual assurances that it was able to deliver satisfactory prints. Fairbanks and his team had several meetings with the Technicolor team and conducted color tests before the final decision was made.[4]

Ultimately, Technicolor provided Fairbanks with four of the seven Technicolor cameras in existence at that time: two cameras side by side for principal photography (one created the domestic and the other the foreign negative), with an additional two cameras kept on hand as backup during production to ensure that there would be no delays should difficulties arise with any one of the cameras used.

Two-color Technicolor was a novelty in Hollywood and had been utilized in sequences in such important films as *The Ten Commandments, The Phantom of the Opera* (1925), and *Ben-Hur: A Tale of the Christ.* To Fairbanks, these sequences were far from satisfactory and had produced glaring, garish results. He had definite ideas about the design of his color film. The limitations of Technicolor were the chief obstacle. The two-color process did not reproduce colors accurately; blues registered as green, and yellows as orange. Fairbanks disliked the bright hues and sought a more subdued approach.

The Black Pirate was the first major Hollywood film designed totally for color in which the experimental and expensive process was first carefully tested. Fairbanks's motivation—beyond the fact that he could not imagine his pirate film without color—was the challenge of further pioneering cinematic art and science. The Technicolor aspect of the production was a questionable selling point with audiences. Some people were fearful of excessive eyestrain from color film. However, Fairbanks was confident the public could be swayed by the undeniable artistry of his production. His compositions—created in an almost painterly fashion—would win over the public to color motion pictures.

In May 1925, Fairbanks and his team, headed by the cinematographer Henry Sharp (who had no previous experience in color photography), commenced four months of Technicolor tests, assisted by members of the Technicolor organization. Technicolor provided the services of Arthur Ball as technical director and George Cave as assistant technical director to assist with all aspects of Technicolor. The following month,

Fairbanks announced his choice of his old friend Albert Parker as director. In addition to having previously directed Fairbanks in the feature films *Arizona* and *The Knickerbocker Buckaroo,* Parker had directed John Barrymore, Norma Talmadge, Gloria Swanson, and Clara Kimbell Young with distinction. Also serving in a vital role was Fred Cavens as fight choreographer. The Swedish-American artist Carl Oscar Borg, best known for his paintings of the American Southwest, and with no previous experience working in the cinema, was engaged as supervising art director. Borg had spent two years in Britain painting maritime pictures and portraits early in his career. Dwight Franklin, an authority on buccaneer life and paintings and a disciple of Howard Pyle, was associate art director. Jack Cunningham, who had prepared the scenario of *Don Q Son of Zorro,* was engaged to shore up the initial treatment. Also on the writing staff was the eccentric British poet Robert Nichols, who ultimately contributed many of the film's intertitles.

The demands of Technicolor necessitated a straightforward production. (In recording the technical aspects of this production, the author has relied heavily upon Rudy Behlmer's authoritative articles on the subject.)[5] The Elton Thomas script was principally drawn from all the buccaneer stories Fairbanks had read or heard in his youth. Fairbanks determined, in his scenario discussions with Lotta Woods and Dr. Arthur Woods, to also include material from "The Black Pirate," a scenario written by Eugene W. Presbrey for the Fairbanks organization in 1923. Ideas from Johnston McCulley's "The Further Adventures of Zorro" were incorporated into *The Black Pirate* as well, albeit in altered form, including the heroine being captured by pirates, the hero swinging through the rigging of a pirate ship, and a race to the rescue by the hero's confederates in a pursuing vessel. The story line of *The Black Pirate* was deliberately simplified. When Fairbanks decided he would do his pirate story in color, he wanted the film to have the overall visual design of the production be akin to an illustrated book by Howard Pyle. Story elements were clearly influenced by Robert Louis Stevenson's *Treasure Island* and James M. Barrie's *Peter Pan.* According to Albert Parker, "the story was produced with color in mind, which is to say that we realized that the color must never dominate the narrative. . . . It has been made a story of situations rather than plot, the main narrative being a bare thread."[6]

Fairbanks did not want to be encumbered with a complicated story, and owing to the cost of Technicolor, he wanted the running time kept short. He reveled in the composition and colors; the film's visual style would incorporate a series of tableaux incorporating all the iconic situations

Fairbanks, the supervising art director, Carl Oscar Borg, and the director, Albert Parker, study a model galleon during preproduction of *The Black Pirate*. "We got the best artists and told them to produce designs for each set," Parker remembered. "Fairbanks would examine them all carefully, mark the parts he liked, and a draughtsman would produce a composite design from the color sketches."

Fairbanks entertains director Albert Parker with a sword-swallowing stunt.

of pirate lore: the duel on the beach (lifted right out of a Pyle illustration), the capture of the ship, walking the plank, and the race to the rescue. As Jeffrey Richards assessed the film in 1977, "[Fairbanks] deliberately designed to create a totally stylized, self-contained, mythic universe. Not based on a classic novel or weighed down with reels of court intrigue, it is entirely a creation of the cinema—a film as light as air. Like the production design, the story content is rigorously stylized, a distillation of all the pirate myths."[7] Admittedly the characters are broadly drawn, with little time spent on character development, but they are all archetypes culled from pirate tales. The appeal of the story is subjugated to the appeal of Fairbanks himself, who dominates the film.

Fairbanks and his crew went to Santa Catalina Island for location tests. The results were unsatisfactory, and it was decided that complete control was required; nearly all the exteriors had to be filmed within the controlled conditions of the Pickford-Fairbanks Studios. Although they were principally inspired by N. C Wyeth's illustrations of Stevenson's *Treasure Island* and Howard Pyle's paintings of pirates, Fairbanks and his crew also made a study of paintings by the Old Masters held at the Huntington Library in Pasadena. Henry Sharp later recalled that the paintings of Rembrandt were an influence. "Rembrandt's great strength was his use of one positive light scale. One central light perspective was always used."[8] Albert Parker recalled that "we found it necessary to work out a definite color scheme (green and brown) and abide by it—rigidly excluding every note that might distract from the whole."[9]

Herbert T. Kalmus remembered: "There was great discussion as to the color key in which this picture would be pitched. We made test prints for Mr. Fairbanks at six different color levels, from a level with slightly more color than black and white, to the most garish rendering of which the Technicolor process was then capable."[10]

Fairbanks himself explained: "Certain colors, such as purple [blue and yellow], cannot be photographed at all. Consequently, the effect is not natural, though many people refer to these pictures as having been photographed in natural colors. Our problem, therefore, became one of overcoming artificiality with artifice."[11]

The vagaries of two-color Technicolor required two sets of costumes and two sets of makeup, because there was a disparity between how they appeared photographed in natural light versus artificial light. Fairbanks himself is wonderfully clad in black to further distinguish him from the colorful cutthroats inhabiting the film. As a costume, it was one of his most inspired: he wears a revealing torn doublet, thigh-

length trousers, seven-league boots turned over at the top into cuffs, and one large earring. So memorable was the Fairbanks costume that Gene Kelly—whose childhood idol was Fairbanks—virtually replicated it for Kelly's magnificent "Pirate Ballet" sequence in Vincente Minnelli's *The Pirate* (1948).

Fairbanks was, as usual, a dynamo. As an interviewer described him in 1926: "It was like watching him on the screen—same panther-like activity, same flashing teeth, same piercing eyes, same everything. His ebulliency was overwhelming. I felt as though I had been whirled about by a particularly vigorous tornado."[12] Ted Reed, Fairbanks's production manager, remembered that even when Carl Oscar Borg and Dwight Franklin were satisfied with results, Fairbanks himself often vetoed them. "Time and time again he did this," Reed declared. "He was determined to get the exact effect on the screen that he wanted, and he was

The island set of *The Black Pirate* on the Pickford-Fairbanks Studios back lot, with Donald Crisp, Sam de Grasse, and Anders Randolf on the "beach." Also visible in the background are sets from other Pickford-Fairbanks productions.

certain from the beginning of just what that effect should be."[13] After visiting the production, the film critic Edwin Schallert wrote in *Picture-Play*, "It was a tedious and painstaking job. Sets were built in all the colors of the rainbow, and test shots were taken. The walls of the studios were painted in patches of blue, green, pink, lavender, orange, mauve, and every other tint that might be thought of. Special attention was also given to the texture of the buildings and costumes."[14]

Albert Parker said that the aim was to "take color out of color,"[15] and that it was Fairbanks's idea "to make a pirate picture that would seem to spectators as something that had been down in the cellars for 300 years, and looked as if it has been cleaned and varnished for theater showing."[16] More than just an artistic choice, the subdued colors assured against complaints of eye strain from color film.[17] By the time the testing phase was completed, over 50,000 feet of negative had been exposed.[18]

Rescuing the distressed damsel: Princess Isobel (Billie Dove) and the Black Pirate.

The most important aspect in casting the leading lady for *The Black Pirate* (one of only two female parts in the entire film) was that she photograph well in Technicolor. For two months Fairbanks tested numerous women for the part. Always in the back of his mind was a Technicolor test of Billie Dove that he had studied, along with her scenes in *Wanderer of the Wasteland*.[19] Seventy years later, Billie Dove recalled receiving a telephone call from Fairbanks while she was filming *The Ancient Highway* (1925) on location in Washington State. "When are you finishing your picture, Billie?" he inquired. "I want you to be my leading lady in my next picture." "As soon as I had completed *The Ancient Highway*, I went to work with Doug," Dove remembered. "I didn't test for the part. They had my costumes and wigs ready for me."[20] As the damsel in distress, Dove conceded that the part required little more

The Black Pirate challenges the leader of the pirate band (Anders Randolf) to a duel, watched by Michel (Sam de Grasse).

than for her to act scared, yet she was satisfied with her performance and proud of her professional association with Fairbanks. Sam de Grasse, who had memorably played the villainous Prince John in *Robin Hood,* was hired to bring his understated playing to the brooding and aloof Michel, the key villain role in *The Black Pirate.* Donald Crisp, fresh from directing as well as acting in *Don Q Son of Zorro,* was engaged to play MacTavish. Crisp later claimed to have assumed some directorial duties during the film's early stages.[21]

The Black Pirate begins with a ruthless band of bloodthirsty buccaneers taking control of a merchant vessel ship and proceeding to loot, pillage, and murder its helpless crew. Among the doomed there are but two survivors: a young nobleman (Fairbanks) and his fatally wounded father, who manage to escape and find refuge on a deserted island. After the father dies in his arms, the son vows vengeance. He sees his opportunity when he encounters the pirate leader and a small party of his crew burying their treasure on the island. Assuming the identity of "the Black Pirate," he proposes to join their cutthroat company. To prove his worthiness, he challenges their sadistic leader (Anders Randolf) to a duel. After skillfully dispatching him, he is embraced by the senior sea dog, MacTavish (Crisp), but not by the slain chief's devious lieutenant, Michel (Sam de Grasse). The Black Pirate offers to further prove his mettle by single-handedly capturing the next merchant ship they encounter. In a dazzling display of strategy and stunts, he takes over the ship and wins a place in the pirate band. A beautiful young princess (Dove) is discovered on board, and the Black Pirate proposes holding the ship and its royal cargo for ransom, thus assuring her temporary safety. While attempting to facilitate her escape, the Black Pirate is discovered by Michel and is denounced to the crew and forced to walk the plank. MacTavish, however, secretly ensures the survival of his friend. The Black Pirate is able to free himself underwater, swim ashore, and return with a rescue party of eager young seamen, who storm the pirate ship and overpower it. The film ends with the Black Pirate revealing his true noble identity, easily securing a royal engagement and a happy ending.

If the preproduction was the most technologically complex and difficult of any Fairbanks film, production went relatively quickly once it started in the summer of 1925. Principal photography for *The Black Pirate* was accomplished in nine weeks, five of which were spent on exteriors. The whole enterprise was artfully accomplished. The beach scenes were photographed on the back lot, although they appear to have been filmed on location. In addition, the production boasts brilliant miniature work involving the various ships used within the film. Their successful integration with the full-scale ships was a major achievement. A huge tank, holding 700,000 gallons of water, was constructed, with airplane propellers creating waves. Indeed, sections of the Pickford-Fairbanks Studios back lot looked like a shipyard, with five "fighting sets," complete with sections of seventeenth-century galleons built under the supervision of Borg and his associates Edward M. Langley and Jack Holden. P. H. L. Wilson, a marine technician, made certain the hulls, rigging, and sails were accurate in every detail. The climactic rescue sequence was filmed off Santa Catalina Island and also included long shots involving large miniature ships. Joseph Dannenberg, who visited Fairbanks at the studio, wrote in *Film Daily:* "Doug is all enthusiasm. . . . He has constant suggestions; constant ideas, for director Albert Parker. He is not too big; not too important to bother with the tiniest of detail. He helped the makeup man go over some tattooing on the chest of one of the most ferocious of the pirates. He never tires."[22] Extras used in the production—cast as pirates—included many prizefighters, wrestlers, and athletes, whom Fairbanks also engaged as a much-needed diversion during the lengthy camera setups. During the filming of one scene, Fairbanks cracked a rib. His was not the only injury. Ted Reed fractured his right leg while inspecting one of the vessels under construction at the studio.[23] Despite the inevitable tensions of the experimental and arduous production, Parker recalled, Fairbanks was nothing less than exemplary:

The Black Pirate leads MacTavish (Donald Crisp), Michel (Sam de Grasse), and four other seadogs.

▷ The Black Pirate is cheered by his fellow cutthroats after he proves himself by capturing a galleon single-handedly.

▷ Nine pirates are no match for Fairbanks.

But you don't know—nobody can know, without working with him—how he is loved and admired by the people he gathers around him, you don't know the power he has developed by which he can get the best that a group of experts have to give, and yet be able to weld their efforts into a splendid unity which has his own, personal stamp on it.

That's not an easy thing to do. For *The Black Pirate,* there were fourteen members of the production personnel, not counting myself and my staff, each of whom had something vital to contribute. Imagine the possibilities for clashes, for jealousy, for friction of all kinds. Yet Doug was able to avoid those things. He does it by keeping an open mind, by always being ready to listen to every one on the staff, and by his quick, precise judgment. If he didn't approve of a suggestion, he would say why not. He'd try it both ways, and then decide which way he thought was best.

He gets the best work out of people by telling them the *result* he wants, and then letting them work it out in their own way. If the result isn't satisfactory, he may order a different method, but he always leaves the actual details to the people hired for the work. For instance, in this pirate picture he wanted a certain effect. The technical staff said it could be obtained by miniature. They were given *carte blanche* to go ahead. The models were made, the scenes taken. They were good, but not quite good enough. "Let's do it life size," Doug said, when he saw the result. Not a word of censure. He knew they had done their best, and that not all experiments along new lines can succeed.[24]

The most celebrated sequence of the film, and perhaps of Fairbanks's entire career, is the moment in which the Black Pirate, when capturing a galleon single-handedly, slashes a line with his knife, catches the end of the mizzen, and swings upward with the wayward sail to the main topsail. He then plunges his knife into the canvas of the topsail and slides down the sail, supported by the hilt of his knife as it severs the canvas in half. He rends the mainsail in the same manner. The feat is so spectacular that Fairbanks repeats it once more with the fore topsail, rendering the ship powerless. The Black Pirate swings through the lines to the forecastle, swivels about a pair of cannons he has commandeered, and holds the crew as helpless as the galleon itself. The sliding down the sails is a grand stunt, building on Robin Hood's celebrated descent down the enormous drapery in *Robin Hood.* The 43-year-old showman is in top physical form, and the appearance of effortlessness, the breathtaking arcs of movements, and the sheer joy with which he

Fairbanks performs the most famous of all his stunts: plunging his knife into the canvas of a galleon's sails and sliding down, while it severs the canvas in half, in *The Black Pirate*. Frame enlargement from a 35 mm nitrate fine-grain master positive.

accomplishes the impossible are ample demonstration of Fairbanks's kinetic genius.

The sequence was achieved with separate sail sets engineered by Robert Fairbanks on the back lot, apart from the various ship settings, and erected on an angle away from the cameras (which were also on an angle). The sails, according to Douglas Fairbanks Jr., were "pre-sliced and then stitched up invisibly. . . . The knife was rigged with piano wire, pulley, and counterweight. . . . He would thrust his knife into the sail and there would be a quick cut. The next cut would be of him holding the special knife connected to the hidden pulley and counterweight."[25] Airplane propellers behind the canvas provided the billowing effect for the sails. As with all of his stunts, the sequence required meticulous preparation and days of practice. In rehearsals, as well as during the actual filming, Fairbanks wore a wire harness, and his arms and legs were taped to prevent friction burns.[26] Although no one doubted

Fairbanks shows off his bronzed physique in 1926—he helped popularize the tanning craze—at a luxuriously appointed seaside tent site he and Pickford owned on a stretch of crescent-shaped beach near Laguna, California. A Santa Monica beach house built the following year at a cost of $100,000 was intended—like the Laguna compound—as a weekend getaway destination.

at the time that he performed the stunt, William K. Everson later maintained that Fairbanks did not do so himself.[27] But the accounts of Albert Parker, Douglas Fairbanks Jr., and Chuck Lewis and the surviving outtakes from the scene itself dispel any claim that Fairbanks did not perform his most famous feat.[28] Fairbanks's bravura stunt was subsequently pirated by a stunt double for Errol Flynn in *Against All Flags* (1952) and by Johnny Depp in *Pirates of the Caribbean* (2006).

One of the immediate effects of the famous sequence was all the injuries sustained by impressionable children imitating their screen idol. Edward Wagenknecht wrote, "one shudders to think how many broken arms and legs he must have been responsible for among the children of America during the years of his vogue."[29] Robert Parrish, a future director and film editor, was one such child. He recalled having seen *The Black Pirate* in his hometown of Columbus, Georgia, and immediately wanting to emulate the spectacular Fairbanks stunt:

As a seven-year-old, I had seen Douglas Fairbanks in *The Black Pirate* plunge a knife into the sail and riding the knife down to the deck. I tried the knife stunt myself that afternoon with a borrowed linen bed sheet. Some friends and I attached it to the limb of an oak tree about ten feet off the ground. I climbed the tree with a butcher's knife in my mouth trying to smile like Fairbanks—I soon tasted blood in my mouth—and pointed the knife at the sheet and jumped. The sheet crashed down upon me like a deflated parachute and the knife flew out of my hand. I landed on the ground

A victorious Black Pirate with his rescue party of eager young seamen, after storming and overpowering the pirate ship in the climax of *The Black Pirate*.

with a broken arm, the wind knocked out of me, and blood running from my Fairbanks grin.[30]

He was, nevertheless, "the hero of the day, coddled by the grownups and admired by my peers."[31]

In another celebrated sequence of the film, directly derived from Peter Pan's mopping-up crew, the rescue party of 120 scantily clad, supercharged sailors submerge a galley, swim in formation underwater at great depth, and rise to the surface in perfect order. Allene Talmey, in her book *Doug and Mary and Others*, provides a detailed account of how this water sequence was achieved without involving water. Fairbanks and his team devised a blue-green background cyclorama depicting the ocean. The 120 extras were suspended in midair by piano wires from a crane and went through the motions of the breast stroke as it carried them from camera left to right. Decorative touches such as seaweed (made of paper and also suspended by wires from the top of the stage) and visible air bubbles completed the illusion. "Audiences marveled at soldiers swimming at the bottom of the sea, and once more Douglas Fairbanks had contributed to movie mechanics and aesthetics," Talmey concluded.[32] Not everyone agreed. Such effects were no more than a "studied prettiness," John Grierson wrote in *Motion Picture News*; "when the boarding party swim under-water to capture the schooner and stick knives in the pirates' innards, they might be a bunch of fairies swimming in the moonlight."[33] Modern audiences inevitably read a homosexual innuendo into the sequences involving the rescue party, but any such interpretation is gainsaid by the innocence of the portrayals. Like the Black Pirate, the underwater seamen are exuberant exponents of Fairbanks's own masculinity.

Pickford was making her masterpiece *Sparrows* (1926) concurrently with *The Black Pirate,* and Fairbanks frequently visited her sets. For the last sequence of *The Black Pirate,* in which Fairbanks's character (revealed to be the Duke of Arnoldo) embraces the princess, Billie Dove was replaced by Mary Pickford—wearing Dove's costume and wig—for the single shot.[34] The reason for the substitution, according to Dove, was simple jealousy; Pickford did not want him kissing another woman. "It wasn't filmed in a close-up; it was shot at some distance from the camera. You really couldn't tell it was her and not me," Dove recalled.[35]

In postproduction, Fairbanks once again enlisted Mortimer Wilson to compose an original score for the film. He reportedly was not entirely satisfied with the results.[36] The carefully crafted score, inspired in part by traditional sea shanties, is in the same spirit as the larger-than-life characters of the romantic fantasy Fairbanks envisioned. However, the main deficiency of Wilson's score is its absence of melodic inspiration. For example, the duel between Fairbanks and Anders Randolf with rapiers and daggers is ill served by the agitato composed by Wilson; it neither supports the action nor develops into anything interesting as a piece of music. The sequence is arguably the finest choreographed and executed swordfight in the silent cinema; its only rival is the swordplay between John Barrymore and Montagu Love in *Don Juan.* The agitato composed by David Mendoza and William Axt for the Vitaphone score accompanying *Don Juan* is fast and exciting, with a rhythmic idea perfectly fitting the action, and leaves spectators on the edge of their seats. Fairbanks's film deserved a score comparable to what Mendoza and Axt achieved with *Don Juan,* but instead of a score punctuating a grand and exciting seafaring romance, Wilson delivered one unworthy of the film (inexplicably, it includes "Camptown Races"). The collaboration between Fairbanks and Wilson—which had lasted three films—sank with *The Black Pirate.*

At nine reels in length, or 8,490 feet (approximately 88 minutes at a suggested projection speed of $87\frac{1}{2}$ feet per minute), the final cut of *The*

Fairbanks and the fight choreographer, Fred Cavens, rehearse the rapiers and daggers fight sequence on the island set during production of *The Black Pirate.*

The same scene as it appears in the film: Fairbanks duels with Anders Randolf.

Black Pirate was the shortest Fairbanks feature since *The Nut*. Fairbanks could scarcely afford it to be a foot longer; as it was, the exhibition prints cost a staggering $170,122.14 (foreign exhibition was especially expensive, because the prints had to be imported from America; in Britain, a print cost four times as much as in the United States). The film's production cost totaled $847,008.46.[37]

The world premiere was held at the Tivoli Cinema in London on March 7, 1926, with the American premiere held the following day. Mordaunt Hall reported on the grander of these two maiden voyages, the celebrity-studded first showing at the Selwyn Theatre in New York City, in the *New York Times:* "The audience was ushered into the realm of piracy by the singing of 'Fifteen Men on a Dead Man's Chest' and afterward by a ghost-like voice that asked everyone to go back to the days of bloodthirsty sea robbers. With its excellent titles and wondrous colored scenes this picture seems to have a Barriesque motif that has been aged in Stevensonian wood."[38] *Photoplay* thought the color achieved its purpose to "emphasize rather than detract from the story value. Nothing has ever been done in colors on the screen that approaches it in beauty and uniformity. . . . Mr. Fairbanks, for the first time in motion pictures, has secured the beautiful effect of mural paintings."[39] *Variety* groused that it was a good thing the running time was short "so that the eye strain doesn't become too trying," and wrote that "in the tale that it spins it's the weakest Fairbanks has ever had. . . . Fairbanks should have done Sabatini's *Captain Blood.*"[40] Rafael Sabatini's novel *Captain Blood* had been published in 1922, and a film version of it had already been produced, as well as of Sabatini's *The Sea Hawk* (both released in 1924, by Vitagraph and First National, respectively). *Variety* missed the point. Sabatini's long, relatively convoluted story encompasses a great deal more than Fairbanks wanted to do.

The Black Pirate opened in Los Angeles as a "dual premiere" at Grauman's Egyptian Theatre with Pickford's *Sparrows*. Edwin Schallert wrote in the *Los Angeles Times* that *The Black Pirate* "lives up to its reputation in being a radical improvement" in the advancement of color cinematography. Moreover, Schallert maintained that the film was "the first feature that has approached portraying adequately something of the picturesqueness of pirates, despite that there have already been a number of so-called pirate pictures."[41] Iris Barry wrote that same year in her book *Let's Go to the Pictures* that the film was "far and away the best colour-film made."[42]

Fairbanks never attempted a feature-length Technicolor film again, although he filmed a Technicolor sequence for his next film. The principal reasons were the enormous costs and the fact that color itself was

Fairbanks pencils his thoughts at the studio during the filming of *The Black Pirate.*

not a sufficient draw at the box office to warrant the expense. Indeed, Fairbanks was very concerned about the money spent versus money received for his Technicolor experiment. Perhaps, however, he started out selling the exhibition rights too cheaply. Joseph M. Schenck encountered Fairbanks with a dazed look in his eyes at the studio one day and inquired what was the matter. Fairbanks said nothing, instead handing him a letter from an exhibitor, who enclosed a check, explaining that he had made such an enormous profit on a one-week engagement with *The Black Pirate* that his conscience troubled him.[43] The film ultimately grossed $1.8 million domestically.

Upon the completion of the film's initial run, *The Black Pirate* remained available for exhibition through United Artists throughout the 1920s, but the advent of sound made it virtually obsolete. Fairbanks deposited film elements from *The Black Pirate* at the Museum of Modern Art in 1938. In 1959, much of this material was transferred to the British Film Institute National Archive in London, which provided better storage conditions.[44] An altered version of the film had been released earlier that decade for television distribution, in black and white, with narration replacing the intertitles and an added musical score. Original Technicolor prints of *The Black Pirate* were quickly deteriorating by 1959. Attempts by the early independent film preservationists John Hampton and John E. Allen to save the film in its original Technicolor form were thwarted by the deteriorating materials.[45] They soon abandoned their efforts, and for many years, the film was available only in black-and-white versions.

In 1970, the British Film Institute National Archive was approached by Douglas Fairbanks Jr. about restoring the film from the surviving materials. Unfortunately, only a reconstruction was possible, because just a portion of the cut original camera negative survived, and all the original Technicolor prints had faded. The film preservationist Harold Brown had the formidable task of assembling a negative—complete with intertitles—primarily from outtakes. Upon the assembly of the negative, Technicolor made new separation masters in its long-obsolete two-color process, and a new negative was created, from which a final print was delivered in June 1972. The world premiere of the reconstruction was held in 1973 as a gala performance to benefit the British Film Institute National Archive.[46] Rudy Behlmer noted that the project was an ambitious undertaking in 1970, when film restoration—let alone a full-scale 1926 two-color Technicolor reconstruction—was not the routine activity it is today. "Some people were surprised to find the dominance of shades of brown, with muted greens and rusts lending support, in the print screened in 1972," Behlmer wrote. "But we know from every account of the original production at that time about the prevalence of 'sepia,' 'wood colors,' and 'prevailing brown tone.' "[47]

Sixty years after the film's initial release, the great British film director Michael Powell assessed *The Black Pirate* and Fairbanks thus: "*The Black Pirate* . . . was two-strip Technicolor and they designed for it. Until *The Thief of Bagdad* [1940] came along, it was the best colour ever seen. Doug was a great producer. . . . Doug was an artist. That was my opinion, but it was Al Parker's too."[48] The novelist Saul Bellow was also one of the film's champions. "Fairbanks's magic remains very fresh and potent in my mind," he recalled in a 1994 interview. "I can vividly recall *The Black Pirate* from when I first saw the film in 1926. . . . Fairbanks was courageous on screen. That was his character. Yet he was just as courageous off screen as a pioneering producer. Of all the major figures from Hollywood's early years, Fairbanks deserves to be better known. His movies are more than highly entertaining. They are high art."[49]

The Black Pirate remains a landmark achievement in the advancement of cinema as an art form and the definitive pirate film of the entire silent film era. The film is also a wonderful showcase for Fairbanks as a leader in the film industry and one of the most creative producers Hollywood has ever known. After the film's successful launch in New York City, Fairbanks and Pickford embarked upon an extended tour abroad, combining business with pleasure. This much-deserved vacation enabled them to assert themselves as the leading citizens of cinema in Europe, a key market. Hollywood's royal couple was received by such diverse leaders as Benito Mussolini and the king and queen of Spain. Fairbanks and Pickford also visited Russia, with a memorable entry into the country via the former czar's private railway car. Enormous crowds (100,000 by Pickford's estimate) greeted them upon their arrival in Moscow.[50] The pair met the celebrated film director Sergei Eisenstein, and they supported the Russian film industry by making a brief unintended appearance in Sergei Komarov's film *Potselui Meri Pikford* (*The Kiss of Mary Pickford*, 1927), which satirized the new phenomenon of film celebrity. Pickford and Fairbanks thought they were posing for Russian newsreel cameras. They had no idea that the footage would serve as the basis for a feature film. Indeed, they tried to suppress the film once they discovered how this footage was being exploited.

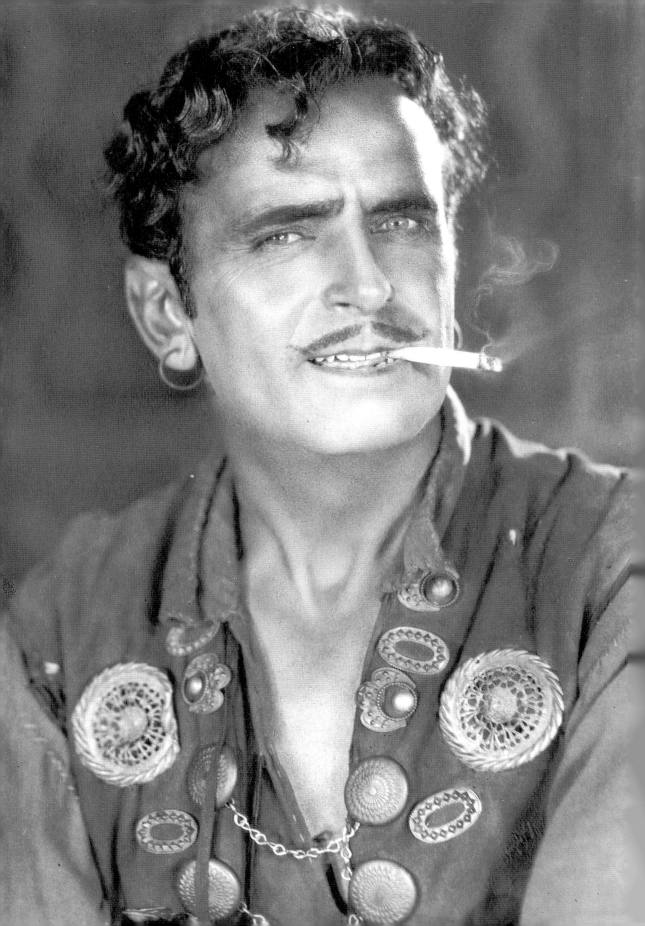

Darkness Falls

Douglas Fairbanks as The Gaucho (1927)

Fairbanks's penultimate silent film, *Douglas Fairbanks as The Gaucho*, is an anomaly among his works. A daring departure, the film is an effort of unanticipated darkness in tone, setting, and character. The spirit of adolescent boyish adventure, the omnipresent characteristic of his prior films, is noticeably absent. It has been replaced by a spiritual fervor and an element of seething sexuality the likes of which had never been seen before in one of his productions. No boy scout here, Fairbanks drinks, smokes, and acts upon his carnal desires with a lascivious glee that would make the Black Pirate blush in Technicolor. The hero of the film—a Byronic hero in the true sense of the term—ultimately finds redemption through religious conversion. *Douglas Fairbanks as The Gaucho* is a frequently misunderstood film, but its dark tone and divinity-versus-carnality story resonate effectively in the twenty-first century. It is, in fact, a near masterwork, and as such, it demands reappraisal.

In 1926, both Doug and Mary were dealing with personal crises that would have a profound effect on them in the years to come. John Fairbanks's health was rapidly declining as a result of his earlier stroke, and Charlotte Pickford, Mary's beloved mother, had terminal breast cancer. She was unwilling to consider a mastectomy, and alternate sources of treatment were being vigorously sought. One of these included a trip to Lourdes, the famous Roman Catholic shrine in southern France. According to publicity materials of the time, Fairbanks visited Lourdes

Fairbanks as the chain-smoking, Byronic hero in *Douglas Fairbanks as The Gaucho*. Photograph by Charles E. Lynch.

himself and witnessed several apparent faith healings.[1] He was intrigued by the shrine's history: a fourteen-year-old peasant girl named Bernadette Soubirous experienced a series of eighteen visions of the Blessed Virgin Mary at the Lourdes grotto in 1858. Since the time of the visions, the waters of the grotto have been used to perform miracle cures, and Fairbanks envisioned the dramatic possibilities of an avarice-versus-faith conflict for one of his films. He was interested in faith and holistic cures as a result of Charlotte Pickford's condition, and the timing was appropriate for such a theme; religious drama held the imagination of the American public. Cecil B. DeMille had found great commercial success with his formula of mixing religion, spectacle, and sex, and the evangelist and media sensation Aimee Semple McPherson was at the height of her popularity.

Fairbanks was perplexed as to what his next project should encompass. Always restless, he appeared to be growing more so with each passing year, as each new challenge was surveyed and conquered. Now the undisputed king of escapist adventure films and hero of boys everywhere, he sought out a scenario with more depth and daring. He wanted to play the sort of character that he had not attempted before, a darker, more visceral rendering of a hero. His restlessness was fed by the increasingly grim atmosphere he encountered daily at Pickfair. Distraught over her mother's health, Mary had begun drinking heavily. This acutely distressed the teetotaler Fairbanks, who was as unhappy about that as he was about his brother's decline.

Stirred with a desire to push his screen persona further than he ever had before, Fairbanks pursued a new screen character and his most atypical hero yet: an outlaw who revels in his nefarious ways with little regard for consequence. He would, of course, find redemption in the end and reform his ways, as called for by both the Hays Code of motion picture production and Fairbanks's own personal code of behavior.[2]

It was a daring idea for Fairbanks, if not necessarily for motion picture audiences of the time. By 1926, filmgoers were primed for "sin and salvation" sagas such as *The Ten Commandments* and *Ben-Hur: A Tale of the Christ*. Sex always sold, and it did not take moviemakers long to realize that it sold even better with a little spiritual reformation at the end. However, Fairbanks's productions had always steered clear of sexual themes and, perhaps partly in order to connect with his audience of boys, Doug often appeared as adolescent in his lovemaking attempts. This gave his films a large part of their appeal, but both Fairbanks and his audience had to grow up sometime, and the premise of debauchers and their deliverance was distinctly in vogue in late 1920s America. It also echoed the Fairbanks theme of character transformation, a hall-

Fairbanks seethes with a demonic sexuality in this portrait from Douglas Fairbanks as The Gaucho.

mark of his films prior to *The Three Musketeers*. This time, however, his conversion would transcend the merely physical and rise to a transformation of the soul.

Assembling his production team was a challenge for him in some respects, because his mood during preproduction was as dark as the film he intended to make. There were, of course, the familiar faces: Carl Oscar Borg and his team of scenic designers; Lotta Woods and Dr. Arthur Woods, respectively, delving into the scenario and research; and Ted Reed as manager of production. Fairbanks's brother Robert continued his role as general manager and overseer of production, which was fortunate, since in November 1926, John Fairbanks finally succumbed to the devastating effects of the stroke he had suffered as a result of the strain of the production of *Robin Hood*, which left him partially paralyzed and virtually speechless. His death was a serious blow to Fairbanks, one that he had difficulty overcoming. His bereavement was acute, and it brought the grim specter of his own mortality sharply into focus. The idea that the amazing gifts he had worked so steadily to maintain could slip away severely distressed Fairbanks, who prized his physical prowess and agility. John Fairbanks's death reverberated through the rest of his life. A brief cameo in King Vidor's comedy *Show People* (1928) depicts Fairbanks as himself clowning at M-G-M's studio commissary, but still wearing the black armband of mourning. Robert Fairbanks noted that it was at this time his brother suddenly began to jokingly complain of feeling old and noted that Douglas had once told him: "When my time comes, I hope it will happen quickly. I can't think of anything more horrible than being ill."[3]

The pall cast by his brother's death bled inevitably into the story Fairbanks was developing. Already what was emerging had a darker perspective than any of his prior works, but now the film took on an almost fatalistic bent. Mortality permeates it from the first scene, in which a young girl plunges to her death (or so it appears) from a cliff, to a mysterious victim of "the Black Doom"—leprosy—lurking in the background.

Fairbanks realized that a deft touch was essential to leaven the film and prevent it from becoming too dark. He therefore made an unexpected but shrewd decision; he hired a top comedy director, F. Richard Jones. Best remembered for directing the comedienne Mabel Normand in several films, including the famous Mack Sennett comedy *Mickey* (1917), Jones also directed the popular *Yankee Doodle in Berlin* (1919) for Sennett. He later served as production supervisor for Hal Roach before his premature death in 1930. He was new to the singular fusion of adventure, comedy, and drama of the Fairbanks films, and Fairbanks considered this an asset; he particularly wanted the freshness of Jones's view. In addition, Jones was known to be a hard worker, and just the sort of whip Fairbanks needed at this critical time in his life and career.

Another new face entering the United Artists Studios lot was the cinematographer Tony Gaudio. As well known for his temperament as for his talent, Gaudio had previously photographed Pickford at the Independent Motion Picture Company in 1911, and had filmed *Kismet* (1920) and a number of Joseph M. Schenck productions. He later shot landmark films such as *Hell's Angels* (1930), *Little Caesar* (1931), and *The Adventures of Robin Hood* (1938). Another addition new to the payroll was none other than Douglas Fairbanks Jr., who had been out of work for some time and appealed to his father through his Uncle Robert for some employment. He was hired to direct a few screen tests at $150 a test. Despite his inexperience, but with the assistance of a veteran cinematographer, he directed two excellent tests of Lupe Velez and Eve Southern, ultimately cast in the film's principal female roles.[4]

In these two women, Fairbanks had not one but two strong female characters for his new film (three if one counts the contribution of Mary Pickford's cameo as the Virgin Mary). Considering that he was loath to share the spotlight with any strong personality, male or female, it is interesting that he chose an actress with the fire and energy of Lupe Velez, or the ethereal beauty of Eve Southern. It was a calculated risk that was rewarded, because in the casting of Velez with Southern, the fire with the ice, the whore with the Madonna, he was hedging his

Fairbanks surrounded by his crew during the production of *Douglas Fairbanks as The Gaucho*. Tony Gaudio, the cinematographer, is on the platform at left, behind the Mitchell NC cameras. F. Richard Jones, the director, is behind Fairbanks. Chuck Lewis, Fairbanks's friend and trainer, is second from the right.

bets with his audience. Originally, Dolores Del Rio had been engaged to play the role of the feisty Mountain Girl but she was replaced by the 17-year-old Velez, who was loaned to Fairbanks by the Hal Roach Studios, when it was determined that an unknown might better serve the production.[5]

Also cast were the veteran Nigel de Brulier (last seen with Fairbanks as Cardinal Richelieu in *The Three Musketeers*), as the Padre, and the prolific character actor Gustav von Seyffertitz, as Ruiz the Usurper. Seyffertitz had appeared previously with Fairbanks in *Down to Earth* and had achieved one of his finest performances the previous year in Pickford's *Sparrows*. Rounding out the cast were Albert MacQuarrie, who had memorably played Colonel Matsado in *Don Q Son of Zorro* and now appeared as the shadowy Victim of the Black Doom, and Geraine Greear (later known as Joan Barclay), as the young shepherdess who becomes the Girl of the Shrine.

"There will be no time element in the story, which might have taken place any time during the last century. Naturally, it will be colorful,

Lupe Velez (holding her pet Chihuahua) with Fairbanks during preproduction at the United Artists Studios in 1927. Her Chihuahua originally helped Velez secure the role of the Mountain Girl. Fairbanks's initial impression of Velez was that she was far too placid for the part. This first impression was quickly dispelled when a member of Fairbanks's crew took Velez's pet as a joke. Upon her discovery of the prank, she became very combative and fiery toward the prankster, and her potential was fully revealed to Fairbanks.

showing the South Americans as we think of them rather than as they are. . . . We have to show the gauchos in colorful costumes and romantic settings," Fairbanks told the *Los Angeles Record* in April 1927.[6] The production rekindled both Fairbanks's infatuation with Latin culture and his fascination with weaponry. This time the accoutrement in question was not a sword, a whip, or a bow and arrows, but a *boleadoras,* or bolas, the weapon of the cowmen of the Argentine pampas. The Fairbanks research team were delighted to find among their reading an account of the gaucho and the bolas by Charles Darwin, who visited the pampas of Argentina on his 1831 scientific expedition and wrote of it in *The Voyage of the Beagle.* Bolas were made of three leather thongs tied together in the shape of a Y, with stone or metal balls at the ends. Darwin wrote:

The balls can be thrown fifty or sixty yards, but with little certainty. This, however, does not apply to a man on horseback; for when the speed of the horse is added to the force of the arm, it is said that they can be whirled with effect to the distance of eighty yards. . . . The Gaucho holds the smallest of the three [weights] in his hand and whirls the other two around his head; then, taking aim, sends them like chain-shot revolving through the air. The balls no sooner strike any object, than, winding around it, they cross each other and become firmly hitched.[7]

As with his prior weaponry, Fairbanks threw himself unreservedly into mastering this new toy, aided by two expert instructors, Nick Milanesio and Andres Rodriguez. One can only speculate how essential a new athletic challenge was to the restless Fairbanks in each new production. He practiced while on horseback as well as standing, throwing the bolas at both upright stakes and moving targets. Just as the sword, the bow, and the whip had served him earlier, the bolas utilized in this production were not merely a prop but an integral part of the alienated character of the Gaucho, who shuns convention to the point of being an outlaw. He is admired—adulated even—but he deflects connection with anyone or anything. He is also noncommittal. His philosophy is summed up by the intertitle in which he proclaims: "Yesterday was yesterday. Today is today. There is no tomorrow until it's today." It is with his bolas that he connects with things; he uses them to reach out and clasp objects that pique his interest, releasing them from his grasp as quickly and deftly when his interest wanes. In this way, Fairbanks's prowess with the bolas is skillful character delineation; Fairbanks was a conscientious actor as well as an astute showman.

Although the Gaucho may have been an untypical role for him to play, there are also subtle similarities between Fairbanks the man and the character he portrays, particularly the sense of isolation. This was to be expected in a motion picture star, but the feeling of living a life apart—even from those closest to him—was something Fairbanks had experienced nearly his entire life. In the most important sense, it was what drove him; it was the fuel of his fire. And the theme of standing apart from those around him reverberates through every character he portrays, from Jeff Hillington, who dreams of life riding the range in *Wild and Woolly,* to the effete Don Diego Vega in *The Mark of Zorro.* However, in no other film is this theme personified as acutely as in *Douglas Fairbanks as The Gaucho* (hereafter *The Gaucho*).

As with all Fairbanks's costume adventures, *The Gaucho* is notable for its exceptional visual design. Credit goes to the supervising art director, Carl Oscar Borg, along with Harry Oliver, Jack Holden, Francesc Cugat, Edward M. Langley, and Mario Larrinaga as associate artists. The sets that they created—the craggy, ivy-covered grotto, the shimmering, spotlessly white steps leading to the shrine, the intricacies of the various shops within the City of the Miracle (an exte-

Fairbanks rehearses with the bolas at the studio during preproduction. The bolas Fairbanks used to practice with are preserved by the Natural History Museum of Los Angeles County.

The bolas-wielding Gaucho single-handedly captures the City of the Miracle from Ruiz's army.

The irrepressible Gaucho, with the omnipresent clouds of smoke about him, raises cigarette lighting and match extinguishing to an art as he sits in a prison cell.

rior set 800 feet in length), the smoky taverns, and the dark prison are all romantically presented and beautiful to behold. The pampas setting was intentionally indeterminate of time or place, and the costumes were likewise created to enhance the artistic effect rather than to reflect realism. Fairbanks is magnificently attired throughout as the swaggering scoundrel with *botas de potro* (a pair of untanned horsehide boots), *bombachos* (flowing trousers buttoned at the ankle), a wide-brimmed hat, a *tirador* (a spangled leather belt with pockets), a long knife, leather armbands, coiled bolas, and an ever-present cigarette dangling from his lips. Ruiz the Usurper, the true villain of the film, is counterintuitively costumed in brilliant white, as are his soldiers, whereas the Gaucho and his band are attired almost exclusively in dark colors.

As cinematographer, Tony Gaudio handles large crowds and intimate scenes with great skill. The unusual camera angles and frequent moving camera show the influence of German cinema on American filmmaking. Gaudio also employs chiaroscuro lighting, creating deep shadows and a marked degree of contrast between darkness and light, thus making the film Fairbanks's darkest both literally and figuratively. In addition to dealing with the challenges of the two-color Technicolor footage, the film employs glass shots,[8] models, and a relatively recent contrivance, the hanging miniature. Requiring the close collaboration of the cinematographer, art directors, and visual effects specialists, the hanging miniature (another first for a Fairbanks film) involves suspending a model set or parts of sets in front of the camera in perfect alignment with the full-scale set in the background. The light out of doors falls on the miniature in the same way it falls on the actual set. A high level of mathematical accuracy is essential for the illusion to be perfect, with the necessary aid of a wide-angle lens, with its inherent extreme depth of field (and focus). When filming commences, the miniature blends into the existing set, giving the appearance of a seamless whole. The hanging miniature combined with a glass shot yields even greater illusions. In *The Gaucho*, the finest example of these two techniques is a distance shot of a group of the Gaucho's men riding their horses down a winding trail on the side of a cliff. The achievement of such visual effects is even more amazing when one considers that all the effects were achieved inside the camera on one negative; the technique of combining images from two or more negatives into one piece of film had not yet arrived. William K. Everson contends that Fairbanks's film boasts "some of the best and most convincing glass shots ever filmed."[9]

The Gaucho begins with a young shepherdess who has fallen to certain death off a precipice being miraculously brought back to life by an apparition of the Blessed Virgin Mary. Ten years pass, and the site where the Virgin appeared becomes a shrine to which sick and displaced people make pilgrimages. The young shepherdess, now known as the Girl of the Shrine, and the local padre are the custodians of the holy site. The town surrounding the shrine, known as the City of the Miracle, grows rich from the grateful gold of the many believers. However, the flood of gold into the town draws the attention of two disreputable characters: Ruiz the Usurper, who hears of the wealth and dispatches his army to confiscate it, and the Gaucho, a notorious outlaw. Hearing of Ruiz's invasion, the Gaucho makes his way to the city to recapture it, meeting the fiery young Mountain Girl along the way, and bringing her along with him and his army of bandits. Disguising himself as one of the Usurper's army, the Gaucho enters the city and single-handedly takes control of it from Ruiz's men. He becomes entranced

The Gaucho confronts the Padre (Nigel de Brulier) in *Douglas Fairbanks as The Gaucho*.

with the Girl of the Shrine, now a beautiful young woman of unearthly allure, and urges her to attend the bacchanalian feast he has planned for that evening. This draws the ire of the jealous Mountain Girl, and later that evening, when she catches the Gaucho alone with the young woman, she attacks her with a knife. The Gaucho defends the Girl of the Shrine and is wounded in the process. At this time, he is assaulted and infected by a crazed victim of "the Black Doom," a shadowy pariah of the city whom the Gaucho had earlier advised to commit suicide rather than live with his affliction. Taking his own advice, the Gaucho flees the city, intending to kill himself; he is prevented from doing so by the Girl of the Shrine, who leads him to the grotto where the Virgin Mary appears to heal him of his affliction. Cured and converted, but now trapped by Ruiz and his men, the Gaucho is imprisoned, along with the Girl of the Shrine and the Padre. Set for execution, the Gaucho, who has been spiritually reborn as a result of his healing, manages to escape the prison and acts swiftly to save the others. Feeling remorse for her actions, the Mountain Girl alerts the Gaucho's men to his plight. He soon joins them, and together they rouse the thousands of cattle that graze outside the city into a thunderous stampede. The cattle storm the city, and through the resulting tempest of dust and debris, the Gaucho and his men enter the city and recapture it from Ruiz. Restoring the shrine to the people, he completes his rehabilitation by proposing marriage to the Mountain Girl, and the two ride off happily together.

The Gaucho defends the Girl of the Shrine (Eve Southern) from the knife and ire of the jealous Mountain Girl (Lupe Velez).

The Pickford-Fairbanks lot, renamed the United Artists Studios, was teeming with activity when production began in the spring of 1927. Joseph M. Schenck had arranged a long-term lease on the lot the previous year, and an administrative building and several new stages were among the improvements built to enlarge the facilities and accommodate Schenck's Art Cinema productions, featuring such stars as Norma Talmadge, Constance Talmadge, and Rudolph Valentino. Pickford had completed production of *My Best Girl* (1927), and her husband invited her to take part in his film, in which she makes an uncredited appearance as the Madonna, shot in two-color Technicolor.

Once again, Technicolor required extensive testing, and after dealing with the arduous process in *The Black Pirate*, Fairbanks was not about to revisit it once more for an entire film. However, he realized that Technicolor would give the religious mysticism of the opening sequence the gravitas the film required. Fortunately, he already knew his wife photographed beautifully in the color process; a test survives of Pickford photographed in two-color Technicolor during the production of *The Black Pirate*.[10] To give the Madonna an appropriate celestial glow, Pickford stood on a pedestal, backed against a plank trimmed to her silhouette, with two bands of leather bristling with a multitude of thin sticks of pliable metal, passed through rollers following the contour of her body, which were moved by a crank concealed in the bottom of the pedestal. The silvery sticks, moving rapidly in two different

The actor Louis Wolheim, the playwright and screenwriter Karl Vollmoller, Pickford (in costume for *My Best Girl*), the actor Emil Jannings, Fairbanks (in costume), and the director Lewis Milestone at the studio during production of *Douglas Fairbanks as The Gaucho*.

directions and illuminated with intense floodlights, provided the illusion of a brilliant radiance emitted by the Madonna herself.[11] Casting Pickford as the Virgin Mary appears to have been a whim of Fairbanks's; it was a choice he believed would appeal to his audience. Pickford regarded it as "a lovely compliment."[12]

It was more than that, however. When Fairbanks visited the *My Best Girl* set one day while Mary was filming a love scene with her leading man, Charles "Buddy" Rogers, he was only able to watch for a few moments before leaving abruptly. The intimacy he witnessed between the two sent a chill through him. "It's more than jealousy," he said, trying to explain his reaction to his brother Robert. "I suddenly felt afraid."[13] Whether his fear was justified or not is beside the point; he felt threatened to the core and needed to reestablish his proper place in his own mind. He did this in two ways: by turning Mary into the Madonna, and by beginning a brief affair with his leading lady, Lupe Velez. H. Bruce "Lucky" Humberstone, who was assistant director on *My Best Girl* (and later on *The Iron Mask* and *Taming of the Shrew*), remembered, "Doug had started a big affair when he was doing *The Gaucho* with Lupe Velez and of course everybody in the studio knew about it."[14] As a result of the affair, the film is charged with an eroticism and sexual energy noticeably absent in other Fairbanks productions. Partly owing to this, the Mountain Girl is the most fully realized of any female character in a Fairbanks film. Velez, later dubbed "the Mexican Spitfire," matches Fairbanks shot

The Gaucho encounters
the Mountain Girl.

for shot; with arms akimbo, chest heaving, and eyes flashing, she is in every respect the equal to Fairbanks's Gaucho. Indeed, one contemporary review even dubbed her "the female Fairbanks."[15]

Sparks of a different sort than the ones achieved for Mary's celestial appearance appear in every scene between Fairbanks and Velez. Their electrifying tango scene, performed early in the film, is reminiscent of Rudolph Valentino's famed dance in *The Four Horsemen of the Apocalypse* and is nearly as potent. Fairbanks may lack Valentino's smoldering sexual ambiguity, but the swaggering self-confidence of his insouciant masculinity captivates. Using the bolas to entwine himself with Velez, Fairbanks smokes through the entire sequence, sneering at her as he clutches his cigarette between his teeth, tucks it with his tongue in the back of his mouth before he leans in to kiss her, and then thrusts it back

The Gaucho uses the bolas to entwine himself with the Mountain Girl as they dance a sexually charged tango.

The Gaucho and the Mountain Girl are frequently bellicose in their romantic scenes in *Douglas Fairbanks as The Gaucho*. One critic described their lovemaking as "a pugilistic encounter." Their animal attraction and carnal combativeness was a fresh approach to Hollywood lovemaking.

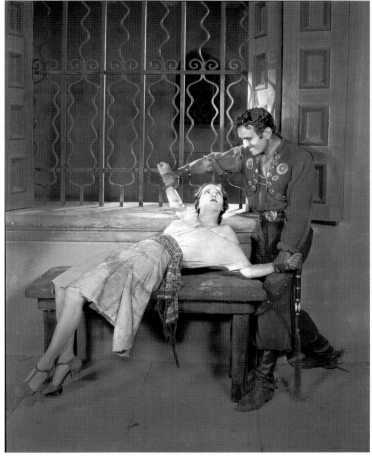

out again, blowing smoke in her face. (The bit with the cigarette was later used by Gene Kelly in Vincente Minnelli's *The Pirate*.) The sexual metaphors are clearly evident, and the two enact their dance with undeniable carnality. The red-hot tango sequence was an important one to Fairbanks, and the choreographer Henry Barsha was specially engaged to make the Americanized tango steps a highlight of the film.[16]

Of the film's spectacular sequences, not least of them the one in which an entire house is pulled off its foundation by a hundred horses, the cattle stampede at the climax is perhaps one of Fairbanks's most memorable. Cattle stampedes were nothing new to films; westerns had employed the device on innumerable occasions with varying degrees of success. Even Buster Keaton had effected comic cattle chaos for *Go West* (1925). Fairbanks understood the art of cinematic illusion better than almost anyone and employed it in his sequences when needed; in order to make hundreds of steers look like thousands, he arranged for a herd of approximately six hundred to appear in the foreground. In the background were miniature models of cattle (affixed to belts and turntables and animated by the pulling of tape), then a painting or enlarged photograph of more cattle.[17] But Fairbanks was also meticulous in the preparation of the sequence to capture authentic cattle calamity. A herd of longhorns was collected in Mexico under the direction of Kenneth Dix, a former ranchman who made a specialty of acquiring herds for film industry work, as well as three hundred horses. Stampeding cattle are impossible to direct, as Fairbanks knew, and he realized that the best way to achieve the effect he wanted was with rapid intercutting. Utilizing wind machines, tight close-ups, glass shots, and undercranking, Fairbanks, Jones, and Gaudio were able to create the desired effect, which was skillfully edited by William Nolan.

Despite all the potential problems involving hundreds of cattle and horses, the production of the film went relatively smoothly. The only reported injury was to Fairbanks, who received a sword wound in the leg during filming of a scene in June 1927. When Fairbanks struck a saber from a soldier, the pommel struck the ground and rebounded, and the point of the blade penetrated Fairbanks's left leg below the knee. He was treated by a medic at the studio's hospital and remained undaunted; it was a minor mishap for a performer famed for allegedly doing his own stunts. Ted Reed recalled in 1956 that Fairbanks "didn't use any doubles until *The Gaucho,* and then only because he failed to show up and Chuck Lewis substituted for him to keep from wasting time."[18] Charles O. "Chuck" Lewis had been captain of the football team at the University of Missouri, an officer in the U.S. Army, and a pentathlon winner in the Los Angeles Olympic tryouts. He was working as a ge-

Fairbanks (at bottom just right of center) poses with the longhorn steers used in the climactic stampede in *Douglas Fairbanks as The Gaucho*. In the background are miniature models of cattle and a painting or enlarged photograph of even more steer. The mountain backdrop was achieved with a glass shot.

ologist when he met Fairbanks in 1922. He became Fairbanks's friend, trainer, and traveling companion for the rest of Fairbanks's life. Some fascinating outtakes and test film survive, revealing Chuck Lewis doubling for Fairbanks in extreme long shots for the sequence in which the Gaucho, having scaled the parabola of a palm tree, swings from tree to tree in a style equal to that of any of the screen Tarzan characters.[19]

The film had the working title *The Gaucho* and publicity materials indicate it was nearly renamed *Over the Andes*. (The suggested billing was: "Douglas Fairbanks as 'The Gaucho' in *Over the Andes*.") However, *Douglas Fairbanks as The Gaucho* prevailed. The world premiere was held at Grauman's Chinese Theatre in Hollywood on November 4, 1927. Fairbanks usually premiered his films in New York City, but he broke with precedent in this case for Grauman's Chinese Theatre, which had opened earlier that year. Fairbanks attended the event, as did nearly

The film exhibitor and showman Sid Grauman assists
Fairbanks and Pickford in the
placing of their footprints and
handprints in cement at the
first ceremony in the fore-
court of Grauman's Chinese
Theatre, April 30, 1927.
Photograph by J.C. Milligan.

every notable celebrity in the film world. The program boasted an elab-
orate prologue, entitled "Argentine Nights," conceived and staged by
Grauman himself. The musical score was compiled and conducted by
Arthur Kay.[20] Edwin Schallert wrote in the *Los Angeles Times*:

The Gaucho may meet with approbation because it is different, and
because it embodies a certain metaphysical interest, which is attractive to certain types of audiences, but it never reaches the high
point of entertainment that one associates with the star except for
more or less fleeting moments. It is nonetheless a praise-worthy
effort at attaining a new objective, the fruits of which will doubtless be shown in some future undertaking of the star.[21]

The New York premiere was held at the Liberty Theatre later that same month. The critical reaction to *The Gaucho* was decidedly mixed. Fairbanks perhaps gives a more startling display of his agility than in any other film, performing "antics that even simians might envy," Mordaunt Hall wrote in his *New York Times* review. He also praised the settings and the supporting cast, criticizing only the clash of darkness and joviality in the film. The character of the Victim of the Black Doom, in particular, was part of a "somber strain" that ultimately left the impression of a "gruesome undertone to an otherwise gay symphony."[22] *Motion Picture* magazine's reviewer addressed the film's religious content:

I had a few uneasy moments at the beginning of this picture when it seemed that Doug Fairbanks had gotten religion rather badly and was determined to convert us all, in Technicolor. But it was all right. It was just a legend that explained the story, and though Doug did get religion a little later on, he did it as quietly, quickly, and inoffensively as we have ever seen done. Don't let this saintly spirit keep you away from *The Gaucho*, for it is merely lurking in the background and doesn't interfere in the least with all the knavery, bravery, love and excitement. . . . Doug, with an amazingly slim waistline, is as acrobatic and impudent and ingenious as ever. . . . It is all just about the best entertainment that I can suggest.[23]

The strongest voice of dissension was Robert E. Sherwood, who expressed his disappointment in *Life* at Fairbanks's choice to use "religion, lust or loathsome disease" in one of his films, adding "there is no place for anything but Douglas Fairbanks—and all the beautiful, preposterous qualities that Douglas Fairbanks represents—in a Douglas Fairbanks film."[24] Despite the mixed response, *The Gaucho*, which had cost roughly $700,000 to make, grossed an impressive $1.4 million.[25]

In his 1973 study of Fairbanks, Richard Schickel writes: "*The Gaucho*, despite Fairbanks' tricks with the bola, was the flattest of the big-scale adventure-romances. Indeed, it is hard to determine just what he thought he was doing here."[26] Other modern critics have been uneasy with the religious aspects of the film. Jeanine Basinger writes that the "maudlin religious motif crowds in on the action," and that the action itself is "stretched to a point that's almost self-satirizing."[27]

Such criticism misses the point; the "self-satirizing" is actually self-parody and completely intentional. By 1927, Fairbanks's increasing restlessness was frequently manifesting itself in ways unimaginable a

The Gaucho dexterously
mounts and dismounts from
his horse (via reverse photography) for the amusement
of the Mountain Girl.

decade earlier. Sporadic absences, occasional extramarital dalliances, and a growing cynicism are a few examples of his increasing lack of interest. The cynicism naturally bled into his on screen attitude, and a sense of self-parody is very much evident in *The Gaucho*. John C. Tibbetts and James M. Welsh, in their study of Fairbanks, recognize the film's exceptional qualities, observing: "Ever since the publication of Byron's *The Corsair*, the popular imagination has been inflamed by tales of proud and cynical heroes who perform daring feats and display little regard for law or authority. . . . *The Gaucho* is one of the earliest attempts in American film to deal with the Byronic style of heroism."[28]

William K. Everson contends: "In a later period, when audiences were no longer confused by the sudden switching of mood and the ultra-rapid segues from slapstick to tragedy, *The Gaucho* would probably have been a much bigger hit."[29] The date of the film's release contributed significantly to its being overlooked. *The Gaucho* had its world premiere in November 1927, one month after *The Jazz Singer*, the film that started the talkie revolution. In a world suddenly captivated by the blending of voice with the visual, the silent *Gaucho* was soon rendered obsolete.

The film's failure to win reappraisal in subsequent decades has been largely owing to the lamentable fact that it has been presented solely in substandard black-and-white prints. Not only did the original contain two-color Technicolor footage, but the prints were tinted. To view *The Gaucho* devoid of color is an alteration to the film not intended by the filmmaker and dampens its power.

Admittedly, *The Gaucho* is far from flawless. The structure of the film is both derivative and confused, and one may lay blame for this on the fact that by this time, Fairbanks was surrounding himself with yes-men, who did not help him by subjecting his ideas to critical scrutiny. *The Gaucho* recycles *Robin Hood,* in that an outlaw saves the people from a usurper; it recycles *The Mark of Zorro,* in that a loner sets himself against an evil oppressor; it recycles *The Black Pirate,* in that the loner captures the ship/city more or less single-handedly.

The scenario fails to develop what drove El Gaucho to become an outlaw, why the population would be sympathetic to such a predatory, carnal character, or what he has gained by his outlaw life, other than a spectacular wardrobe. Nor is it explained what sustains El Gaucho's private army; the viewer does not see any of them doing normal cowboy work (or anything constructive at all, for that matter). The huge herd of cattle is established by only one quick shot early in the film; otherwise, it is simply a last-minute plot device. El Gaucho seems to have absolute control over his band but is completely aloof from them, except for his first lieutenant, played by Charles Stevens. The viewer does not know why Ruiz is a "usurper" rather than an ordinary tyrant, like the governor in *The Mark of Zorro,* or what he has usurped and how he keeps the army behind him. Fairbanks created a plot full of holes. One does not even see a logical development of El Gaucho's love for the Mountain Girl that would reasonably end in marriage.

In motion, Fairbanks is still beautiful to behold. One suspects that a primary reason he embraced this story was that he imagined throwing the bolas, leaping on and off horses, and vaulting walls with his customary exuberance. Although Fairbanks is beginning to look middle-aged, he executes these stunts amazingly. Despite the film's structural flaws, *The Gaucho* nevertheless succeeds as a character study that successfully integrates daring thematic ideas. The film also fascinates as autobiography; mirroring Fairbanks's own personality, the Gaucho is an unconventional, self-absorbed hero filled with self-doubt. *The Gaucho* indicates a range Fairbanks has hitherto not been credited as possessing. The film is unlike any other that he produced, a work in which theme, not technology, was the experiment, with an artist at the peak of his maturity who was willing to push the scope of emotion rather than the scope of the physical production. Fairbanks would never again attempt the depth and daring he displays here. "Everything is a situation, and he [Fairbanks] plays for the big moment, then snaps the curtain," Allene Talmey wrote presciently in 1927. "There are no third acts for him."[30]

Hail and Farewell

The Iron Mask (1929)

The motion picture industry was changing rapidly in 1928, and the 45-year-old Fairbanks was seriously contemplating his place within it. The erstwhile innovator intuitively recognized that talking motion pictures called for something completely different, yet he had little enthusiasm for pioneering the new technology. Instead, Fairbanks embarked on his last silent film and last great endeavor, *The Iron Mask*, a sequel to *The Three Musketeers*, which drew upon his favorite screen character to summon from himself and his team one final swashbuckling adventure that displayed his unmistakable high standards. This time, however, he placed particular emphasis on historical authenticity, a quality he believed *The Three Musketeers* lacked.[1] Fairbanks's final portrayal of d'Artagnan, coupled with the film's story of the end of the musketeer tradition, plays like a farewell to the silent cinema itself. As a valedictory to the silent screen, *The Iron Mask* is unsurpassed. In one of his few departures from playing a young man—and with fewer characteristic stunts—Fairbanks conjures up his most multidimensional and moving screen portrayal in a film that is perhaps the supreme achievement of its genre.

When audiences at the Warner Theatre in New York City heard Al Jolson utter the phrase "You ain't heard nothin' yet" on October 6, 1927, the world that Douglas Fairbanks had ruled changed forever. *The Jazz Singer*, a silent film with a synchronized musical score and scenes

Fairbanks, in costume as the youthful d'Artagnan, revisits his favorite role in *The Iron Mask*. Photograph by Charles E. Lynch.

of recorded singing, sound effects, and dialogue, premiered; and its sound waves reverberated throughout the motion picture industry. The new technology perfectly tapped into the current American obsession with radio, and its contagion spread quickly to Hollywood. Reaction among the United Artists partners was mixed. Chaplin was defiant. After completion of *The Circus* (1928), he quickly began preproduction for yet another silent film, *City Lights*, which he released in 1931, four years into the sound era. In contrast, Pickford readily embraced the "talkies." Her husband was not quite so eager. "My father did not care for sound films," Douglas Fairbanks Jr. remembered. "He liked to tell a story visually. He thought of his films—silent films—as essentially pantomime and ballet . . . rather than as an actor, he saw himself as an athletic dancer leaping with graceful and visually effective movement across the adventures of history. Sound for his purposes was too literal, too realistic, and too restricting."[2]

Fairbanks turned a deaf ear to the growing noise surrounding him and forged ahead to produce one last silent film. He was determined to mount the finest production possible and leave silent cinema and the romantic costume film he had perfected in a triumphant blaze of glory. This last gasp of silent cinema was also the period of the superproduction: F. W. Murnau's *Sunrise* (1927), William Wellman's *Wings* (1927), Clarence Brown's *The Trail of '98* (1928), and Erich von Stroheim's *The Wedding March* (1928), to name a few. Surely part of Fairbanks's motivation was to compete against and better such films as these, in addition to topping himself. "Doug seemed to be under some sort of compulsion to make this picture one of his best productions," Allan Dwan, whom Fairbanks hired to direct the lavish production, later observed. "He had always meticulously supervised every detail of his pictures, but in this one I think he eclipsed himself. It was as if he knew this was his swan song."[3] It is unsurprising, therefore, that he chose his favorite literary character to make his grand exit. A romantic adventure, not far removed from nineteenth-century opera, *The Iron Mask* contains an element of pathos without precedent in Fairbanks's work. The older d'Artagnan of *The Iron Mask* correctly exudes authority and a touch of wistfulness in contrast to the exuberant bullyboy of *The Three Musketeers*. D'Artagnan can still perform wondrous feats, but now his silver hair belies the athletic prowess, the lines of age crease his pliant and expressive face, and while he still saves the day, and the future of France, in this film—for the first time—he pays the ultimate price for his heroism: he dies. Indeed, nearly every major character from 1921's *The Three Musketeers* shares this fate in *The Iron Mask*. The film, like *The Gaucho*, is unmistakably dark in tone. It is as if Fairbanks is bidding

farewell not only to the art form he had pioneered and perfected, but also to the best part of himself and his work.

In addition to Dwan (directing his tenth and last film for Fairbanks), Fairbanks assembled a top-notch team—a combination of the familiar and the unknown, the veteran and the novice—that helped propel him to heights he had not previously attempted, while at the same time providing him with an all-important safety net. Henry Sharp—on loan from M-G-M—was hired as cinematographer, and the reliable Fred Cavens was again engaged to choreograph all the swordplay and fight sequences. Cavens was also instrumental in teaching proper bearing and the ceremonious bow to all the men in the cast. Several of the original cast members of *The Three Musketeers* repeated their roles in *The Iron Mask:* Marguerite de la Motte as Constance, Nigel de Brulier as Cardinal Richelieu, Lon Poff as Father Joseph, Charles Stevens as d'Artagnan's servant, Planchet, and Léon Bary as Athos. Noticeably absent, however, was the original Aramis, Eugene Pallette, who had gained so much weight in the intervening years that he was replaced by Italian actor Gino Corrado. George Siegmann, the original Porthos, died during the film's preproduction, and Stanley J. Sandford, a tall, heavy-set actor best remembered for his work in silent comedies, filled the large shoes (and costume) of Porthos. Others new to the Fairbanks lot were Ulrich Haupt as the villainous de Rochefort, Dorothy Revier as Milady de Winter, and Belle Bennett as Anne of Austria, the queen mother.

D'Artagnan is frustrated at not having a private moment with Constance (Marguerite de la Motte).

D'Artagnan kisses Constance good-bye.

Adolphe Menjou, launched with his success in Chaplin's *A Woman of Paris* (1923), was not available to reprise the small role of Louis XIII, which went instead to Rolfe Sedan. Rounding out the cast was 20-year-old William Bakewell in the important dual role of Louis XIV and his evil twin brother.

With such an impressive array of talent on hand, and the film taking on increasing importance for him personally, Fairbanks was ever more determined to make sure it had every possible opportunity for success. *The Three Musketeers* was effectively banned in France as a result of a French version, *Les trois mousquetaires,* directed by Henri Diamant-Berger. Fairbanks determined that his new film would not share the fate of its predecessor. In order to make the film appealing to French audiences, he engaged the septuagenarian French artist Maurice Leloir, a recognized authority on the period of Louis XIV and the illustrator of the 1894 Calmann Lévy edition of Dumas *père*'s novel *Les trois mousquetaires,* as production consultant. Leloir, a watercolorist, illustrator, museum founder, costume historian, and theater designer, was personally wooed by Fairbanks. "Mr. Fairbanks in person arrived at my door," Leloir writes. "'I know your Dumas illustrations,'" Fairbanks said, "'but I thought you and he were contemporaries. Weren't you his friend?' 'Who, me and d'Artagnan?'" Leloir joked. "'Yes, I was a friend of Dumas, Dumas *fils*, his son.'"[4] Cinema was a new challenge for the 74-year-old Leloir, who left France on June 20, 1928, and returned after filming ended on December 14 of the same year. For the sum of $25,000, Leloir was responsible for the film's costume design and properties, although Fairbanks consulted him on nearly every detail of the historical aspects of the production, even having him give lessons in seventeenth-century French manners and deportment to a decidedly twentieth-century American cast. Upon his return to France, Leloir assembled his memoirs and sketches into a book, *Cinq mois à Hollywood avec Douglas Fairbanks,* an invaluable record of the production history of *The Iron Mask* and Hollywood filmmaking of the period.

The British painter and stage designer Laurence Irving, grandson of the legendary actor Sir Henry Irving, was recommended to Fairbanks by Edward Knoblock and served as principal art director on *The Iron Mask.* Like Leloir, Irving was a newcomer to films. William Cameron Menzies, who had created the Arabian Nights atmosphere of Fairbanks's *The Thief of Bagdad,* was the consulting production designer to United Artists Studios. Irving acknowledged his debt to Menzies, saying: "The little that I know I learnt from Menzies who, throughout my stay in Hollywood was an assiduous philosopher, guide, and friend who went out of his way to initiate me into the mysteries of his craft in which he has no equal."[5] Irving's assignment was the design of fifty-four sets possessing a scaled authenticity and heightened romanticism seldom undertaken in American film. He explained the process two years later:

As many as two drawings a day [are] made.... Working under the art director are a number of craftsmen who are to supply these details and supervise the construction of a set. To them the art director hands over his drawing which is projected in plan and elevation in such a way that, photographed through a lens of a given angle, the set will appear exactly on the screen as it does in the drawing. To achieve this result building in forced perspective is frequently resorted to. The hall of the convent, by reducing the arches, or groining of a ceiling in order or by making a line of windows of reducing sizes may be made to appear thirty or forty feet in length when in reality its depth is but fifteen feet.... [With the help of the miniature expert,] we can save a great deal of time and money.... [To] build [a] street with a palace rising from the hill behind it, it is necessary only to build such parts in full scale as are needed to cover the action which takes place before them.... An imaginary line is traced across the drawing, everything below which will be built in full-scale and everything above it in miniature.... After the full-scale work has been completed, the camera is set up on a solid platform. Now the miniature man gets to work. On a light framework suspended a few feet in front of the camera, he begins to build the remaining portions of the drawing, in perfect proportion and detail, the textures faithfully reproduced in tiny scale. The same lighting will fall on both the full-scale and the miniature scene. [The miniaturist's work] is so perfectly blended that the line of demarcation is indistinguishable.[6]

Not all of the designer's efforts were realized. Irving recalled the challenges in conveying the impact of a set through a fixed camera and onto a cinema screen:

Lavish scale is apt to dwindle to unimportance on the screen. I well remember a thrilling night when we were shooting the interior of the palace. A set which cost $70,000 to build and heaven knows how much to light and populate with actors, was ultimately cut out altogether because it held up the action of the story. Exquisitely costumed courtiers, soldiers, kings, and princes thronged the floor. The colour and movement was beautiful. The

The superb design for the street of St. Germain-en-Laye in *The Iron Mask*, with the palace rising behind it, as conceived by Laurence Irving. The constructed set occupied nearly three acres of the studio lot, and the palace seen in the distance was achieved with a hanging miniature.

King Louis XIII (Rolfe Sedan) and his court anticipate the arrival of his heir. Note the scale and detail of Laurence Irving's sets. Photograph by Charles E. Lynch.

following afternoon we [watched] the rushes. What we saw on the screen was barely recognisable as the gorgeous spectacle of the night before.[7]

In addition to Menzies, Irving was assisted by a team of talented artists, including Carl Oscar Borg, Ben Carré, Harold W. Miles, David S. Hall, Edward M. Langley, Wilfred Buckland, and Jack Holden. Ben

Carré, on loan from Fox Film Corporation, had created the drawings for the Paris Opera House underworld in *The Phantom of the Opera*. Carré's primary function was the design of the classic Louis XIII–inspired interiors. In his unpublished memoirs, he recalls designing two sets to accommodate Fairbanks's stunts. The first, for a scene in which Fairbanks crashes through a casement window, was built with glass panes made of sugar and the frame of balsa wood. The other was the exterior of the Convent at Mantes, where Constance is taken prisoner by Milady de Winter. Carré writes:

It was difficult even in those days to find a site free of telegraph poles and buildings. We found one near Sunset [Boulevard] by the ocean. The set showed the stone walls of the convent with barred windows on the second and third floors facing a tree-lined road. The worrying part for the set builder was a reinforced tree facing Constance's window. The script stated: "d'Artagnan climbs the tree. Leaping from branch to branch, he stops level with the window. He leaps through space and lands on the window ledge, clinging on to the iron bars. De Winter rushes to the window to stab d'Artagnan who recoils, falling backwards through the branches, to be caught by the musketeers." The tree had to be strong enough to support Fairbanks so I used camouflaged iron straps but avoided too much foliage. There was no safety net—he had to be caught for real. The climb, the jump and the fall were straight takes—platforms were brought in only for the setup or closer shots.[8]

Working from their respective designs, it then fell upon the shoulders of Fairbanks's elder brother Robert to meticulously reproduce their vision in wood, stone, and plaster. Douglas Fairbanks Jr. witnessed this himself at the studio:

My father tended to be extravagant. Nothing would be spared to give his films the finest cast, designs, and costumes. He spent as much as could be afforded. It was to give the films a special something that nobody else could give and also provide a background for his type of picture, which was really his own mixture of pantomime and dance. It was the responsibility of my Uncle Robert to fulfill my father's vision yet keep a tight rein on expenditures. My uncle, as an engineer by profession, had the intelligence and the training to achieve everything my father wanted constructed as efficiently as possible. *The Iron Mask* is second only to *The Thief of Bagdad* in terms of design. In fact, it may have been a more daunting task than *Bagdad*. *The Thief of Bagdad* was pure fantasy. *The Iron Mask* attempts to authentically recreate a specific time and place.[9]

No matter how grand the scale or opulent the surroundings created, however, nothing on the set could ever compete with the towering presence, magnetism, and sincerity of purpose of Fairbanks himself. William Bakewell remembered:

As a kid growing up in Hollywood, I used to go over to the Pickford-Fairbanks Studios all the time. Whenever I heard he was shooting a picture, and wasn't in school, I looked through the wire fence around the back lot on Formosa [Avenue] to catch a glimpse of him. That's when I really felt the call to be an actor. Watching him at work. No question about it. You can imagine the thrill I had a few years later to hear from my agent that I was to work for the great Douglas Fairbanks. It was an incredible experience. It was everything I had ever hoped and imagined it to be—and then some. He was my hero. He was every boy's hero! A giant among men. Doug was d'Artagnan, Robin Hood, and Zorro.[10]

"There was absolutely no cheating on quality," Bakewell recalled.[11] This and the relaxed, convivial atmosphere at the studio made a deep impression on him. "In many respects, it was more like play than work, the romance and pageantry of the subject matter being approached by Doug and his staff with a relish and enthusiasm that was infectious."[12]

This infectious sense of enthusiasm and fun made visiting the set—a very common practice during most of the open-air filming—almost de rigueur on this particular production for celebrities who found themselves in Los Angeles. The most notable of such guests was one Lieutenant Windsor, better known as Prince George, the youngest son of Britain's King George V.[13] A serving officer in the Royal Navy, Prince George absented himself without leave from his ship in Santa Barbara to visit Fairbanks in Hollywood on September 12, 1928. Fairbanks played a scene before the cameras and revealed such tricks as the set's windowpanes made of sugar, through which Fairbanks was able to propel himself unscathed. In addition, a rodeo was hurriedly organized for the future Duke of Kent's entertainment. Following afternoon tea served by Pickford in her bungalow, the prince enjoyed a dinner party at Pickfair with Chaplin, John Gilbert, Greta Garbo, Gloria Swanson, and Billie Dove among the guests.[14] Bakewell remembered:

William Bakewell in his dual role as Louis XIV (top) and his evil twin (bottom).

Throughout the filming of *The Iron Mask*, a sporadic stream of visitors made its way to the Fairbanks set to watch the shooting. Doug was always a charming and gracious host-guide, going to great lengths to explain every facet of the scene in progress. Usually, especially in the cases of guests of distinction, he would invite them to luncheon in his studio bungalow. Often I was asked to join them during my lunch hour, and I sat one day with the distinguished journalist, Arthur Brisbane, and on another, with a cousin of the King of Spain.

"One for All—All for One": the homoerotic suggestion conveyed by the musketeers' sleeping arrangement in *The Iron Mask* was lost on most contemporary audiences, but it surfaces immediately with twenty-first-century viewers. Left to right: Aramis, Athos, d'Artagnan, and Porthos.

[After playing a game of "Doug"] we would usually head for Fairbanks' dressing room and a steam bath before leaving for the day. . . . Invariably, some of Fairbanks' cronies would drop around for a visit in his dressing room at the end of the day. Usually on hand were the screen writer, Tom Geraghty, Charlie Chaplin, theater-owner Sid Grauman. . . . Once Doug had dried off after his steam and a plunge in ice-cold water, he would chat enthusiastically with his friends. I recall watching him lather his chest with soap during one of those bull-sessions and proceed to shave it carefully with a straight-edged razor. "This is common practice in the Orient," he remarked as he nimbly stroked away. However it sounds, it was all completely masculine, for Doug's physique was his stock-in-trade and he went all out to keep it in sleek, deeply tanned, photogenic condition . . . he was built like a bronzed sculpture.[15]

A bronzed sculpture that moved. The stunts, in particular, were carefully constructed to appear as though effortless. They were performed with a rare grace and rhythm that were uniquely his own. Dwan recalled: "Of course, when Doug did any of his stunts, he was essentially graceful. That's one thing he struggled for, and I insisted upon. There was never to be any evidence of effort on his part. Everything we did was based on a measurement of his reach . . . anybody else would be stretching. What we were after in all the stunts was a grace and agility—like a ballet dancer."[16]

Surviving outtakes from *The Iron Mask* reveal many of the secrets of these outstanding sequences. Carefully camouflaged within set pieces are well-placed handholds, making Fairbanks's climbs and vaults appear effortless. For the sword fights, the cinematographer, Henry Sharp, used varying camera speeds to achieve the facile dexterity and lightness of foot. Stairs, tables, and walls were specially built "Doug-size" so that he could elegantly bound over them. So skilled were these craftsmen in achieving these effects that even viewed with today's jaded eyes, they inspire spontaneous applause from large audiences. Two very successful revivals of *The Iron Mask*—a 1953 theatrical reissue and a sumptuous mounting with live orchestral accompaniment in 1999—bear out this assertion.[17]

With the working title of *Twenty Years After*, the scenario of *The Iron Mask* incorporated episodes from *The Three Musketeers* (Fairbanks utilized only half of Dumas's novel in his 1921 film) with events from Dumas's two sequels to *The Three Musketeers: Twenty Years After* and *The Vicomte de Bragelonne, or Ten Years Later*. (*The Man in the Iron Mask* is the third part of the *Vicomte de Bragelonne* trilogy.) The central pivot of Fairbanks's original draft was the supposed twin brother of Louis XIV, who is substituted for the real king. Dr. Arthur Woods conducted the initial historical research, and Lotta Woods wove the most exciting elements of Dumas, plucked by Fairbanks and Dwan from the various texts, into a cohesive scenario over a six-month period. Further embellishments by advisors and gagmen were incorporated into the swashbuckler.[18] Dwan recalled that all of Fairbanks's key collaborators worked on the scenario. "The credit went to Elton Thomas—Doug's middle names—and Lotta Woods. Lotta put it on paper—the big secretary. 'Elton Thomas' was twenty people."[19] Known for weaving historical facts together with intrigue from his own imagination, Dumas *père* based his torturous iron mask on an actual device purportedly used during the reign of Louis XIV. *The Iron Mask* begins in the France of 1638, with Louis XIII on the throne anticipating the birth of his son, the future monarch. Once again, Cardinal Richelieu figures heavily in the dramatic proceedings. Upon the discovery of a royal twin birth, and fearing that there being two future claimants to the crown might precipitate a revolution, Richelieu covertly arranges for the younger twin to be dispatched to a remote location. The sinister de Rochefort, however, devises a scheme to kidnap the child from the kidnappers and groom him in his own conspiracy to switch heirs and seize control of the throne. When the day arrives, the other twin—now the youthful king of France—is imprisoned in a fiendish iron mask device and sent to a remote castle. The second twin, now a power-hungry man driven to in-

For once, too late to save the heroine: Constance dies in d'Artagnan's arms as nuns from the convent look on. Photograph by Charles E. Lynch.

sanity by de Rochefort, assumes the throne in his place. D'Artagnan, discovering the duplicity, summons the other three musketeers for one final adventure, in which they rescue the imprisoned young king, dispose of the mad twin, save France, and, one by one, lose their lives in the line of duty. The film ends with d'Artagnan's spirit rising from his lifeless body and rejoining his three great friends as they march off together into the clouds to experience new, unearthly adventures. "There is greater adventure beyond," the last intertitle reads. Ever the optimist, Fairbanks concludes his elegy to the silent cinema, not with the conventional title "The End," but with "The Beginning."

The fourteen-week production, which began in August 1928, proceeded smoothly and efficiently at the United Artists Studios, with location work in and around Los Angeles.[20] This was largely owing to Dwan's executive talent and engineering skills. Although very much a status-conscious director, he modified his methods when working with Fairbanks, whom he considered a friend. As for Fairbanks, any question on his part of Dwan's direction on the set was mollified by the

Brilliant yet simple lighting techniques in *The Iron Mask* add immeasurably to the sinister proceedings as de Rochefort captures the young Louis XIV and imprisons him in the torturous iron mask. It was, in effect, "a shadowgraph—the play of light on the unornamented surface of a flight of stairs and a wall on which was thrown a monstrous shade of the figures and instruments menacing the victim," Laurence Irving recalled. Photograph by Charles E. Lynch.

producer-star inquiring, "Vous avez raison?" (Fairbanks meant "Do you have a reason?" and was blissfully unaware that the idiom translates as "Are you correct?")[21] According to Irving, although Dwan "was nominally director, his contribution was mainly executive, just as Douglas's pseudonym Elton Thomas was a portmanteau title for himself and all those who had elaborated his original treatment of the two novels."[22] Few, aside from astute observers like Irving, noticed that behind the ebullient veneer, Fairbanks was showing signs of slowing down:

I realised he was approaching the end of a road that he had indeed paved with gold, that the grueling task of filmmaking had lost its charm, and that, having a fertile nest egg, he should end his career with the fine flourish our film promised to be. He was, by nature, restless, and year by year he found it harder to exert the self-discipline to submit himself to the grueling traffic of the studio each film demanded. Every morning, as he donned the iron-grey wig and submitted to the makeup man painting the thickening flesh below the chin a deeper yellow to deceive the relentless eye of the camera, his reflection in the mirror tempted him to quit while he was in the prime of life and on the pinnacle of fame.[23]

Another sign of Fairbanks's slowing down is, perhaps, the fact that in *The Iron Mask*, more than in any of his other costume films, he relegates himself mostly to part of an ensemble. He has foregrounded scenes, of course, but fairly few of them; this is not a star vehicle. This point is amplified by Fairbanks's decision to have almost no close shots of himself. Most of the time, he is shown at full or three-quarter length, probably to soften the impact of his aging. Especially in the first half hour of the film, until the audience grows accustomed to his appearance, the preponderance of long shots and absence of close-ups of the star is quite striking. One could argue that this is to showcase the stunning sets, but Fairbanks does not allow himself to be overwhelmed by the sets in his other costume films, including *Robin Hood*, also directed by Dwan. The ensemble nature is also emphasized by the use of stars such as Belle Bennett in modest supporting parts.

Near completion of the film, Fairbanks felt compelled to make some concession to film exhibitors who wanted sound motion pictures. Sound equipment for the United Artists Studios lot was installed midway through the production of *The Iron Mask*, and although there was no way that the primitive technology could accommodate the sweeping grandeur of the film he was just finishing, Fairbanks was an astute producer. He was financially as well as emotionally invested in this film and wanted to give it every opportunity for success. He therefore reconciled himself to the use of "talking, but with no dialogue" as he described it.[24] His character would speak directly to the audience in two filmed sequences, at the first and second halves of the film. William Bakewell remembered that by this point in Hollywood, "every silent in production had to have a sequence in sound. Fairbanks decided they ought to have a prologue, with a tapestry featuring d'Artagnan and the musketeers. . . . Well everybody was nervous about it. On the day it was filmed people were coming in from all over the lot but they wouldn't let them in. Doug was a professional man of the theater, and even he was uptight about the whole thing."[25]

Fairbanks, dressed as d'Artagnan and flanked by the three musketeers, breaks the tapestry *tableau vivant*, waves his sword, and delivers his prologue speech in verse, a reworking of material written years before by Edward Knoblock:

Out of the shadows of the past
As from a faded tapestry
Of Time's procession slow and vast
I step, to bid you bear with me
The while your fancy I engage
To look upon another age.
An age when on the human tide
The plumed wave of chivalry
Rose to its summit,
Sweeping wide across a Nation's mighty sea.
France never shone a brighter power
Than in this high romantic hour.
So come with me to France of old,
To fiery days when hearts beat high
When blood was young, and hate was bold
And sword crossed sword to do or die.
For love and honor gloried them,
And friendship reached its peak with men.
Friends were friends in those brave days—
Athos, Porthos, Aramis, I
Graved our hearts with a mystic phrase
Bound out lives with a mystic tie
Come, stir your soul with our ringing call
of "All for One, and One for All."
Come on! Come on! Come on![26]

There were four sound systems used in Hollywood in 1928: Warner Bros. had Vitaphone; Fox had Movietone; RCA had Photophone; and United Artists used Western Electric. All of these early systems came with cumbersome recording equipment, and the technicians had little experience in the new medium of talking pictures. One of the technicians on *The Iron Mask* was Edward Bernds, who had seen Fairbanks "at his carefree, prankish best during the silent filming of *The Iron Mask*. Then I saw what the coming of sound did to him when we filmed a talking prologue." Bernds remembered:

Doug ... sprang into the foreground and delivered his prologue speech. We did the scene over and over. . . . Finally, we got a complete take, and, as was the barbaric custom in those days, we played it back. Sound equipment was touchy and inefficient

D'Artagnan rescues Louis XIV in *The Iron Mask*. One of the iron masks made for the production has been preserved by the Natural History Museum of Los Angeles County. The one used in the actual film was kept by William Bakewell as a keepsake.

then. Sometimes speed would go out of control. When we made the playback for Doug, we had a "runaway" on the wax [disc] play-back machine, just fast enough to give Doug a girlish falsetto. Mercifully, somebody pulled the loudspeaker plug, but I think Doug never really recovered from the shock of hearing that gib-berish runaway version.[27]

Indeed, it is likely that Fairbanks never did recover from that ini-tial shock. It was not the innovation that stopped him; it was the limi-tation. He found the process of sound film unsatisfying. Nevertheless, he was sufficiently satisfied with the two talking sequences to retain them, pleased that he was able to deliver a product exhibitors were able to promote as containing "talking" sequences without any dialogue at all in direct action within the film.

The Iron Mask was released in two versions to ensure the widest pos-sible success. The "sound" version had a superb symphonic musical score by the accomplished musician and composer Hugo Riesenfeld, replete with a male chorus singing the film's theme song, "One for All—All for One," sound effects, and two synchronized speeches by Fair-banks (the prologue and the one that begins the second half of the film) recorded on an optical sound track using the Western Electric Sys-tem.[28] For those movie theaters not yet equipped for sound, it was also released in a silent version without the speeches. The world premiere of *The Iron Mask* was held on February 21, 1929 at the Rivoli Theatre in New York City. The *New York Times* called the film "a crackerjack enter-tainment that never wearies."[29] *Variety* reported "Rollicking and excel-lent box-office fare."[30] *Photoplay* magazine pithily proclaimed: "It is adroit. It is imaginative. It is resplendent. There is the characteristic Fairbanks breadth and sweep and stunts. And it is his best job of story-telling."[31] *The Iron Mask* received a big premiere at the Cathay Circle

Theater in Los Angeles with both Fairbanks and Pickford in attendance and to great acclaim.[32]

Yet despite overwhelmingly positive reviews, and grossing an impressive $1.5 million, *The Iron Mask* was considered only a moderate financial success, owing to its approximately $1 million production cost. Having virtually defined the swashbuckler as a cinematic genre, Fairbanks was also the one to usher out its initial cycle. Hollywood began to concentrate on talk-laden original scripts, static adaptations of Broadway plays, and musicals, and action films were momentarily cast aside. When d'Artagnan bids farewell to his earthly existence in the final moments of *The Iron Mask,* Fairbanks also appears to be bidding farewell, not only to that character, but to Zorro, the Thief of Bagdad, the Black Pirate, and all the other romantic roles of his swashbuckling past. It would have been a superb swan song to his life and career, had that only been the case. However, Fairbanks had nearly a dozen more years to live, and time and conditions would compel him to exit less gracefully from the stage that he loved so dearly. But it was a different stage. It was, in every respect, the "sound" stage. In early 1928, as the first United Artists Studios sound stage was being erected, he appeared to know that the end of an era had arrived. Laurence Irving noted the change:

The prop men and the electricians, everybody, were all cheerful, bronzed Californians. The studios were brightly lit, and whenever a scene was played a nice little orchestra played to encourage the actors to get into the right mood. And then gradually there appeared these pale, harassed charges from almost outer space, who were of course the minions of the Western Electric Company who were installing the first sound stage.

Douglas came to my room one day and said, "Let's go down and have a look at the sound stage." We walked down and the doors of the big studios were open, and instead of seeing a nice bright place where everybody was extremely happy working, it was a ghastly sort of cave hung with blankets, no lights, the whole of the floor covered with serpentine wires and cables, and then these menacing microphones. . . .

As he took this in, Douglas laid his hand on my arm, as he often did when he spoke to me, and he said, "Laurence, the romance of motion picture making ends here."[33]

Whether it was the romance of motion picture making, or Fairbanks's own romance with picture making that ended with *The Iron Mask*, one thing is certain. Fairbanks never again made the same emo-

Fairbanks reads *Film Weekly* during a rare moment of relaxation during production of *The Iron Mask*.

Fairbanks created his own obituary on film at the conclusion of *The Iron Mask*. When d'Artagnan dies, his spirit rises from his mortal remains and is reunited with the three musketeers. They march to heaven as they marched in life—together—with d'Artagnan in the middle. Here the musketeers Aramis, Athos, d'Artagnan, and Porthos are amused by the mourners surrounding d'Artagnan's earthly body.

tional and artistic investment in one of his films. He and his team had created a fitting valedictory to the age of silent cinema. They had dared to reach for the moon one last time, and had captured it; it is a beautifully mounted, superbly executed, swashbuckling adventure. Fairbanks's remaining films reveal his magic only in brief flashes. To paraphrase the film's prologue speech, which might also serve as his own epitaph, film never had "a brighter power" than Douglas Fairbanks. *The Iron Mask* was his last "high, romantic hour."

Sound and Fury

Taming of the Shrew (1929) and Marital Strife

Douglas Fairbanks and Mary Pickford were two of the biggest stars in Hollywood. When they co-starred in a major production for the first time, it was a publicist's dream. The world's best-known couple, at last appearing together on screen in the new medium of "talkies," with dialogue from the greatest writer of the language, William Shakespeare, were sure to be a box office bonanza; Doug and Mary in *Taming of the Shrew* were an unbeatable combination. Petruchio was an ideal role for Fairbanks's flamboyant and insouciant screen persona. "America's Sweetheart" was equally well suited as the beautiful, proud, and independent Katherina (renamed Katherine for the film). The production combined the financial resources of the two superstar producers and employed the finest artisans, technicians, and supporting players available. It was thought certain to be the most triumphant production that Hollywood had ever known. Instead, it was a box office disappointment, ushering in the swift decline of both careers and the disintegration of Hollywood's storybook marriage. What went so horribly wrong?

In January 1929, Fairbanks had just completed *The Iron Mask* and was undecided about what his inaugural effort in the "talkies" should entail. Pickford, on the other hand, was the first major silent film star to undertake an all-talking film. Her first foray, *Coquette* (1929), had all

Petruchio and Katherine in the final scene of *Taming of the Shrew*. Asked why such boisterous material was chosen for his screen pairing with his wife, Fairbanks answered: "So much has been written about the romance and marriage of Mary Pickford and myself, and so much of it has been oversweet, that to have filmed a romantic love story would have been, to say the least, bad taste." Photograph by Charles E. Lynch.

the earmarks of great success; it had been a hit on Broadway in 1928, and the part of Norma Besant was feminine yet strong. Out of an all-consuming need to work, Pickford had literally cut ties with her past; she had shorn her famous curls on June 21, 1928, three months after her mother's death. *My Best Girl,* her last silent film, was already out of its first-run release. Her fans mourned the loss of the golden curls, and so too did Fairbanks, who cried when he saw her after the deed was done.[1] Pickford maintained that her bob gave her the freedom to try new things, and *Coquette* went on to great commercial success when it was released in April 1929. For Fairbanks, the loss of the curls—and the loss of the silent cinema—portended an uneasy and uncertain future. Eventually, as Laurence Irving surmised, Fairbanks's "irrepressible ebullience got the better of him. Possible, after all, romance and the making of talking pictures were not incompatible. Mary's quiet persistence may have shamed him into making a show of defiance."[2]

The public had long been clamoring for an on-screen collaboration between the two; and, fortuitously, Fairbanks and Pickford had seen and enjoyed a production of *The Taming of the Shrew* in Los Angeles in January. They jointly concluded that this would make an ideal vehicle for their long-anticipated co-starring screen venture.[3] Furthermore, it would reenergize both their careers. They would co-produce, co-finance, and co-star as Shakespeare's famously combative co-dependent couple, Katherina and Petruchio, on a swift six-week production schedule and with an intended budget of $504,000. "Their aim was high, and their purpose admirable," Irving observes.[4] They would bring Shakespeare to the screen, elevating motion picture dialogue to the highest level, perhaps even with Technicolor. Innovation was always an essential hallmark of the superior productions to which Fairbanks aspired. It would be a new Doug and Mary!

It was appropriate that Fairbanks turned to Shakespeare for his first talkie. His first exposure to theater had been the recitation of Shakespeare soliloquies in the grand manner of his father. There was also the added allure that Shakespearean comedy afforded him full license to unleash his flamboyant acting style, replete with expansive gestures, and a barking light baritone speaking voice. The film would also be the first talking film adaptation of a work by Shakespeare.[5]

With the decision made by both Fairbanks and Pickford to go forward, Sam Taylor was promptly engaged to write the screen adaptation and direct the production. Taylor had directed Pickford in her two previous films, and she was especially keen on having him back to assuage her misgivings about attempting Shakespeare as an immediate follow-up to *Coquette.* Initially, Fairbanks believed that Taylor was an excellent choice for the film. They conceived it as a crowd-pleasing comedy, and Taylor had enjoyed a long and fruitful association with Harold Lloyd as both director and writer; their collaborations included such Lloyd classics as *Safety Last!* (1923) and *The Freshman* (1925). Moreover, he was a graduate of Fordham University, an uncommon distinction among Hollywood's roster of largely untutored directors.

Taylor examined notable adaptations of the play, including those by David Garrick and Augustin Daly, and excised characters, subplot, and dialogue that "held up the action." Thomas Patton, a Shakespearean authority, and John Craig, an authority on variant readings of the text, served as consultants.[6] The choice was also made—in the tradition of E. H. Sothern and Julia Marlowe—to have Katherine be aware of Petruchio's scheme and seek to placate him. This is conveyed in the film by having Katherine overhear Petruchio's "Thus have I politely begun my reign" soliloquy, which he speaks to his dog, Troilus.

Karl Struss was signed on as cinematographer, and he provided the film with some camera movements uncommon in the typically stilted early talkies, including some impressive traveling shots. The Fairbanks alumni William Cameron Menzies and Laurence Irving were engaged to jointly design the costumes and sets, the three major sets being the interior of Baptista's home, a church, and Petruchio's country house, all erected on the main sound stage at United Artists Studios. Although the sets and costumes were originally designed for Technicolor, the idea of color was abandoned when it became clear that it would be too expensive even for the deep pockets of a Pickford-Fairbanks co-production.

Irving remembered that even at this relatively early stage of production, disturbing tensions were beginning to surface on the lot. He wrote in his autobiography:

Bill [Menzies] and I were soon aware of tensions engendered by the fusion of the Fairbanks and Pickford organisations to handle a production in which stardom was to be shared and expenses equally borne. The rival retinues felt their loyal duty was to guard the interests of their employers. The old, easy relationship . . . was bedeviled by the need to get their joint approval of my designs in terms of costs. Douglas's signature on a drawing was no longer a laissez-passer.[7]

Rehearsals commenced on June 6, 1929, with Constance Collier, then working as an elocution teacher in Hollywood, serving as Pickford's vocal coach for Shakespearean speech delivery. Earle Browne, an actor and friend of Fairbanks's since his Broadway days, was put on the

Fairbanks with the art director,
Laurence Irving, and his wife,
Rosalind, during production.

Fairbanks (his arms crossed in defiance) and Pickford, their
marriage under intense strain,
pose for a portrait in costume
during production. Photograph by
Nickolas Muray.

Fairbanks as the swashbuckling Petruchio. Photograph by
Charles E. Lynch.

payroll as dramatic coach. Whether out of confidence or bravado, Fairbanks felt that no such coaching was necessary in his case. He simply
drew upon his own theatrical training and memories of his theatrical
hero, Tomasso Salvini, for inspiration.

The filming of *Taming of the Shrew* began on June 24, 1929, and, almost from the start, Fairbanks was moody, willful, and defiant. The
challenges of sound film and the changes they wrought turned his natural ebullience into petulance. Unlike many screen actors of the time,
Fairbanks did not suffer from "mike fright." He was a Broadway-trained
actor who had no fear of the microphone or of how his voice would reg-
ister. Rather, Fairbanks was annoyed by what was lost.

Since there could be no "mood" musicians on the set, the concert
violinist Chico de Verdi and his ensemble no longer perfumed the air

for Fairbanks with favorite songs like "La Violetera" and "Flor de Mal" during filming. The casual camaraderie on the set and the encouraging laughter of the crew had been replaced by a tense atmosphere, with unfamiliar sound technicians and the absolute necessity of quiet on the set. Indeed, the very way Fairbanks moved across a set was a cause of some difficulty. During the earlier scenes the energetic Fairbanks, accustomed to bounding through silent films, nearly wrecked recording apparatus with his reckless abandon. As a result, an entire new stairway was boxed in and filled with sawdust to deaden his footfalls.[8] The sound engineer Edward Bernds remembered that multiple cameras (encased in massive soundproof camera booths) with microphones perched above the set were used to record the film, the same methodology employed by Taylor for *Coquette*. *Taming of the Shrew* was recorded sound on film, with wax discs for playback on the set.[9] Yet despite these advanced techniques in sound recording, "talkies" were uncomfortable, cumbersome, and awkward for Fairbanks. In silent films, he had been the complete master of every aspect of production. He no longer had this degree of control with the new technology of sound. Control had been replaced by consternation. Fairbanks decided early on that he loathed the laborious and cumbersome process of sound film production.

Fairbanks also quickly came to dislike the director, for whom he had initially had such high hopes. H. Bruce "Lucky" Humberstone, the assistant director, remembered:

Fairbanks took a tremendous disliking to Sam Taylor. Now whether that was because Doug felt that Sam was Mary's director and was sloughing him off or whether he just didn't like him, I don't know. You could say that Sam was a very dull man because he didn't have a sense of humor, even though he was a comedy director. He was just a perfect, quiet, gentleman and Doug Fairbanks was a happy-go-lucky, he loved life, and, well, they just didn't go.[10]

And then there was Pickford. Humberstone recalled that relations between Fairbanks and Pickford were very strained at the time; in fact, they were not talking to each other at all. "It was unbelievable to be on the set with them at that time. I had known them for a couple years, I had eaten with them in their dining room, I was on the sets with them, and now they're not talking to one another!"[11]

It was during the production of the film, Pickford recalled in her autobiography, that she was confronted with a different man from the one she knew and loved:

Fairbanks and director Sam Taylor rehearse a scene.

I saw a completely new Douglas, a Douglas who no longer cared apparently about me or my feelings. . . . The strange new Douglas acting opposite me was being another Petruchio in real life, but without the humor or the tongue-in-cheek playfulness of the man who broke Katherine's shrewish spirit. . . . The usual call at the studio was for "nine o'clock make-up." But Douglas somehow managed to stretch out the daily ritual of his sun bath and calisthenics so that I would be waiting on the set for him till nearly noon. This delay, incidentally, cost us both about thirty dollars a minute.[12]

According to Pickford, when Fairbanks did eventually show up, he would not always know his lines, so they had to be written on large blackboards off camera. Their working habits were completely at odds. Pickford was industrious; she needed to know that she was using her time constructively and had little tolerance for his practical jokes on the set. For Fairbanks, work had to be play; he otherwise had great difficulty engaging in it. As was his lifelong pattern, he avoided disagreements or confrontations. If a tense situation presented itself, he might play "Doug," practice or perfect a stunt or trick, send for sandwiches, orchestrate a prank on the set (a hot-wired chair on the set rigged to give an unsuspecting visitor an electric shock was his favorite joke during the film's production), or call off production for the day and go home. Not only did this offend Pickford's work ethic; as co-producer, it offended her frugal nature. Furthermore, the tensions of the workday inevitably followed them both home. Pickford no longer had her mother to advise and comfort her. She felt dominated by Fairbanks both at the studio and at Pickfair, and her private drinking, which had escalated with her mother's final illness and death, continued unabated. Laurence Irving confirmed it was an unhappy time:

I kept (as much as I could) off the studio floor where the morbid atmosphere became increasingly tense with antagonisms. Sam was losing grip and the confidence of Douglas and Mary, whose forbearance with each other's temperamental foibles was being eroded by assiduous Iagos. At times, it seemed as though a mischievous sprite incited Douglas to ruin scenes for the hell of it, in mockery of the medium in which he realised Mary had a professional edge on him. He would not bother to learn his words, relying on huge placards to prompt him from off stage.[13]

When the silence was occasionally broken between the couple, it was usually Fairbanks challenging Pickford's judgment in front of the crew. On at least one occasion, according to Pickford, Fairbanks refused to do a retake at her request. Perhaps he thought it an unnecessary waste of time. Whatever the reason, the fact remains that Fairbanks had always been meticulous in making the final product as good as he possibly could. He had never been neglectful in his work, but now he sometimes arrived on the set unprepared. Pickford was totally defeated by the experience. "The making of that film was my finish. My confidence was completely shattered, and I was never again at ease before the camera or microphone."[14] As for Fairbanks, he had simply ceased to care.

Contradicting other accounts, Karl Struss remembered Fairbanks never being late to the set and playing only a few scenes using cue cards.[15] He recalled one particular event of the type that caused a schism between husband and wife: "I do recall one afternoon when who should appear but Doug's man, his valet, with a tray of sandwiches and a pitcher of lemonade. He passed it all around as though he were serving at a formal lawn party. Everything stopped while we nibbled on our sandwiches and sipped our lemonade. Miss Pickford was aghast at this waste of time."[16]

In an interview with George Pratt nearly thirty years after the film's initial release, Pickford was still uneasy about *Taming of the Shrew*. She was unhappy with her performance in the film and felt she had been taken advantage of by Fairbanks. "Douglas gave a magnificent performance [but] he'd been studying it since he was seven. . . . I wasn't fair to myself when I took Katherine on."[17] A strange confession, considering

Petruchio dressed ridiculously for his wedding.

the widely held belief that, of the two, she was the great dramatic talent, while he was a "personality" performer. Her assessment of their performances is correct. Fairbanks emerges triumphant in *Taming of the Shrew*, with excellent delivery of his dialogue and impeccable timing, while she fares less well; she lacks the fire the part requires and her small, tight speaking voice is somewhat lost in the proceedings.

After six tense weeks, principal photography finally wrapped on August 5, 1929. During the postproduction phase, the notorious screen credit "By William Shakespeare. Additional Dialogue by Sam Taylor" was supposedly created at the instruction of the director, despite the pleas of Laurence Irving.[18] However, surviving original prints bear the credit, "Adapted and directed by Sam Taylor."[19] Kevin Brownlow has speculated that the infamous credit existed in the print exhibited at

Katherine attempts to calm
an irascible Petruchio.

the world premiere held at the London Pavilion on November 14, 1929,
and, based on audience reaction, was expeditiously altered immediately thereafter.[20]

The New York City premiere was held at the Rivoli Theatre on November 29, 1929. Mordaunt Hall of the *New York Times* gave the film a favorable review (the newspaper later named the film one of the "Ten Best
of the Year").[21] Fairbanks on the whole received excellent reviews; better than his wife's. Sime Silverman wrote in *Variety:* "A money picture,
easily, for it's worth 75 ¢ for anyone to see Mary Pickford and Douglas
Fairbanks do this kind of stuff in a vastly extravagant burlesque of Bill
Shakespeare's best laugh. The two stars often turn that into a howl. So
many ballyhoo and exploitation angles, there's not one town where it
should fall down."[22] *Photoplay* wrote: "Here is the long anticipated co-

starring appearance of Mary and Doug. It has been hailed as the event of the decade. Splendidly acted, picturesquely mounted, it is a lot of fun in addition. . . . Doug is a boisterous woman tamer in the best manner of [the French aesthetician of movement François] Delsarte. His line delivery is excellent."[23] Edwin Schallert wrote in his review for the *Los Angeles Times:* "Petruchio is unquestionably the dominant character in the production, and in his talkie debut in this role, Fairbanks is certain to achieve a popular impression among all who do not take their Shakespeare *too* seriously. He is undoubtedly destined for distinct success in the audible medium, because he has reinforced his very vital personality with the spoken word."[24]

There was some disappointment with the film. Alexander Bakshy wrote in *The Nation:* "As it stands, Mr. Fairbanks' adaptation is merely a silent picture of the conventional pattern with the sub-titles spoken by the actors instead of being read by the audience."[25]

The reviews of the time were cemented in early film histories. Paul Rotha, who wrote the first notable criticism of Fairbanks's oeuvre the following year, nevertheless praised his performance:

The Petruchio of *Taming of the Shrew,* jackboot on head and apple-core in hand, was a symbol of the romance of Fairbanks. It needed a great man to carry off that costume with grandeur. I can think of no other personality in the cinema who could have so displayed the courage of his convictions. In the same way that Chaplin is the centralised character of his work, so is Fairbanks the sole *raison d'être* of his pictures. Despite the presence of his wife, he dominated *Taming of the Shrew.*[26]

Notwithstanding the good reviews the film received and the excellent reviews for Fairbanks himself, the stock market crash of October 1929 hurt the film at the box office. Unlike Pickford, Fairbanks also lost money—over $1 million—in the crash. His glowing reviews were no match for the advent of sound, the unhappy production of the film, and the unraveling of their marriage. Although he was still a millionaire, the crash was another affront to Fairbanks, for as Richard Schickel has noted, it "challenged all the verities about pluck, luck, and hard work that had formed such intellectual underpinnings as had sustained him."[27]

The general public did not have the money to spend on Doug and Mary, and those who did had wanted a more romantic vehicle from Hollywood's royal couple. The public's curiosity in seeing how the two worked together was—after nearly ten years' wait—satisfied. Dissatisfied with the film itself, audiences now focused their attention on the newer crop of film stars. The production cost of *Taming of the Shrew* (not including prints or advertising costs) was $578,191.56, exceeding its initial $504,000 budget by nearly $75,000, and it grossed a disappointing $1 million domestically,[28] whereas *Coquette* had grossed over $1.4 million,[29] and Harold Lloyd's first talkie, *Welcome Danger* (1929), grossed nearly $3 million worldwide.[30]

Despite her steadfast unhappiness with the film, Pickford allowed *Taming of the Shrew* to be shown at the Cinémathèque française in Paris in 1965, where it was met with rousing cheers and applause. She was persuaded by the audience reaction to reissue the film, and Matty Kemp, the head of the Mary Pickford Company, prepared a "modified" version in 1966, replacing the main titles, cutting footage, and recording a new musical score and new sound effects. He also altered the film's visual rhythm by optical printing; pulling close-ups and medium shots out of master shots.[31] At the time of the reissue, Pickford told the *Los Angeles Times* that Fairbanks was the real star of the film,[32] an assessment borne out by more recent critics, who have nonetheless also seen the film as the beginning of his artistic eclipse. David Robinson develops this view of Fairbanks:

He was dashing, funny, had a good voice and spoke his lines with the attack and relish of a trained Shakespearean actor. But a voice, even a good one, was not necessarily a gift to the idols of the silent screen. It may have been that while the vast sets of *Robin Hood* and *The Thief of Bagdad* could not dwarf him, a voice did—merely by removing that magical difference which set apart the silent stars, to whom eyes and face and mind were nature, by bringing him back to human scale.[33]

Taming of the Shrew has never received the recognition it deserves as the first talking film of a Shakespeare play. It was not only technically superior to the majority of talking pictures in 1929 but would unquestionably be the finest translation onto film of Shakespeare for some time to come.

As a reenactment of the Pickford-Fairbanks marriage, *Taming of the Shrew* continues to fascinate as a rather grim comedy. The two willful, larger-than-life personalities working at cross-purposes and conveying their resentment and frustration to each other through blatant one-upmanship and harsh wounds is both the movie and the marital union. According to Pickford, the storybook romance had been showing signs of discord for some time: "I first began to sense the change in Douglas as far back as 1925, not toward me, but in a general restlessness and nervous impatience. There were spells when nothing satisfied him—his house, his work, his friends. Several times I had to refuse to go to Europe with him. I found I just couldn't keep up the pace with a man whose very being had become motion, no matter how purposeless."[34]

Contrary to Pickford's suggestion, their marital tribulations stemmed from something more than Fairbanks's mid-life crisis. Fairbanks was always a man in motion; he had always been impulsive and restless. What had held the Pickford-Fairbanks marriage together for nearly ten years was their work. Once their work began to recede—and with an increasing amount of time available to be spent together—the couple discovered that their respective interests beyond motion pictures really did not coincide. Heretofore, when calamity assaulted their house, they had retreated into the shadow-land of their work and the social obligations that it engendered. Talkies removed that last bastion, and it was the final, lethal blow.

So what went horribly wrong? The combination of the assault of sound and the stresses of life brought about irreconcilable differences between man and wife and between performer and audience. Although they were such visionaries in their professional field, they lacked the requisite skills to adapt and move forward in their personal lives. As a result, they drifted into separate worlds: Fairbanks into the public arena for nearly a decade of purposeless travel; Pickford into a private existence of alcoholism and disillusionment; both equally aimless, and equally empty.

Sliding Downhill

When a man finds himself sliding downhill, he should do everything
to reach bottom in a hurry and pass out of the picture.

Douglas Fairbanks

D
ouglas Fairbanks's great success followed the trajectory of the decade he epitomized.[1] After ascending with the Roaring Twenties, he likewise plummeted with them when the Wall Street crash precipitated a worldwide depression. *Taming of the Shrew,* his first talking picture, premiered in London a scant two weeks after Black Friday to deafening public disapproval and box office disappointment. In addition, Fairbanks lost over a million dollars in the stock market. He adopted a cavalier manner and joked that he owned "stocks with fallen arches."[2] Nonetheless, his confidence as an actor was shaken, and his signature optimism about an America of infinite possibilities, which had been the foundation of his star image, was seriously challenged. He was confronted with a floundering career, a foundering marriage, the burgeoning importance of talking motion pictures, which were alien to his way of working, advancing middle age, and a significantly diminished personal fortune. Fairbanks handled his current adversity in his customary fashion: he ran. This time, however, the movement was literally a wandering of the world. The final decade of his life consisted of one desperate journey after another; he spanned the globe searching for a haven where he might regroup and rebuild his shattered confidence and reclaim the social and professional preeminence he had so suddenly and unceremoniously lost. During this swift, steady downhill slide, with forgettable performances and too much time spent on the golf links, Fairbanks was, however, able to accomplish

A formal portrait of father and son, 1934. Photograph by George Hurrell.

Fairbanks on the golf links, ca. 1928. Fairbanks was always ranked a long hitter among amateurs. He sometimes played as many as fifty-four holes in a day. He mostly enjoyed playing in matches with famous golfers such as Bobby Jones and Walter Hagen or famous amateurs such as the Prince of Wales.

several noteworthy off-screen achievements that were of lasting importance to the cinema.

One of his greatest contributions was helping create the Academy of Motion Picture Arts and Sciences, which was founded in May 1927. The brainchild of Fairbanks and Louis B. Mayer, the Academy numbered thirty-six members at its formation and included production executives and film luminaries of the period. Fairbanks not only was a founding member but also was elected its first president, a position he held from May 1927 to October 1929.

While Fairbanks's notion for the Academy was the creation of primarily an academic institution, his colleagues in the enterprise had other ideas. The first presentation of the art deco–style statuettes (they were not yet called the Oscar) given as awards of merit took place at

Fairbanks informally presents Janet Gaynor with her Academy Award at the United Artists Studios prior to the formal presentation held at the Hollywood Roosevelt Hotel on May 16, 1929.

Fairbanks's studio office. A dinner ceremony and "official" presentation of the awards followed at the Roosevelt Hotel in Hollywood on May 16, 1929. Fairbanks envisioned the dinner ceremony as a fundraising tool; tickets could be sold for it, and the profits derived from the sale could be funneled into further film research and development. The Blossom Room of the Roosevelt Hotel (one of Fairbanks's numerous investments of his pre-crash capital) was selected as the site of the first Academy Awards ceremony. It was not long before the annual awards for merit became the primary focus of the enterprise and not, as was Fairbanks's intent, the study and development of film arts and sciences. He began to lose interest in the venture and stepped down as president.

Fairbanks gives the introductory lecture for a course entitled "Photoplay Appreciation," taught at USC, February 6, 1929. At his right is the university's president, Rufus Bernhard von KleinSmid.

Through the Academy of Motion Picture Arts and Sciences, Fairbanks (whose intellectual pretensions had once prompted him to falsely advertise himself as a former student of Harvard University) was instrumental in developing the first university-level curriculum devoted exclusively to the study of film. Fairbanks himself gave the introductory lecture and inaugural address for a course in "Photoplay Appreciation" sponsored by the Academy and taught by the University of Southern California beginning February 6, 1929. The course developed into the first film school in the United States, known today as the USC School of Cinematic Arts.

Although he presented himself as an expert in the study of film, Fairbanks, at this time, admitted to being a student as well. He investigated the new technology of sound film and how it might be best utilized. He explained to one critic that he had been "looking for a new formula. The old patterns will not fit. . . . Just as Griffith showed us the essence of the silent picture technique in *The Birth of a Nation*, someone is going to create a standard of talking picture method. It has not come yet, and when it does arrive, it will be shaped either consciously or unconsciously by rhythm." In particular, he cited the work of Sergei Eisenstein, who was adapting his concepts of montage to sound film, as well as that of Walt Disney, as among the best in utilizing the new technology. The Disney animated short subjects, he believed, "get their tremendous appeal from the perfect rhythm, in comedy tempo. . . . It is not mere synchronization; it is more than that; it is a rhythmic, swinging, lilting thing, with what musicians call the proper accent-structure."[3]

Originally, Fairbanks had intended his next screen vehicle to be a talking version of *If I Were King*, Justin Huntly McCarthy's play based on the life of the French poet François Villon, which had twice previously been made as a silent film, most memorably *The Beloved Rogue* (1927), starring John Barrymore.[4] After the disappointing reception of *Taming of the Shrew*, however, and with the production of the film musical of the Villon story, *The Vagabond King* (1930), Fairbanks's interest in producing this project waned. Unsure of his next step and wanting to fulfill his distribution obligations to United Artists, he accepted an unusual offer from the producer Joseph M. Schenck to star in a film musical.

Schenck's working relationship with Fairbanks had extended beyond the United Artists boardroom for several years. He had the highest regard for Fairbanks, and he once asserted that Fairbanks "knows more about making pictures than all of us put together."[5] Schenck had partially financed Fairbanks's last two silent films (their combined negative costs were $2,522,000 of which $2,170,000 was provided by Schenck, while Fairbanks contributed $352,000), from which he received a cumulative profit of $130,000, while Fairbanks pocketed $370,000 from the profits, along with a salary as both actor and scenario writer exceeding $100,000 per film.[6] For this new musical project, Fairbanks agreed to a flat salary of $300,000, making him, in essence, an actor for hire for the first time since his days with Triangle–Fine Arts. (Pickford had negotiated similar terms with Schenck to star in *Kiki* [1931], receiving the same salary and stance.) The proposed vehicle was a musical comedy entitled *Reaching for the Moon* (it bore no resemblance to Fairbanks's 1917 Artcraft comedy of the same name), with original songs by the great American songwriter Irving Berlin.

As a result of the phenomenal box office success of *The Broadway Melody* (1929), musicals were all the rage. People not only wanted films to talk now; they wanted them to sing. Having failed to gauge the public barometer with *Taming of the Shrew*, Fairbanks was determined to give audiences what they wanted this time, despite his personal misgivings about the project. His only previous experience with musical comedy had been *Fantana*, a Broadway musical of 1905. It had not been his most pleasurable experience in the theater. Fairbanks's anxieties were allayed somewhat when he was assured that his role in this project required little in the way of singing. Despite Fairbanks's limited participation in the musical numbers, *Reaching for the Moon* was to have eight Berlin songs: "Brokers Ensemble" (the opening number), "A Toast to Prohibition," "If You Believe," "How Much I Love You," "Do You Believe

Fairbanks and the director, Edmund Goulding, clown around the office set during production of *Reaching for the Moon* (1930). The desk used by Fairbanks's character, Larry Day, featured sixteen telephones and two stock market ticker tape machines. Photograph by John Miehle.

Larry Day (Fairbanks) with his valet, Roger (Edward Everett Horton), in *Reaching for the Moon*. The film contains several amusing homosexual allusions between the two characters.

Your Eyes or Do You Believe My Baby," "When the Folks High-Up Do the Mean Low-Down!" "The Little Things in Life," and the lilting waltz "Reaching for the Moon," as the film's theme song.[7]

Berlin's original story idea, which was developed by Fairbanks,[8] evolved into a scenario concerning an Amelia Earhart–like aviatrix, Vivien Benton (Bebe Daniels), being romanced by Wall Street tycoon Larry Day (Fairbanks) aboard an ocean liner bound for Europe in the final days before the Wall Street crash of 1929. Embarking on his ocean voyage as a prince of finance, Day disembarks a pauper as a result of the crash, which takes place while they are at sea. Daniels, a silent film star with a flair for comedy (she had once been Harold Lloyd's leading lady), had recently demonstrated her singing talents in the film musical *Rio Rita* (1929) and was an excellent choice for the aviatrix. Edward Everett Horton in the role of Larry Day's fey valet, Roger, was equally well cast, and he deftly delivered dialogue peppered with double entendres designed to titillate the audience. (This was before the Motion Picture Production Code became strictly enforced in 1934 and its vigilance removed such suggestiveness from the American screen.)

John W. Considine Jr. was originally hired to direct but was quickly replaced by Edmund Goulding, whose previous film work included directing the Greta Garbo–John Gilbert vehicle *Love* (1927) and writing the story for *The Broadway Melody*.[9] According to June MacCloy, who appeared in the film as Kitty, Vivien Benton's confidante, the production was a congenial one, with Fairbanks the ardent Anglophile and consummate snob insisting the entire cast and crew break at four P.M. each day for an elaborate afternoon tea, complete with fine caviar, sandwiches, and scones.[10] The film boasted memorable art deco sets by William Cameron Menzies. Not surprisingly, the main sets (the vast deck and staterooms of an ocean liner) were transformed into a personal gymnasium by the brash, backslapping Larry Day to showcase his athleticism.

In addition to directing, Goulding was also revising the script, much to Fairbanks's and particularly Irving Berlin's dismay. Not only did he eliminate some of Berlin's songs; he devised the scenario's hoary romantic comedy contrivance of an aphrodisiac (called "Angel's Breath" in the film). Goulding's most noteworthy contribution to the project was his engaging a young mellow-voiced crooner named Bing Crosby to take part in "When the Folks High-Up Do the Mean Low-Down!" It was one of Crosby's earliest film appearances and a highlight of the film.

Reaching for the Moon previewed late in 1930, a year that saw more than seventy musicals released (most of which were critical and commercial failures). After initial previews, audience reaction to the film prompted Schenck to make a decision that virtually guaranteed its ruin; he authorized the removal of all but one of the original Berlin numbers, the Daniels and Crosby song "When the Folks High-Up Do the Mean Low-Down!" The result was a musical comedy without the music. Taking his cue from his Larry Day screen character, Fairbanks boarded the SS *Belgenland* on December 29, 1930 (the night of the film's premiere), and set sail for the Far East. He timed the trip to spare himself the mortification of the mixed critical reception that he correctly anticipated for his come-back film. Mordaunt Hall in the *New York Times* charitably described the film as "Buffoonery deluxe, a soupçon of musical comedy plot, a hybrid conception of French farce, streaks of sentiment, acrobatics and clever modernistic settings."[11] Sid Silverman of *Variety* called the film "fair and light entertainment," mentioning only in passing that the Berlin songs had been removed after previews.[12]

Although the reviews were mixed, public reaction was not. *Reaching for the Moon* failed at the box office, the first Fairbanks film to show a loss. The film's flimsy plot, made unappealing by Schenck's excision of the musical numbers, was one problem. Moreover, Depression-era audiences were unable to identify with Fairbanks's careless, carefree Wall Street tycoon. Fairbanks's new screen image proved troublesome. In a talking film with a modern, naturalistic setting, his performance style was artificial. His exaggerated and stylized gestures and flourishes, so effective in silent cinema, were incongruous in sound film. He also appeared older (despite the wig and heavy lacquer of makeup) and, even more distressing, he seemed unrelaxed on screen. His uneasiness with the new medium made his audience uncomfortable watching him.

Since he was no longer able to entertain himself by entertaining others, travel now became Fairbanks's one diversion. As always, movement calmed him; but he still had professional obligations to meet. Ingeniously, he found a way to deal with his personal needs and discharge his professional obligations by producing a feature-length comic travelogue entitled *Around the World with Douglas Fairbanks* (1931).[13]

Not only was the project an ideal way to combine work with play, always a Fairbanks prerequisite; it was also a perfect excuse for him to travel extensively without generating the unfavorable publicity inevitably sparked by extended trips without Pickford. The film was made at a cost of $117,866.60 and consists of footage of the perpetually peripatetic screen adventurer's tour of Hawaii, Japan, Hong Kong, China, the Philippines, Cambodia, Thailand, and India.[14] Fairbanks assembled a crew consisting of his friends the director Victor Fleming, the cinematographer Henry Sharp, and Chuck Lewis, his trainer. The narrative, filled with topical references and insensitive, flippant comments, was

Fairbanks (using a golf club as a pointer) flanked by director Victor Fleming (left), his friend and trainer, Chuck Lewis (right), and cinematographer Henry Sharp (second from right) in *Around the World with Douglas Fairbanks* (1931).

supplied during postproduction by his most forgiving critic and generous admirer, Robert E. Sherwood.

"My sole idea is to have a good time," Fairbanks proclaims at the outset of this desultory travelogue. His hollow narrative premise is that the world (i.e., the modern-day world of the Great Depression) is "essentially funny." His dilettantish forays into the diverse cultures and lifestyles he encounters on his travels treat them as little more than comic fodder. The film's other escapist idea, which serves to justify its fragmented nature, is that "absolutely anything can happen." Fairbanks's provincial viewpoint is augmented by footage filmed at his West Hollywood studio, visual effects, and even Disney animation (one scene depicts "Hollywood's most famous star," Mickey Mouse, dancing to Thai music). Fairbanks even reprises his glory days by trotting out his old Indian rope trick from *The Thief of Bagdad*, along with that film's flying carpet, which he employs as a narrative deus ex machina to seamlessly transport himself back to Hollywood once it becomes apparent that the eighty-minute goal for his around-the-world adventure is a trifle too ambitious, even for Douglas Fairbanks. One is left with the impression that Fairbanks views the world (or wants his audience to see him as someone who still views the world) as his oyster: his personal playground and golf course. Indeed, at one point, he muses, "One thing that appeals to me about the world is that you can play around it with a mashie—good courses everywhere."

A portrait of a natty Fairbanks during production of *Around the World with Douglas Fairbanks*.

The barely disguised nature of Fairbanks's underlying middle-aged sadness, as well as the slight nature of the film itself, was disappointing to many, including Joseph M. Schenck, who objected to what he viewed as substandard and unacceptable product for a UA release. Despite Schenck's objections, *Around the World with Douglas Fairbanks* was released by United Artists, with the world premiere held November 19, 1931, at the Rivoli Theatre in New York City. Critical reaction to the film was mixed. *Variety*'s reviewer was typical in criticizing its "murderous padding" and lack of distinction.[15]

Fairbanks was so pleased with the film, however, that even before it was released, he took a slow boat to China on November 17, 1931, accompanied by his brother Robert, the director Lewis Milestone, and the humorist Robert Benchley, in order to make another escapist travelogue. The party got as far as Rome, but then returned to America on December 23 after receiving reports of the box-office failure of *Around the World with Douglas Fairbanks* (which eventually grossed a paltry $200,000). The film is seldom revived outside of the Museum of Modern Art, and even that institution has little enthusiasm for its charge. "Except perhaps from a sociological point of view, it is a film of no importance," the former MoMA film curator Eileen Bowser observes.[16] Its only value may be as documentation of how painful Fairbanks found the aging process.[17]

Given the vast, unfamiliar lands that were at his disposal to explore as he pleased, the thought of being confined to a sound stage in Hollywood was loathsome to Fairbanks, but professional obligations beckoned. *Mr. Robinson Crusoe* (1932), his last personal production, was designed to meet his responsibilities in the least demanding way. The film was conceived as an inexpensive travelogue masquerading as a narrative film.

Fairbanks chartered Joseph M. Schenck's luxurious schooner, *The Invader,* and sailed from San Francisco for Tahiti, insulated by his most faithful cronies and yes-men, the writer Tom Geraghty, the actor Earle Browne, and Chuck Lewis. He felt safe enough in their company to also bring along his new leading lady, the Spanish actress Maria Alba, with whom he was discreetly having an extramarital affair. The affable A. Edward Sutherland, who had previously worked with Chaplin and W. C. Fields, and Max Dupont were also brought aboard, as director and cinematographer, respectively.

A modern adaptation of Daniel Defoe's novel *The Life and Adventures of Robinson Crusoe,* the film concerns the adventurous exploits of Steve Drexel (Fairbanks), enjoying a cruise with two companions. He wagers he can survive marooned on a desert island for a month. His friends readily take him up on the bet. Drexel jumps ship, accompanied only by his faithful dog, and creates a paradise for himself on an uninhabited tropical island, conquering both the elements and neighboring natives, and easily wins the bet with his friends.

According to Sutherland, the key personnel drew no salary but worked for a percentage of the film's profits, with island natives hired in minor roles and as extras when needed. While the economy of the location shooting appealed to Fairbanks at the outset, the hazards of filming in the tropical humidity soon wreaked havoc with the production. The sound equipment became inoperable, and filming continued without sound. Whether by accident or design, Fairbanks was back in silent pictures. "We had to shoot every scene with somebody in

Fairbanks with the writer, Tom Geraghty, the director, A. Edward Sutherland, and unidentified members of the crew during production of *Mr. Robinson Crusoe* in Tahiti.

Fairbanks as Steve Drexel, a modern-day Robinson Crusoe, in *Mr. Robinson Crusoe* (1932).

movement, or putting his hand up to his face, so that we could dub it when we got back to the studio," Sutherland remembered. "This meant hours and weeks in the cutting room, trying to fit lips to words. The sound equipment wasn't very good, and in the heat and dampness of Tahiti, it just broke; it was ruined."[18]

Free from the hated dialogue that had so confined his type of film, Fairbanks should have been in his element. And yet, despite the primarily visual aspect of the film, his customary ebullience is not in evidence; his character is a hypomanic middle-aged man. The film does contain some minor charm redolent of his earlier comedies, particularly *Down to Earth* (1917), with its celebration of the natural life, as well as the contraptions in *The Nut*. Echoes of the latter film are particularly evident when Fairbanks's character tames the wilderness by creating a treetop haven equipped with several ingenious time-saving devices, including an elaborate catapult, which is put to excellent use in the film's climax to hold off irate natives.

Despite these clever bits, no one involved with the production had any illusions about the film's quality. It was a far cry from Fairbanks's previous high standards—little more than "a glorified travelogue," according to Sutherland.[19] Fairbanks's former enthusiasm and meticulous preparation collapsed into apathy. During production, Sutherland asked him, "Why don't you direct yourself?" He replied, "I haven't the patience."[20]

Fairbanks's lack of patience was partly owing to his preoccupation with the bare-breasted native island women. Far away from "America's Sweetheart" and the nosey Hollywood gossip columnists, he gave full rein to his hitherto constrained libido. (Douglas Fairbanks Jr. wryly noted that he had several unacknowledged half-siblings on Tahiti as a result of *Mr. Robinson Crusoe*.)[21]

With approximately 70 percent of *Mr. Robinson Crusoe* completed, the crew returned to Hollywood, where the arduous task of postproduction dubbing was undertaken. Alfred Newman was hired to create the musical score and provided the film's only artistically distinguished component. One of Newman's themes was so distinctive that he later incorporated it into his musical score for *The Hurricane* (1937), where it became a popular song called "Moon of Manakoora."

The world premiere of *Mr. Robinson Crusoe* was held on September 21, 1932, at the Rivoli Theatre in New York City. Mordaunt Hall gave the film a charitable review in the *New York Times,* writing: "The film is done in Mr. Fairbanks' best vein. It is artful, jolly and imaginative, and one never thinks while watching the laughable incidents that the lone man on the island was always accompanied by a camera crew."[22] *Variety,* however, was less generous, declaring the film "one of Douglas Fairbanks' minor efforts" and noting: "The talk sustaining the action is practically a 70-minute monolog by Fairbanks; others in the cast doing pantomime most of the time."[23]

As was commonplace in early sound film, a hybrid version of the talking film was prepared for foreign distribution with intertitles replacing the spoken dialogue, but the musical sound track and other sound effects were retained. *Mr. Robinson Crusoe,* with its predominant one-character narrative, was an ideal film for this hybrid treatment, and it is this version of the film that is most readily available today for viewing in authorized prints. Although the Museum of Modern Art possesses an archival print of the film with dialogue as originally intended, it nevertheless chose to make only the hybrid version available in its Circulating Film Library, because of the film's "old-fashioned air that makes titles seem more appropriate."[24]

Fairbanks's incessant globe-trotting inevitably fueled speculation about his marriage to Pickford. While Fairbanks charged from Indochina to Tibet to London, Pickford seldom left the grounds of Pickfair. The separation, although not official, was emotional as well as physical. However, hopes of reconciliation were frequently rekindled, particularly on the occasion of Fairbanks's return to Pickfair in 1932 for the Olympic Games, held that summer in Los Angeles. (He was instrumental, through his international sports contacts, in securing the Olympic Games for Los Angeles.) Pickford, in anticipation of his return, supervised renovations to Pickfair. Most impressive of the renovations during this period was the installation of an elaborate mahogany bar formerly housed in the Union Saloon in Auburn, California. The "Western Bar" was Pickford's Christmas gift to Fairbanks that year. Although Fairbanks had been wanting to sell the house—and was still an avowed teetotaler—he nonetheless loved the gift and its romantic evocations of the western frontier. He frequently entertained athletes and international celebrities visiting for the Olympic Games that summer in the newly refurbished Pickfair. However, these cosmetic transformations were insufficient to dissuade him from keeping on the move.

Although he was gracious in his acceptance of the reconstructed Wild West saloon from Pickford, Fairbanks's tolerance of her own imbibing was reaching its limit. In the past, he had looked away as she had retreated to the solitude of her bedroom, where he knew she quietly drank. Her slow withdrawal from the world and her losing battle with alcoholism were unbearable to him. As Chuck Lewis observed, "All Doug ever wanted was a sober Mary."[25] No longer able to tolerate her

Harold Lloyd, Chaplin, and Fairbanks help promote the Olympic Games held in Los Angeles in the summer of 1932. Photograph by K. O. Rahmn.

continued excesses with alcohol, not to mention her extramarital affair with her former leading man Charles "Buddy" Rogers, he left Pickfair after Christmas 1932 and, notwithstanding a short interlude suggestive of détente rather than reconciliation in the autumn the following year, seldom returned.[26] His brother Robert had forecast the destructive effects these protracted journeys would have on the marriage some years before, saying of his brother's solo ventures: "I don't like it at all. Douglas is establishing a dangerous precedent."[27]

Years of divisions and reunions, of separations and reconciliations, had left Fairbanks weary. Of his father and stepmother's union, Douglas Fairbanks Jr. surmised: "It became a tragic competition between the two of them in those last years. They would try and outdo each other with respect to whose pride had been hurt most and who would give in first."[28] Inextricably tied yet irrevocably divided, Pickford ultimately filed for divorce on December 8, 1933, citing Fairbanks's relentless travel and the mental anguish the separations caused her. Infidelity was not mentioned.

Fairbanks skis in St. Moritz, Switzerland, while Mary Pickford sues for divorce in Los Angeles, December 1933.

Fairbanks assumes his signature stance, with his fists on his hips and his head tilted back in joyous laughter, one last time as the title character in *The Private Life of Don Juan* (1934).

Fairbanks turned fifty in 1933. He had told his son that year that he hoped " 'to die soon—but violently, in an accident of some kind.' He added that he had done just about everything he had wanted to do in his life at least twice, that now he woke in the morning he couldn't think of anything new to do. He was bored with life and prepared to die, but not to linger."[29] He had aged enormously in just a few years. The ultimate insult, late middle age, was devastating to one who had placed such importance upon the ideal of limitless youth. Too preoccupied fighting her own demons, his wife of thirteen years was not willing to support his illusions any longer. A young (she was not yet thirty), blonde, slender former chorus girl, whom he had met in the spring of 1931 at a party in London for King Alfonso XIII of Spain, was willing to take on the role. The fact that she was also the estranged wife of Lord Ashley, the heir to the Earl of Shaftesbury, made the liaison all the more appealing to him.

Fairbanks had always been drawn to the titled classes. He was an unapologetic Anglophile, and he had more success than any other actor of his generation in accessing the inner circles of Britain's aristocracy and associating with members of the royal family (he counted the Prince of Wales and the Duke and Duchess of Kent among his friends).[30] He had entry to castles, palaces, stately homes, country houses, hunting lodges, and gentlemen's clubs. It was a natural progression that he should be charmed by and forge an emotional attachment to the former Sylvia Hawkes, now Lady Ashley and known to intimates as "Silky."

Fairbanks was also charmed that year by leading British director-producer Alexander Korda, whose *Private Life of Henry VIII* (1933), starring Charles Laughton, had been released by United Artists to great critical success. Korda approached Fairbanks with the possibility of tailoring a project of similar stature specifically for him. The film he proposed was about Don Juan and was based on Henri Bataille's play *L'homme à la rose*, in which the great lover grows old and tired of his wanton wanderings and longs for peace and tranquility. *The Private Life of Don Juan* (1934), a comedy containing a meditation on celebrity and age, was Fairbanks's swan song.

The project appeared to be ideally suited for Fairbanks at this point in his career. It was a return, of sorts, to the costume film—the genre at which he had always excelled—and the mythic lover Don Juan was the type of larger-than-life figure befitting the silent screen's Zorro, d'Artagnan, and Robin Hood. Furthermore, Fairbanks would have no need to apologize for his age; the story confronted the idea of life for the great lover past his prime. The script was credited to the playwright Frederick Lonsdale and Lajos Biró, and the cast included the dazzling

Fairbanks, actress Patricia Hilliard, and director-producer Alexander Korda during production of *The Private Life of Don Juan*.

young beauty Merle Oberon (who became Mrs. Alexander Korda in 1939). Korda directed, and his personal participation suggested a promising film. For Fairbanks, the most appealing aspect of the assignment was that it afforded him the opportunity to be with Sylvia. He also delighted in the idea of assuming the role of an English country squire and rented North Mimms Park, an estate in Hertfordshire, approximately forty-five minutes from London, with a manor capable of accommodating up to fifty houseguests, making an appropriately stately backdrop to entertain and impress Sylvia and her chic social circle.

Notwithstanding all this, Fairbanks unavoidably found himself at one of the lowest emotional ebbs of his life. He had serious misgivings about a film project that drew attention to him as being past his prime. Furthermore, he was weary of acting—both on screen and off—and tired of the years of drifting. Depression-prone throughout his life, he wired Pickford, who remained his sole anchor, in despair on February 24, 1934: "HIPPER DEAR PASSING THROUGH WORST PERIOD I HAVE KNOWN TRYING TO PULL MYSELF TOGETHER TO START PICTURE LOVE DUBER."[31]

He rallied sufficiently to see the filming at Elstree Studios through to the end. The film's plot struck a nerve with him. Don Juan effects a reconciliation with his estranged spouse in the final reel, and Fairbanks secretly hoped that this would also be the outcome for himself and Pickford. Alas, events conspired against it. During production of *The Private Life of Don Juan,* Sylvia's husband, Lord Ashley, petitioned for divorce, citing Fairbanks as co-respondent. Fairbanks did not con-

Mary Pickford leaves the witness stand after testifying in the divorce action brought by her against Fairbanks, January 10, 1935.

test the proceedings and was required to pay court costs of approximately $10,000.

While she was able to tolerate his infidelities so long as they remained private, once they became a matter of public record, Pickford found the situation untenable. The provisional divorce decree she obtained on January 10, 1935, was intended as a wake-up call of sorts to Fairbanks. It might easily have been rescinded had he returned to Pickfair. However, despite entreaties from Fairbanks for some kind of reconciliation (one last-minute opportunity to reunite was lost as a result of a mislaid telegram), the final divorce decree was granted on January 10, 1936. The terms of the settlement allowed Pickford to continue to reign as owner of Pickfair, while Fairbanks retained Rancho Zorro and their Santa Monica beach house.

The Private Life of Don Juan premiered at the London Pavilion on September 5, 1934, and elicited mixed critical reaction on both sides of the Atlantic. André Sennwald wrote in the *New York Times* that Fairbanks's presence in the film created "a lamentable air of anachronism. . . . He whom we loved for his reckless swagger and airy movement now finds himself trapped and forced to play the actor. It is a poor fate for one who was once so free, and it is not always pleasant to watch."[32] Furthermore, audiences identified the aging roué Don Juan with Fairbanks, whose infidelity was making headlines. Pickford loyalists and those unhappy with their fallen swashbuckling idol sometimes referred to Lady Ashley as "Lady Ashcan."[33] The film was a resounding box office failure, and Fairbanks's embarrassment over the disappointing results was acute. It was during this period of his life that he confided to Raoul Walsh, "There's nothing as humiliating as being a has-been."[34]

The eclipse of his reputation at that time is underscored by an anecdote recalled by another director from Fairbanks's halcyon days. As Fairbanks and Albert Parker strolled down Park Lane in London in the early 1930s, an anonymous pedestrian passed by them and said, "Goodnight, Doug," as he walked past and turned down Brook Street. Fairbanks responded, "Goodnight, fella," and said to Parker, "You see? They still remember me." The bittersweetness of the moment struck Parker, who, in relating the story to the director Michael Powell some time later, remarked, "And only five years before he had been the greatest star in the world."[35]

Less than three months after his divorce from Pickford became final, Fairbanks married Sylvia at the American Embassy in Paris on March 7, 1936. He was content now merely to follow Sylvia in search of a good time. They were soon fixtures in international society and were photographed by the press while in Britain for the social season, Saint Moritz for skiing trips, and Berlin for the 1936 Olympic Games. With the advent of World War II in Europe in September 1939, their globe-trotting came to an abrupt end. They arrived in New York to attend the World's Fair that autumn and subsequently retreated to Fairbanks's elegant beach house at 705 Ocean Front in Santa Monica, California.

No longer able to be a citizen of the world or play a leading role on the world stage, Fairbanks sought secondary interests to fill the hours not occupied by the demands of Sylvia's social schedule. He toyed with the idea of producing projects that might involve his son, whose career had flourished in inverse proportion to his own precipitous decline. In a series of important films, notably Howard Hawks's *The Dawn Patrol* (1930) and Mervyn LeRoy's *Little Caesar*, Douglas Fairbanks Jr. had found success in cynical, antihero formulas that were the antithesis of his father's romantic, idealized heroics. At last able to surrender his need to be the preeminent Fairbanks, Douglas Fairbanks Sr. took pride in his son's accomplishments and sought to develop scripts on which they could jointly participate, with his son as star and himself as producer. *The Adventures of Marco Polo* was one of these. Fairbanks had been nurturing the idea for a decade before eventually growing weary of the project and selling his interests in the property to his United Artists partner Samuel Goldwyn. (In 1937 Goldwyn produced the film, released in 1938, with Gary Cooper in the title role.) Another project, *The Californian*, never went beyond some tentative treatments.[36]

Fairbanks visits Douglas Fairbanks Jr. on the set of *Jump for Glory* (1937; retitled *When Thief Meets Thief* for American distribution) at Britain's Worton Hall Studios in 1936. The Criterion production was directed by Raoul Walsh, who had directed the elder Fairbanks's *The Thief of Bagdad*.

Fairbanks's Rancho Zorro, the 3,000 acres of land near Del Mar, California, intended as a country home to which he might eventually retire, as he originally visualized it, drawn by the architect Carl Jules Weyl, ca. 1927.

Other minor preoccupations of this period included Fairbanks's legal battle with the Internal Revenue Service regarding tax refunds he had received totaling $175,927, which the government deemed erroneous (Fairbanks eventually lost his case in 1939), and Rancho Zorro, 3,000 acres of land near Del Mar, California, that he had purchased for $100,000 in October 1926, intending it as a country home to which he might eventually retire. The Depression forced him to abandon his romantic plans for a grand hacienda, and without sufficient funds to develop the property and have it serve as an outlet for his creative energy during his retirement, he lost interest in it.

Another preoccupation at this time, and much more significant to his legacy, was the preservation of his great body of work. Iris Barry, the first curator of the Museum of Modern Art's Film Library, approached Fairbanks and inquired if he might consider depositing his film archives with the museum in order to safeguard them for future generations. Fairbanks consented, and the majority of the collection arrived by ship in New York City in 1938. Fairbanks's own collection was vast (approximately 2,700,000 feet of film) and included not only all of his films but multiple prints in many cases, as well as preprint materials, outtakes, and private material. The acquisition of the Douglas Fairbanks Collection was a major achievement in the legitimization of the fledgling MoMA Film Library, although Fairbanks appears to have come to have reservations about his decision. Film preservation in America began with MoMA, and, at this period, it was in its technological infancy. Unfortunately, ideal storage facilities for nitrate film did not exist at the time of the Fairbanks donation and many of the Fairbanks films sent

Fairbanks and his third wife, Sylvia, the former Lady Ashley, attend the opening night celebration of the new Museum of Modern Art building (and the museum's tenth anniversary) in New York City, May 1939. After Farbanks's premature death at the age of 56, Sylvia—best known for her marriages to aristocrats and movie stars—counted Clark Gable among her three subsequent husbands.

MoMA no longer exist, including complete versions of six of his Artcraft comedies,[37] while others were rescued only after they had seriously deteriorated.

Douglas Fairbanks Jr. celebrated his thirtieth birthday on Saturday, December 9, 1939, with a family gathering that included his father and Sylvia. The following day, after attending the USC-UCLA football game with Sylvia, Fairbanks complained of severe indigestion, and on Monday, he experienced chest pains. His physician, Dr. Phillip Sampson, was summoned to the beach house and diagnosed Fairbanks as having experienced a heart attack. Sampson prescribed nearly six months of bed rest, along with the abstention of all activities that might cause excitement. It was Fairbanks's death sentence. "He just lost the will to live right at that moment," remembered his son. "He couldn't visualize himself being bedridden."[38] In a conversation with his brother earlier in the day, Fairbanks requested that should anything happen to him, he was to communicate the message "By the clock" to Pickford. On Monday night, attended by James Taylor, a male nurse, and with his bull mastiff, Polo, in his room, Fairbanks asked at 11 P.M. for the lights to be dimmed and the window opened so that he might hear the ocean. Taylor inquired how he was feeling. Fairbanks grinned one last time and answered, "I've never felt better."[39] Less than two hours later, at 12:45 A.M. on Tuesday, December 12, 1939, Taylor heard Polo growl ominously. He reentered the master bedroom and found Fairbanks dead. Mary Pickford was informed of the news of his passing while in Chicago with Charles "Buddy" Rogers, whom she had married in 1937, and issued a statement:

Douglas's sudden going is a great shock and a deep sorrow to his family and friends but I am sure it will prove a consolation to us all to recall the joy and the glorious spirit of adventure that he gave to the world. He has passed from our mortal life quickly and spontaneously as he did everything in life, but it is impossible to believe that vibrant and gay spirit could ever perish.[40]

Approximately one hundred invited guests, including some of the most notable figures in Hollywood, crammed into the Wee Kirk o' the Heather, a small chapel at Forest Lawn Memorial Park in Glendale, for the funeral service, while two thousand people stood quietly outside. No eulogy or formal words were spoken. The 23rd and 121st Psalms were read, as well as a passage from the eighth chapter of Romans. Chico de Verdi and an ensemble of other musicians who had worked as Fairbanks's "mood" musicians in silent films played Brahms's "Lullaby," Gounod's "Ave Maria," and the Spanish songs Fairbanks had loved. Fairbanks's body remained in a receiving vault at Forest Lawn until a suitable memorial could be constructed.

After his premature death, the world continued to be reminded of him above all by the fame of Douglas Fairbanks Jr., who played swashbuckling roles in pictures like *The Prisoner of Zenda* (1937), George Stevens's *Gunga Din* (1939), *The Corsican Brothers* (1941), and *Sinbad the Sailor* (1947), and who was further distinguished by his real-life derring-do as a naval officer in World War II. In a tribute that would have made his father especially proud, and not a little envious, Douglas Fairbanks Jr. was awarded an honorary knighthood in 1949 by King George VI for his efforts to foster Anglo-American relations. He put the pioneering spirit he inherited from his father to work in the new

Charles Chaplin delivers a eulogy for Fairbanks at the dedication of his white marble memorial at Hollywood Memorial Park (now Hollywood Forever Cemetery), May 23, 1941.

medium of television, producing, hosting, and occasionally starring in *Douglas Fairbanks Jr. Presents* (also known as *The Rheingold Theater*), an anthology series that lasted five seasons (1953–57). His efforts to keep his father's memory alive included producing sound versions of *The Black Pirate*, *The Gaucho*, and *The Iron Mask*, as well as funding the British Film Institute's reconstruction of *The Black Pirate* in Technicolor. Douglas Fairbanks Jr. died on May 7, 2000, in New York City at the age of ninety. He was interred in the same crypt as his father, their lives and legacies inescapably linked.

The $40,000 memorial to Douglas Fairbanks that Sylvia Fairbanks had commissioned was unveiled on May 23, 1941, on what would have been his fifty-eighth birthday, and his remains were transferred to Hollywood Memorial Park (now Hollywood Forever Cemetery). The magnificent memorial, designed and erected by Howard Seidell, was a fitting tribute to the man who had helped define the heroic tradition of Hollywood silent cinema and who had been instrumental in shaping the art of the motion picture. The Reverend Neal Dodd, an Episcopal pastor, officiated, and Charles Chaplin read the lines from Shakespeare's *Hamlet* inscribed on the sarcophagus: "Good night, sweet prince, / And flights of angels sing thee to thy rest!" Chaplin eulogized the man he later called the closest friend he had ever had to the 1,500 people in attendance.[41]

However eloquent Chaplin's tribute may have been, Douglas Fairbanks had presented his own, most fitting eulogy with his last silent swashbuckler. In *The Iron Mask*, he truly bade farewell as the Fairbanks that the world had known and loved and the Fairbanks he wished them to remember: ever youthful, energetic, and vibrant with life. And through cinema's magical fusion of light and shadow, on a screen five times larger than life, he still bursts forth: riding the wind-blown sails of a Spanish galleon, scaling the heights of a castle drawbridge, deftly defeating an army of adversaries with the slice of a sword, and flying through the air on the back of a winged horse. He joyously taunts viewers to join him, to cast grown-up cares aside and be children again, delighted in the adventure of life and all its wondrous possibilities. The inimitable Fairbanks, contained in his greatest films, remains among the richest pleasures of the cinema. One viewing, and he leaps to life again.

Notes

PROLOGUE

1. William Bakewell, interview with the author, 1992. For a variation of this same idea, see William Bakewell, *Hollywood Be Thy Name* (Metuchen, N.J., 1991), 36.
2. Douglas Fairbanks Jr., interview with the author, 1993.
3. Jean Epstein, *Cinema* (Paris, 1921), 88.
4. Douglas Fairbanks Jr., interview with the author, 1993. His notion of his father as a series of masks was first developed in his *Vanity Fair* profile of Douglas Fairbanks, entitled "Dad" (ca. 1930). A typescript is held in the Douglas Fairbanks Jr. Collection, Howard Gotlieb Archival Research Center, Boston University.
5. Douglas Fairbanks Jr., *The Salad Days* (Garden City, N.Y., 1988), 23.
6. Douglas Fairbanks Jr., interview with the author, 1993.
7. Douglas Fairbanks Jr. called his father an "incorrigible exaggerator" (*Salad Days*, 16). In her memoir *Sunshine and Shadow* (Garden City, N.Y., 1955), Mary Pickford remembered Fairbanks as "the sort of raconteur who would never spoil a story for the lack of a few facts" (289).

A BAD CASE OF ST. VITUS' DANCE

1. Ralph Hancock and Letitia Fairbanks, *Douglas Fairbanks: The Fourth Musketeer* (New York, 1953), 23. Letitia Fairbanks Smoot was Douglas Fairbanks's niece.
2. Ibid., 29.
3. Douglas Fairbanks Jr., *The Salad Days* (Garden City, N.Y., 1988), 8.
4. Curiously, Lazarus Ulman was a Baptist minister during and after the Civil War. Douglas Fairbanks Jr., letter to Richard Schickel, March 27, 1972, 2, Richard Schickel Papers, 1953–86, Wisconsin Historical Society.
5. The author is indebted to the pioneer researches of Thomas L. Jones and Keri Leigh, who delved into the early life of H. Charles Ulman and published their findings with "The Sword of Zorro's Father," *North South Trader's Civil War* 30, no. 5 (2004): 20–26.
6. Hancock and Fairbanks, *Douglas Fairbanks*, 13.
7. Douglas Fairbanks Jr., interview with the author, 1993. See also Douglas Fairbanks Jr., *Salad Days*, 12.
8. Hancock and Fairbanks, *Douglas Fairbanks*, 64.
9. Douglas Fairbanks Jr. Collection, Howard Gotlieb Archival Research Center, Boston University.
10. Hancock and Fairbanks, *Douglas Fairbanks*, 40.

11. Frederick Warde, *Fifty Years of Make-Believe* (New York, 1920), 269–70.

12. The September 1900 Richmond run of *The Duke's Jester* is generally accepted as Fairbanks's stage debut. However, the *New York Dramatic Mirror* of September 9, 1899, lists him among the Warde Company, scheduled to open in Philadelphia on September 11, 1899, and in "Personal Reminiscences," *The Theatre* 25, no. 194 (April 1917): 220, Fairbanks himself said he had made his debut as François in *Richelieu*.

13. Alistair Cooke, *Douglas Fairbanks: The Making of a Screen Character* (New York, 1940), 13.

14. Douglas Fairbanks, "Let Me Say This for the Films," *Ladies' Home Journal,* September 1922, 13.

15. In several interviews between 1910 and 1921, and later in his official biography, prepared by United Artists Corporation, Fairbanks claimed to have been a student at Harvard, but the Harvard University Archives has no record of his ever attending the university, and his son maintained it was one of his many "fanciful tales about his early life" (interview with the author, 1993).

16. Hancock and Fairbanks, *Douglas Fairbanks,* 80.

17. William A. Brady, *Showman* (New York, 1937), 262.

18. Ibid., 262–63.

19. Douglas Fairbanks, *Youth Points the Way* (New York, 1924), 1–2. On Fairbanks's doodling the word "success," see also Frank Case, *Tales of a Wayward Inn* (New York, 1938), 91; Hancock and Fairbanks, *Douglas Fairbanks,* 169; and Mary Pickford, *Sunshine and Shadow* (Garden City, N.Y., 1955), 222–23.

20. Fairbanks Jr., interview with the author, 1994.

21. Brady, *Showman,* 264–65.

22. Fairbanks, "Let Me Say This for the Films," 13.

23. Fairbanks appears to have made another early film appearance during this period, a lost one-reel film entitled *Our Mutual Girl, Chapter 47: Our Mutual Girl at Yale-Princeton Game* (1914). According to a synopsis by Marc Edmund Jones of the Mutual house organ *Reel Life* (December 5, 1914), Margaret, "The Mutual Girl" (Norma Phillips), meets Douglas Fairbanks (playing himself), who invites her into his red Stutz racing car and takes her for a spin at breakneck speed. Fairbanks's appearance concludes with a title reading: "I have to get to the theater. I've a matinee to-day, drat it, or I'd go all the way [to the game] with you."

24. Case, *Tales,* 82.

25. Peter Bogdanovich, *Allan Dwan: The Last Pioneer* (New York, 1971), 42.

THE MACHINE FOR ESCAPE

1. At Fairbanks's suggestion, Buster Keaton later took on the role of Bertie in *The Saphead* (1920).

2. Douglas Fairbanks, "Let Me Say This for the Films," *Ladies' Home Journal,* September 1922, 13.

3. Alistair Cooke, *Douglas Fairbanks: The Making of a Screen Character* (New York, 1940), 14.

4. Douglas Fairbanks Jr., interview with the author, 1993.

5. Douglas Fairbanks Jr., interview with the author, 1994. The remark has often been attributed to D. W. Griffith, but without confirmation of source.

6. Jeanine Basinger, *Silent Stars* (New York, 1999), 105.

7. "Triangle Debut," *New York Times,* September 24, 1915, 2.

8. Harry and Roy Aitken Papers, 1909–1940, Wisconsin Center for Film and Theater Research.

9. John Emerson and Anita Loos, "Photoplay Writing," *Photoplay* 13, no. 5 (April 1918): 81.

10. Cooke, *Douglas Fairbanks,* 22.

11. Anita Loos quoted in Louella Parsons, "Louella Parsons Tells How 'Doug' was Guiding Genius in Early Days," unsourced clipping in the Douglas Fairbanks Memorial Album, 1939. Douglas Fairbanks Collection, Margaret Herrick Library, Academy of Motion Picture Arts and Sciences.

12. Cooke, *Douglas Fairbanks,* 16.

13. "His Picture in the Papers," *Variety,* February 4, 1916, 24.

14. Peter Bogdanovich, *Allan Dwan: The Last Pioneer* (New York, 1971), 42.

15. Ibid.

16. Arthur Lennig, *The Silent Voice* (Albany, N.Y., 1966), 45.

17. Kevin Brownlow, *Behind the Mask of Innocence* (New York, 1990), 102.

18. Charles Chaplin, *My Autobiography* (London, 1964), 212.

19. Charles Chaplin, interview with Richard Meryman, 1966, quoted in Jeffrey Vance, *Chaplin: Genius of the Cinema* (New York, 2003), 159.

20. "Fairbanks at $15,000 Weekly Tops All Picture Salaries," *Variety* 45, no. 7 (January 12, 1917): 3.

21. Ralph Hancock and Letitia Fairbanks, *Douglas Fairbanks: The Fourth Musketeer* (New York, 1953), 140.

22. "Fairbanks Endeavors to Break Contract with Triangle," *Motion Picture News* 15, no. 4 (January 27, 1917): 546.

DOUG

1. Epigraph: Douglas Fairbanks, *Laugh and Live* (New York, 1917), 9.
2. Alistair Cooke, *Douglas Fairbanks: The Making of a Screen Character* (New York, 1940), 17–22.
3. Ibid., 16.
4. Douglas Fairbanks Jr., interview with the author, 1994.
5. Delight Evans, "Gee Whiz," *Photoplay* 13, no. 1 (December 1917): 30.
6. Cooke, *Douglas Fairbanks,* 17.
7. Alfred Gheri, "Réflexions sur l'art de Douglas Fairbanks," *Cinéa-Ciné pour tous* (Paris), November 1, 1927, quoted in Cooke, *Douglas Fairbanks,* 16.
8. Douglas Fairbanks Jr., interview with the author, 1994.
9. "Film Industry Working for Liberty Loan," *Moving Picture World* 36, no. 4 (April 27, 1918): 519–21.
10. *Wild and Woolly* pressbook.
11. John Emerson and Anita Loos, "Photoplay Writing," *Photoplay* 13, no. 5 (April 1918): 81–82.
12. John C. Tibbetts, "Glen MacWilliams: Following the Sun with a Veteran Hollywood Cameraman," *American Classic Screen* 3, no. 3 (January–February 1979): 35.
13. William K. Everson, *American Silent Film* (New York, 1978), 8.
14. Peter Bogdanovich, *Allan Dwan: The Last Pioneer* (New York, 1971), 45–48; Tibbetts, "Glen MacWilliams," 35–36; and *A Modern Musketeer* pressbook.
15. Douglas Fairbanks, "Douglas Fairbanks' Own Page," *Photoplay* 13, no. 3 (February 1918): 40, and "Why I Was Disappointed in the Grand Canyon," *Ladies' Home Journal,* February 1918, 18.
16. Douglas Fairbanks Jr., interview with the author, 1994.
17. Cooke, *Douglas Fairbanks,* 30.
18. Alice Belton Evans, "He Knows What He Wants and He Does It," *National Board of Review Magazine* 3, no. 1 (January 1928): 5.
19. "A Modern Musketeer," *Variety,* January 4, 1918, 40.
20. *A Modern Musketeer* was long thought to survive only as a fragment (only the first three reels were preserved by the Museum of Modern Art), but the missing reels were eventually located, and MoMA, the Danish Film Institute, and Lobster Films jointly restored the film in 2006. Only the first two reels of *He Comes Up Smiling* are known to exist in 2008.

PICKFAIR

1. Epigraph: Adela Rogers St. Johns, "The Married Life of Doug and Mary," *Photoplay* 31, no. 3 (February 1927): 35.
2. The sobriquet "America's Sweetheart" was coined for Pickford by David J. "Pop" Grauman (father of Sid) in 1914 when he presented Edwin S. Porter's *Tess of the Storm Country* (1914) at his San Francisco theater.
3. Mary Pickford, *Sunshine and Shadow* (Garden City, N.Y., 1955), 95.
4. Ibid., 199.
5. Anita Loos, *A Girl Like I* (New York, 1966), 166–67.
6. Douglas Fairbanks Jr., *The Salad Days* (Garden City, N.Y., 1988), 46.
7. Alistair Cooke, *Douglas Fairbanks: The Making of a Screen Character* (New York, 1940), 21.
8. Allene Talmey, *Doug and Mary, and Others* (New York, 1927), 36.
9. Cary Grant, "Archie Leach," *Ladies' Home Journal,* January–February 1963, 142. Fairbanks's popularization of the suntan after World War I was the result of the unconditional love and acceptance he received from Pickford. With her encouragement, he made a virtue out of his swarthy complexion (which he had hitherto thought to be an ineradicable blemish). Indeed, private correspondence survives between the couple in which Fairbanks is referred to as Pickford's "black baby." Mary Pickford Collection, Margaret Herrick Library, Academy of Motion Picture Arts and Sciences.
10. Lord Mountbatten, 1977 interview with Kevin Brownlow and David Gill for the documentary *Hollywood* (1980). Transcript courtesy of Kevin Brownlow.
11. Booton Herndon, *Mary Pickford and Douglas Fairbanks: The Most Popular Couple the World Has Ever Known* (New York, 1977), 194.
12. Talmey, *Doug and Mary, and Others,* 33.
13. Herndon, *Mary Pickford and Douglas Fairbanks,* 202.

1. Tino Balio, *United Artists: The Company Built by the Stars* (Madison, Wis., 1976), 14.

2. Joseph Henabery, *Before, in and after Hollywood: The Life of Joseph E. Henabery* (Lanham, Md., 1997), 183.

3. Ibid., 184.

4. Ibid., 153.

5. "*His Majesty the American,*" *Variety*, October 31, 1919.

6. Julian Johnson, "*His Majesty the American,*" *Photoplay* 17, no. 1 (December 1919): 117.

7. Louis Weadock, engaged as an apprentice in the scenario department of the Fairbanks organization, was present at the studio during preproduction of *When the Clouds Roll By*. His ideas proved unsatisfactory, and he was no longer affiliated with Fairbanks before the completion of the film. Curiously, although Weadock receives no screen credit, he is named as having assisted Fairbanks with the scenario on the Certificate of Copyright Registration submitted to the U.S. Copyright Office. His employment with the Douglas Fairbanks Pictures Corporation ended acrimoniously, and Fairbanks paid Weadock $500 to settle a claim of libel. Douglas Fairbanks Collection, Margaret Herrick Library, Academy of Motion Picture Arts and Sciences.

8. "Technical Effects for *When the Clouds Roll By*," *Literary Digest*, July 3, 1920, 75.

9. "*When the Clouds Roll By*," *Variety*, January 2, 1920; Burns Mantle, "*When the Clouds Roll By*," *Photoplay* 17, no. 4 (March 1920): 67.

10. Alistair Cooke, "The Films of Douglas Fairbanks," *Museum of Modern Art Film Library Bulletin*, ser. 8 (1941).

11. *The Mollycoddle* pressbook.

12. Ibid.

13. "*The Mollycoddle*," *New York Times*, June 14, 1920, 13.

14. Burns Mantle, "*The Mollycoddle*," *Photoplay* 18, no. 4 (September 1920): 67. *Dancin' Fool* (1920), an Artcraft production starring Wallace Reid, also contains an animated sequence.

15. "*The Mollycoddle*," *New York Times*, June 14, 1920, 13.

16. Fairbanks later regretted his documentary approach to the Hopi dances. "I think that if I were to do *The Mollycoddle* over again, I had rather idealize it just a bit and rely a little more upon the imagination that some of the great painters have put in depicting the Indian and the West," he wrote in 1922. "You cannot get what Frederic Remington saw and painted by merely photographing the actual." Fairbanks, "Let Me Say This for the Films," *Ladies' Home Journal*, September 1922, 118.

17. *The Mollycoddle* pressbook.

18. Ibid.

19. Booton Herndon, *Mary Pickford and Douglas Fairbanks: The Most Popular Couple the World Has Ever Known* (New York, 1977), 233–35.

20. "*The Mollycoddle*." *Variety*, June 18, 1920.

21. Burns Mantle, "*The Mollycoddle*," *Photoplay* 18, no. 4 (September 1920): 66–67.

22. Douglas Fairbanks, "One Reel of Autobiography," *Collier's*, June 18, 1921, 11.

23. *The Nut* pressbook.

24. Douglas Fairbanks Collection, Margaret Herrick Library, Academy of Motion Picture Arts and Sciences.

25. "*The Nut*," *Variety*, March 11, 1921.

26. *The Nut* pressbook.

27. Ibid.

28. J. Theodore Reed quoted in P. Felten, "Reminiscence," *Films in Review* 14, no. 3 (March 1963): 190.

29. *The Nut* pressbook.

30. Burns Mantle, "*The Nut*," *Photoplay* 19, no. 4 (March 1921): 62.

MAKING HIS MARK: *The Mark of Zorro*

1. Dennis F. "Cap" O'Brien to Douglas Fairbanks Pictures Corporation, letter dated May 7, 1920. United Artists Corporation Records, 1919–65, Wisconsin Center for Film and Theater Research.

2. Douglas Fairbanks Jr., interview with the author, 1993, and Mary Pickford, *Sunshine and Shadow* (Garden City, N.Y., 1955), 221. Ruth Allen appeared with Fairbanks on Broadway in *Hawthorne of the U.S.A.* and had small roles in *Wild and Woolly* and *Down to Earth*.

3. Douglas Fairbanks, "Let Me Say This for the Films," *Ladies' Home Journal*, September 1922, 120.

4. "The Old Plaza Church as It Appeared in 1830: Reconstructed for Douglas Fairbanks' Production Entitled *The Mark of Zorro*," *Los Angeles Times*, November 14, 1920, § 8.

5. John C. Tibbetts and James M. Welsh, *His Majesty the American: The Films of Douglas Fairbanks, Sr.* (Cranbury, N.J., 1977), 123–24.

6. UA advertisement in *Motion Picture News* 23, no. 1 (December 25, 1920): 9.
7. Douglas Fairbanks Collection, Margaret Herrick Library, Academy of Motion Picture Arts and Sciences.
8. "The Mark of Zorro," *New York Times*, November 29, 1920, 20.
9. "The Mark of Zorro," *Variety*, December 3, 1920, 32.
10. Carl Sandburg, *The Movies Are: Carl Sandburg's Film Reviews and Essays, 1920–1928* (Chicago, 2000), 39.
11. Gary Carey, *Doug & Mary: A Biography of Douglas Fairbanks and Mary Pickford* (New York, 1977), 114.
12. "*Mark of Zorro* Most Delightful Film She Has Ever Seen, Says Elinor Glyn," *Moving Picture World* 49, no. 5 (April 2, 1921): 478.
13. Frederick James Smith, "The Celluloid Critic," *Motion Picture Classic* 11, no. 6 (February 1921): 46.
14. Bob Kane remembered that Fairbanks's Zorro costume, secret lair, and dual identity inspired Batman. "As a kid, my idol was Douglas Fairbanks, Sr. His Zorro was a big influence on Batman. . . . He was a fop by day and a crusader at night. . . . He'd put on a mask, cape, and sword and ride out of his secret cave at night" (interview with the author, 1994). Fairbanks was also a direct influence on the creation of Superman; see Dennis Dooley, "The Man of Tomorrow and the Boys of Yesterday," in Dennis Dooley and Gary Engle, eds., *Superman at Fifty: The Persistence of a Legend* (Cleveland, 1987), 30.
15. For an authoritative examination of this subject, see Gaylyn Studlar's Fairbanks chapter, "Building Mr. Pep: Boy Culture and the Construction of Douglas Fairbanks," in id., *This Mad Masquerade: Stardom and Masculinity in the Jazz Age* (New York, 1996), 10–89.
16. Gavin Lambert, "Fairbanks and Valentino: The Last Heroes," *Sequence*, Summer 1949, 77.

THE GREAT LEAP: *The Three Musketeers*

1. Charles Chaplin, *My Autobiography* (London, 1964), 212–213. See also Mary Pickford, *Sunshine and Shadow* (Garden City, N.Y., 1955), 198.
2. Richard Schickel, *His Picture in the Papers: A Speculation on Celebrity in America, Based on the Life of Douglas Fairbanks, Sr.* (New York, 1973), 75
3. Arthur Edeson in an unsourced clipping held by the Margaret Herrick Library, Academy of Motion Picture Arts and Sciences. The author is grateful to Robert S. Birchard for this information.
4. Douglas Fairbanks, "Kind of Crazy," *Motion Picture Magazine* 24, no. 10 (November 1922): 43, 94.
5. "Fairbanks Makes D'Artagnan into a French Cowboy," *Literary Digest*, September 17, 1921, 28.
6. Douglas Fairbanks, "Why Big Pictures?" *Ladies' Home Journal*, April 1924, 104, states: "For the *Musketeers* we did have a ready-made story, but we only took part of the book. I would like to do the whole over now; for when I saw it last time I was not satisfied." See also Maurice Leloir, *Cinq mois à Hollywood avec Douglas Fairbanks* (Paris, 1929), 9.
7. *The Three Musketeers* pressbook.
8. Ibid.
9. Douglas Fairbanks Jr., interview with the author, 1994.
10. *The Three Musketeers* pressbook.
11. Adolphe Menjou and M. M. Musselman, *It Took Nine Tailors* (New York, 1948), 91.
12. Ibid., 92.
13. Ralph Hancock and Letitia Fairbanks, *Douglas Fairbanks: The Fourth Musketeer* (New York, 1953), 176.
14. Ibid., 181.
15. Alison Smith, "The Screen in Review," *Picture-Play* 15, no. 4 (December 1921): 62.
16. Douglas Fairbanks Jr., interview with the author, 1994.
17. Fairbanks, "Kind of Crazy," 94.
18. "The Three Musketeers," *Variety*, September 2, 1921, 61.
19. "The Three Musketeers," *New York Times*, August 29, 1921, 14.
20. "Fairbanks Makes D'Artagnan into a French Cowboy," 28.
21. "The Three Musketeers," *Photoplay* 20, no. 5 (November 1921): 60.
22. Robert E. Sherwood, "The Three Musketeers," *Life* 78, no. 2029 (September 22, 1921): 22.
23. The production figure includes release prints ($47,954.51), which ordinarily would not be considered part of production cost or "negative" cost. Further complicating the issue is a less detailed document dated December 14, 1928, among Fairbanks's professional papers, which claims that the production cost of the film was substantially less: $451,314.19. It is the same document that records that the film's cumulative gross profits (up to November 11, 1928) were $1,409,476.51. As late as 1928, Fairbanks and the United Artists Paris office were still attempting to negotiate a reasonable rights arrangement with Henri Diamant-Berger to distribute *The Three Musketeers* in France. Douglas Fairbanks Collection, Margaret Herrick Library, Academy of Motion Picture Arts and Sciences. Fairbanks recalled that in French-speaking territories where the film could be distributed, there was "much minute criticism of the film—criticism which so often ended with the words: '*Jamais Dumas; toujours Douglas*' ('Never Dumas; always

Douglas')." Douglas Fairbanks, "Let Me Say This for the Films," *Ladies' Home Journal,* September 1922, 13. Edward Knoblock held the same opinion. "Douglas gave a brilliant performance, suiting the character of d'Artagnan to himself and not himself to the character." Edward Knoblock, *Round the Room* (London, 1939), 309.

24. Vachel Lindsay, *The Art of the Moving Picture* (New York, 1922), xviii, 16.
25. Alistair Cooke, "The Films of Douglas Fairbanks," *Museum of Modern Art Film Library Bulletin,* ser. 8 (1941).

SCALING THE HEIGHTS: *Douglas Fairbanks in Robin Hood*

1. Grace Kingsley, "*Robin Hood* Down to Date," *Los Angeles Times,* November 29, 1920, § 2, 3.
2. Peter Bogdanovich, *Allan Dwan: The Last Pioneer* (New York, 1971), 53.
3. Robert Florey, "Le Film," *Montreal,* October 1922, 6–11, as quoted in Kevin Brownlow, *The Parade's Gone By . . .* (New York, 1968), 248.
4. Robert E. Sherwood, ed., *The Best Moving Pictures of 1922–1923* (Boston, 1923), 38.
5. Adele Whitely Fletcher, "The Man Who Made *Robin Hood,*" *Motion Picture Magazine,* February 1923, 99.
6. Alistair Cooke, *Douglas Fairbanks: The Making of a Screen Character* (New York, 1940), 28.
7. Marc Wanamaker, interview with the author, 2006.
8. Rudy Behlmer, ed., "From Legend to Film," *The Adventures of Robin Hood* (Madison, Wis., 1979), 16.
9. Sherwood, *Best Moving Pictures of 1922–1923,* 42.
10. "How Douglas Fairbanks Produces His Pictures," *New York Times,* June 7, 1925, § 8, 4.
11. Ibid.
12. Florey, quoted in Brownlow, *Parade's Gone By . . . ,* 250–51.
13. Allan Dwan in an interview with Kevin Brownlow, 1964, quoted in Brownlow, *Parade's Gone By . . . ,* 251.
14. Ibid.
15. Fletcher, "Man Who Made *Robin Hood,*" 25, 99.
16. *Douglas Fairbanks in Robin Hood* pressbook.
17. "What Photography Means to *Robin Hood,*" *American Cinematographer* 3, no. 9 (December 1922): 7.
18. Ibid., 8, and Allan Dwan, "Notes from a Talk to Photoplay Students at Columbia University" held by the Margaret Herrick Library, Academy of Motion Picture Arts and Sciences.
19. "What Photography Means to *Robin Hood,*" 8, 22.
20. A glass shot is a painting of a foreground or background on glass placed in front of the camera lens and aligned precisely with the full-scale set. In the case of *Douglas Fairbanks in Robin Hood,* it provided the illusion of even taller towers and battlements.
21. David Chierichetti, *Mitchell Leisen: Hollywood Director* (Los Angeles, 1995), 26.
22. Ibid., 24.
23. Ralph Hancock and Letitia Fairbanks, *Douglas Fairbanks: The Fourth Musketeer* (New York, 1953), 50.
24. Douglas Fairbanks Collection, Margaret Herrick Library, Academy of Motion Picture Arts and Sciences.
25. Hancock and Fairbanks, *Douglas Fairbanks,* 197.
26. Outtakes from *Douglas Fairbanks in Robin Hood* are held by the George Eastman House as well as by private film collectors.
27. Enid Bennett, interview with Kevin Brownlow, 1967, quoted in Brownlow, *Parade's Gone By . . . ,* 254.
28. Hancock and Fairbanks, *Douglas Fairbanks,* 191.
29. Douglas Fairbanks, "Kind of Crazy," *Motion Picture Magazine* 24, no. 10 (November 1922): 94.
30. Edward Wagenknecht, *The Movies in the Age of Innocence* (Norman, Okla., 1962), 185.
31. Brownlow, *Parade's Gone By . . . ,* 257.
32. *Douglas Fairbanks in Robin Hood* pressbook.
33. Hancock and Fairbanks, *Douglas Fairbanks,* 198–99.
34. Based on the accounts in the *Douglas Fairbanks in Robin Hood* pressbook and Charles Chaplin, *My Autobiography* (London, 1964), 213.
35. Dwan, "Notes from a Talk to Photoplay Students at Columbia University," 6.
36. Dennis James, interview with the author, 1993, and id., "Performing with Silent Films," in Clifford McCarty, ed., *Film Music 1* (New York, 1989), 70–74. A copy of Schertzinger's *Robin Hood* score is held by the Margaret Herrick Library, Academy of Motion Picture Arts and Sciences.
37. Allan Dwan quoted in Richard Schickel, *His Picture in the Papers: A Speculation on Celebrity in America, Based on the Life of Douglas Fairbanks, Sr.* (New York, 1973), 100.
38. The production cost figure includes release prints ($32,480.74), which ordinarily would not be considered part of production cost or "negative" cost. The film's "exploitation" expenditure (included in the production cost figure) was $105,990.93. Douglas Fairbanks Collection, Margaret Herrick Library, Academy of Motion Picture Arts and Sciences.

39. Tino Balio, *United Artists: The Company Built by the Stars* (Madison, Wis., 1976), 45.
40. Unfortunately, the surviving accounting records held in the Douglas Fairbanks Collection, Margaret Herrick Library, Academy of Motion Picture Arts and Sciences, are far from complete.
41. Hancock and Fairbanks, *Douglas Fairbanks*, 195.
42. *Douglas Fairbanks in Robin Hood* pressbook.
43. Robert E. Sherwood, quoted in "*Robin Hood* Rides upon the Screen," *Literary Digest,* November 18, 1922, 32.
44. "*Robin Hood* a Great Spectacle," *New York Times,* October 31, 1922, 4.
45. Carl Sandburg, *The Movies Are: Carl Sandburg's Film Reviews and Essays, 1920–1928* (Chicago, 2000), 147.
46. Edwin Schallert, "*Robin Hood* Superb Film," *Los Angeles Times,* October 19, 1922, § 2, 1.
47. "*Robin Hood* Wins *Photoplay* Magazine 1922 Gold Medal of Honor," *Photoplay* 25, no. 1 (December 1923): 61.
48. René Clair, *Cinema Yesterday and Today* (New York, 1972), 61.
49. Vachel Lindsay, "The Great Douglas Fairbanks," *Ladies' Home Journal,* August 1926, 12.
50. Sherwood, *Best Moving Pictures of 1922–1923,* 44.
51. Alistair Cooke, "The Films of Douglas Fairbanks," *Museum of Modern Art Film Library Bulletin,* ser. 8 (1941).
52. Schickel, *His Picture in the Papers,* 80.
53. Jeanine Basinger, *Silent Stars* (New York, 1999), 121.
54. MoMA has held material on *Robin Hood* since 1938. Indeed, the film was the first Fairbanks film to appear in the MoMA circulating film collections; it is listed in the catalogs titled *The Museum of Modern Art Film Library Bulletin* (1938–39) and *The Museum of Modern Art Film Library Bulletin* (1940). The author is grateful to Ron Magliozzi of the Department of Film, MoMA, for this information.
55. "Add Scenes to Play," *Los Angeles Times,* June 30, 1923, § 2, 9.

APOGEE: *The Thief of Bagdad*

1. The production cost of *The Thief of Bagdad* has been the source of speculation for decades. In "The Films of Douglas Fairbanks," *Museum of Modern Art Film Library Bulletin,* ser. 8 (1941), Alistair Cooke asserts that *The Thief of Bagdad* cost $2 million; Douglas Fairbanks Jr. told the author in a 1994 interview that it cost "nearly two million dollars"; and Eileen Whitfield, *Pickford: The Woman Who Made Hollywood* (Lexington, Ky., 1997), 211, quotes Mary Pickford, a reliable source for all financial matters, as saying *The Thief of Bagdad* "cost a million seven hundred thousand." The film's actual $1,135,654.65 production cost is revealed in this book for the first time. Douglas Fairbanks Collection, Margaret Herrick Library, Academy of Motion Picture Arts and Sciences.
2. Sara Redway, "Doug Hoists the Black Flag About Pirates and Pictures," *Motion Picture Magazine,* June 1926, 94, and also Ralph Hancock and Letitia Fairbanks, *Douglas Fairbanks: The Fourth Musketeer* (New York, 1953), 202.
3. Raoul Walsh, *Each Man in His Time: The Life Story of a Director* (New York, 1974), 163.
4. Raoul Walsh in a 1973 interview with Richard Schickel for the documentary *The Men Who Made the Movies* (1974). Transcript courtesy of Richard Schickel.
5. Gary Carey, *Doug & Mary: A Biography of Douglas Fairbanks and Mary Pickford* (New York, 1977), 142–43. Fairbanks was, however, a discreet ladies' man.
6. Jeanine Basinger, *Silent Stars* (New York, 1999), 123.
7. *The Arabian Nights* (also known as *The Thousand and One Nights*), translated by Sir Richard Francis Burton as *The Book of a Thousand Nights and a Night* (1885), as quoted in Hancock and Fairbanks, *Douglas Fairbanks,* 203.
8. Edward Wagenknecht, interview with the author, 1994, and id., *The Movies in the Age of Innocence* (Norman, Okla., 1962), 186.
9. Douglas Fairbanks Jr., interview with the author, 1994. The concept of a theme for the Fairbanks productions began in earnest with *The Three Musketeers* ("A rolling stone gathers no moss"). The theme of *Robin Hood* was "When the cat's away the mice will play." Fairbanks explained his views regarding thematic ideas in "As Douglas Fairbanks Sees the Film Play Tomorrow," *Christian Science Monitor,* October 17, 1922: "It's a game of mine to try to find the truth that will apply to each picture I see. Because unless a picture expresses some persistent truth it is valueless as a work of art."
10. "How 'Doug' Keeps Self Fit," *New York Times,* July 19, 1925, 2.
11. Douglas Fairbanks, "Films for the Fifty Million," *Ladies' Home Journal,* April 1924, 47.
12. Douglas Fairbanks Jr., *The Salad Days* (Garden City, N.Y., 1988), 96.
13. Walsh, *Each Man in His Time,* 165.
14. Douglas Fairbanks Jr., letter to Richard Schickel, March 27, 1972, 12, Richard Schickel Papers, 1953–86, Wisconsin Historical Society.
15. David Sharpe, quoted in the *Los Angeles Mirror,* February 27, 1952.
16. Don Ryan, "Fantasy Arrives on the Screen," *Picture-Play,* May 1924.
17. John C. Tibbetts and James M. Welsh, *The Encyclopedia of Novels into Film* (New York, 1998), 142.

18. Fairbanks, "Films for the Fifty Million," 47.
19. Douglas Fairbanks, "Translating Fantasy into Pictures," *The Thief of Bagdad* souvenir book, 1924.
20. David Chierichetti, *Mitchell Leisen: Hollywood Director* (Los Angeles, 1995), 30–31.
21. Fairbanks, "Films for the Fifty Million," 27.
22. Fritz Lang in a 1975 interview with Gene D. Phillips, S.J., reprinted in Barry Keith Grant, ed., *Fritz Lang Interviews* (Jackson, Miss., 2003), 178.
23. Douglas Fairbanks Jr., letter to Richard Schickel, March 27, 1972, 7, Richard Schickel Papers, 1953–86, Wisconsin Historical Society.
24. Jan-Christopher Horak, interview with the author, 2003.
25. Coy Watson Jr., *The Keystone Kid: Tales of Early Hollywood* (Santa Monica, Calif., 2001), 215, and interview with the author, 2001.
26. "The Mechanical Marvels of *The Thief of Bagdad*," *Science and Invention*, May 1924, 12–13.
27. "Troubles of a Bagdad Thief," *New York Times*, March 2, 1924, § 8, 6.
28. Walsh, *Each Man in His Time*, 165.
29. Ibid., 167.
30. *The Thief of Bagdad* pressbook.
31. Ibid.
32. "A Higher Order of Music for the Movies," *Literary Digest*, July 19, 1924, 26.
33. Ibid.
34. Martin Marks in *The Oxford History of World Cinema*, ed. Geoffrey Nowell-Smith (Oxford, 1996), 189.
35. Gillian Anderson, *Music for Silent Films, 1894–1929: A Guide* (Washington, D.C., 1988), xli. In an interview with the author in 1993, Anderson remarked that Wilson's score to *The Thief of Bagdad* "may be the finest of the contemporary silent film scores."
36. *The Thief of Bagdad* pressbook.
37. Herbert Howe, "Mary Pickford's Favorite Stars and Films," *Photoplay* 25, no. 2 (January 1924): 28.
38. Mordaunt Hall, "Arabian Nights Satire: *The Thief of Bagdad*," *New York Times*, March 19, 1924, 19.
39. Ibid.
40. The *New York Herald Tribune* as quoted in *The Thief of Bagdad* pressbook.
41. "*The Thief of Bagdad*," *Photoplay* 25, no. 6 (May 1924): 54.
42. Robert E. Sherwood, "*The Thief of Bagdad*," *Life* 83, no. 2161 (April 3, 1924): 32.
43. Carl Sandburg, *The Movies Are: Carl Sandburg's Film Reviews and Essays, 1920–1928* (Chicago, 2000), 242–43.
44. Vachel Lindsay, "The Great Douglas Fairbanks," *Ladies' Home Journal*, August 1926, 12, 114.
45. Benjamin B. Hampton, *A History of the Movies* (New York, 1931), 231.
46. Wagenknecht, *Movies in the Age of Innocence*, 186.
47. Jean Goudal in Paul Hammond, ed., *The Shadow and Its Shadow: Surrealist Writings on the Cinema* (San Francisco, 2000), 93.
48. Maurice Bardèche and Robert Brasillach, *The History of Motion Pictures*, trans. and ed. Iris Barry (New York, 1938), 291.
49. Alistair Cooke, *Douglas Fairbanks: The Making of a Screen Character* (New York, 1940), 29–30.
50. Cooke, "Films of Douglas Fairbanks."
51. Alexander Walker, *Stardom: The Hollywood Phenomenon* (New York, 1970), 113–14.
52. David Robinson, "The Hero," *Sight & Sound* 42, no. 2 (Spring 1973): 101.
53. Richard Schickel, interview with the author, 2006.
54. Kevin Brownlow and John Kobal, *Hollywood: The Pioneers* (New York, 1979), 9.
55. Michael Powell, *A Life in Movies: An Autobiography* (London, 1986), 513. Documentation survives regarding the agreement between the Elton Corporation and London Film Productions, Ltd., dated September 24, 1938, to license "a sound and talking motion picture" based on Fairbanks's *The Thief of Bagdad*. Compensation to the Elton Corporation was $20,000, and a producer's share of gross receipts in excess of $1 million. Douris Corporation Records—Douglas Fairbanks Files, Margaret Herrick Library, Academy of Motion Picture Arts and Sciences.
56. Douglas Fairbanks Jr. told the author in 1993 that *The Thief of Bagdad* was his father's favorite among his films, while *The Mark of Zorro* was "close to the top." *The Thief of Bagdad* was also his own favorite among his father's films.

THE SON ALSO RISES: *Don Q Son of Zorro*

1. By following *The Mark of Zorro* with *Don Q Son of Zorro*, Fairbanks did more than help popularize film sequels. His portrayal of both father and son in *Don Q Son of Zorro* inaugurated a formula and was duplicated the following year by Rudolph Valentino in *The Son of the Sheik* (1926).

2. *Don Q Son of Zorro* pressbook.

3. Ibid.

4. Douglas Fairbanks Jr., interview with the author, 1993, and *Don Q Son of Zorro* pressbook.

5. Henry Sharp, ASC Clubhouse interview, 1963, courtesy of the American Society of Cinematographers and the University of Southern California.

6. Douglas Fairbanks Jr., *The Salad Days* (Garden City, N.Y., 1988), 104.

7. Ralph Hancock and Letitia Fairbanks, *Douglas Fairbanks: The Fourth Musketeer* (New York, 1953), 31, 36, 206–207.

8. Paul Rotha, *The Film Till Now* (London, 1930), 108.

9. Mary Astor, *My Story: An Autobiography* (Garden City, N.Y., 1959), 83.

10. Ibid.

11. Alistair Cooke, *Douglas Fairbanks: The Making of a Screen Character* (New York, 1940), 25.

12. "How Douglas Fairbanks Produces His Pictures," *New York Times,* June 7, 1925, § 8, 4.

13. Booton Herndon, *Mary Pickford and Douglas Fairbanks: The Most Popular Couple the World Has Ever Known* (New York, 1977), 240.

14. The production cost figure includes release prints ($58,712.27), which ordinarily would not be considered part of production cost or "negative" cost. Douglas Fairbanks Collection, Margaret Herrick Library, Academy of Motion Picture Arts and Sciences.

15. *Don Q Son of Zorro* pressbook.

16. Mordaunt Hall, "A Chip of the Old Block," *New York Times,* June 16, 1925, 24.

17. "*Don Q Son of Zorro,*" *Variety,* June 17, 1925, 35.

18. Edwin Schallert, "*Don Q* Great Popular Hit," *Los Angeles Times,* January 30, 1926, A9.

19. "*Don Q,*" *Photoplay* 29, no. 3 (August 1925): 51.

20. "*Don Q Son of Zorro,*" *Motion Picture Classic,* August 1925.

21. Iris Barry, review of *Don Q Son of Zorro, Spectator,* September 19, 1925, as quoted in Eileen Bowser, ed., *Film Notes* (New York, 1969), 56–57.

22. Alexander Walker, *Stardom: The Hollywood Phenomenon* (New York, 1970), 115.

23. Douglas Fairbanks Jr., *Salad Days,* 30, and interview with the author, 1993.

24. Douglas Fairbanks Jr., interview with the author, 1993.

25. Douglas Fairbanks Jr., *Salad Days,* 30–31.

26. Ibid., 30.

27. Brian Connell, *Knight Errant: A Biography of Douglas Fairbanks, Jr.* (London, 1955), 16.

28. Douglas Fairbanks Jr., interview with the author, 1993.

29. Connell, *Knight Errant,* 33.

30. Douglas Fairbanks Jr., *Salad Days,* 32, and interview with the author, 1993.

31. Connell, *Knight Errant,* 34.

32. Douglas Fairbanks Jr., *Salad Days,* 90.

33. Douglas Fairbanks Jr., interview with the author, 1993.

34. Frank Thompson, ed., *Henry King, Director: From Silents to 'Scope* (Los Angeles, 1995), 64.

35. Hancock and Fairbanks, *Douglas Fairbanks,* 244.

36. Douglas Fairbanks Jr., interview with the author, 1993. See Connell, *Knight Errant,* 42, for the consistency of Douglas Fairbanks Jr.'s version of events. However, the chronology is incorrect in Connell's version. See Douglas Fairbanks Jr., *Salad Days,* 107, for confirmation that he received his first car as a gift from his father for his sixteenth birthday.

37. The book is in the Douglas Fairbanks Jr. Collection, Howard Gotlieb Archival Research Center, Boston University.

38. Frances Hughes, "Filmland's Royal Family, Second Edition," *Photoplay* 36, no. 6 (November 1929): 37, 96.

39. Joan Crawford with Jane Kesner Ardmore, *A Portrait of Joan* (Garden City, N.Y., 1962), 75.

40. Douglas Fairbanks Jr., *Salad Days,* 155

41. Pickford quoted in Connell, *Knight Errant,* 40.

DERRING-DO: *The Black Pirate*

1. Aljean Harmetz, "Jackie Coogan—Remember?" *New York Times,* April 2, 1972, 11. A scenario by Eugene W. Presbrey entitled "The Black Pirate," dated April 1923, survives in the Douris Corporation Records—Douglas Fairbanks Files, Margaret Herrick Library, Academy of Motion Picture Arts and Sciences.

2. Douglas Fairbanks, "Color Pictures Detract from Drama, Says Doug," *New York Morning Telegraph,* September 9, 1923.

3. Herbert T. Kalmus, "Technicolor Adventures in Cinemaland," *Journal of the Society of Motion Picture Engineers,* December 1938, 569–70.

4. Ibid., 570.
5. Rudy Behlmer, "*The Black Pirate* Weighs Anchor," *American Cinematographer* 73, no. 5 (May 1992): 34–40, and "High Style on the High Seas," *American Cinematographer* 73, no. 4 (April 1992): 34–40.
6. *The Black Pirate* pressbook.
7. Jeffrey Richards, *Swordsmen of the Screen: From Douglas Fairbanks to Michael York* (London, 1977), 250.
8. Henry Sharp, ASC Clubhouse interview, 1963, courtesy of the American Society of Cinematographers.
9. Dunham Thorp, "How Fairbanks Took the Color Out of Color," *Motion Picture Classic* 23, no. 3 (May 1926): 29, 87.
10. Kalmus, "Technicolor Adventures in Cinemaland," 570.
11. Edwin Schallert, "Yo, Ho, and a Bottle of Rum!" *Picture-Play Magazine* 23, no. 6 (February 1926): 17.
12. R. J. B. Denby, "Doug Shoots Tomorrow's Perfect Film," *Liberty,* May 15, 1926.
13. Schallert, "Yo, Ho, and a Bottle of Rum!" 17.
14. Ibid.
15. Thorp, "How Fairbanks Took the Color Out of Color," 28.
16. *The Black Pirate* pressbook.
17. Thorp, "How Fairbanks Took the Color Out of Color," 89, and *The Black Pirate* pressbook.
18. *The Black Pirate* pressbook.
19. Ibid.
20. Billie Dove, interview with the author, 1994.
21. "Donald Crisp Signed to Direct De Mille Productions," *Moving Picture World* 78, no. 6 (February 6, 1926): 554, is the one contemporary reference to Crisp as director of *The Black Pirate.* See also Booton Herndon, *Mary Pickford and Douglas Fairbanks: The Most Popular Couple the World Has Ever Known* (New York, 1977), 237.
22. Joseph Dannenberg, "Moving Fast," *Film Daily* 34, no. 9 (October 11, 1925), 8.
23. *The Black Pirate* pressbook.
24. John Addison Elliott, "A Hero to His Own Director" (unsourced clipping in the Mary Pickford Collection, Margaret Herrick Library, Academy of Motion Picture Arts and Sciences).
25. Douglas Fairbanks Jr., interview with the author, 1994.
26. Ibid., corroborated by *The Black Pirate* pressbook and R. J. B. Denby, "Doug Shoots Tomorrow's Perfect Film," *Liberty,* May 15, 1926. See also Behlmer, "*The Black Pirate* Weighs Anchor," 34.
27. William K. Everson, "Stunt Men," *Films in Review* 6, no. 8 (October 1955): 394–402, and id., interview with the author, 1993.
28. Albert Parker in a conversation with Kevin Brownlow, 1960; Douglas Fairbanks Jr., interview with the author, 1994; and Charles O. Lewis in Herndon, *Mary Pickford and Douglas Fairbanks,* 238. The 3,623 feet of outtakes from *The Black Pirate* have been preserved by the Library of Congress.
29. Edward Wagenknecht, *The Movies in the Age of Innocence* (Norman, Okla., 1962), 183.
30. Robert Parrish, interview with the author, 1991.
31. Robert Parrish, *Growing Up in Hollywood* (New York, 1976), 8.
32. Allene Talmey, *Doug and Mary, and Others* (New York, 1927), 34–35.
33. John Grierson, "Putting Atmosphere in Pictures," *Motion Picture News* 34, no. 23 (December 4, 1926): 2141–42.
34. Billie Dove, interview with the author, 1994.
35. Ibid., corroborated by Douglas Fairbanks Jr., interview with the author, 1994.
36. Mordaunt Hall, "Mr. Fairbanks's New Picture: *The Black Pirate,*" *New York Times,* March 9, 1926, 21.
37. The production cost figure includes release prints ($170,122.14), which ordinarily would not be considered part of production cost or "negative" cost. Douglas Fairbanks Collection, Margaret Herrick Library, Academy of Motion Picture Arts and Sciences.
38. Mordaunt Hall, "Fairbanks's Pirate Film Whimsical and Beautiful," *New York Times,* March 14, 1926, 5.
39. "*The Black Pirate,*" *Photoplay* 29, no. 6 (May 1926): 48.
40. "*The Black Pirate,*" *Variety,* March 10, 1926, 21.
41. Edwin Schallert, "Doug's Color Picture Exerts Rare Spell of Entertainment," *Los Angeles Times,* May 9, 1926, H2.
42. Iris Barry, *Let's Go to the Pictures* (London, 1926), 45.
43. Ralph Hancock and Letitia Fairbanks, *Douglas Fairbanks: The Fourth Musketeer* (New York, 1953), 210. Fairbanks, a shrewd and sometimes ruthless businessman, quickly remedied this, and exhibitors were soon complaining about the profits he was stripping from them. See James R. Quirk, "Speaking of Pictures," *Photoplay* 31, no. 1 (December 1926): 27.
44. Nigel Andrews, "Resurrecting the Pirate," *BFI News,* January 1973, 3, and "London Curator Lindgren re Rohauer: Print Never Lost, He Just Needs to Pay," *Variety,* March 15, 1972.
45. John Hampton, letter to Alan Martin, August 11, 1959, author's collection.
46. Andrews, "Resurrecting the Pirate," 3, and information provided to the author by Nigel Algar and Sonia Genaitay of the British Film Institute. In 1984, the BFI National Archive revisited their reconstruction work on *The Black*

Pirate and a new color negative and print were produced. However, neither the 1973 nor the 1984 reconstruction has reproduced the color—glowing like the old masterpieces on which the cinematography was based—of the original nitrate prints from the 1920s.

47. Behlmer, "*The Black Pirate* Weighs Anchor," 40.
48. Michael Powell, *A Life in Movies: An Autobiography* (London, 1986), 454.
49. Saul Bellow, interview with author, 1994.
50. Mary Pickford, *Sunshine and Shadow* (Garden City, N.Y., 1955), 279.

DARKNESS FALLS: *Douglas Fairbanks as The Gaucho*

1. *Douglas Fairbanks as The Gaucho* pressbook. In an interview with the author in 1994, Douglas Fairbanks Jr. offered a different account: "It was my stepmother [Mary Pickford] who visited the shrine. And she mentioned it to my father."
2. In 1927, the Motion Picture Producers and Distributors of America, under the direction of its president, Will H. Hays, published its first set of guidelines (familiarly known as the "Don'ts and Be Carefuls") to govern film production. Fairbanks did not think much of Hays. He thought him an "official fixer" rather than an "uplifter of the movies." See "Fairbanks Turns on Hays," *New York Times,* January 27, 1923, 16.
3. Ralph Hancock and Letitia Fairbanks, *Douglas Fairbanks: The Fourth Musketeer* (New York, 1953), 213.
4. Douglas Fairbanks Jr., interview with the author, 1994. He made an additional $200 during postproduction by writing several intertitles, three of which, according to him, were retained for the film.
5. When Lupe Velez turned eighteen years old on July 18, 1927, her contract was renegotiated. Douglas Fairbanks Collection, Margaret Herrick Library, Academy of Motion Picture Arts and Sciences.
6. Dan Thomas, "Dolores Del Rio Chosen by 'Doug,'" *Los Angeles Record,* April 19, 1927.
7. Charles Darwin, *The Voyage of the Beagle,* as quoted in Ralph Hancock and Letitia Fairbanks, *Douglas Fairbanks: The Fourth Musketeer* (New York, 1953), 211.
8. On glass shots, see page 314, n. 20.
9. William K. Everson, interview with the author, 1993.
10. The footage has been preserved by the George Eastman House.
11. Maurice Leloir, *Cinq mois à Hollywood avec Douglas Fairbanks. Films muets, films parlants, par Max de Cuvillon* (Paris, 1929), 64.
12. Scott Eyman, *Mary Pickford: America's Sweetheart* (New York, 1990), 170.
13. Hancock and Fairbanks, *Douglas Fairbanks,* 214.
14. H. Bruce "Lucky" Humberstone, interview with David Shepard, 1983. Transcript courtesy of the Directors Guild of America, Inc. In an interview with the author in 2006, Shepard recalled: "It did not make it into the recorded Humberstone oral history, but Lucky told me several times that one of those big packing crates in *My Best Girl* was fixed up with a mattress and that Mary and Buddy would quite openly slip in for a quick tryst between set-ups. If the whole set knew, Doug probably would have known also."
15. "The Gaucho," *Variety,* November 9, 1927, 18.
16. Grace Kingsley, "Henley Will Direct Haines," *Los Angeles Times,* March 19, 1927, 12.
17. Based on the accounts of Maurice Leloir in Leloir, *Cinq mois à Hollywood,* 60, and the Hollywood miniature specialist William Davidson contained in Raymond Lee, "Old Doug Fairbanks Enjoyed His Jokes," *Los Angeles Times* (Valley ed.), July 5, 1953.
18. J. Theodore Reed quoted in P. Felten, "Reminiscence," *Films in Review* 14, no. 3 (March 1963): 190.
19. Outtakes from the film have been preserved by various private collectors.
20. Fairbanks originally hired Louis F. Gottschalk to compose and compile a musical score for *Douglas Fairbanks as The Gaucho.* Gottschalk's score proved unsatisfactory, and Arthur Kay was engaged to compile a score for the film's premiere engagement. However, it was the thematic music cue sheet, compiled by Ernst Luz, that served as the basis for most cinema musicians who accompanied the film during its original release. Douglas Fairbanks Collection, Margaret Herrick Library, Academy of Motion Picture Arts and Sciences.
21. Edwin Schallert, "*Gaucho* Opens Glamorfully," *Los Angeles Times,* November 7, 1927, A7.
22. Mordaunt Hall, "An Argentine Cowboy," *New York Times,* November 22, 1927, 32.
23. "The Gaucho," *Motion Picture Magazine* 35, no. 2 (March 1928): 60.
24. Robert E. Sherwood, "The Gaucho," *Life* 90, no. 2354 (December 15, 1927): 26.
25. Tino Balio, *United Artists: The Company Built by the Stars* (Madison, Wis., 1976), 93.
26. Richard Schickel, *His Picture in the Papers: A Speculation on Celebrity in America, Based on the Life of Douglas Fairbanks, Sr.* (New York, 1973), 112.
27. Jeanine Basinger, *Silent Stars* (New York, 1999), 128.

28. John C. Tibbetts and James M. Welsh, *The Encyclopedia of Novels into Film* (New York, 1998), 156.
29. William K. Everson, *American Silent Film* (New York, 1979), 285.
30. Allene Talmey, *Doug and Mary, and Others* (New York, 1927), 37.

HAIL AND FAREWELL: *The Iron Mask*

1. Maurice Leloir, *Cinq mois à Hollywood avec Douglas Fairbanks. Films muets, films parlants, par Max de Cuvillon* (Paris: J. Peyronnet, 1929), 9.
2. Douglas Fairbanks Jr., interview with the author, 1994.
3. Ralph Hancock and Letitia Fairbanks, *Douglas Fairbanks: The Fourth Musketeer* (New York, 1953), 221.
4. Leloir, *Cinq mois à Hollywood avec Douglas Fairbanks*, 11. Translated from the French by the author.
5. Laurence Irving, "Designing for Film," a lecture given at the invitation of the Architectural Association in February 1930. Transcript courtesy of John H. B. Irving and Kevin Brownlow. The excerpt—intended to be spoken—has been edited slightly for publication.
6. Ibid.
7. Ibid.
8. Ben Carré, "Memoir of an Art Director" (unpublished MS) quoted in *The Iron Mask* Channel Four Television program book, 1999, 7.
9. Douglas Fairbanks Jr., interview with the author, 1994.
10. William Bakewell, interview with the author, 1992.
11. Ibid.
12. William Bakewell, *Hollywood Be Thy Name* (Metuchen, N.J., 1991), 39.
13. Prince George (1902–1942) was the fourth son of George V and Queen Mary; he should not be confused with his elder brother, Prince Albert Frederick Arthur George, Duke of York, subsequently King George VI.
14. See Alma Whitaker, "Lieut. Windsor Slips One Over," *Los Angeles Times,* September 13, 1928, A1, and Laurence Irving, *Designing for the Movies: The Memoirs of Laurence Irving* (Lanham, Md., 2005), 49–52.
15. Bakewell, *Hollywood Be Thy Name*, 40–42.
16. Allan Dwan, 1977 interview with Kevin Brownlow and David Gill for the documentary *Hollywood* (1980). Transcript courtesy of Kevin Brownlow.
17. *The Iron Mask* was reissued in 1953 and distributed by Lippert Pictures. The 1953 reissue version, produced by Odyssey Productions, features a musical score by Allan Gray and a narration, replacing the original intertitles, written by Richard Llewellyn and spoken by Douglas Fairbanks Jr. The 1999 version of *The Iron Mask,* produced by Photoplay Productions for Britain's Channel 4 in association with the Douris Corporation, features a musical score by Carl Davis and restores Fairbanks's two speeches to the film.
18. "For All Eternity" by Elton Thomas (Fairbanks), a fifty-one-page first draft from a treatment by Jack Cunningham, and "The Further Adventures of d'Artagnan," as revised by Lotta Woods, survive in the Douris Corporation Records—Douglas Fairbanks Files, Margaret Herrick Library, Academy of Motion Picture Arts and Sciences.
19. Peter Bogdanovich, *Allan Dwan: The Last Pioneer* (New York, 1971), 82.
20. Author's interviews with William Bakewell, Edward Bernds, Douglas Fairbanks Jr., Robert Parrish, and Dorothy Revier.
21. See H. Bruce Humberstone, interview with David Shepard, 1983, for Dwan's manner on the set of *The Iron Mask.* For Fairbanks's "Vous avez raison?" see Booton Herndon, *Mary Pickford and Douglas Fairbanks: The Most Popular Couple the World Has Ever Known* (New York, 1977), 48 and 241.
22. Irving, *Designing for the Movies*, 32.
23. Ibid., 39.
24. *The Iron Mask* pressbook.
25. William Bakewell, interview with the author, 1992.
26. Edward Knoblock wrote the verse for exhibitors presenting *The Three Musketeers* for use as a prologue in presentations of the film. Unsigned article. "Edward Knoblock Writes Prologue," *New York Morning Telegraph,* August 21, 1921. The text of the speech follows the punctuation as reprinted in the *Iron Mask* souvenir book.
27. Edward Bernds, *Mr. Bernds Goes to Hollywood* (Lanham, Md., 1999), 72–73. Rumors persist that Fairbanks's voice registered high and a voice double was used for his two speeches. The author's interviews with Edward Bernds, William Bakewell, and Douglas Fairbanks Jr. leave no doubt that this was not the case. However, one can see Fairbanks's lip movements do not exactly match the voice in the prologue speech. This was no doubt the result of using another sound take. The voice used in the film is unquestionably the voice of Douglas Fairbanks.
28. *The Iron Mask* was also released with the sound track dubbed onto Vitaphone discs.
29. Mordaunt Hall, "*The Iron Mask,*" *New York Times,* February 22, 1929, 18.

30. Sid Silverman, "*The Iron Mask*," *Variety*, February 27, 1929.
31. "*The Iron Mask*," *Photoplay* 35, no. 3 (February 1929): 53.
32. Edwin Schallert, "*Iron Mask* Is Distinct Event," *Los Angeles Times*, March 14, 1929, A11.
33. Laurence Irving, 1979 interview with Kevin Brownlow and David Gill for the documentary *Hollywood* (1980). Transcript courtesy of Kevin Brownlow. See also Irving, *Designing for the Movies*, 40–41.

SOUND AND FURY: *Taming of the Shrew*

1. Mary Pickford, *Sunshine and Shadow* (Garden City, N.Y., 1955), 294.
2. Laurence Irving, *Designing for the Movies: The Memoirs of Laurence Irving* (Lanham, Md., 2005), 43.
3. Scott Eyman, *Mary Pickford: America's Sweetheart* (New York, 1990), 192.
4. Irving, *Designing for the Movies*, 43. Pickford is quoted in the *Taming of the Shrew* pressbook conveying the film's high purpose: "It somehow seems an advance toward a higher standard in talkie dialogue, and there is something really worth while and constructive in this idea."
5. Douglas Fairbanks Jr., interview with the author, 1993.
6. Irving, *Designing for the Movies*, 69, and the *Taming of the Shrew* pressbook.
7. Irving, *Designing for the Movies*, 69.
8. *Taming of the Shrew* pressbook.
9. Edward Bernds in an interview with the author, 1994. See also id., *Mr. Bernds Goes to Hollywood* (Lanham, Md., 1999), 85, and Scott Eyman, *The Speed of Sound: Hollywood and the Talkie Revolution, 1926–1930* (New York, 1997), 275–76.
10. H. Bruce Humberstone, interview with David Shepard, 1983.
11. Ibid.
12. Pickford, *Sunshine and Shadow*, 311.
13. Irving, *Designing for the Movies*, 70.
14. Pickford, *Sunshine and Shadow*, 312.
15. Scott Eyman, *Five American Cinematographers* (Metuchen, N.J., 1987), 13–14.
16. Booton Herndon, *Mary Pickford and Douglas Fairbanks: The Most Popular Couple the World Has Ever Known* (New York, 1977), 271.
17. Mary Pickford, interviews with George Pratt, ca. 1957. Transcript courtesy the Richard and Ronay Menschel Library, George Eastman House.
18. Irving, *Designing for the Movies*, 70.
19. The Library of Congress holds preservation material of the silent version of *Taming of the Shrew* (created for foreign markets as well as American cinemas not yet equipped for sound) and the sound version. The Museum of Modern Art also has material on the film, deposited by Fairbanks in 1938.
20. Kevin Brownlow, *Mary Pickford Rediscovered* (New York, 1999), 235.
21. Mordaunt Hall, "A Shakespearean Farce," *New York Times*, November 30, 1929, 23.
22. Sime Silverman, "*Taming of the Shrew*," *Variety*, December 4, 1929, 15.
23. "*Taming of the Shrew*," *Photoplay* 36, no. 6 (November 1929): 53.
24. Edwin Schallert, "*Taming of the Shrew*: Comedy of Action," *Los Angeles Times*, December 22, 1929, H2.
25. Alexander Bakshy, "Films: Mostly 'For the Family,'" *The Nation* 129, December 25, 1929, 784.
26. Paul Rotha, *The Film Till Now* (London, 1930), 108.
27. Richard Schickel, *His Picture in the Papers: A Speculation on Celebrity in America, Based on the Life of Douglas Fairbanks, Sr.* (New York, 1973), 123.
28. Douglas Fairbanks Collection, Margaret Herrick Library, Academy of Motion Picture Arts and Sciences.
29. Tino Balio, *United Artists: The Company Built by the Stars* (Madison, Wis., 1976), 92.
30. Jeffrey Vance, *Harold Lloyd: Master Comedian* (New York, 2002), 165.
31. Matty Kemp, interview with the author, 1995.
32. Phillip Scheuer, "1929 *Shrew*—A Sweetheart of a Picture," *Los Angeles Times*, October 23, 1966, Calendar 9.
33. David Robinson, "The Hero," *Sight & Sound* 42, no. 2 (Spring 1973): 102.
34. Pickford, *Sunshine and Shadow*, 309.

SLIDING DOWNHILL

1. Epigraph: Ralph Hancock and Letitia Fairbanks, *Douglas Fairbanks: The Fourth Musketeer* (New York: Holt, 1953), 238.
2. Douglas Fairbanks Jr., interview with the author, 1993.

3. Scott Eyman, *The Speed of Sound: Hollywood and the Talkie Revolution, 1926–1930* (New York, 1997), 273. See also Robert Herring, "Interview with Douglas Fairbanks," *Close Up* 6, no. 6 (June 1930): 504–8.

4. Grace Kingsley, "First National Gets Comedian," *Los Angeles Times,* April 23, 1929, A10.

5. Frank Case, *Tales of a Wayward Inn* (New York, 1938), 89.

6. Wisconsin Center for Film and Theater Research, United Artists Corporation Records, 1919–65.

7. The Irving Berlin Collection at the Library of Congress Music Division holds all of the songs Berlin wrote—and duly submitted for copyright in various states of completion—for *Reaching for the Moon.* Further information was supplied by Miles Kreuger of the Institute of the American Musical, based on Kreuger's telephone interview with Irving Berlin in September 1972.

8. Douglas Fairbanks, letter to Joseph M. Schenck, June 28, 1930, Douris Corporation Records—Douglas Fairbanks Files, Margaret Herrick Library, Academy of Motion Picture Arts and Sciences.

9. H. Bruce Humberstone in an interview with Jim Desmarias, 1983. Transcript courtesy of Directors Guild of America, Inc.

10. June MacCloy, interview with the author, 1999.

11. Mordaunt Hall, "Mr. Fairbanks in Modern Attire," *New York Times,* December 30, 1930, 24.

12. Sid Silverman, *"Reaching for the Moon,"* *Variety,* January 7, 1931.

13. The title *Around the World in 80 Minutes with Douglas Fairbanks* was inexplicably used in advertising and publicity materials.

14. Douglas Fairbanks Collection, Margaret Herrick Library, Academy of Motion Picture Arts and Sciences.

15. "Around the World in 80 Minutes," *Variety,* November 24, 1931.

16. Eileen Bowser, ed., *Film Notes* (New York, 1969), 80.

17. "A case can be made that Fairbanks was beginning to suffer from masked depression in 1931. It is well known that such depressions increase the susceptibility of individuals to coronary artery disease, as would ultimately be Fairbanks's case," the psychiatrist Stephen M. Weissman postulated in an interview with the author, 2006.

18. Reminiscences of A. Edward Sutherland in an interview with Bob and Joan Franklin, 1959, in the Columbia University Oral History Research Office Collection, 146. Transcript courtesy of the CUOHROC.

19. Ibid., 147.

20. Ibid.

21. Douglas Fairbanks Jr., interview with the author, 1993. A. Edward Sutherland disputed claims of Fairbanks's promiscuity during the film's production; see Booton Herndon, *Mary Pickford and Douglas Fairbanks: The Most Popular Couple the World Has Ever Known* (New York, 1977), 288.

22. Mordaunt Hall, "On a Desert Island," *New York Times,* September 22, 1932, 25.

23. "Mr. Robinson Crusoe," *Variety,* September 27, 1932.

24. Bowser, ed., *Film Notes,* 84.

25. Herndon, *Mary Pickford and Douglas Fairbanks,* 292.

26. Charles "Buddy" Rogers, interview with the author, 1997. See also Herndon, *Mary Pickford and Douglas Fairbanks,* 285.

27. Hancock and Fairbanks, *Douglas Fairbanks,* 227.

28. Douglas Fairbanks Jr., interview with the author, 1993.

29. Douglas Fairbanks Jr., *The Salad Days* (Garden City, N.Y., 1988), 347.

30. The rarefied circles enjoyed by Fairbanks is illustrated with the following story. "Hello Doug," Chaplin said one morning. "How's the duke?" "What duke?" asked Fairbanks. "Oh," shrugged Chaplin. "Any duke." Quoted in Charles Lockwood, *Dream Palaces: Hollywood at Home* (New York, 1981), 115.

31. Douglas Fairbanks, cable to Mary Pickford, February 24, 1934. Mary Pickford Collection, Margaret Herrick Library, Academy of Motion Picture Arts and Sciences.

32. André Sennwald, *"The Private Life of Don Juan,"* *New York Times,* December 10, 1934, 16.

33. Douglas Fairbanks Jr., interview with the author, 1993. See also Herndon, *Mary Pickford and Douglas Fairbanks,* 292.

34. Hancock and Fairbanks, *Douglas Fairbanks,* 263.

35. Michael Powell, *A Life in Movies: An Autobiography* (London, 1986), 513.

36. Douglas Fairbanks Jr., interview with the author, 1993.

37. Alistair Cooke, interview with the author, 1993, and private source.

38. Douglas Fairbanks Jr., interview with the author, 1994.

39. Ibid.; Hancock and Fairbanks, *Douglas Fairbanks,* 275.

40. "Douglas Fairbanks Dies in His Sleep," *New York Times,* December 13, 1939, 30.

41. "Tribute Paid to Fairbanks," *Los Angeles Times,* May 26, 1941, 12.

Douglas Fairbanks Filmography

COMPILED BY TONY MAIETTA

Triangle Film Corporation/Fine Arts Film Company

THE LAMB (1915)

Premiere: September 23, 1915, at the Knickerbocker Theatre, New York City. Length: five reels. Distributed by Triangle Film Corporation. Produced by Fine Arts Film Company. Director: William Christy Cabanne. Supervision: D. W. Griffith. Screenplay: William Christy Cabanne. Story: Granville Warwick [D. W. Griffith]. Cinematography: William E. Fildew. Music arranged and adapted by Joseph Carl Breil.

Cast: Douglas Fairbanks (Gerald, Son of the Idle Rich), Seena Owen (Mary, the American Girl), Alfred Paget (Bill Cactus, Her Model Type of Man), Monroe Salisbury (Wealthy Miner), Kate Toncray (Gerald's Mother), Edward Warren (Gerald's Valet), Charles Eagle Eye (Himself), William E. Lowery (Yaqui Chief), Lillian Langdon (Mary's Mother), Tom Kennedy (White Hopeless), Charles Stevens.

DOUBLE TROUBLE (1915)

Premiere: October 31, 1915, at the Knickerbocker Theatre, New York City. Length: five reels. Distributed by Triangle Film Corporation. Produced by Fine Arts Film Company. Director: William Christy Cabanne. Supervision: D. W. Griffith. Screenplay: William Christy Cabanne. Adapted from the novel by Herbert Quick. Original Treatment: Ben Hecht. Cinematography: William E. Fildew. Music arranged and adapted by Joseph Carl Breil. Intertitles: Anita Loos.

Cast: Douglas Fairbanks (Florian Amidon and Eugene Brassfield), Richard Cummings (Judge Blodgett), Olga Grey (Madame Leclaire), Margery Wilson (Elizabeth Waldron), Gladys Brockwell (Daisy Scarlett), Monroe Salisbury (Hotel Clerk), W. E. Lowery (Politician), Tom Kennedy (Politician), Kate Toncray (Working Man's Wife), Lillian Langdon (Mrs. Waldron), Charles Stevens.

HIS PICTURE IN THE PAPERS (1916)

Premiere: February 10, 1916, at the Knickerbocker Theatre, New York City. Length: five reels. Distributed by Triangle Film Corporation. Produced by Fine Arts Film Company. Director: John Emerson. Supervision: D. W. Griffith. Screenplay: Anita Loos, John Emerson. Cinematography: George W. Hill. Assistant directors: Erich von Stroheim, Emmett Flynn.

Cast: Douglas Fairbanks (Pete Prindle), Clarence Handyside (Proteus Prindle), Rene Boucicault (Pansy Prindle), Jean Temple (Pearl Prindle), Charles Butler (Cassius Cadwalader), Homer Hunt (Melville), Loretta Blake (Christine Cadwalader), Helena Rupport (Olga), Erich von Stroheim (Gangster), Nick Thompson.

THE HABIT OF HAPPINESS (1916)

Premiere: March 12, 1916, at the Knickerbocker Theatre, New York City. Length: five reels. Distributed by Triangle Film Corporation. Produced by Fine Arts Film Company. Director: Allan Dwan. Supervision: D. W. Griffith. Screenplay: Allan Dwan, Shannon Fife. Story: Douglas Fairbanks. Cinematography: Victor Fleming. Music arranged and adapted by Hugo Riesenfeld.

Cast: Douglas Fairbanks (Sunny Wiggins), Grace Rankin (Clarice Wiggins), George Backus (Mr. Wiggins), Dorothy West (Elsie Pepper), Macey Harlan (Forster), George Fawcett (Jonathon Pepper), William Jefferson (Jones), Margery Wilson, Adolphe Menjou.

THE GOOD BAD MAN (1916)

Premiere: April 21, 1916, at the Rialto Theatre, New York City. Length: five reels. Distributed by Triangle Film Corporation. Produced by Fine Arts Film Company. Director: Allan Dwan. Supervision: D. W. Griffith. Story: Douglas Fairbanks. Cinematography: Victor Fleming.

Cast: Douglas Fairbanks ("Passin' Through"), Mary Alden (Jane Stuart, His Mother), George Beranger (Thomas Stuart, His Father), Sam de Grasse (Bud Frazer, later "The Wolf"), Doc Cannon (Bob Emmons, Marshal), Joseph Singleton ("The Weasel"), Bessie Love (Amy, His Daughter), Fred Burns (Sheriff), Charles Stevens.

REGGIE MIXES IN (1916)

Premiere: May 28, 1916, at the Rialto Theatre, New York City. Length: five reels. Distributed by Triangle Film Corporation. Produced by Fine Arts Film Company. Director: William Christy Cabanne. Supervision: D. W. Griffith. Screenplay: Roy Somerville. Story: Robert M. Baker. Cinematography: William E. Fildew.

Cast: Douglas Fairbanks (Reggie Van Deuzen), Joseph Singleton (Old Pickleface, His Valet), Bessie Love (Agnes), W. E. Lowery (Tony), Wilbur Higby (Gallagher, The Cabaret Proprietor), Frank Bennett (Sammy the Dude), A. D. Sears (Sylvester Ringrose), Lillian Langdon (Susan, Reggie's Aunt), Alma Rubens (Lemona Reighley), Alberta Lee (Agnes's Mother), Tom Wilson (Bouncer).

THE MYSTERY OF THE LEAPING FISH (1916)

Released: June 11, 1916. Length: two reels. Distributed by Triangle Film Corporation. Produced by Triangle Film Corporation. Director: John Emerson. Supervision: D. W. Griffith. Story: Tod Browning. Intertitles: Anita Loos. "Leaping Fish" patented by J. P. McCarty. Cinematography: John W. Leezer. Assistant cinematographer: Karl Brown.

Cast: Douglas Fairbanks (Coke Ennyday), Bessie Love (Inane, the Little Fish-Blower of Short Beach), A. D. Sears (Gentleman Rolling in Wealth), Alma Rubens (His Female Accomplice), Charles Stevens (Japanese Accomplice), George Hall (Japanese Accomplice), Tom Wilson (I. M. Keene, Chief of the Secret Service), Joe Murphy (Footman on Car), Bennie Zeidman.

FLIRTING WITH FATE (1916)

Premiere: June 25, 1916, at the Rialto Theatre, New York City. Length: five reels. Distributed by Triangle Film Corporation. Produced by Fine Arts Film Company. Director: William Christy Cabanne. Supervision: D. W. Griffith. Screenplay: William Christy Cabanne. Story: Robert M. Baker. Cinematography: William E. Fildew.

Cast: Douglas Fairbanks (August Holliday), Howard Gaye (Roland Dabney), Jewel Carmen (Gladys Kingsley), W. E. Lawrence (Harry Hansum, Augy's Friend), George Beranger (Automatic Joe), Dorothy Haydel (Phyllis), Lillian Langdon (Mrs. Kingsley), Wilbur Higby (Landlord), J. P. McCarty (Detective).

THE HALF BREED (1916)

Premiere: July 9, 1916, at the Rialto Theatre, New York City. Length: five reels. Distributed by Triangle Film Corporation. Produced by Fine Arts Film Company. Director: Allan Dwan. Supervision: D. W. Griffith. Screenplay: Anita Loos. Adapted from "In the Carquinez Woods" by Bret Harte. Cinematography: Victor Fleming.

    Cast: Douglas Fairbanks (Lo Dorman), Alma Rubens (Teresa), Sam de Grasse (Sheriff Dunn), Tom Wilson (Curson), Frank Brownlee (Winslow Wynn), Jewel Carmen (Nellie), George Beranger (Jack Brace).

MANHATTAN MADNESS (1916)

Premiere: September 10, 1916, at the Rialto Theatre, New York City. Length: Five reels. Distributed by Triangle Film Corporation. Produced by Fine Arts Film Company. Director: Allan Dwan. Supervision: D. W. Griffith. Screenplay: Charles T. Dazey. Based on a story by E. V. Durling. Cinematography: Victor Fleming.

    Cast: Douglas Fairbanks (Steve O'Dare), Jewel Carmen (The Girl), George Beranger (The Butler), Ruth Darling (The Maid), Eugene Ormonde (Count Marinoff), Macey Harlan (The Villain), Warner P. Richmond (Jack Osborne), Albert MacQuarrie, Norman Kerry, Adolphe Menjou.

AMERICAN ARISTOCRACY (1916)

Premiere: November 5, 1916, at the Rialto Theatre, New York City. Length: five reels. Distributed by Triangle Film Corporation. Produced by Fine Arts Film Company. Director: Lloyd Ingraham. Supervision: D. W. Griffith. Screenplay: Anita Loos. Cinematography: Victor Fleming. Assistant Cinematographer: Glen MacWilliams.

    Cast: Douglas Fairbanks (Cassius Lee), Charles DeLima (Leander Hick), Jewel Carmen (Geraldine Hick), Albert Parker (Percy Horton), Arthur Ortego (Delgado), Douglas Fairbanks Jr. (Newspaper Boy), Charles Stevens (Mexican), Truman Newberry.

THE MATRIMANIAC (1916)

Premiere: December 3, 1916, at the Rialto Theatre, New York City. Length: five reels. Distributed by Triangle Film Corporation. Produced by Fine Arts Film Company. Director: Paul Powell. Supervision: D. W. Griffith. Screenplay: Anita Loos, John Emerson. Story: Octavus Roy Cohen and J. U. Giesy. Cinematography: Victor Fleming. Assistant cinematographer: Glen MacWilliams.

    Cast: Douglas Fairbanks (Jimmie Conroy), Constance Talmadge (Marna Lewis), Wilbur Higby (Col. T. H. Lewis), Clyde Hopkins (Wally Henderson), Fred Warren (Reverend Thomas Timothy Tubbs), Winifred Westover (Maid), Monte Blue (Assistant Hotel Manager), Charles Stevens (Conroy's Wedding Witness).

THE AMERICANO (1916)

Premiere: December 24, 1916, at the Rialto Theatre, New York City. Length: five reels. Distributed by Triangle Film Corporation. Produced by Fine Arts Film Company. Director: John Emerson. Supervision: D. W. Griffith. Screenplay: Anita Loos, John Emerson. Based on the novel *Blaze Derringer* by Eugene P. Lyle Jr. Cinematography: Victor Fleming. Assistant cinematographer: Glen MacWilliams. Editor: William Shea.

    Cast: Douglas Fairbanks (Blaze Derringer), Alma Rubens (Juana de Castalar), Spottiswoode Aitken (Presidente Hernando de Castalar), Carl Stockdale (Salza Espada), Tote Du Crow (Alberto de Castille), Charles Stevens (Colonel Gargaras), Mildred Harris (Stenographer), Lillian Langdon (Señora de Castille), Tom Wilson ("Whitey").

Artcraft Film Corporation/Famous Players–Lasky Corporation

IN AGAIN—OUT AGAIN (1917)

Premiere: April 22, 1917, at the Rialto Theatre, New York City. Length: five reels. Distributed by Artcraft Film Corporation. Produced by Douglas Fairbanks Pictures Corporation. Director: John Emerson. Producer: Douglas Fairbanks. Screenplay:

Anita Loos. Cinematography: Victor Fleming. Assistant cinematographer: Glen MacWilliams. Assistant director: Jack Scott. Editor: William Shea. General manager: John Fairbanks.

Cast: Douglas Fairbanks (Teddy Rutherford), Arline Pretty (Janie Smith, The Sheriff's Daughter), Walter Walker (Her Father), Arnold Lucy (Amos Jennings Ford, Pacifist), Helene Greene (Pacifice, His Daughter), Homer Hunt (Henry Pinchit), Albert Parker (Jerry), Bull Montana (The Burglar), Ada Gilman (His Mother), Frank Lalor (The Druggist), Betty Tyrel (The Nurse), Spike Robinson (The Trusty), Erich von Stroheim.

WILD AND WOOLLY (1917)

Premiere: June 24, 1917, at the Rialto Theatre, New York City. Length: five reels. Distributed by Artcraft Pictures Corporation. Produced by Douglas Fairbanks Pictures Corporation. Director: John Emerson. Producer: Douglas Fairbanks. Screenplay: Anita Loos. Based on a story by H. B. Carpenter. Cinematography: Victor Fleming. Assistant Cinematographer: Glen MacWilliams. Second unit director: Joseph Henabery. Editor: William Shea. Consultant: Ed Burns. General manager: John Fairbanks.

Cast: Douglas Fairbanks (Jeff Hillington), Eileen Percy (Nell Larrabee), Walter Bytell (Hollis J. Hillington), Joseph Singleton (Judson, Hillington's Butler), Calvin Carter (Bitter Creek Hotel Keeper), Forest Seabury (Banker), J. W. Jones (Lawyer), Charles Stevens (Pedro), Sam de Grasse (Steve Shelby), Tom Wilson (Engineer), Bull Montana (Bartender), Monte Blue, Ed Burns, Ruth Allen, James Wharton James

DOWN TO EARTH (1917)

Premiere: August 5, 1917, at the Rialto Theatre, New York City. Length: five reels. Distributed by Artcraft Pictures Corporation. Produced by Douglas Fairbanks Pictures Corporation. Director: John Emerson. Producer: Douglas Fairbanks. Screenplay: Anita Loos and John Emerson. Based on a story by Douglas Fairbanks. Cinematography: Victor Fleming. Assistant cinematographer: Glen MacWilliams. Editor: William Shea. Second unit director: Joseph Henabery. General manager: John Fairbanks.

Cast: Douglas Fairbanks (Billy Gaynor), Eileen Percy (Ethel Forsythe), Charles K. Gerrard (Charlie Riddle), Gustav von Seyffertitz (Dr. Jollyem), Charles McHugh (Dr. Samm), William H. Keith (Mr. Carter), Ruth Allen (Lydia Fuller-Jermes), Fred Goodwins (Gordan Jinny), Florence Mayon (Mrs. Helfer-Eaton), Herbert Standing (A. D. Speptic), David Porter (Joseph Hackenkoff), Bull Montana (Wild Man).

THE MAN FROM PAINTED POST (1917)

Premiere: October 1, 1917, at the Rialto Theatre, New York City. Length: five reels. Distributed by Artcraft Pictures Corporation. Produced by Douglas Fairbanks Pictures Corporation. Director: Joseph Henabery. Producer: Douglas Fairbanks. Screenplay: Douglas Fairbanks. Based on the story "Silver Slippers" by Jackson Gregory. Cinematography: Harris Thorpe. Assistant cinematographer: Glen MacWilliams. Assistant director: Millard Webb. Editor: William Shea. General manager: John Fairbanks.

Cast: Douglas Fairbanks ("Fancy Jim" Sherwood), Eileen Percy (Jane Forbes), Frank Campeau ("Bull" Madden), Frank Clark (Toby Madden), Herbert Standing (Warren Bronson), William Lowery (Charles Ross), Rhea Haines (Wah-na Madden), Charles Stevens (Tony Lopez), Monte Blue (Slim Carter), Tommy Grimes, Sam Brownell, John Judd, H. A. Strickland, Ed Burns, Prairie Rose.

REACHING FOR THE MOON (1917)

Premiere: November 18, 1917, at the Rialto Theatre, New York City. Length: five reels. Distributed by Artcraft Pictures Corporation. Produced by Douglas Fairbanks Pictures Corporation. Director: John Emerson. Producer: Douglas Fairbanks. Screenplay: Anita Loos and John Emerson. Cinematography: Victor Fleming, Sam Landers. Assistant Cinematographer: Glen MacWilliams. Art director: Wilfred Buckland. Editor: William Shea. Technical director: Erich von Stroheim. General manager: John Fairbanks.

Cast: Douglas Fairbanks (Alexis Caesar Napoleon Brown), Richard Cummings (Old Bingham, His Boss), Millard Webb (Mr. Mann), Eileen Percy (Elsie Merrill), Eugene Ormonde (Minister of Vulgaria), Frank Campeau (Black Boris), Bull Montana (Conspirator), Charles Stevens (Agent of Black Boris), Baron Moncheur, James Gustafos Whitely, Erich von Stroheim.

A MODERN MUSKETEER (1917)

Premiere: December 28, 1917, at the Rivoli Theatre, New York City. Length: five reels. Distributed by Artcraft Pictures Corporation. Produced by Douglas Fairbanks. Director: Allan Dwan. Producer: Douglas Fairbanks. Screenplay: Allan Dwan. Based on the story "D'Artagnan of Kansas" by E. P. Lyle Jr. Cinematography: Hugh McClung, Harris Thorpe. Assistant cinematographer: Glen MacWilliams. Editor: William Shea. General manager: John Fairbanks.

Cast: Douglas Fairbanks (Ned Thacker / d'Artagnan), Marjorie Daw (Elsie Dodge), Kathleen Kirkham (Her Mother), Frank Campeau (Chin-de-dah, Navajo Chief), Eugene Ormonde (Forrest Vandeeter), Tully Marshall (James Brown), Edythe Chapman (Mrs. Thacker), Zasu Pitts (Kansas Girl), Charles Stevens, James Mason, Art Acord, Johnny Judd, Shorty Kelso, Tommy Grimes.

HEADIN' SOUTH (1918)

Premiere: March 10, 1918, at the Rivoli Theatre, New York City. Length: five reels. Distributed by Artcraft Film Corporation. Produced by Douglas Fairbanks Pictures Corporation. Director: Arthur Rosson. Supervising Director: Allan Dwan. Producer: Douglas Fairbanks. Screenplay: Allan Dwan. Cinematography: Hugh McClung, Harris Thorpe. Assistant cinematographers: Glen MacWilliams, Len Powers, Connie De Roo. Editor: William Shea. General manager. John Fairbanks.

Cast: Douglas Fairbanks ("Headin' South"), Frank Campeau ("Spanish" Joe), Katherine MacDonald (The Girl), James Mason (Aide), Marjorie Daw, Ruth Mason, Johnny Judd, Tommy Grimes, Art Acord, Hoot Gibson, Ed Burns.

MR. FIX-IT (1918)

Premiere: April 21, 1918, at the Rivoli Theatre, New York City. Length: five reels. Distributed by Famous Players–Lasky Corporation/Artcraft Film Corporation. Produced by Douglas Fairbanks Pictures Corporation. Director: Allan Dwan. Producer: Douglas Fairbanks. Screenplay: Allan Dwan. Based on a story by Ernest Butterworth. Cinematography: Hugh McClung, Glen MacWilliams. Editor: William Shea. General manager: John Fairbanks.

Cast: Douglas Fairbanks (Dick Remington, "Mr. Fix-It"), Wanda Hawley (Mary McCollough), Marjorie Daw (Marjorie Threadwell), Frank Campeau (Uncle Henry Burroughs), Katherine MacDonald (Georgiana Burroughs), Leslie Stuart (Reginald Burroughs), Ida Waterman (Aunt Agatha Burroughs), Alice Smith (Aunt Priscilla Burroughs), Mrs. H. R. Hancock (Aunt Laura Burroughs), Mr. Russell (Butler Jarvis), Fred Goodwins (Gideon Van Tassell), Margaret Landis (Olive Van Tassell).

SAY! YOUNG FELLOW (1918)

Premiere: June 16, 1918, at the Rivoli Theatre, New York City. Length: five reels. Distributed by Famous Players–Lasky Corporation/Artcraft Film Corporation. Produced by Douglas Fairbanks Pictures Corporation. Director: Joseph Henabery. Producer: Douglas Fairbanks. Screenplay: Joseph Henabery. Cinematography: Hugh McClung, Glen MacWilliams. Editor: William Shea. Intertitles: J. Theodore Reed. General manager: John Fairbanks.

Cast: Douglas Fairbanks (The Young Fellow), Marjorie Daw (The Girl), Frank Campeau (The Villain), Edythe Chapman (A Sweet Spinster), James Neill (A Kindly Bachelor), Ernest Butterworth.

BOUND IN MOROCCO (1918)

Premiere: July 28, 1918, at the Rivoli Theatre, New York City. Length: five reels. Distributed by Famous Players–Lasky Corporation/Artcraft Film Corporation. Produced by Douglas Fairbanks Pictures Corporation. Director: Allan Dwan. Producer: Douglas Fairbanks. Screenplay: Allan Dwan. Cinematography: Hugh McClung, Glen MacWilliams. Editor: William Shea. General manager: John Fairbanks.

Cast: Douglas Fairbanks (George Travelwell), Pauline Curley (Ysail), Edythe Chapman (Her Mother), Tully Marshall (Ali Pah Shush), Frank Campeau (Basha El Harib, Governor of the Province of Harib), Jay Dwiggins (Kaid Mahedi el Menebhi, Lord High Ambassador to Court of El Harib), Fred Burns (Chief of the Bandits), Marjorie Daw, Albert MacQuarrie.

HE COMES UP SMILING (1918)

Premiere: September 8, 1918, at the Rivoli Theatre, New York City. Length: five reels. Distributed by Famous Players–Lasky Corporation/Artcraft Film Corporation. Produced by Douglas Fairbanks Pictures Corporation. Director: Allan Dwan. Producer: Douglas Fairbanks. Screenplay: Frances Marion. Adapted from the play by Byron Ongley and Emil Nyitray and the novel by Charles Sherman. Cinematography: Hugh McClung, Glen MacWilliams. Editor: William Shea. General manager: John Fairbanks.

Cast: Douglas Fairbanks (Jerry Martin, "The Watermelon"), Herbert Standing (Mike), Bull Montana (Baron Bean, A Tramp), Albert MacQuarrie (Batchelor, A Stockbroker), Marjorie Daw (Billy Bartlett), Frank Campeau (John Bartlett, Her Father), Jay Dwiggins (The General), Kathleen Kirkham (Louise, His Daughter), Billy Elmer.

ARIZONA (1918)

Premiere: December 15, 1918, at the Rivoli Theatre, New York City. Length: five reels. Distributed by Famous Players–Lasky Corporation/Artcraft Film Corporation. Produced by Douglas Fairbanks Pictures Corporation. Director: Albert Parker. Producer: Douglas Fairbanks. Screenplay: J. Theodore Reed. Adapted from Augustus Thomas's play *Arizona*. Cinematography: Hugh McClung, Glen MacWilliams. Editor: William Shea. Technical director: James P. Hogan. General manager: John Fairbanks.

Cast: Douglas Fairbanks (Lieutenant Denton), Theodore Roberts (Canby), Kate Price (Mrs. Canby), Frederick Burton (Colonel Bonham), Harry Northrup (Captain Hodgeman) Frank Campeau (Kellar), Kathleen Kirkham (Estrella), Marjorie Daw (Bonita), Marguerite de la Motte (Lena), Raymond Hatton (Tony), Robert Boulder (Doctor), Albert MacQuarrie (Lieutenant Hatton).

THE KNICKERBOCKER BUCKAROO (1919)

Premiere: May 25, 1919, at the Rivoli Theatre, New York City. Length: seven reels. Distributed by Famous Players–Lasky Corporation/Artcraft Film Corporation. Produced by Douglas Fairbanks Pictures Corporation. Director: Albert Parker. Producer: Douglas Fairbanks. Screenplay: Elton Banks [Douglas Fairbanks], Joseph Henabery, Frank Condon. Scenario editor: J. Theodore Reed. Cinematography: Hugh McClung, Glen MacWilliams. Editor: William Shea. Art direction: Max Parker. General manager: John Fairbanks. Production manager: Robert Fairbanks.

Cast: Douglas Fairbanks (Teddy Drake), Marjorie Daw (Mercedes), William Wellman (Henry, Her Brother), Frank Campeau (Sheriff, A Crook), Edythe Chapman (Teddy's Mother), Albert MacQuarrie (Manuel Lopez, The Bandit), J. Theodore Reed (A New York Clubman), James Mason, Ernest Butterworth.

United Artists Corporation

HIS MAJESTY THE AMERICAN (1919)

Released: September 1, 1919. New York premiere: October 24, 1919, at the Capitol Theatre, New York City. Length: eight reels. Distributed by United Artists Corporation. Produced by Douglas Fairbanks Pictures Corporation. Director: Joseph Henabery. Producer: Douglas Fairbanks. Story: Joseph Henabery. Cinematography: Victor Fleming and Glen MacWilliams. Art director: Max Parker. General manager: John Fairbanks.

Cast: Douglas Fairbanks (William Brooks), Lillian Langdon (Princess Marguerite), Marjorie Daw (Felice, Comtesse of Montenac), Jay Dwiggins (Grotz), Sam Sothern (King Phillipe IV), Frank Campeau (Grand Duke Sarzeau), Boris Karloff (Soldier).

WHEN THE CLOUDS ROLL BY (1919)

Premiere: December 28, 1919, at the Rivoli Theatre, New York City. Length: six reels. Distributed by United Artists Corporation. Produced by Douglas Fairbanks Pictures Corporation. Director: Victor Fleming. Producer: Douglas Fairbanks. Story: Douglas Fairbanks. Scenario: Tom J. Geraghty. Cinematography: William McGann and Harris Thorpe. Art director: Edward M. Langley. Art titles painted by Henry Clive. Assistant director: J. Theodore Reed. General manager: John Fairbanks.

Cast: Douglas Fairbanks (Daniel Boone Brown), Albert MacQuarrie (Hobson), Ralph Lewis (Curtis Brown), Frank Campeau (Mark Drake), Herbert Grimwood (Dr. Ulrich Metz), Daisy Robinson (Bobby De Vere), Kathleen Clifford (Lucette Bancroft), Bull Montana (Nightmare Apparition), Babe London (Switchboard Operator).

THE MOLLYCODDLE (1920)

Premiere: June 13, 1920, at the Mark Strand Theatre, New York City. Length: six reels. Distributed by United Artists Corporation. Produced by Douglas Fairbanks Pictures Corporation. Director: Victor Fleming. Producer: Douglas Fairbanks. Story: Harold McGrath. Scenario editor: Tom J. Geraghty. Cinematography: Harris Thorpe and William McGann. Art director: Edward M. Langley. Assistant director: J. Theodore Reed. Technical director: Robert Fairbanks. General manager: John Fairbanks.

Cast: Douglas Fairbanks (Richard Marshall III / Richard Marshall IV / Richard Marshall V), Wallace Beery (Henry Van Holkar), Paul Burns (Samuel Levinski), Morris Hughes (Patrick O'Flanigan), George Stewart (Ole Olsen), Ruth Renick (Virginia Hale), Adele Farrington (Mrs. Warren), Betty Bouton (Molly Warren), Charles Stevens (Yellow Horse), Lewis Hippe (First Mate), Albert MacQuarrie (Driver of "Desert Yacht"), Bull Montana (Fish House Worker).

THE MARK OF ZORRO (1920)

Premiere: November 29, 1920, at the Capitol Theatre, New York City. Length: seven reels. Distributed by United Artists Corporation. Produced by Douglas Fairbanks Pictures Corporation. Director: Fred Niblo. Producer: Douglas Fairbanks. Scenario: Eugene Mullin and Douglas Fairbanks, based on the story "The Curse of Capistrano" by Johnston McCulley published in *All-Story Weekly*. Cinematography: William McGann and Harris Thorpe. Art director: Edward M. Langley. Assistant director: J. Theodore Reed. Fight Choreographers: H. J. Uyttenhove, Richard Talmadge. Master of properties: Harry Edwards. General manager: John Fairbanks. Production manager: Robert Fairbanks.

Cast: Douglas Fairbanks (Don Diego Vega / Zorro), Marguerite de la Motte (Lolita), Robert McKim (Captain Juan Ramon), Noah Beery (Sergeant Gonzales), Charles Hill Mailes (Don Carlos Pulido), Claire McDowell (Dona Catalina), Snitz Edwards (Tavern Keeper), Sydney De Grey (Don Alejandro), George Periolat (Governor Alvarado), Walt Whitman (Fray Felipe), Tote Du Crow (Bernardo), Charles Stevens (Peon beaten by Sergeant Gonzales), Noah Beery Jr. (Brave Boy).

THE NUT (1921)

Premiere: March 6, 1921, at the Mark Strand Theatre, New York City. Length: six reels. Distributed by United Artists Corporation. Produced by Douglas Fairbanks Pictures Corporation. Director: J. Theodore Reed. Producer: Douglas Fairbanks. Story: Kenneth Davenport. Scenario: William Parker and Lotta Woods. Cinematography: Harris Thorpe, William McGann, Charles Warrington. Art director: Edward M. Langley. General manager: John Fairbanks. Production manager: Robert Fairbanks.

Cast: Douglas Fairbanks (Charlie Jackson), Marguerite de la Motte (Estrell Wynn), William Lowery (Philip Feeney), Gerald Pring ("Gentleman George"), Morris Hughes (Pernelius Vanderbrook Jr.), Barbara La Marr (Claudine Dupree), Sydney De Grey (Vanderbrook Steward), Mary Pickford (Party Guest), Gwynne Pickford (Child in Wax Museum), Kenneth Davenport (Managing Editor), William Parker (City Editor), Richard Talmadge (Party Guest), Fred Kelsey (Judge), Charles Stevens (Feeney Henchman).

THE THREE MUSKETEERS (1921)

Premiere: August 28, 1921, at the Lyric Theatre, New York City. Length: twelve reels. Distributed by United Artists Corporation. Produced by Douglas Fairbanks Pictures Corporation. Director: Fred Niblo. Producer: Douglas Fairbanks. Adapted by Edward Knoblock from the novel *The Three Musketeers* by Alexandre Dumas. Cinematography: Arthur Edeson. Art director: Edward M. Langley. Music: Louis F. Gottschalk. Costumes: Edward Knoblock. Master of costumes: Paul Burns. Wigs: Zan Zak. Master of properties: Harry Edwards. Editor: Nellie Mason. Scenario editor: Lotta Woods. Fight choreographer: H. J. Uyttenhove. Assistant director: Doran Cox. Technical director: Frank England. Electrician: Bert Wayne. General manager: John Fairbanks. Production manager: Robert Fairbanks.

Cast: Douglas Fairbanks (d'Artagnan), Léon Bary (Athos), George Siegmann (Porthos), Eugene Pallette (Aramis), Adolphe Menjou (Louis XIII), Nigel de Brulier (Cardinal Richelieu), Mary MacLaren (Anne of Austria), Thomas Holding (George Villiers, Duke of Buckingham), Marguerite de la Motte (Constance Bonacieux), Willis Robards (Captain de Tréville), Boyd Irwin (de Rochefort), Barbara La Marr (Milady de Winter), Lon Poff (Father Joseph), Walt Whitman (d'Artagnan's Father), Sidney Franklin (Bonacieux), Charles Belcher (Bernajoux), Charles Stevens (Planchet), Jean de Limur (extra).

DOUGLAS FAIRBANKS IN ROBIN HOOD (1922)

Premiere: October 18, 1922, at Grauman's Egyptian Theatre, Hollywood. Length: eleven reels. Distributed by United Artists Corporation. Produced by Douglas Fairbanks Pictures Corporation. Director: Allan Dwan. Producer: Douglas Fairbanks. Story: Elton Thomas [Douglas Fairbanks]. Cinematography: Arthur Edeson. Supervising art director: Wilfred Buckland. Associate art directors: Irvin J. Martin, Edward M. Langley. Music: Victor Schertzinger. Editor: William Nolan. Costume designer: Mitchell Leisen. Assistant director: Richard Rosson. Scenario editor: Lotta Woods. Research director: Dr. Arthur Woods. Fight choreographer: H. J.Uyttenhove. Assistant cinematographer: Charles Richardson. Scenic artists: Mahlon Blaine. Wardrobe mistress: Mabel Thomas. Technical director: Robert Fairbanks. Production manager: Robert Fairbanks. General manager: John Fairbanks.

    Cast: Douglas Fairbanks (Earl of Huntingdon / Robin Hood), Wallace Beery (Richard the Lion-Hearted), Sam de Grasse (Prince John), Enid Bennett (Lady Marian Fitzwalter), Paul Dickey (Sir Guy of Gisbourne), William Lowery (High Sheriff of Nottingham), Roy Coulson (King's Jester), Billie Bennett (Lady Marian's Serving Woman), Merrill McCormick (Henchman to Prince John), Wilson Benge (Henchman to Prince John), Ann Doran (Page), Robert Florey (Peasant), Charles Stevens (Victim of Robin Hood), Willard Louis (Friar Tuck), Alan Hale (Little John), Maine Geary (Will Scarlet), Lloyd Talman (Allan-a-Dale).

THE THIEF OF BAGDAD (1924)

Premiere: March 18, 1924, at the Liberty Theatre, New York City. Length: fifteen reels. Distributed by United Artists Corporation. Produced by Douglas Fairbanks Pictures Corporation. Director: Raoul Walsh. Producer: Douglas Fairbanks. Story: Elton Thomas [Douglas Fairbanks], inspired by *The Arabian Nights.* Cinematography: Arthur Edeson. Associate cinematographers: Richard Holahan, P. H. Whitman, Kenneth MacLean. Art director: William Cameron Menzies. Consulting art director: Irvin J. Martin. Associate artists: Anton Grot, Paul Youngblood, H. R. Hopps, Harold W. Grieve, Park French, William Utwich, Edward M. Langley. Music: Mortimer Wilson. Editor: William Nolan. Costume designer: Mitchell Leisen. Master of wardrobe and properties: Paul Burns. Assistant director: James O'Donohue. Master electrician: Albert Wayne. Still photographer: Charles Warrington. Titles: George Sterling. Scenario editor: Lotta Woods. Research director: Dr. Arthur Woods. Consultant: Edward Knoblock. Acting general manager: Harry D. Buckley. Company manager: Norris Wilcox. Technical director: Robert Fairbanks. Director of mechanical effects: Hampton Del Ruth. Technicians: Howard MacChesney, Clinton Newman, Walter Pallman, J. C. Watson. Production manager: J. Theodore Reed.

    Cast: Douglas Fairbanks (Ahmed, the Thief of Bagdad), Snitz Edwards (His Evil Associate), Charles Belcher (Holy Man), Julanne Johnston (Princess), Anna May Wong (Mongol Slave), Winter-Blossom (Slave of the Lute), Etta Lee (Slave of the Sand Board), Brandon Hurst (Caliph), Tote Du Crow (His Soothsayer), Sojin (Mongol Prince), K. Nambu (His Counselor), Sadakichi Hartmann (His Court Magician), Noble Johnson (Indian Prince), Mathilde Comont (Persian Prince), Charles Stevens (His Awaker), Sam Baker (Sworder), Charles Sylvester (Eunuch), Scott Mattraw (Eunuch), Jess Weldon (Eunuch), Jesse Lasky Jr. (Boy).

DON Q SON OF ZORRO (1925)

Premiere: June 15, 1925, at the Globe Theatre, New York City. Length: eleven reels. Distributed by United Artists Corporation. Produced by The Elton Corporation. Director: Donald Crisp. Producer: Douglas Fairbanks. Story: Jack Cunningham, based on the novel *Don Q's Love Story* by Kate and Hesketh Prichard. Cinematography: Henry Sharp. Supervising art director: Edward M. Langley. Art directors: Francesc Cugat, Anton Grot, Harold Miles. Consulting artist: Harry Oliver. Music: Mortimer Wilson. Makeup: Percy and Ernest Westmore. Editor: William Nolan. Associate cinematographer: E. J. Vallejo. Lighting effects: William S. Johnson. Assistant director: Frank Richardson. Scenario editor: Lotta Woods. Research director: Dr. Arthur Woods. Fight choreographer: Fred Cavens. Master of wardrobe: Paul Burns. Master of properties: Howard MacChesney. Technical effects: Ned Mann. Casting director: Albert MacQuarrie. General manager: Robert Fairbanks. Production manager: J. Theodore Reed.

    Cast: Douglas Fairbanks (Don Cesar de Vega and Zorro, his father), Mary Astor (Dolores de Muro), Jack McDonald (General de Muro), Donald Crisp (Don Sebastian), Stella De Lanti (Queen), Warner Oland (Archduke), Jean Hersholt (Don Fabrique Borusta), Albert MacQuarrie (Colonel Matsado), Lottie Pickford Forrest (Lola), Charles Stevens (Robledo), Tote Du Crow (Bernardo), Martha Franklin (Duenna), Juliette Belanger (Dancer), Roy Coulson (Her Admirer),

Enrique Acosta (Ramon), Phil Gastrock (Man with Knife), Phil Sleeman (Guest at Archduke's Ball), Princess de Bourbon (Tavern Keeper's Daughter), Baron Gosta Wreda (Man in Students' Club).

THE BLACK PIRATE (1926)

Premiere: March 7, 1926, at the Tivoli Cinema in London. Length: nine reels. Distributed by United Artists Corporation. Produced by The Elton Corporation. Director: Albert Parker. Producer: Douglas Fairbanks. Story: Elton Thomas [Douglas Fairbanks]. Adapted by Jack Cunningham. Cinematography: Henry Sharp. Supervising art director: Carl Oscar Borg. Associate artists: Edward M. Langley, Jack Holden. Technicolor staff: Arthur Ball, George Cave. Music: Mortimer Wilson. Makeup: George Westmore. Film editor: William Nolan. Scenario editor: Lotta Woods. Research director: Dr. Arthur Woods. Marine technician: P. H. L. Wilson. Fight choreographer: Fred Cavens. Consultants: Dwight Franklin, Robert Nichols. General manager: Robert Fairbanks. Production manager: J. Theodore Reed.

Cast: Douglas Fairbanks (Duke of Arnoldo / Black Pirate), Billie Dove (Princess Isobel), Tempe Pigott (Duenna), Donald Crisp (MacTavish), Sam de Grasse (Michel), Anders Randolf (Pirate Captain), Charles Stevens (Powder Man), Charles Belcher (Chief Passenger), John Wallace, Fred Becker, E. J. Ratcliffe.

DOUGLAS FAIRBANKS AS THE GAUCHO (1927)

Premiere: November 4, 1927, at Grauman's Chinese Theatre in Hollywood. Length: ten reels. Distributed by United Artists Corporation. Produced by The Elton Corporation. Director: F. Richard Jones. Producer: Douglas Fairbanks. Story: Elton Thomas [Douglas Fairbanks]. Cinematography: Tony Gaudio. Supervising art director: Carl Oscar Borg. Associate artists: Harry Oliver, Jack Holden, Francesc Cugat, Edward M. Langley, Mario Larrinaga. Master of costumes and properties: Paul Burns. Editor: William Nolan. Associate cinematographer: Abe Scholtz. Assistant directors: William J. Cowen, Lewis R. Foster. Scenario editor: Lotta Woods. Research director: Dr. Arthur Woods. Consultants: Wallace Smith, Eugene P. Lyle Jr. Main title courtesy of Joseph B. Harris. Stills photographer: Charles E. Lynch. Technician: William Davison. General manager: Robert Fairbanks. Production manager: J. Theodore Reed.

Cast: Douglas Fairbanks (Gaucho), Lupe Velez (Mountain Girl), Geraine Greear (Girl of the Shrine as a Child), Eve Southern (Girl of the Shrine), Gustav von Seyffertitz (Ruiz the Usurper), Michael Vavitch (Usurper's First Lieutenant), Charles Stevens (Gaucho's First Lieutenant), Nigel de Brulier (Padre), Albert MacQuarrie (Victim of the Black Doom), Mary Pickford (Blessed Virgin Mary).

THE IRON MASK (1929)

Premiere: February 21, 1929, at the Rivoli Theatre in New York City. Length: nine reels. Distributed by United Artists Corporation. Produced by The Elton Corporation. Director: Allan Dwan. Producer: Douglas Fairbanks. Story: Elton Thomas [Douglas Fairbanks], based on *The Three Musketeers* and *The Man in the Iron Mask* by Alexandre Dumas and the memoirs of d'Artagnan, Richelieu, and de Rochefort. Cinematography: Henry Sharp. Supervising art director: Laurence Irving. Art directors: Carl Oscar Borg, Ben Carré, Edward M. Langley, Harold W. Miles, Wilfred Buckland, David S. Hall, Jack Holden. Consulting production designer: William Cameron Menzies. Costume designer: Maurice Leloir. Costumes: Gilbert Clark, Mary Hallett, and Western Costume Company. Makeup: Fred C. Ryle. Historical supervision: Maurice Leloir. Musical arrangement: Hugo Riesenfeld. Song "One for All—All for One": music by Hugo Riesenfeld and Louis Alter, with lyrics by Jo Trent. Assistant director: H. Bruce Humberstone. Assistants: Sherry Shourds, Vinton Vernon. Technical director: William M. Reineck. Associate cinematographer: Warren Lynch. Master of wardrobe and properties: Paul Burns. Assistant master of wardrobe: S. L. Chalif. Properties: Paul Roberts. Interior decorator: Burgess Beall. Technical effects: Walter Pallman. Editor: William Nolan. Scenario editor: Lotta Woods. Research director: Dr. Arthur Woods. Fight choreographer: Fred Cavens. Stills photographers: Charles E. Lynch, Fred Grossi. Chief electrician: J. W. Montgomery. Consultants: Jack Cunningham, Earle Browne. Production assistant: Charles O. Lewis. Sound recordist: Edward Bernds. General manager: Robert Fairbanks.

Cast: Douglas Fairbanks (d'Artagnan), Léon Bary (Athos), Stanley J. Sandford (Porthos), Gino Corrado (Aramis), Belle Bennett (Anne of Austria, the Queen Mother), Marguerite de la Motte (Constance), Dorothy Revier (Milady de Winter), Vera Lewis (Madame Peronne), Rolfe Sedan (Louis XIII), William Bakewell (Louis XIV and His Twin Brother), Gordon Thorpe (Young Prince and His Twin Brother), Nigel de Brulier (Cardinal Richelieu), Ulrich Haupt (de Rochefort), Lon Poff (Father Joseph), Charles Stevens (Planchet), Henry Otto (King's Valet), Robert Parrish (Page), Leo White (Bun-Tossing Baker).

Reissue version premiere: May 26, 1953, Strand Theatre, New York City. Distributed by Lippert Pictures. Produced by Odyssey Pictures Corporation. Producers: Douglas Fairbanks Jr. and Sol Lesser. Music: Allan Gray, conducted by Ludo Philipp. Narrative: Richard Llewellyn. Narrative spoken by Douglas Fairbanks Jr.

TAMING OF THE SHREW (1929)

Premiere: November 14, 1929, at the London Pavilion. Length: eight reels. Distributed by United Artists Corporation. Produced by The Pickford Corporation and The Elton Corporation. Director: Sam Taylor. Producer: Mary Pickford and Douglas Fairbanks. Adapted by Sam Taylor from *The Taming of the Shrew* by William Shakespeare. Cinematography: Karl Struss. Art directors: William Cameron Menzies and Laurence Irving. Assistant director: H. Bruce Humberstone. Dramatic coach: Earle Browne. Production staff: Walter Mayo. Editor: Allen McNeil. General manager: Robert Fairbanks.

Cast: Mary Pickford (Katherine), Douglas Fairbanks (Petruchio), Edwin Maxwell (Baptista Minola), Joseph Cawthorn (Gremio), Clyde Cook (Grumio), Geoffrey Wardwell (Hortensio), Dorothy Jordan (Bianca), Charles Stevens (Servant).

Reissue version released November 1966 at the Lytton Center in New York City and the Tivoli Plaza Theatre, Los Angeles. Distributed by Cinema Classics. Produced by Mary Pickford Corporation. Producer: Matty Kemp. Editor: John F. Link.

REACHING FOR THE MOON (1930)

Premiere: December 29, 1930, at the Criterion Theatre, New York City. Distributed by United Artists Corporation. Produced by Feature Productions. Director: Edmund Goulding. Producer: Joseph M. Schenck. Based on story with music by Irving Berlin. Writer: Edmund Goulding. Additional dialogue: Elsie Janis. Cinematography: Ray June and Robert Planck. Editors: Lloyd Nosler, Hal C. Kern. Art director: William Cameron Menzies. Decorations: Julia Heron. Fashions: David Cox. Gowns: Howard Greer. Recording supervisor: J. Theodore Reed. Recording: Oscar Lagerstrom. Musical direction: Alfred Newman. Assistant director: Lonnie D'Orsa.

Cast: Douglas Fairbanks (Larry Day), Bebe Daniels (Vivien Benton), Edward Everett Horton (Roger), Claud Allister (Sir Horace Partington Chelmsford), Jack Mulhall (Jimmy Carrington), Walter Walker (James Benton), June MacCloy (Kitty), Helen Jerome Eddy (Secretary), Bing Crosby (Singer), Luana Walters, Kate Price, Emmett Corrigan, Phil Tead, Adrienne d'Ambricourt.

AROUND THE WORLD WITH DOUGLAS FAIRBANKS (1931),
also known as AROUND THE WORLD IN 80 MINUTES WITH DOUGLAS FAIRBANKS

Premiere: November 19, 1931, at the Rivoli Theatre in New York City. Distributed by United Artists Corporation. Produced by The Elton Corporation. Scenario: Douglas Fairbanks. Director: Douglas Fairbanks, Victor Fleming. Producer: Douglas Fairbanks. Narrative: Robert E. Sherwood. Narrative spoken by Douglas Fairbanks. Cinematography: Henry Sharp. General manager: Robert Fairbanks.

Cast: Douglas Fairbanks, Victor Fleming, Henry Sharp, Charles O. Lewis, Duke Kahanamoku, Sojin, Sessue Hayakawa, Dr. Mei Lim-Fang, General Emilio Aguinaldo, King Prajadhipok of Siam, Mickey Mouse.

MR. ROBINSON CRUSOE (1932)

Premiere: September 21, 1932, at the Rivoli Theatre in New York City. Distributed by United Artists Corporation. Produced by Douglas Fairbanks. Director: A. Edward Sutherland. Producer: Douglas Fairbanks. Story: Elton Thomas. Screen adaptation: Tom Geraghty. Cinematography: Max Dupont. Music: Alfred Newman. Editor: Robert Kern. Technical effects: Walter Pallman. General manager: Robert Fairbanks. Production managers: Charles O. Lewis, Harry Ham.

Cast: Douglas Fairbanks (Steve Drexel), William Farnum (William Belmont), Earle Browne (Professor August Carmichale), Maria Alba (Saturday).

THE PRIVATE LIFE OF DON JUAN (1934)

Premiere: September 5, 1934, at the London Pavilion. Distributed by United Artists Corporation. Produced by London Film Productions. Director: Alexander Korda. Producer: Alexander Korda. Based on Henri Bataille's play *L'homme à la* rose. Story and dialogue: Frederick Lonsdale and Lajos Biró. Lyrics: Arthur Wimperis. Cinematography: Georges Périnal. Art director: Vincent Korda. Musical compositions: Ernst Toch. Musical direction: Muir Mathieson. "The Don Juan Serenade" by Michael Spolianski. Sound director: A. W. Watkins. Supervising editor: Harold Young. Editor: Stephen Harrison. Costumes: Oliver Messel and B. J. Simmons & Co. Camera: Osmond Borradaile. Special effects: Ned Mann. Architect: F. Hallam. Assistant director: G. Boothby. Technical direction: Marqués de Portago. Production manager: David B. Cunynghame.

Cast: Douglas Fairbanks (Don Juan), Merle Oberon (Antonita), Bruce Winston (Her Manager), Gina Malo (Pepitta), Benita Hume (Dolores), Binnie Barnes (Maid), Melville Cooper (Leporello), Owen Nares (An Actor), Heather Thatcher (Actress), Diana Napier (Lady of Sentiment), Joan Gardner (Young Lady of Romance), Gibson Gowland (Her Poor Husband), Barry Mackay (Young Man of Romance), Claude Allister (Duke), Athene Seyler (Middle-Aged Lady), Hindle Edgar (Jealous Husband), Natalie Paley (His Poor Wife), Patricia Hilliard (Young Girl in Love), Lawrence Grossmith (Her Uncle), Clifford Heatherley (Don Juan's Masseur), Morland Graham (His Doctor), Edmund Breon (Playwright), Betty Hamilton (Wife of a Tired Businessman), Rosita Garcia (Another Wife of Another Tired Businessman), John Brownlee (Singer), Elsa Lanchester (Maid).

Other Film Appearances

OUR MUTUAL GIRL, CHAPTER 47: OUR MUTUAL GIRL AT YALE–PRINCETON GAME (1914)

Released: December 7, 1914. Length: one reel. Distributed by Mutual Film Corporation.

Cast: Norma Phillips (Margaret, the Mutual Girl), Douglas Fairbanks (Himself), William J. O'Neil (Ralph Hamilton), Arthur Forbes (Aaron Burr Edwards), Harry G. Weir (Judge Pendleton), Francis Leonard (Pennington), and George Graham (Doctor).

THE MARTYRS OF THE ALAMO (1915)

Released: November 21, 1915. Length: five reels. Distributed by Triangle Film Corporation. Produced by Fine Arts Film Company. Director: William Christy Cabanne. Production Supervised by D. W. Griffith. Screenplay: William Christy Cabanne and Theodosia Harris. Cinematography: William E. Fildew. Music arranged and adapted by Joseph Carl Briel.

Cast: Sam de Grasse (Silent Smith), Walter Long (Santa Anna), A. D. Sears (David Crockett), Alfred Paget (James Bowie), Fred Burns (Captain Dickinson), John Dillon (Colonel Travis), Juanita Hansen (Old Soldier's Daughter), Ora Carew (Mrs. Dickinson), Tom Wilson (Sam Houston), Augustus Carney (Old Soldier of Revolutionary War), Douglas Fairbanks (three small roles).

INTOLERANCE (1916)

Premiere: September 5, 1916, at the Liberty Theatre, New York City. Length: fourteen reels. Distributed by Wark Producing Company. Produced by Wark Producing Company. Director: D. W. Griffith. Producer: D. W. Griffith. Screenplay: D. W. Griffith. Cinematography: G. W. Bitzer. Assistant cinematographer: Karl Brown. Music arranged and adapted by Joseph Carl Briel and D. W. Griffith.

Cast: Lillian Gish (Woman Who Rocks the Cradle), Mae Marsh (Dear One), Robert Harron (Boy), Josephine Crowell (Catherine de Medici), Constance Talmadge (Marguerite de Valois / The Mountain Girl), Alfred Paget (Prince Belshazzar), Seena Owen (Princess Beloved), Douglas Fairbanks (extra).

ALL-STAR PRODUCTION OF PATRIOTIC EPISODES FOR THE SECOND LIBERTY LOAN (1917), also known as WAR RELIEF

Released: October 1917. Length: split reel. Distributed by Paramount Pictures. Produced by National Association of the Motion Picture Industry. Director: Marshall Neilan.

Promotional short subject for the second Liberty Loan bond drive with President Woodrow Wilson, Douglas Fairbanks, Mary Pickford, William S. Hart, Julian Eltinge, Raymond Hitchcock, and Theodore Roberts.

SWAT THE KAISER (1918)

Distributed by Federal Reserve. Length: split reel. Produced by Douglas Fairbanks Pictures Corporation. Producer: Douglas Fairbanks. Director: Joseph Henabery.

Promotional short subject for the third Liberty Loan bond drive with Douglas Fairbanks (Democracy), Bull Montana (Prussianism), Tully Marshall, Gustav von Seyffertitz, E. Lyons Gleason, Helen McKern.

SIC 'EM, SAM (1918)

Released: September 14, 1918. Length: split reel. Distributed by Federal Reserve. Produced by Douglas Fairbanks Pictures Corporation. Producer: Douglas Fairbanks. Director: Albert Parker.

Promotional short subject for the fourth Liberty Loan bond drive with Douglas Fairbanks.

HOLLYWOOD (1923)

Released: August 19, 1923. Length: eight reels. Distributed by Paramount Pictures. Produced by Famous Players–Lasky. Director: James Cruze. Producer: Jesse L. Lasky. Screenplay: Frank Condon. Adapted by Tom Geraghty. Cinematography: Karl Brown.

Cast: Hope Drown (Angela Whitaker), Luke Cosgrave (Joel Whitaker), George K. Arthur (Lem Lefferts), Roscoe Arbuckle (Fat Man in Casting Office), and Charles Chaplin, Cecil B. DeMille, Sid Grauman, Lloyd Hamilton, William S. Hart, Pola Negri, Jack Pickford, Will Rogers, Gloria Swanson, and Douglas Fairbanks as themselves.

DOROTHY VERNON OF HADDON HALL (1924)

Released: March 15, 1924. Length: ten reels. Distributed by United Artists Corporation. Produced by Mary Pickford Company. Director: Marshall Neilan. Producer: Mary Pickford. Screenplay: Waldemar Young. Adapted from the novel by Charles Major. Cinematography: Charles Rosher. Art directors: Harold Grieve, Anton Grot, Irvin J. Martin, Harry Oliver, H. W. Miles. Costume designers: Mitchell Leisen, Sophie Wachner. Fight choreographer: Fred Cavens. Music: Victor Schertzinger.

Cast: Mary Pickford (Dorothy Vernon), Allan Forrest (Sir John Manners), Anders Randolf (Sir George Vernon), Marc McDermott (Sir Malcolm Vernon), Carrie Daumery (Lady Vernon), Lottie Pickford (Jennie Faxton), Wilfred Lucas (Earl of Rutland), Clare Eames (Queen Elizabeth), Estelle Taylor (Mary, Queen of Scots), Courtenay Foote (Earl of Leicester), Colin Kenny (Dawson).

Fairbanks doubles for Allan Forrest's bare back in one sequence.

DOUGLAS FAIRBANKS AT HOME (1925)

One-reel film with Douglas Fairbanks, Charles O. Lewis, Lotta Woods, and Douglas Fairbanks Jr. The majority of this film is of Fairbanks not at home but at the Pickford-Fairbanks Studios, and it mostly features his associates. However, the film includes some precious footage of Fairbanks practicing with the Australian stock whip for *Don Q Son of Zorro*.

POTSELUI MERI PIKFORD (THE KISS OF MARY PICKFORD) (1927)

Released: September 9, 1927, in the Soviet Union. Length: six reels. Director: Sergei Komarov. Screenplay: Sergei Komarov, Vadim Shershenevich.

Cast: Igor Ilyinsky (Goga Palkin), Anel Sudakayvich (Dusya Galkina), and Mary Pickford and Douglas Fairbanks as themselves.

CHARACTER STUDIES (1927)

One-reel film believed to have been made for a private party in 1925 (and given a theatrical release by Educational Pictures in 1927) with Carter De Haven, Buster Keaton, Harold Lloyd, Roscoe Arbuckle, Rudolph Valentino, Douglas Fairbanks (attired as Robin Hood), and Jackie Coogan.

SHOW PEOPLE (1928)

Released: October 20, 1928. Length: nine reels. Distributed by Metro-Goldwyn-Mayer. A Marion Davies Production for Metro-Goldwyn-Mayer. Director: King Vidor. Producer: Irving Thalberg. Screenplay: Agnes Christine Johnston, Laurence Stallings. Continuity: Wanda Tuchock. Intertitles: Ralph Spence. Cinematography: John Arnold. Art director: Cedric Gibbons. Editor: Hugh Wynn. Costume designer: Henrietta Frazer.

   Cast: Marion Davies (Peggy Pepper), William Haines (Billy Boone), Dell Henderson (Colonel Pepper), Paul Ralli (Andre), Tenen Holtz (Casting Director), Harry Gribbon (Comedy Director), Sidney Bracy (Dramatic Director), Polly Moran (Maid), Albert Conti (Producer), and John Gilbert, King Vidor, William S. Hart, Norma Talmadge, Charles Chaplin, and Douglas Fairbanks as themselves.

HOLIDAY IN MEXICO (1929)

A Technicolor one-reel promotional film of Douglas Fairbanks and Mary Pickford playing golf at a resort in Mexico.

ALI BABA GOES TO TOWN (1937)

Released: October 29, 1937. Distributed by Twentieth Century–Fox. Director: David Butler. Executive producer: Darryl F. Zanuck. Producer: Laurence Schwab. Screenplay: C. Graham Baker, Gene Fowler, Gene Towne, Harry Tugend, Jack Yellen. Cinematography: Ernest Palmer. Art director: Bernard Herzbrun. Music: Robert Russell Bennett. Editor: Irene Morra. Costumes: Herschel McCoy, Gwen Wakeling.

   Cast: Eddie Cantor (Ali Baba / Aloysius "Al" Babson), Tony Martin (Yusuf), Roland Young (Sultan), June Lang (Princess Miriam), Gypsy Rose Lee (Sultana), John Carradine (Ishak), Virginia Field (Dinah), and Dolores del Rio, Tyrone Power, Cesar Romero, Ann Sothern, Shirley Temple, and Douglas Fairbanks as themselves.

Outtakes and Private Material

The Museum of Modern Art was the repository for all of Douglas Fairbanks's outtakes and private material dating from 1919 to 1932 as a result of his deposit agreement with MoMA commencing in 1938. However, much of the deposited outtakes and private material was not subsequently preserved or retained by MoMA.

   MoMA has preserved six short private films with such descriptive titles as *Doug and Mary in Tokyo*, *Leaving for Europe*, *Spanish People at Pickfair*, *Trip Around the World*, and *Angkor and India*. These films were photographed by the cinematographer Henry Sharp in 35 mm as private records of Fairbanks's travels.

   The George Eastman House was the recipient of a significant collection of Fairbanks outtakes from MoMA. The George Eastman House holds outtakes from *The Mark of Zorro*, *The Nut*, and *Douglas Fairbanks in Robin Hood*, as well as color tests from *The Black Pirate* and *Taming of the Shrew*.

   The British Film Institute and the Library of Congress both hold outtakes from *The Black Pirate*. The Library of Congress also holds private Fairbanks material in its Mary Pickford Collection, including *Mary Pickford's Cousin's Wedding* (1925). Other private Fairbanks material can be found in the holdings of the Mary Pickford Foundation, the Chaplin family's Roy Export Company Establishment, and The Harold Lloyd Trust.

   Outtakes from *Douglas Fairbanks in Robin Hood*, *The Thief of Bagdad*, *Don Q Son of Zorro*, *Douglas Fairbanks as The Gaucho*, *The Iron Mask*, and *Mr. Robinson Crusoe* also survive as the possessions of private collectors.

Douglas Fairbanks's Broadway Appearances, 1902–1915

COMPILED BY TONY MAIETTA

Only Douglas Fairbanks's Broadway appearances are listed here; his touring productions, summer stock, and "A Regular Business Man" vaudeville act are omitted.

Her Lord and Master (play) by Martha Morton
    February 24, 1902–April 1902, Manhattan Theatre
    Produced by Henry C. Pierce
    Role: Lord Canning

A Rose o' Plymouth-Town (play) by Beulah Marie Dix and Evelyn Greenleaf Sutherland
    September 29, 1902–October 1902, Manhattan Theatre
    Produced by W. G. Smyth
    Role: Philippe de la Noye

The Pit (play) adapted by Channing Pollock from the novel by Frank Norris
    February 10, 1904–April 1904, Lyric Theatre
    Produced by William A. Brady
    Role: Landry Court

Two Little Sailor Boys (play) by Walter Howard
    May 2, 1904–May 1904, Academy of Music
    Role: Jack Jolly

Fantana (musical) book by Robert B. Smith and Sam S. Shubert; lyrics by Robert B. Smith; additional music by Gus Edwards; additional lyrics by Vincent Bryan
    January 14, 1905–September 1905, Lyric Theatre
    Produced by Sam and Lee Shubert
    Role: Fred Everett

A Case of Frenzied Finance (play) by Kellett Chambers
    April 3, 1905–April 1905, Princess Theatre
    Produced by William A. Brady
    Role: Bennie Tucker

As Ye Sow (play) by the Rev. John M. Snyder
    December 25, 1905–January 1906, Garden Theatre
    Produced by William A. Brady and Joseph R. Grismer
    Role: Lute Ludlam

Clothes (play) by Channing Pollock and Avery Hopwood
    September 11, 1906–December 1906, Manhattan Theatre
    Produced by William A. Brady
    Role: Thomas Smith, Jr.

The Man of the Hour (play) by George Broadhurst
    December 4, 1906–January 1908, Savoy Theatre
    Produced by William A. Brady and Joseph R. Grismer
    Role: Perry Carter Wainwright

All for a Girl (play) by Rupert Hughes
    August 22, 1908–September 1908, Bijou Theatre
    Produced by William A. Brady and Joseph R. Grismer
    Role: Harold Jepson

A Gentleman from Mississippi (play) by Harrison Rhodes and Thomas A. Wise
    September 29, 1908–September 1909, Bijou Theatre
    Produced by William A. Brady and Joseph R. Grismer
    Role: Bud Haines

The Cub (play) by Thompson Buchanan
    November 1, 1910–November 1910, Collier's Comedy Theatre
    Produced by William A. Brady
    Role: Steve Oldham

The Lights o' London (play revival) by George R. Sims
    May 1, 1911–May 1911, Lyric Theatre
    Produced by William A. Brady
    Role: Philosopher Jack

A Gentleman of Leisure (play) by John Stapleton and P. G. Wodehouse
    August 24, 1911–October 1911, Playhouse Theatre (subsequently moved to Globe Theatre and Herald Square Theatre)
    Produced by William A. Brady
    Role: Edgar Willoughby Pitt

Officer 666 (play) by George M. Cohan
    1912, Gaiety Theatre
    Produced by George M. Cohan and Sam Harris
    Role: Travers Gladwin (Fairbanks replaces Wallace Eddinger)

Hawthorne of the U.S.A. (play) by James Bernard Fagan
    November 4, 1912–January 1913, Astor Theatre
    Produced by George M. Cohan and Sam Harris
    Role: Anthony Hamilton Hawthorne

The New Henrietta (play) by Winchell Smith and Victor Mapes based on *The Henrietta* by Bronson Howard
    December 22, 1913–February 1914, Knickerbocker Theatre
    Produced by Charles Frohman and Klaw & Erlanger
    Role: Bertie Van Alstyne

He Comes Up Smiling (play) by Byron Ongley and Emil Nyitray based on a novel by Charles Sherman
    September 16, 1914–November 1914, Liberty Theatre
    Produced by A. H. Woods
    Role: Jerry Martin.

The Show Shop (play) by James Forbes
    December 31, 1914–May 1915, Hudson Theatre
    Produced by Selwyn & Company
    Role: Jerome Belden

Bibliography

BOOKS, BROCHURES, AND MANUSCRIPTS

Aitken, Roy E., as told to Al P. Nelson. *The Birth of a Nation Story.* Middleburg, Va.: Denlinger, 1965.

Allen, Frederick Lewis. *The Big Change: America Transforms Itself, 1900–1950.* New York: Harper & Brothers, 1952.

Amid, John. *With the Movie Makers.* Boston: Lothrop, Lee & Shepard, 1923.

Anderson, Gillian. *Music for Silent Films, 1894–1929: A Guide.* Foreword by Eileen Bowser. Washington, D.C.: Library of Congress, 1988.

Astor, Mary. *A Life on Film.* Introduction by Sumner Locke Elliott. New York: Delacorte Press, 1971.

———. *My Story: An Autobiography.* Garden City, N.Y.: Doubleday, 1959.

Atkinson, Brooks. *Broadway.* New York: Macmillan, 1970.

Bakewell, William. *Hollywood Be Thy Name.* Metuchen, N.J.: Scarecrow Press, 1991.

Balio, Tino. *United Artists: The Company Built by the Stars.* Madison: University of Wisconsin Press, 1976.

Ball, Eustace Hale. *The Gaucho.* New York: Grosset & Dunlap, 1927.

Bardèche, Maurice, and Robert Brasillach. *The History of Motion Pictures.* Translated and Edited by Iris Barry. New York: Norton, 1938.

Barry, Iris. *D. W. Griffith: American Film Master.* New York: Museum of Modern Art, 1940.

———. *Let's Go to the Pictures.* London: Chatto & Windus, 1926.

Basinger, Jeanine. *Silent Stars.* New York: Knopf, 1999.

Beauchamp, Cari. *Without Lying Down: Frances Marion and the Powerful Women of Early Hollywood.* New York: Scribner, 1997.

Behlmer, Rudy, ed. *The Adventures of Robin Hood.* Introduction by Rudy Behlmer. Madison: University of Wisconsin Press, 1979.

Berg, A. Scott. *Goldwyn.* New York: Knopf, 1989.

Bergen, Ronald. *The United Artists Story.* New York: Crown, 1986.

Bernds, Edward. *Mr. Bernds Goes to Hollywood.* Lanham, Md.: Scarecrow Press, 1999.

Birchard, Robert S. *Cecil B. DeMille's Hollywood.* Foreword by Kevin Thomas. Lexington: University Press of Kentucky, 2004.

Bitzer, G. W. *Billy Bitzer, His Story.* Introduction by Beaumont Newhall. New York: Farrar, Straus & Giroux, 1973.

Bodeen, DeWitt. *From Hollywood: The Careers of 15 Great American Stars.* South Brunswick, N.J.: A. S. Barnes, 1976.

Bogdanovich, Peter. *Allan Dwan: The Last Pioneer.* New York: Praeger, 1971.

Bowser, Eileen, ed. *Film Notes.* New York: Museum of Modern Art, 1969.

———. *The Transformation of Cinema.* Berkeley: University of California Press, 1994.

Brady, William A. *Showman*. New York: Dutton, 1937.

Braudy, Leo. *The Frenzy of Renown: Fame and Its History*. New York: Oxford University Press, 1986.

Bronner, Edwin. *The Encyclopedia of the American Theatre 1900–1975*. New York: A. S. Barnes, 1980.

Brown, Karl. *Adventures with D. W. Griffith*. Edited by Kevin Brownlow. New York: Farrar, Straus & Giroux, 1973.

Brownlow, Kevin. *Behind the Mask of Innocence*. New York: Knopf, 1990.

——. *Mary Pickford Rediscovered*. New York: Harry N. Abrams, 1999.

——. *The Parade's Gone By . . . .* New York: Knopf, 1968.

——. *The War, the West and the Wilderness*. New York: Knopf, 1979.

Brownlow, Kevin, and John Kobal. *Hollywood: The Pioneers*. New York: Knopf, 1979.

Burton, Richard. *The Arabian Nights: Tales from a Thousand and One Nights*. Introduction by A. S. Byatt. New York: Modern Library, 2004.

Card, James. *Seductive Cinema: The Art of Silent Film*. New York: Knopf, 1994.

Carey, Gary. *Anita Loos: A Biography*. New York: Knopf, 1988.

——. *Doug & Mary: A Biography of Douglas Fairbanks and Mary Pickford*. New York: Dutton, 1977.

Carré, Ben. "Memoir of an Art Director." Manuscript.

Case, Frank. *Tales of a Wayward Inn*. New York: Frederick A. Stokes, 1938.

Chaplin, Charles. *My Autobiography*. London: Bodley Head, 1964.

Chaplin, Lita Grey, and Jeffrey Vance. *Wife of the Life of the Party*. Introduction by Sydney Chaplin. Lanham, Md.: Scarecrow Press, 1998.

Cherchi Usai, Paolo, ed. *The Griffith Project*, vol. 8: *Films Produced in 1915*. London: British Film Institute, 2004.

——. *The Griffith Project*, vol. 9: *Films Produced in 1916–1918*. London: British Film Institute, 2005.

Chierichetti, David. *Mitchell Leisen: Hollywood Director*. Los Angeles: Photoventures Press, 1995.

Clair, René. *Cinema Yesterday and Today*. Translated from the French by Stanley Appelbaum. Edited by R. C. Dale. New York: Dover, 1972.

Connell, Brian. *Knight Errant: A Biography of Douglas Fairbanks, Jr.* London: Hodder & Stoughton, 1955.

Cooke, Alistair. *Douglas Fairbanks: The Making of a Screen Character*. New York: Museum of Modern Art, 1940.

Cooper, Miriam, with Bonnie Herndon. *Dark Lady of the Silents: My Life in Early Hollywood*. Indianapolis: Bobbs-Merrill, 1973.

Crawford, Joan, with Jane Kesner Ardmore. *A Portrait of Joan*. Garden City, N.Y.: Doubleday, 1962.

Crowther, Bosley. *The Great Films: 50 Golden Years of Motion Pictures*. New York: Putnam, 1967.

Cushman, Robert. *Tribute to Mary Pickford*. Washington, D.C.: American Film Institute, 1970.

Daniels, Bebe, and Ben Lyon. *Life with the Lyons: The Autobiography of Bebe Daniels and Ben Lyon*. London: Odhams Press, 1953.

Davies, Marion. *The Times We Had*. New York: Bobbs-Merrill, 1975.

Dippie, Brian W., ed. *Charles M. Russell, World Painter: Letters 1887–1926*. Forth Worth, Tex.: Amon Carter Museum, 1993.

Dobson, R. B., and J. Taylor. *Rymes of Robyn Hood: An Introduction to the English Outlaw*. London: Heinemann, 1976.

Dooley, Dennis, and Gary Engle, eds. *Superman at Fifty: The Persistence of a Legend*. Cleveland: Octavia Press, 1987.

Douglas Fairbanks: Film Tribute to a Legendary Hero. Retrospective brochure. Washington, D.C.: American Film Institute, 1974.

Drew, William M. *Speaking of Silents: First Ladies of the Screen*. Vestal, N.Y.: Vestal Press, 1989.

Dwan, Allan. "Notes from a Talk to Photoplay Students at Columbia University." Manuscript. Margaret Herrick Library, Academy of Motion Picture Arts and Sciences.

Eisenschitz, Bernard. *Douglas Fairbanks*. Paris: Anthologie du Cinéma, 1969.

Eisner, Lotte H. *Fritz Lang*. Translated by Gertrud Mander. Edited by David Robinson. London: Secker & Warburg, 1976.

——. *The Haunted Screen: Expressionism in German Cinema and the Influence of Max Reinhardt*. Translated by Roger Greaves. London: Thames & Hudson, 1969.

Emerson, John, and Anita Loos. *How to Write Photoplays*. Philadelphia: George W. Jacobs, 1923.

Epstein, Jean. *Cinéma*. Paris: Éditions de la Sirène, 1921.

Everson, William K. *American Silent Film*. New York: Oxford University Press, 1978.

Eyman, Scott. *Ernst Lubitsch: Laughter in Paradise*. New York: Simon & Schuster, 1993.

——. *Five American Cinematographers*. Metuchen, N.J.: Scarecrow Press, 1987.

——. *Lion of Hollywood: The Life and Legend of Louis B. Mayer*. New York: Simon & Schuster, 2005.

——. *Mary Pickford: America's Sweetheart*. New York: Donald I. Fine, 1990.

——. *The Speed of Sound: Hollywood and the Talkie Revolution, 1926–1930*. New York: Simon & Schuster, 1997.

Fairbairn, William Ewart. *Scientific Self-Defence*. Introduction by Douglas Fairbanks. New York: D. Appleton, 1931.

Fairbanks, Douglas. *Assuming Responsibilities*. New York: Britton, 1918.

——. *Douglas Fairbanks: In His Own Words*. Edited by Keri Leigh. Lincoln, Neb.: iUniverse, 2006.

—— [as Elton Thomas]. *Douglas Fairbanks in Robin Hood*. Booklet edited by Lotta Woods. Los Angeles: Douglas Fairbanks Pictures Corporation, 1922.

——. *Initiation and Self-Reliance.* New York: Britton, 1918.

——. *Laugh and Live.* New York: Britton, 1917.

——. *Making Life Worth While.* New York: Britton, 1918.

——. *My Secret Success.* Los Angeles, 1922.

——. *Profiting by Experience.* New York: Britton, 1918.

——. *Taking Stock of Ourselves.* New York: Britton, 1918.

——. *Wedlock in Time.* New York: Britton, 1918.

——. *Whistle and Hoe—Sing as We Go.* New York: Britton, 1918.

——. *Youth Points the Way.* Preface by James E. West. New York: D. Appleton, 1924.

Fairbanks, Douglas, and Edward Knoblock. *The Three Musketeers.* Los Angeles: Douglas Fairbanks Pictures Corporation, 1921.

Fairbanks, Douglas, Jr. *A Hell of a War.* New York: St. Martin's Press, 1993.

——. *The Salad Days.* Garden City, N.Y.: Doubleday, 1988.

Fishwick, Marshall W. *American Heroes: Myth and Reality.* Introduction by Cal Carmer. Washington, D.C.: Public Affairs Press, 1954.

Florey, Robert. *Douglas Fairbanks, sa vie, ses films, ses aventures.* Paris: Jean-Pascal, 1926.

——. *La Lanterne magique.* Preface by Maurice Bessy. Lausanne: Cinémathèque suisse, 1966.

Ford, Charles. *Douglas Fairbanks, ou La Nostalgie de Hollywood.* Paris: France-Empire, 1980.

Frohman, Daniel. *Daniel Frohman Presents: An Autobiography.* New York: Claude Kendall & Willoughby Sharp, 1935.

Gates, MacBurney. *The Black Pirate.* New York: Grosset & Dunlap, 1926.

Gish, Lillian, with Ann Pinchot. *The Movies, Mr. Griffith, and Me.* Englewood Cliffs, N.J.: Prentice-Hall, 1969.

Goldman, Herbert G. *Jolson: The Legend Comes to Life.* New York: Oxford University Press, 1988.

Goldwyn, Samuel. *Behind the Screen.* New York: George H. Doran, 1923.

Grant, Barry Keith, ed. *Fritz Lang Interviews.* Jackson: University Press of Mississippi, 2003.

Griffith, D. W. *The Man Who Invented Hollywood: The Autobiography of D. W. Griffith.* Edited by James Hart. Louisville, Ky.: Touchstone, 1972.

Hammond, Paul, ed. *The Shadow and Its Shadow: Surrealist Writings on the Cinema.* San Francisco: City Lights Books, 2000.

Hampton, Benjamin B. *A History of the Movies.* New York: Covici, Friede, 1931.

Hancock, Ralph, and Letitia Fairbanks. *Douglas Fairbanks: The Fourth Musketeer.* New York: Holt, 1953.

Hanson, Patricia King, ed. *The American Film Institute Catalog of Motion Pictures Produced in the United States: Feature Films, 1911–1920, Film Entries.* Berkeley: University of California Press, 1988.

Hart, William S. *My Life East and West.* Boston: Houghton Mifflin, 1929.

Hays, Will H. *The Memoirs of Will H. Hays.* Garden City, N.Y.: Doubleday, 1955.

Henabery, Joseph. *Before, in and after Hollywood: The Life of Joseph E. Henabery.* Edited by Anthony Slide. Lanham, Md.: Scarecrow Press, 1997.

Herndon, Booton. *Mary Pickford and Douglas Fairbanks: The Most Popular Couple the World Has Ever Known.* New York: Norton, 1977.

Higgins, Steven. "Introduction." In *Still Moving: The Film and Media Collections of the Museum of Modern Art.* New York: Museum of Modern Art, 2006.

Hodges, Graham Russell Gao. *Anna May Wong: From Laundryman's Daughter to Hollywood Legend.* New York: Palgrave Macmillan, 2004.

Hofstadter, Richard. *From Bryan to F.D.R.* New York: Knopf, 1955.

Hopper, DeWolf, with Wesley Winans Stout. *Once a Clown, Always a Clown.* Boston: Little, Brown, 1927.

Hopper, Hedda. *From Under My Hat.* Garden City, N.Y.: Doubleday, 1952.

Hughes, Glenn. *A History of the American Theatre: 1700–1950.* New York: Samuel French, 1951.

Hughes, Laurence A. *The Truth about the Movies by the Stars.* Hollywood, Calif.: Hollywood Publishers, 1924.

Irving, Laurence. *Designing for the Movies: The Memoirs of Laurence Irving.* Introduction by John H. B. Irving. Lanham, Md.: Scarecrow Press, 2005.

Jacobs, Lewis. *The Rise of the American Film: A Critical History.* New York: Harcourt, Brace, 1939.

Jamison, Kay Redfield. *Touched with Fire: Manic-Depressive Illness and the Artistic Temperament.* New York: Free Press, 1994.

Janis, Elsie. *So Far, So Good!* New York: Dutton, 1932.

Jones, Howard Mumford. *The Age of Energy.* New York: Viking, 1971.

Kalmus, Herbert T., with Eleanore King Kalmus. *Mr. Technicolor.* Absecon, N.J.: Magic Image Film Books, 1993.

Kauffmann, Stanley, ed., with Bruce Henstell. *American Film Criticisms from the Beginnings to Citizen Kane.* New York: Liveright, 1972.

Keaton, Buster, with Charles Samuels. *My Wonderful World of Slapstick.* Garden City, N.Y.: Doubleday, 1960.

Kennedy, Matthew. *Edmund Goulding's Dark Victory: Hollywood's Genius Bad Boy.* Madison: University of Wisconsin Press, 2004.

Kerr, Walter. *The Silent Clowns*. New York: Knopf, 1975.

Knight, Arthur. *The Liveliest Art: A Panoramic History of the Movies*. New York: Macmillan, 1957.

Knoblock, Edward. *Round the Room*. London: Chapman & Hall, 1939.

Koszarski, Richard. *An Evening's Entertainment: The Age of the Silent Feature Picture, 1915–1928*. Berkeley: University of California Press, 1994.

Lahue, Kalton C. *Dreams for Sale: The Rise and Fall of the Triangle Film Corporation*. South Brunswick, N.J.: A. S. Barnes, 1971.

———. *Gentlemen to the Rescue: The Heroes of the Silent Screen*. South Brunswick, N.J.: A. S. Barnes, 1972.

Lasky, Jesse L., with Don Weldon. *I Blow My Own Horn*. Garden City, N.Y.: Doubleday, 1957.

Lasky, Jesse L., Jr. *Whatever Happened to Hollywood?* New York: Funk & Wagnalls, 1973.

Leider, Emily W. *Dark Lover: The Life and Death of Rudolph Valentino*. New York: Farrar, Straus & Giroux, 2003.

Lejeune, C. A. *Cinema*. London: A. Maclehose, 1931.

Leloir, Maurice. *Cinq mois à Hollywood avec Douglas Fairbanks. Films muets, films parlants, par Max de Cuvillon*. Paris: J. Peyronnet, 1929.

Lennig, Arthur. *The Silent Voice*. Albany: Faculty-Student Association of the State University of New York, 1966.

Lindsay, Vachel. *The Art of the Moving Picture*. New York: Macmillan, 1922.

Lloyd, Harold, with Wesley W. Stout. *An American Comedy*. New York: Longmans, Green, 1928.

Lockwood, Charles. *Dream Palaces: Hollywood at Home*. New York: Viking Press, 1981.

Loos, Anita. *A Girl Like I*. New York: Viking Press, 1966.

———. *Kiss Hollywood Goodbye*. New York: Viking, 1975.

Love, Bessie. *From Hollywood with Love*. Introduction by Kevin Brownlow. London: Elm Tree Books, 1977.

Marchand, Leslie A. *Byron*. New York: Knopf, 1957.

Marion, Frances. *Off with Their Heads: A Serio-Comic Tale of Hollywood*. New York: Macmillan, 1972.

Mast, Gerald. *The Comic Mind: Comedy and the Movies*. Indianapolis: Bobbs-Merrill, 1973.

McCabe, John. *George M. Cohan: The Man Who Owned Broadway*. Garden City, N.Y.: Doubleday, 1973.

McCarty, Clifford, et al., eds. *Film Music 1*. New York: Garland, 1989.

Menjou, Adolphe, and M. M. Musselman. *It Took Nine Tailors*. Foreword by Clark Gable. New York: McGraw-Hill, 1948.

Miller, Alice. *Prisoners of Childhood*. Translated from the German by Ruth Ward. New York: Basic Books, 1981.

Mills, C. Wright. *The Power Elite*. New York: Oxford University Press, 1956.

Montagu, Ivor. *With Eisenstein in Hollywood*. New York: International Publishers, 1969.

Moore, Colleen. *Silent Star*. Garden City, N.Y.: Doubleday, 1968.

Morris, Edmund. *The Rise of Theodore Roosevelt*. New York: Coward, McCann & Geoghegan, 1979.

———. *Theodore Rex*. New York: Random House, 2001.

Nelson, Al P., and Mel R. Jones. *A Silent Siren Song: The Aitken Brothers' Hollywood Odyssey, 1905–1926*. New York: Cooper Square Press, 2000.

Niven, David. *Bring On the Empty Horses*. New York: Putnam, 1975.

Noone, John. *The Man behind the Iron Mask*. New York: St. Martin's Press, 1988.

Nowell-Smith, Geoffrey, ed. *The Oxford History of World Cinema*. Oxford: Oxford University Press, 1996.

O'Dell, Scott. *Representative Photoplays Analyzed*. Hollywood, Calif.: Palmer Institute of Authorship, 1924.

Osborne, Robert. *80 Years of the Oscar: The Official History of the Academy Awards*. New York: Abbeville Press, 2008.

Parrish, Robert. *Growing Up in Hollywood*. New York: Harcourt Brace Jovanovich, 1976.

Parsons, Louella O. *The Gay Illiterate*. Garden City, N.Y.: Doubleday, Doran, 1944.

Pickford, Mary. *The Demi-Widow*. New York: Bobbs-Merrill, 1935.

———. *My Rendezvous with Life*. New York: H. C. Kinsey & Co., 1935.

———. *Sunshine and Shadow*. Foreword by Cecil B. DeMille. Garden City, N.Y.: Doubleday, 1955.

———. *Why Not Try God?* New York: H. C. Kinsey & Co., 1934.

Powell, Michael. *A Life in Movies: An Autobiography*. London: Heinemann, 1986.

Pratt, George C. *Spellbound in Darkness*. Greenwich, Conn.: New York Graphic Society, 1973.

Prichard, Kate, and Hesketh Prichard. *Don Q's Love Story*. New York: Grosset & Dunlap, 1925.

Pruzhan, Irina. *Léon Bakst: Set and Costume Designs, Book Illustrations, Paintings, and Graphic Works*. New York: Viking, 1987.

Pyle, Howard. *Howard Pyle's Book of Pirates*. New York: Harper & Brothers, 1921.

Ramsaye, Terry. *A Million and One Nights: A History of the Motion Picture*. 2 vols. New York: Simon & Schuster, 1926.

Richards, Jeffrey. *Swordsmen of the Screen: From Douglas Fairbanks to Michael York*. London: Routledge & Kegan Paul, 1977.

Robinson, David. *Chaplin: His Life and Art*. London: Penguin Books, 2001.

———. *From Peep Show to Palace: The Birth of American Film*. Foreword by Martin Scorsese. New York: Columbia University Press, 1996.

———. *Hollywood in the Twenties.* New York: A. S. Barnes, 1968.

Rotha, Paul. *The Film Till Now.* London: Jonathan Cape, 1930.

———. *Love, Laughter, and Tears: My Hollywood Story.* Garden City, N.Y.: Doubleday, 1978.

Salt, Barry. *Film Style & Technology.* London: Starword, 1992.

Sandburg, Carl. *The Movies Are: Carl Sandburg's Film Reviews and Essays, 1920–1928.* Edited by Arnie Bernstein. Introduction by Roger Ebert. Chicago: Lake Claremont Press, 2000.

Schickel, Richard. *D. W. Griffith: An American Life.* New York: Simon & Schuster, 1984.

———. *The Fairbanks Album.* Foreword by Douglas Fairbanks Jr. Boston: New York Graphic Society, 1975.

———. *His Picture in the Papers: A Speculation on Celebrity in America, Based on the Life of Douglas Fairbanks, Sr.* New York: Charterhouse, 1973.

———. *Intimate Strangers: The Culture of Celebrity in America.* Chicago: I. R. Dee, 2000.

———. *Schickel on Film: Encounters—Critical and Personal—with Movie Immortals.* New York: Morrow, 1989.

Schouvaloff, Alexander. *Léon Bakst: The Theatre Art.* London: Sotheby's, 1991.

Seldes, Gilbert. *The Seven Lively Arts.* New York: Harper & Brothers, 1924.

Shakespeare, William. *The Taming of the Shrew.* The Arden Edition of the Works of William Shakespeare. Edited by Brian Morris. London: Routledge, 1989.

Sherwood, Robert E., ed. *The Best Moving Pictures of 1922–1923.* Boston: Small, Maynard, 1923.

Skal, David J., and Elias Savada. *Dark Carnival: The Secret World of Tod Browning.* New York: Anchor Books, 1995.

Slide, Anthony. *The Kindergarten of the Movies: A History of the Fine Arts Company.* Metuchen, N.J.: Scarecrow Press, 1980.

Spencer, Charles. *Léon Bakst.* New York: St. Martin's Press, 1973.

———. *The World of Serge Diaghilev.* New York: Viking, 1979.

Stebbins, Genevieve. *Delsarte System of Expression.* New York: Dance Horizons, 1977.

Sternberg, Joseph von. *Fun in a Chinese Laundry.* New York: Macmillan, 1965.

St. Johns, Adela Rogers. *The Honeycomb.* Garden City, N.Y.: Doubleday, 1969.

Studlar, Gaylyn. "Douglas Fairbanks: Thief of the Ballet Russes." In *Bodies of the Text: Dance as Theory, Literature as Dance,* ed. Ellen Goellner and Jacqueline Shea Murphy, 107–24. New Brunswick, N.J.: Rutgers University Press, 1994.

———. *This Mad Masquerade: Stardom and Masculinity in the Jazz Age.* New York: Columbia University Press, 1996.

Sullivan, Mark. *Our Times: The United States, 1900–1925.* 6 vols. New York: Scribner, 1935.

Swanson, Gloria. *Swanson on Swanson.* New York: Random House, 1980.

Talmey, Allene. *Doug and Mary, and Others.* New York: Macy-Masius, 1927.

Thompson, Frank, ed. *Henry King, Director: From Silents to 'Scope.* Los Angeles: Directors Guild of America, 1995.

Thompson, Frank T. *Lost Films: Important Movies That Disappeared.* Secaucus, N.J.: Carol Publishing, 1996.

Thompson, Kristin. "Fairbanks without the Moustache: A Case for the Early Films." In *The Path to Hollywood, 1911–1920,* eds. Paolo Cherchi Usai and Lorenzo Codelli, 156–92. Rome: Edizioni Biblioteca dell'Immagine, 1988.

Tibbetts, John C., and James M. Welsh. *The Encyclopedia of Novels into Film.* New York: Facts on File, 1998.

———. *His Majesty the American: The Films of Douglas Fairbanks, Sr.* Cranbury, N.J.: A. S. Barnes, 1977.

Truffaut, François. *Hitchcock.* London: Secker & Warburg, 1967.

Ulman, Emory Washburn. *Young Lawyer U. N. Truth's First Case.* Foreword by Douglas Fairbanks. Brooklyn, N.Y.: Cullinan, 1922.

Vaknin, Samuel. *Malignant Self Love: Narcissism Revisited.* Prague: Narcissus Publications, 2005.

Vance, Jeffrey. *Chaplin: Genius of the Cinema.* New York: Harry N. Abrams, 2003.

———. *Harold Lloyd: Master Comedian.* New York: Harry N. Abrams, 2002.

Vidor, King. *A Tree Is a Tree.* New York: Harcourt, Brace, 1953.

Wagenknecht, Edward. *The Movies in the Age of Innocence.* Norman: University of Oklahoma Press, 1962.

———. *Stars of the Silents.* Metuchen, N.J.: Scarecrow Press, 1987.

Walker, Alexander. *The Shattered Silents: How the Talkies Came to Stay.* London: Elm Tree Books, 1978.

———. *Stardom: The Hollywood Phenomenon.* New York: Stein & Day, 1970.

Walsh, Raoul. *Each Man in His Time: The Life Story of a Director.* New York: Farrar, Straus & Giroux, 1974.

Warde, Frederick. *Fifty Years of Make-Believe.* New York: International Press Syndicate, 1920.

Wasson, Haidee. *Museum Movies: The Museum of Modern Art and the Birth of Art Cinema.* Berkeley: University of California Press, 2005.

Watson, Coy, Jr. *The Keystone Kid: Tales of Early Hollywood.* Santa Monica, Calif.: Santa Monica Press, 2001.

Wellman, William. *A Short Time for Insanity.* New York: Hawthorn, 1974.

Whitfield, Eileen. *Pickford: The Woman Who Made Hollywood.* Lexington: University of Kentucky, 1997.

Windeler, Robert. *Sweetheart: The Story of Mary Pickford.* New York: Praeger, 1973.

Wollen, Peter. *Raiding the Icebox: Reflections on Twentieth-Century Culture.* Bloomington: Indiana University Press, 1993.

Zukor, Adolph, with Dale Kramer. *The Public Is Never Wrong.* New York: Putnam, 1953.

"Add Scenes to Play." *Los Angeles Times,* June 30, 1923, §2, 9.

"*American Aristocracy.*" *Variety,* October 27, 1916.

Ames, Hector. "Always Up Against It Is Douglas Fairbanks." *Motion Picture Classic,* July 1916, 18, 64.

Andrews, Nigel. "Resurrecting the Pirate." *BFI News,* no. 3 (January 1973): 3.

"*Around the World in 80 Minutes.*" *Variety,* November 24, 1931.

"As Douglas Fairbanks Sees the Film Play Tomorrow." *Christian Science Monitor,* October 17, 1922.

Bakshy, Alexander. "Films: Mostly 'For the Family.'" *The Nation* 129 (December 25, 1929): 784.

Bates, Billy. "The Pickford-Fairbanks Wooing." *Photoplay* 18, no. 1 (June 1920): 70, 73–74, 113.

Behlmer, Rudy. "*The Black Pirate* Weighs Anchor." *American Cinematographer* 73, no. 5 (May 1992): 34–40.

———. "High Style on the High Seas." *American Cinematographer* 73, no. 4 (April 1992): 34–40.

———. "Robin Hood on the Screen." *Films in Review* 16, no. 2 (February 1965): 91–102.

———. "Swordplay on the Screen." *Films in Review* 16, no. 6 (June–July 1965): 362–75.

———. "Technicolor." *Films in Review* 25, no. 6 (June–July 1964).

Belasco, David. "Mary Pickford Came to Me." *Photoplay* 9, no. 1 (December 1915): 27–34.

Benthall, Dwinelle. "Our Unofficial Ambassadors." *Motion Picture Magazine,* June 1927, 38–39, 104, 116–17.

B.L. "A Dressing Room Chat with Douglas Fairbanks." *Theatre,* 1912.

"*The Black Pirate.*" *Photoplay* 29, no. 6 (May 1926): 48.

"*The Black Pirate.*" *Variety,* March 10, 1926, 21.

Bodeen, DeWitt. "Douglas Fairbanks." *Focus on Film,* no. 5 (Winter 1970): 17–30.

"Bonanza in Junk Pile." *New York Times,* November 27, 1952.

Brewster, Eugene V. "Why Color Pictures and Talking Movies Can Never Be Universal." *Motion Picture Magazine,* June 1926, 5.

Brown, Geoff. "Return of the Roguish Hero." *The Times* (London), August 7, 1998.

Brownlow, Kevin, et al. "Fairbanks: *L'acrobatico sorriso.*" *Cinegrafie,* no. 11. Ancona: Transeuropa, 1998.

"Business of Directing a Fairbanks Photoplay." *Motion Picture Magazine* 15, no. 3 (April 1918): 56–57.

Calhoun, Dorothy. "How Can Doug Stay Away from Hollywood?" *Motion Picture Magazine* 47, no. 1 (February 1934): 40–41, 82–83.

"Chaplin Wealth at Top." *New York Times,* July 8, 1932.

Cohn, Alfred A. "A Photo Interview with Douglas Fairbanks." *Photoplay* 12, no. 5 (October 1917): 36–39.

Connolly, Myles E. "Douglas Fairbanks." *Boston Post,* October 16–November 27, 1920.

Cooke, Alistair. "The Films of Douglas Fairbanks." *Museum of Modern Art Film Library Bulletin,* ser. 8 (1941).

Corliss, Richard. "The King of Hollywood." *Time* 147, no. 25 (June 17, 1996).

"Crawford Romance May Bud." *Los Angeles Times,* January 15, 1928, C13.

Creel, George. "A 'Close-Up' of Douglas Fairbanks." *Everybody's Magazine* 35, no. 6 (December 1916): 729–38.

Crisler, B. R. "Gossip of the Films." *New York Times,* November 1, 1936.

Dannenberg, Joseph. "Moving Fast." *Film Daily* 34, no. 9 (October 11, 1925): 1, 8.

Denby, R. J. B. "Doug Shoots Tomorrow's Perfect Film." *Liberty,* May 15, 1926, reprinted Spring 1975, 16–17.

Devon, Louis. "Douglas Fairbanks: Unique and Great Star, 1883–1939." *Films in Review* 27, no. 5 (May 1976): 267–83.

"Director Tells of Making Fairbanks' New Prismatic Pirate Production." *New York Times,* March 7, 1926, 5.

"*Don Q.*" *Photoplay* 29, no. 3 (August 1925): 51.

"*Don Q* Score Is Pleasing." *New York Times,* July 4, 1925, 12.

"*Don Q Son of Zorro.*" *Motion Picture Classic,* August 1925.

"*Don Q Son of Zorro.*" *Variety,* June 17, 1925, 35.

"Donald Crisp Signed to Direct De Mille Productions." *Moving Picture World* 78, no. 6 (February 6, 1926): 554.

"Douglas Fairbanks and William A. Brady Part." *New York Times,* October 6, 1911, 13.

"Douglas Fairbanks Bridges Centuries in His Recent Period Play Productions." *Los Angeles Times,* November 22, 1925, C29.

"Douglas Fairbanks Dies in His Sleep." *New York Times,* December 13, 1939, 29–30.

"Douglas Fairbanks Hurt." *New York Times,* October 14, 1925, 31.

"Douglas Fairbanks in Fine Arts Pictures." *Moving Picture World* 26, no. 1 (October 2, 1915): 86.

"Douglas Fairbanks in New Role." *New York Times,* October 10, 1913, 11.

"Douglas Fairbanks Settles Tax." *New York Times,* May 9, 1939, 29.

"Douglas Fairbanks Uses New Weapon, the Bolas." *New York Times,* October 16, 1927, 6.

"'Doug' Psychoanalyzes the Grin." *New York Times,* August 2, 1925.

"*Down to Earth.*" *Variety,* August 10, 1917.

Dyer, Braven. "Entries Slated to Close Wednesday for Southern California Junior Olympic Games." *Los Angeles Times,* April 7, 1929, A3.

"Edward Knoblock Writes Prologue." *New York Morning Telegraph*, August 21, 1921.

Ellis, Carlyle. "The Meaning of 'Griffith-Supervised.'" *Motography*, January 15, 1916, 115–16.

Emerson, John, and Anita Loos. "Photoplay Writing." *Photoplay* 13, no. 3 (February 1918): 51–52.

———. "Photoplay Writing." *Photoplay* 13, no. 4 (March 1918): 53–54.

———. "Photoplay Writing." *Photoplay* 13, no. 5 (April 1918): 81–82, 122.

"Enid Bennett Crowns Doug." *Los Angeles Times*, October 15, 1922, §3, 32.

Evans, Alice Belton. "He Knows What He Wants and He Does It." *National Board of Review Magazine* 3, no. 1 (January 1928): 4–5, 10.

Evans, Delight. "Gee Whiz." *Photoplay* 13, no. 1 (December 1917): 30.

———. "Mary Pickford, the Girl." *Photoplay* 14, no. 2 (July 1918): 90–91, 111.

Evans, Harry. "*The Iron Mask.*" *Life* 93, no. 2419 (March 15, 1929): 25.

Everson, William K. "Stunt Men." *Films in Review* 6, no. 8 (October 1955): 394–402.

Fairbanks, Douglas. "The Academy's Plans." *Academy Magazine* 1, no. 1 (November 1927).

———. "The Big Adventure." *Boys' Life*, June, 1928, 17, 51.

———. "Color Pictures Detract from Drama, Says Doug." *New York Morning Telegram*, September 9, 1923.

———. "Combining Play with Work." *American Magazine*, July 1917, 33–34, 102.

———. "The Development of the Screen." *Moving Picture World*, July 21, 1917.

———. "Douglas Fairbanks." *Los Angeles Times*, April 23, 1929, C6.

———. "Douglas Fairbanks' Own Page." *Photoplay* 12, no. 6 (November 1917): 87.

———. "Douglas Fairbanks' Own Page." *Photoplay* 13, no. 1 (December 1917): 54.

———. "Douglas Fairbanks' Own Page." *Photoplay* 13, no. 2 (January 1918): 107.

———. "Douglas Fairbanks' Own Page." *Photoplay* 13, no. 3 (February 1918): 40.

———. "Douglas Fairbanks' Own Page." *Photoplay* 13, no. 4 (March 1918): 84.

———. "Douglas Fairbanks' Own Page." *Photoplay* 13, no. 5 (April 1918): 63.

———. "Douglas Fairbanks Says Talkies Will Become Better and Cheaper." *Christian Science Monitor*, April 9, 1929.

———. "Films for the Fifty Million." *Ladies' Home Journal*, April 1924, 27, 47.

———. "How I Keep Running on High." *American Magazine*, August 1922, 36–39.

———. "A Huge Responsibility." *Ladies' Home Journal*, May 1924, 36–37.

———. "If I Were Bringing Up Your Children." *Woman's Home Companion*, July 1919, 24, 88.

———. "If I Were Fifteen." *Boys' Life* 16, no. 4 (April 1926): 7, 47.

———. "Kind of Crazy." *Motion Picture Magazine* 24, no. 10 (November 1922): 42–43, 94.

———. "Let Me Say This for the Films." *Ladies' Home Journal*, September 1922, 13, 117–18, 120.

———. "Listen My Children and You Shall Hear." *Arcadian Observer* 1, no. 6 (September 7, 1918): 5.

———. "The Magic Carpet of My Life as Told to Stuart Jackson." *Pictures and Picturegoer*, March 18, 1933–April 1, 1933.

———. "Making Film History." *Graphic*, November 2, 1928.

———. "One Reel of Autobiography." *Collier's*, June 18, 1921, 10–11, 26.

———. "Personal Reminiscences." *Theatre* 25, no. 194 (April 1917): 220–22.

———. "Robinson Crusoe, 1932–1933." *Boys' Life*, January 1933.

———. "Sunrise and Other Things." *Boys' Life*, January 1924, 59, 62.

———. "Those Guileless Ruralites." *Green Book*, August 1912.

———. "What Is Love?" *Photoplay* 27, no. 3 (February 1925): 36–37.

———. "Why Big Pictures?" *Ladies' Home Journal*, March 1924, 7, 103–4.

———. "Why I Was Disappointed in the Grand Canyon." *Ladies' Home Journal*, February, 1918, 18–19.

"Fairbanks at $15,000 Weekly Tops All Picture Salaries." *Variety* 45, no. 7 (January 12, 1917): 3.

"Fairbanks Endeavors to Break Contract with Triangle." *Motion Picture News* 15, no. 4 (January 27, 1917): 546.

"Fairbanks Estate Put at $2,318,651." *New York Times*, October 7, 1940, 27.

"Fairbanks Faces Suit for Breaking Contract." *Motion Picture News* 15, no. 9 (March 3, 1917): 1368.

"Fairbanks Has an Unusual Role in *Headin' South.*" *Paramount Artcraft Progress-Advance* 4, no. 13 (February 21, 1918): 257.

"Fairbanks Has Society Role in Next Artcraft Picture." *Paramount Artcraft Progress-Advance* 4, no. 15 (March 7, 1918): 297.

"Fairbanks Loses Revision Suit." *New York Times*, December 9, 1922.

"Fairbanks Makes D'Artagnan into a French Cowboy." *Literary Digest*, September 17, 1921, 28–29.

"Fairbanks Negatives Discovered in Cache." *Hollywood Reporter*, November 28, 1952.

"Fairbanks Retires from Triangle." *Moving Picture World* 13, no. 4 (January 27, 1917): 537.

"Fairbanks Returns to Become Producer." *New York Times*, January 8, 1936, 22.

"Fairbanks Rites to Be Tomorrow." *New York Times*, December 14, 1939, 34.

"Fairbanks Seeks Basic Truths for the Screen." *New York Morning Telegraph*, December 24, 1922.

"Fairbanks Spurns Talkies." *New York Times*, July 18, 1931, 192.

"Fairbanks's Brother Dies." *New York Times*, November 21, 1926, 15.

"Fairbanks's Cameraman Joins Colors." *Paramount Artcraft Progress-Advance* 4, no. 12 (February 14, 1918): 237.

"Fairbanks's Feats Daring and Novel." *Paramount Artcraft Progress-Advance* 4, no. 14 (February 28, 1918): 277.

"Fairbanks's New Screen Voice." *New York Times*, February 3, 1929, 112.

"Fairbanks's Wicked Whip." *New York Times*, May 31, 1925, 2.

"Fairbanks to Tour for Third Loan." *Paramount Artcraft Progress-Advance* 4, no. 17 (March 21, 1918): 329.

"Fairbanks Turns on Hays." *New York Times*, January 27, 1923, 16.

"Fairbanks Turns Professor." *Los Angeles Times*, February 7, 1929, A5.

"Fairbanks Wants to Make a Few Pictures in South America." *Motion Picture News* 13, no. 25 (June 24, 1916): 3884.

"Fairbanks Was an Old Man in '96." *Photoplay* 11, no. 6 (May 1917): 34.

Felten, P. "Reminiscence." *Films in Review* 14, no. 3 (March 1963): 190.

"Film Industry Working for Liberty Loan." *Moving Picture World* 36, no. 4 (April 27, 1918): 519–21.

"Film Snags Hurdled by Douglas Fairbanks." *New York Times*, November 20, 1927, 3.

"Film Stars See Mussolini." *New York Times*, May 11, 1926, 29.

Fletcher, Adele Whitely. "The Man Who Made *Robin Hood.*" *Motion Picture Magazine* 25, no. 1 (February 1923): 24–25, 99.

"*Flirting with Fate.*" *Variety*, June 30, 1916.

Florey, Robert. "Le Film." *Montreal*, October 1922, 6–11.

Frohman, Ray W. "Charlie Chaplin." *Los Angeles Herald*, December 2, 1919.

"*The Gaucho.*" *Motion Picture Magazine* 35, no. 2 (March 1928): 60.

"*The Gaucho.*" *Photoplay* 32, no. 2 (January 1928): 53.

"*The Gaucho.*" *Variety*, November 9, 1927, 18.

Gheri, Alfred. "Réflexions sur l'art de Douglas Fairbanks," *Cinéa-Ciné pour tous* (Paris), November 1, 1927.

"*The Good Bad Man.*" *Variety*, April 14, 1916.

Gow, Gordon. "Doug." *Films and Filming* 19, no. 8 (May 1973): 34–40.

Grant, Cary. "Archie Leach" (pt. 1 of 3). *Ladies' Home Journal*, January–February 1963, 50–53, 133–34, 136, 138, 140, 142.

Grant, Paul. "John, Anita, and the Giftie." *Photoplay* 13, no. 1 (December 1917): 48–50.

Grierson, John. "Putting Atmosphere in Pictures." *Motion Picture News* 34, no. 23 (December 4, 1926): 2141–42.

"*The Habit of Happiness.*" *Variety*, March 24, 1916, 29.

"*The Half Breed.*" *Variety*, July 21, 1916.

Hall, Mordaunt. "Arabian Nights Satire: *The Thief of Bagdad.*" *New York Times*, March 19, 1924, 19.

———. "An Argentine Cowboy." *New York Times*, November 22, 1927, 32.

———. "A Chip of the Old Block." *New York Times*, June 16, 1925, 24.

———. "Fairbanks's Pirate Film Whimsical and Beautiful." *New York Times*, March 14, 1926, 5.

———. "*The Iron Mask.*" *New York Times*, February 22, 1929, 18.

———. "Mr. Fairbanks in Modern Attire." *New York Times*, December 30, 1930, 24.

———. "Mr. Fairbanks's New Picture: *The Black Pirate.*" *New York Times*, March 9, 1926, 21.

———. "On a Desert Island." *New York Times*, September 22, 1932, 25.

———. "A Shakespearean Farce." *New York Times*, November 30, 1929, 23.

Harmetz, Aljean. "Jackie Coogan—Remember?" *New York Times*, April 2, 1972, 1, 11.

"The Headline Career of Mary and Doug." *Motion Picture Classic*, March 1933, 68.

Herring, Robert. "Interview with Douglas Fairbanks." *Close Up* 6, no. 6 (June 1930): 504–8.

"A Higher Order of Music for the Movies." *Literary Digest*, July 19, 1924, 26–27.

"*His Majesty the American.*" *Variety*, October 31, 1919, 57.

"*His Picture in the Papers.*" *Variety*, February 4, 1916, 24.

Hornblow, Arthur, Jr. "Douglas Fairbanks, Dramatic Dynamo: An Interview with a K.O. Athlete Who Has Just Left the Triangle Company and Joined the Artcraft." *Motion Picture Classic*, March 1917, 47–48.

Hournon, Jean. "Maurice Leloir: Une carrière aux multiples facettes." *Petit Journal de l'Exposition Maison Fournaise*, 1995.

"How 'Doug' Keeps Self Fit." *New York Times*, July 19, 1925, 2.

"How Doug Made *The Thief of Bagdad.*" *Photoplay* 25, no. 6 (May 1924): 60–61.

"How Douglas Fairbanks Produces His Pictures." *New York Times*, June 7, 1925, 4.

Howe, Herbert. "Mary Pickford's Favorite Stars and Films." *Photoplay* 25, no. 2 (January 1924, 28–29): 105–7.

"Huge Film Pact Planned." *Los Angeles Times*, October 14, 1924, A1.

Hughes, Frances. "Filmland's Royal Family, Second Edition." *Photoplay* 36, no. 6 (November 1929): 37, 96.

"*The Iron Mask.*" *Photoplay* 35, no. 3 (February 1929): 53.

"*Iron Mask* Due Soon." *Los Angeles Times*, February 24, 1929, C14.

Johnson, Julian. "*His Majesty the American.*" *Photoplay* 17, no. 1 (December 1919): 117.

———. "*The Knickerbocker Buckaroo.*" *Photoplay* 16, no. 3 (August 1919): 57–58.

Jones, Thomas L., and Keri Leigh. "The Sword of Zorro's Father." *North South Trader's Civil War* 30, no. 5 (2004): 20–26.

Kalmus, H. T. "Technicolor Adventures in Cinemaland." *Journal of the Society of Motion Picture Engineers*, December 1938, 564–84.

Kendall, Read. "Fairbanks Mourned in Hollywood." *Los Angeles Times*, December 13, 1939, 1, 6.

King, Susan. "Restoring a Silent Treasure." *Los Angeles Times*, June 11, 2002.

Kingsley, Grace. "First National Gets Comedian." *Los Angeles Times*, April 23, 1929, A10.

———. "Henley Will Direct Haines." *Los Angeles Times*, March 19, 1927, 12.

———. "*Robin Hood* Down to Date." *Los Angeles Times*, November 29, 1920, § 2, 3.

Lachmund, Marjorie Gleyre. "Douglas Fairbanks Discourses on Work and Play." *Motion Picture Classic*, December 1917, 54.

Lambert, Gavin. "Fairbanks and Valentino: The Last Heroes." *Sequence*, no. 8 (Summer 1949): 77–80.

Lane, Tamar. "Mechanical Marvels of *The Thief of Bagdad*." *Science and Invention*, May 1924, 12–13.

Lang, Harry. "Young Doug." *Photoplay* 38, no. 6 (November 1930): 65, 146–47.

Lee, Raymond. "Old Doug Fairbanks Enjoyed His Jokes." *Los Angeles Times*, July 5, 1953.

Lindsay, Vachel. "The Great Douglas Fairbanks." *Ladies' Home Journal*, August 1926, 12, 114.

———. "*The Thief of Bagdad*." *Michigan Quarterly Review* 31 (Spring 1992): 231, 240.

Little, Barbara. "The Pirates Are Coming." *Picture-Play*, March 1923, 47.

"London Curator Lindgren re Rohauer: Print Never Lost, He Just Needs to Pay." *Variety*, March 15, 1972.

Lowe, Joshua. "*The Lamb*." *Variety*, October 1, 1915, 18.

———. "*Reggie Mixes In*." *Variety*, June 2, 1916, 16.

"Making the Photoplay Unreal: How Science and Art Have Produced a Screen Fantasy." *Scientific American*, March 1924, 169.

"*The Man from Painted Post*." *Variety*, October 5, 1917.

"*Manhattan Madness*." *Variety*, September 22, 1916.

Manners, Dorothy. "What Is Doug Doing?" *Motion Picture Magazine* 41, no. 1 (February 1931): 55, 90.

Mantle, Burns. "*The Mollycoddle*." *Photoplay* 18, no. 4 (September 1920): 66–67.

———. "*The Nut*." *Photoplay* 19, no. 4 (March 1921): 62

———. "*When the Clouds Roll By*." *Photoplay* 17, no. 4 (March 1920): 67.

"*The Mark of Zorro*." *New York Times*, November 29, 1920, 20.

"*The Mark of Zorro*." *Variety*, December 3, 1920, 32.

"*Mark of Zorro* Most Delightful Film She Has Ever Seen, Says Elinor Glyn." *Moving Picture World* 49, no. 5 (April 2, 1921): 478.

"Mary Pickford Reveals Break with Husband Douglas Fairbanks." *New York Times*, July 3, 1933, 1.

"Mary Too Busy to Be in Court." *Los Angeles Times*, June 6, 1925, 5.

McCulley, Johnston. "The Curse of Capistrano" (5 parts), *All-Story Weekly* 100, no. 2-101, no. 2 (August 9, 1919–September 6, 1919).

———. "The Further Adventures of Zorro" (6 parts), *Argosy All-Story Weekly* 142, no. 4-143, no. 3 (May 6, 1922–June 10, 1922).

Mercer, Janet. "The Fairbanks' Social War Is On!" *Photoplay* 50, no. 2 (August 1936): 22–23, 96.

Minchinton, John. "Homespun Superman." *Films and Filming* 1, no. 3 (December 1954): 13.

"*A Modern Musketeer*." *Variety*, January 4, 1918, 40.

"*The Mollycoddle*." *New York Times*, June 14, 1920, 13.

"*The Mollycoddle*." *Variety*, June 18, 1920.

"*Mr. Robinson Crusoe*." *Variety*, September 27, 1932, 17.

"Mrs. Woodrow Wilson Sees Douglas Fairbanks in *A Modern Musketeer*." *Paramount Artcraft Progress-Advance* 4, no. 10 (January 31, 1918): 197.

Naylor, Hazel Simpson. "The Fairbanks Scale of Americanism." *Motion Picture Magazine* 17, no. 1 (February 1919): 30–32.

Noël, Benoît. "Maurice Leloir: De Guy de Maupassant à Douglas Fairbanks." *Petit Journal de l'Exposition Maison Fournaise*, 1995.

Nugent, Frank. "A Man and an Illusion." *New York Times*, December 17, 1939, 127.

"*The Nut*." *Variety*, March 11, 1921.

Nye, Myra. "Music Treat for Children." *Los Angeles Times*, July 19, 1923, § 2, 1.

"The Old Plaza Church as It Appeared in 1830: Reconstructed for Douglas Fairbanks' Production Entitled *The Mark of Zorro*." *Los Angeles Times*, November 14, 1920, § 8, 1.

"The One and Only 'Doug' Himself." *Woman's Home Companion*, July 1919, 52.

Paddock, Charles W. "Fairbanks at 50." *Physical Culture*, May 1931, 40–41, 124.

Parker, Eleanor. "How Douglas Fairbanks Keeps Fit." *Correct Eating*, April 1929, 11–12, 37.

"Passing of Actor Mourned by Celebrities of Screen." *Los Angeles Times*, December 13, 1939, 7.

Pickford, Mary, and Douglas Fairbanks. "The Inside of the Bowl." *Liberty*, November 9, 1929.

———. "Our Trip around the World" (10 parts). *New York World Syndicate*, 1930.

"Picture Stars in Pageant." *Los Angeles Times*, October 7, 1926, 10.

Quirk, James R. "Speaking of Pictures." *Photoplay* 31, no. 1 (December 1926): 27.

Rall, Pearl. "Fairbanks' First Thousand." *Los Angeles Evening Express*, August 27, 1921.

"The Real Robin Hood." *Los Angeles Times*, October 8, 1922, §3, 33.

"*Reaching for the Moon.*" *Photoplay* 39, no. 3 (February 1931): 53.

Redway, Sara. "About Pirates and Pictures." *Motion Picture Magazine* 31, no. 5 (June 1926): 27, 94, 97.

"*Robin Hood.*" *Photoplay* 22, no. 2 (January 1923): 64.

"*Robin Hood* a Great Spectacle." *New York Times*, October 31, 1922, 15.

"*Robin Hood* Bests King Richard." *Los Angeles Times*, June 12, 1922, §2, 1.

"*Robin Hood* Rides upon the Screen." *Literary Digest*, November 18, 1922, 32–33.

"*Robin Hood* Wins *Photoplay* Magazine 1922 Gold Medal of Honor." *Photoplay* 25, no. 1 (December 1923): 61.

Robinson, David. "The Hero." *Sight & Sound* 42, no. 2 (Spring 1973): 98–102.

"Rohauer Completes His Acquisition of Fairbanks Pix; Bows at Berlin Fest." *Variety*, February 23, 1972.

Ryan, Don. "Fantasy Arrives on the Screen." *Picture-Play*, May 1924.

Schallert, Edwin. "Academy Head Issue to Fore." *Los Angeles Times*, September 23, 1928, C11.

———. "*Don Q* Great Popular Hit." *Los Angeles Times*, January 30, 1926, A9.

———. "Doug Rubs the Magic Lamp." *Picture-Play*, September 1923, 87.

———. "Doug's Color Picture Exerts Rare Spell of Entertainment." *Los Angeles Times*, May 9, 1926, H2.

———. "Fairbanks Felt Artistry Cure-All for Film Industry." *Los Angeles Times*, December 13, 1939, 6.

———. "Film Banquet Is Dazzling." *Los Angeles Times*, July 11, 1924, A9.

———. "*Gaucho* Opens Glamorfully." *Los Angeles Times*, November 7, 1927, A7.

———. "*Iron Mask* Is Distinct Event." *Los Angeles Times*, March 14, 1929, A11.

———. "Radios." *Los Angeles Times*, December 2, 1920, §3, 4.

———. "*Robin Hood* Superb Film." *Los Angeles Times*, October 19, 1922, §2, 1.

———. "Speed Mania Is General." *Los Angeles Times*, March 22, 1925, D11.

———. "*Taming of the Shrew*: Comedy of Action." *Los Angeles Times*, December 22, 1929, H2.

———. "*Three Musketeers.*" *Los Angeles Times*, September 1, 1921, §3, 4.

———. "Yo, Ho, and a Bottle of Rum!" *Picture-Play* 23, no. 6 (February 1926): 16–17, 108.

Scheuer, Phillip K. "1929 *Shrew*—A Sweetheart of a Picture." *Los Angeles Times*, October 23, 1966, Calendar 9.

———. "Fairbanks, Pickford Return in *Shrew.*" *Los Angeles Times*, November 4, 1966, §4, 20.

Schickel, Richard. "Doug Fairbanks: Superstar of the Silents." *American Heritage* 23, no. 1 (December 1971): 4–12, 92–99.

Sennwald, André. "*The Private Life of Don Juan.*" *New York Times*, December 10, 1934, 16.

Sherwood, Robert E. "*The Black Pirate.*" *Life* 87, no. 2264 (March 25, 1926): 26.

———. "*Don Q.*" *Life* 83, no. 2227 (July 9, 1925): 24.

———. "*The Gaucho.*" *Life* 90, no. 2354 (December 15, 1927): 26.

———. "*Robin Hood.*" *Life* 80, no. 2089 (November 16, 1922): 24.

———. "*The Thief of Bagdad.*" *Life* 83, no. 2161 (April 3, 1924): 32.

———. "*The Three Musketeers.*" *Life* 78, no. 2029 (September 22, 1921): 22.

Silverman, Sid. "*The Iron Mask.*" *Variety*, February 27, 1929.

———. "*Reaching for the Moon.*" *Variety*, January 7, 1931.

Silverman, Sime. "*Robin Hood.*" *Variety*, October 30, 1922, 40.

———. "*Taming of the Shrew.*" *Variety*, December 4, 1929, 15.

"Simplicity Marks Fairbanks Rites." *New York Times*, December 16, 1939, 17.

Smith, Alison, "The Screen in Review." *Picture-Play* 15, no. 4 (December 1921): 61–63.

Smith, Frederick James. "The Celluloid Critic." *Motion Picture Classic* 11, no. 6 (February 1921): 46–47.

———. "Roping Doug Fairbanks Into an Interview." *Motion Picture Classic*, September 1917, 46–47.

Sorgenfrei, Robert. "Did Douglas Fairbanks Attend Mines?" *Mines Magazine*, July–August 1999.

St. Johns, Adela Rogers. "Artistic Efficiency—That's Dwan." *Photoplay* 18, no. 3 (August 1920): 56–57, 109.

———. "The Married Life of Doug and Mary." *Photoplay* 31, no. 3 (February 1927): 34–35, 134–35.

———. "The Real Tragedy of Doug and Mary." *Liberty*, February 10, 1934, 6–9.

"Stars Discuss Film Combine." *Los Angeles Times*, February 22, 1923, §2, 20.

"Swashbuckling with Doug on a Painted Ocean." *Literary Digest*, April 10, 1926, 36–38, 42.

"*Taming of the Shrew.*" *Photoplay* 36, no. 6 (November 1929): 53.

"*Taming of the Shrew.*" *The Times* (London), November 15, 1929, 12.

"*Taming of the Shrew.*" *Variety*, November 2, 1966.

Tarkington, Booth. "Booth Tarkington Sends Us Word About Douglas Fairbanks" (insert in Douglas Fairbanks, "Combining Play with Work"). *American Magazine*, July 1917, 33.

Taylor, Charles K. "Doug Gets Away With It." *Outlook*, April 14, 1926, 560–62.

———. "The Most Popular Man in the World." *Outlook*, December 24, 1924, 683.

"Technical Effects for *When the Clouds Roll By.*" *Literary Digest,* July 3, 1920, 75.

"They're Just Shooting Douglas Fairbanks," *Photoplay* 11, no. 4 (March 1917): 109.

"*The Thief of Bagdad.*" *Photoplay* 25, no. 6 (May 1924): 54.

"*The Thief of Bagdad.*" *Variety,* March 26, 1924.

Thomas, Dan. "Dolores Del Rio Chosen by 'Doug.'" *Los Angeles Record,* April 19, 1927.

Thorp, Dunham. "How Fairbanks Took the Color Out of Color." *Motion Picture Classic* 23, no. 3 (May 1926): 28–29, 87–89.

"*The Three Musketeers.*" *New York Times,* August 29, 1921, 14.

"*The Three Musketeers.*" *Photoplay* 20, no. 5 (November 1921): 60.

"*The Three Musketeers.*" *Variety,* September 2, 1921, 61.

Tibbetts, John C. "The Choreography of Hope." *Film Comment* 32, no. 3 (May–June 1996): 50–55.

———. "Glen MacWilliams: Following the Sun with a Veteran Hollywood Cameraman." *American Classic Screen* 3, no. 3 (January–February 1979): 32–39.

———. "Splendidly Self-Propelled: Douglas Fairbanks' *The Gaucho.*" *Films in Review* 47, no. 7–8 (July–August 1996): 96–101.

"Triangle Debut." *New York Times,* September 24, 1915, 2.

"Tribute Paid to Fairbanks." *Los Angeles Times,* May 26, 1941, 12.

"Troubles of a Bagdad Thief." *New York Times,* March 2, 1924, 5.

Von Harleman, G. P. "Douglas Fairbanks Bids Goodbye to California." *Moving Picture World* 13, no. 1 (January 6, 1917): 85.

Wallace, David H. "That Personality of Douglas Fairbanks." *New York,* August 1913.

"What Photography Means to *Robin Hood.*" *American Cinematographer* 3, no. 9 (December 1922): 7–8, 22.

"When 'Doug,' the Gaucho, Hurls His Trusty Bolas." *Literary Digest,* December 31, 1927, 26, 31–32.

"*When the Clouds Roll By.*" *Variety,* January 2, 1920.

Whitaker, Alma. "Lieut. Windsor Slips One Over." *Los Angeles Times,* September 13, 1928, A1.

"Why Douglas Fairbanks Smiles." *New York Times,* February 4, 1917, 7.

"*Wild and Woolly.*" *Variety,* June 22, 1917, 23.

Williams, Dick. "Sound Stage Legends." *Mirror,* February 27, 1952.

Woollcott, Alexander. "The Strenuous Honeymoon." *Everybody's,* November 1920.

AUTHOR'S INTERVIEWS

Gillian Anderson, 1993.

Suzanne Menzies Antles, 1994.

William Bakewell, 1992.

Tino Balio, 2003.

Joan Barclay (aka Geraine Greear), 1994.

Rudy Behlmer, 2006.

Saul Bellow, 1994.

Edward Bernds, 1994.

Malcolm Boyd, 1996.

Mary Brian, 1999.

Herman Brix (aka Bruce Bennett), 1999.

James Card, 1994.

Gaylord Carter, 1991.

Diana Serra Cary, 1999.

Lita Grey Chaplin, 1995.

Alistair Cooke, 1993.

Pauline Curley, 1994.

Carl Davis, 1996.

Ann Doran, 1996.

Billie Dove, 1994.

William K. Everson, 1993.

Douglas Fairbanks Jr., 1991–95.

Lillian Gish, 1991.

Jan-Christopher Horak, 2003.

John H. B. Irving, 1999.

Robert Israel, 2006.

Dennis James, 1993.

Cammilla Johnson Jones, 1996.
Bob Kane, 1994.
Matty Kemp, 1995.
Miles Kreuger, 2007.
Betty Lasky, 1996.
Loyal Lucas, 1998.
June MacCloy, 1999.
Virginia Cherrill Martini, 1995.
Joseph M. Newman, 2002.
Robert Parrish, 1991.
Dorothy Revier, 1992.
Hal Roach, 1991.
Charles "Buddy" Rogers, 1997.
Richard Schickel, 2006.
David Shepard, 2006.
Gore Vidal, 2005.
Edward Wagenknecht, 1994.
Marc Wanamaker, 2006.
Coy Watson Jr., 2001.
Stephen M. Weissman, 2006.
Fay Wray, 2000.

ARCHIVAL INTERVIEWS

Charles Chaplin in an interview with Richard Meryman, 1966, Roy Export Company Establishment and Richard Meryman.
Allan Dwan in a 1977 interview with Kevin Brownlow and David Gill for the documentary *Hollywood* (1980), Kevin Brownlow Collection.
Allan Dwan Oral History, courtesy the Louis B. Mayer Library, American Film Institute.
Joseph Henabery in an interview with Kevin Brownlow, 1964, Kevin Brownlow Collection.
H. Bruce "Lucky" Humberstone in interviews with Jim Desmarias and David Shepard, 1978 and 1983, Directors Guild of America, Inc.
Laurence Irving in a 1979 interview with Kevin Brownlow and David Gill for the documentary *Hollywood* (1980), Kevin Brownlow Collection.
Lord Mountbatten in a 1977 interview with Kevin Brownlow and David Gill for the documentary *Hollywood* (1980), Kevin Brownlow Collection.
Mary Pickford in an interview with Arthur B. Friedman, 1958, Columbia University Oral History Research Office Collection.
Mary Pickford in an interview with George Pratt, ca. 1957, courtesy of the Richard and Ronay Menschel Library, George Eastman House.
Henry Sharp in an interview conducted by the ASC Clubhouse, 1963, American Society of Cinematographers.
A. Edward Sutherland in an interview with Bob and Joan Franklin, 1959, Columbia University Oral History Research Office Collection.
Raoul Walsh in an interview with Robert Bookman/Richard Schickel, 1973, Richard Schickel Collection.

MISCELLANEOUS

Harry and Roy Aitken Papers, 1909–40, Wisconsin Center for Film and Theater Research.
Archives of the Archdiocese of Denver, Colorado.
Rudy Behlmer Collection, Margaret Herrick Library, Academy of Motion Picture Arts and Sciences.
The Black Pirate souvenir program (1926).
Alistair Cooke Collection, Howard Gotlieb Archival Research Center, Boston University.
Harry Crocker Collection, Margaret Herrick Library, Academy of Motion Picture Arts and Sciences.
Douglas Fairbanks as The Gaucho Grauman's Chinese Theatre world premiere program (November 4, 1927).
Douglas Fairbanks as The Gaucho souvenir program (1927).
Douglas Fairbanks Collection, Margaret Herrick Library, Academy of Motion Picture Arts and Sciences.

Douglas Fairbanks Jr. Collection, Howard Gotlieb Archival Research Center, Boston University.

Douglas Fairbanks Jr., "Dad." Typescript of a *Vanity Fair* personality sketch of Douglas Fairbanks, ca. 1930. Douglas Fairbanks Jr. Collection, Howard Gotlieb Archival Research Center, Boston University.

Douglas Fairbanks Memorial Album, 1939. Douglas Fairbanks Collection, Margaret Herrick Library, Academy of Motion Picture Arts and Sciences.

Douris Corporation Records—Douglas Fairbanks Files, Margaret Herrick Library, Academy of Motion Picture Arts and Sciences.

Robert Florey Collection, Margaret Herrick Library, Academy of Motion Picture Arts and Sciences.

Tom Geraghty Collection, Margaret Herrick Library, Academy of Motion Picture Arts and Sciences.

Tom J. Geraghty Papers, Manuscript Division, Library of Congress.

Anton Grot Papers (collection 956), Department of Special Collections, Young Research Library, UCLA.

Harvard University Libraries and Archives.

Joseph and Jeanne Henabery Collection, Margaret Herrick Library, Academy of Motion Picture Arts and Sciences.

Jean Hersholt Collection, Margaret Herrick Library, Academy of Motion Picture Arts and Sciences.

The Iron Mask Channel Four Television program book (1999).

The Iron Mask souvenir program (1929).

Laurence Irving, "Designing for Film." A lecture given at the invitation of the Architectural Association in February 1930. Transcript courtesy of John H. B. Irving and Kevin Brownlow.

National Archives, Civil War Records Division.

Merle Oberon Collection, Margaret Herrick Library, Academy of Motion Picture Arts and Sciences.

Paramount Artcraft Progress-Advance, 1917–19.

Paramount Pictures Collection, Margaret Herrick Library, Academy of Motion Picture Arts and Sciences.

Mary Pickford Collection, Margaret Herrick Library, Academy of Motion Picture Arts and Sciences.

Mary Pickford Institute for Film Education.

Pressbooks: *The Lamb, His Picture in the Papers, The Good Bad Man, Reggie Mixes In, The Half Breed, Manhattan Madness, American Aristocracy, In Again—Out Again, Wild and Woolly, Down to Earth, The Man from Painted Post, Reaching for the Moon, A Modern Musketeer, Headin' South, Say! Young Fellow, He Comes Up Smiling, Arizona, The Knickerbocker Buckaroo, His Majesty the American, When the Clouds Roll By, The Mollycoddle, The Mark of Zorro, The Nut, The Three Musketeers, Douglas Fairbanks in Robin Hood, The Thief of Bagdad, Don Q Son of Zorro, The Black Pirate, Douglas Fairbanks as The Gaucho, The Iron Mask, Taming of the Shrew, Reaching for the Moon, Around the World with Douglas Fairbanks (aka Around the World in 80 Minutes with Douglas Fairbanks), Mr. Robinson Crusoe, The Private Life of Don Juan.*

Richard Schickel Papers, 1953–86, Wisconsin Historical Society.

The Thief of Bagdad souvenir program (1924).

The Thief of Bagdad Thames Television program book (1984).

Triangle/Reliance Film Corporation Records, 1912–23, New York Public Library.

United Artists Corporation Records, 1919–65, Wisconsin Center for Film and Theater Research.

Adolph Zukor Collection, Margaret Herrick Library, Academy of Motion Picture Arts and Sciences.

Acknowledgments

This book is dedicated to Sandra Vance.

It began in the Manhattan office of Douglas Fairbanks Jr. in 1993. Mr. Fairbanks was the ideal collaborator, an invaluable source, filled with vivid, firsthand information. Moreover, he made available to me all of his personal and professional papers, scrapbooks, and photographs, many of which are now held by Boston University, where I was a graduate student at the time. I had several lengthy sessions with Mr. Fairbanks working on this book and am indebted to him for his steadfast support.

I moved to Los Angeles in 1994, and because of Mr. Fairbanks's declining health in the next few years, and his death in 2000, our collaboration on this book ended. Eleven years later, in arranging this book project with the Academy of Motion Picture Arts and Sciences and University of California Press, I was fortunate enough to find a new collaborator in Tony Maietta. It proved an ideal partnership, and if this book is better written than my previous efforts, it is in no small measure owing to Tony's participation. In addition, Tony headed the research not previously undertaken and compiled the Fairbanks filmography and Broadway stage listings.

Principal thanks also go to the Academy of Motion Picture Arts and Sciences for commissioning me to prepare this volume. It is a great privilege, offered to few film historians, to write a book for the Academy, particularly on a subject as important to it as its first president. I am grateful to the Academy's current president, Sid Ganis, and to its executive director, Bruce Davis, its executive administrator, Ric Robertson, and its associate executive administrator, Mikel Gordon, for the opportunity.

The opportunity to prepare this volume would not have presented itself had it not been for the efforts of Robert Cushman, photograph curator and photographic services administrator of the Margaret Herrick Library of the Academy of Motion Picture Arts and Sciences. In addition to being a prime mover in the realization of this book, he served as photographic editor, as well as carefully reading the text and improving it with his suggestions. Robert and I selected the images, and the photograph preservationist Manoah Bowman had the formidable responsibility of printing images from original camera negatives, scanning negatives and original prints, and removing all the imperfections caused by the ravages of time. In every instance, Manoah enhanced the images.

I am also grateful to executives and staff of the Margaret Herrick Library for their kindness and support, in particular, Linda Harris Mehr, Barbara Hall, Howard Prouty, Sandra Archer, Stacey Behlmer, Jenny Romero, and Libby Wertin.

A special debt of gratitude is due to Vera Fairbanks, widow of Douglas Fairbanks Jr., who not only donated all of the Douglas Fairbanks Sr. material previously held at Boston University (thus creating the Academy's treasured Douglas Fairbanks Collection) but also proved wonderfully supportive and helpful in the preparation of this book. If a photograph or document was needed, Vera Fairbanks was never too busy to assist in the search in order to make this book the best it could possibly be.

I am grateful to the generosity extended by Gary Dartnall of the Douris Corporation for establishing the corporation's Douglas Fairbanks Files at the Margaret Herrick Library and making available Fairbanks materials controlled by Douris.

David Shepard exceeded any ordinary call of friendship and scholarship in order to make certain this was the best Fairbanks book possible, given its space restrictions. David provided films from his vast collection, put me in contact with people who always proved helpful, and carefully read the text and greatly improved it with his encyclopedic knowledge of film, as well as his expert editorial suggestions.

In addition to David, I feel very fortunate to have had the help of prominent film historians to assist with the preparation of the text. First among these is Rudy Behlmer, the foremost authority on screen swashbuckling, who proved an invaluable help. In addition to finding inspiration from his own published work, he generously provided research material from his monumental files, footage, and advice; he carefully read every chapter. Other film historians who contributed ideas, materials, or support over the years include Tino Balio, Robert S. Birchard, Eileen Bowser, Kevin Brownlow, the late James Card, the late William K. Everson, Scott Eyman, Tom Gunning, Jan-Christopher Horak, Constance Brown Kuriyama, Emily W. Leider, Russell Merritt, David Robinson, Anthony Slide, David Stenn, and the late Edward Wagenknecht.

Dr. Stephen M. Weissman's expertise as a psychiatrist and biographer proved invaluable. He read every chapter, challenged long-held notions, contributed wonderful ideas, and helped formulate all of the psychological views contained within the text.

I have been privileged to have known the authors who have made important contributions to the understanding of Douglas Fairbanks. They have all—at one time or another—been my teachers. I am grateful to the late Alistair Cooke, author of the pioneering study *Douglas Fairbanks: The Making of a Screen Character;* John C. Tibbetts and James M. Welsh, authors of *His Majesty the American: The Films of Douglas Fairbanks, Sr.;* and especially Richard Schickel, whose *His Picture in the Papers: A Speculation of Celebrity in America, Based on the Life of Douglas Fairbanks, Sr.* is a cornerstone not only of Fairbanks scholarship but also of cultural studies.

I am indebted to the following personnel who assisted me in the research and writing of the text: Marc Wanamaker of Bison Archives; Nigel Algar and Sonia Genaitay of the British Film Institute; Cecilia Cenciarelli of the Cineteca Bologna; Thaddeus Napp of the Directors Guild of America; Patrick Loughney and Nancy Kauffman of the George Eastman House; the late Howard Gotlieb, Margaret Goostray, and, more recently, Ryan Hendrickson of the Howard Gotlieb Archival Research Center, Boston University; Miles Kreuger of the Institute of the American Musical; Steven Higgins, Ron Magliozzi, and Charles Silver of the Museum of Modern Art's Department of Film; Beth Werling of the Natural History Museum of Los Angeles County; Hugh Munro Neely of the Mary Pickford Institute for Film Education; John Martello of The Players; Todd Wiener of the UCLA Film and Television Archive; Robert Rosen, dean of the UCLA School of Theater, Film, and Television; Ned Comstock of the USC Cinematic Arts Library; Maxine Ducey and Dorinda Hartmann of the Wisconsin Center for Film and Theater Research; and Helmut M. Knies and Harry Miller of the Wisconsin Historical Society.

I am grateful to Michael Pogorzelski, Brian Meacham, and Chris Fedak of the Academy Film Archive for arranging the viewing of 35 mm archival prints from the Academy's own holdings, as well as the holdings of the Library of Congress and the George Eastman House; to Tim Lanza of the Douris Corporation for viewing 35 mm release prints; Kitty Cleary of the Museum of Modern Art's Circulating Film Library for viewing 16 mm release prints; Valarie Schwan of USC Moving Image Archive for viewing 16 mm archival prints; and Serge Bromberg of Lobster Films for viewing an assortment of Fairbanks rarities in digital formats.

I would also like to record with particular appreciation the support I have received, in friendship, interest, and encouragement, from Josephine Chaplin and Kate Guyonvarch of Association Chaplin, Ben Baker, Julie Bontier, Justin Chambers, Vincent De Paul, Karyn Gerhard, Herbert G. Goldman, Randy Haberkamp, James and Kristine Hall, Michelle Hall, Jon Hall, Suzanne Lloyd of The Harold Lloyd Trust, Nick Harvill, Sam Hayes, Alba Francesca and James Karen, Hanna M. Kennedy, Bruce Lawton, Jerry Lewis, Anthony and Jane Maietta, Jeffery Masino, Albert Maysles, Matthew McCarty, Randall Meadows, Peter Nickowitz, Karen Norwood, the late Robert E. Patterson, David Pierce, Steve Randisi, Scott Rivers, Steven Smith, James Thiérrée, Yuri Tsivian, Elisa Urbanelli, George Thomas Vance, and Bill Daly of Warner Bros. Pictures. A special acknowledgment to the late Mary Pickford, whose response to my first fan letter provided early encouragement. A salute to Jon S. Bouker Jr.—a friend of many years—who shared my early enthusiasm for Fairbanks. A heartfelt thank-you to my grandmother, Edith A. Patterson, and my sister, Megan Vance.

Finally, I would like to extend my gratitude to the book's sponsoring editor, Mary C. Francis, project editor, Dore Brown, and designer, Claudia Smelser.

Jeffrey Vance
Los Angeles, California, 2008

Index

Italicized page numbers refer to illustrations.

DESIGNER AND COMPOSITOR   Claudia Smelser
TEXT   10.5/14 Filosofia
DISPLAY   Filosofia
INDEXER   Sharon Sweeney
PRINTER AND BINDER   Friesens Corporation